Object-Oriented Artificial Intelligence Using C++

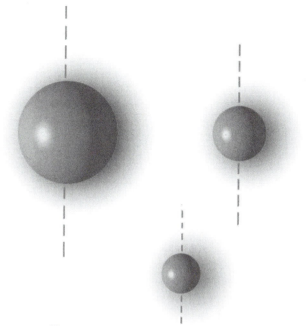

OBJECT-ORIENTED ARTIFICIAL INTELLIGENCE USING C++

KIM W. TRACY

Bell Labs
Lucent Technologies, Inc.
North Central College

PETER BOUTHOORN

Gröningen University

COMPUTER SCIENCE PRESS

AN IMPRINT OF W. H. FREEMAN AND COMPANY • New York

Acquisitions Editor: Richard Bonacci
Project Editor: Penelope Hull
Text Designer: Patrice Sheridan
Cover Designer: HRS
Illustration Coordinator: Susan Wein
Illustration: NuGraphic Design, Inc.
Production Coordinator: Paul Rohloff
Composition: Peng Olaguera
Manufacturing: R R Donnelley & Sons Company

Library of Congress Cataloging-in-Publication Data
Tracy, Kim W.
        Object-oriented artificial intelligence using C++ / Kim W. Tracy, Peter
Bouthoorn.
        p.   cm.
        Includes bibliographical references and index.
        ISBN 0-7167-8294-4 (hard cover)
        1. Artificial Intelligence—Data Processing. 2. Object-oriented programming
(Computer science) 3. C++ (Computer program language)
        I. Bouthoorn, Peter. II. Title.
        Q336.T72 1997
        006.3—dc20   96-33964
                                                                                     CIP

Printed in the United States of America
First printing, 1996

Computer Science Press
An imprint of W. H. Freeman and Company
41 Madison Avenue, New York, NY 10010
Houndmills, Basingstoke RG21 6XS, England

TO KATHLEEN AND ROBERT

CONTENTS

PREFACE

Facilitating the use of large and complex programs has made object orientation one of the preferred programming paradigms for computer scientists. As such, it is a paradigm that artificial intelligence (AI) programmers find suitable for addressing many of the problems they face. This book is designed to make the techniques of an object-oriented approach to artificial intelligence accessible to a broad audience. By using object-oriented design, AI techniques are more easily understood and integrated into the work of people who already use an object-oriented language.

PURPOSE

The book grew out of our frustration in finding a textbook that provides an object-oriented introduction to artificial intelligence. Many computer science departments are moving to incorporate the object-oriented paradigm (usually with C++) throughout their undergraduate curriculums, but there has been no textbook that uses an object-oriented approach to AI and supplies a base library of AI algorithms. Without a textbook and supporting structure, the introductory object-oriented AI course has been difficult to teach.

This text, therefore, has two primary goals:

1. To provide an object-oriented introduction to artificial intelligence for computer science curriculums that use an object-oriented (and usually C++) approach

2. To provide C++ libraries that can easily be used for integrating AI algorithms into new and existing projects

In introducing the reader to the field of artificial intelligence using C++ as the language of implementation, the focus of the book is on the key concepts and techniques of AI and their application to various problems. The core of the book provides readers with a fundamental understanding of AI that will enable them to understand the more advanced topics they encounter in this book and in other AI literature.

The book provides the C++ source code for the algorithms presented in the text, as well as much more underlying code to support the AI algorithms. The C++ programs have been tested using Borland's C++ 3.1 and 4.0 and Gnu C++'s gcc compiler. The code should be easily portable to other compilers, as long as the compilers support templates, which are used heavily in the code. Much of the code is listed in the text itself and can be obtained electronically from the authors.

The choice of C++ as the language to implement the algorithms is not accidental. C++ is the most widely used and understood object-oriented programming language. While other object-oriented languages, such as the Common Lisp Object System (CLOS) and SmallTalk, may arguably be better object-oriented environments, C++ is still by far the most popular choice of industry for designing real systems.

AUDIENCE

The book is primarily designed for undergraduate and graduate students with strong backgrounds in computer science but not necessarily in artificial intelligence. The book can also benefit professional computer scientists who need to understand the techniques and concepts central to AI, particularly those who wish to use an object-oriented programming language. The text is most useful for a first course in artificial intelligence for students who know the C or C++ programming language. Brief overviews of C++ and object-oriented design are given, but readers who have previously studied those topics will gain maximum benefit from the book.

After completing this book, the reader should be able to meet the following learning objectives:

- Understand the basic concepts of artificial intelligence
- Understand and be able to apply object-oriented design in AI applications
- Understand the current theory in several application areas of artificial intelligence
- Write object-oriented artificial intelligence programs in C++

Readers should also be able to pursue their own artificial intelligence interests beyond the scope of this book. It is hoped that the examples and algorithms in this book will create excitement about the enormous potential of AI techniques.

USING THE BOOK

An introductory course in artificial intelligence can cover most of this book in a single semester or quarter. The chapters are in the order they are presented in Kim Tracy's course. The first eight chapters are the core and should be covered in sequence; the remaining chapters are on advanced topics and are independent of one another. For a quarter course, it is best to cover the first six chapters and then a selection of at least three of the remaining chapters.

Numerous exercises apply and expand on the concepts and techniques presented in each chapter. The exercises build on readers' already sound foundation in mathematics and computer science. The book also provides many programming exercises of varying difficulty. We recommend that readers do all of the warm-up problems to ensure that they understand the concepts. Readers should also attempt to do some of the homework problems and programming assignments.

The warm-up problems problems are targeted at understanding the material presented and should take less than 10 minutes each. The homework problems usually take more than 10 minutes each, and some may take a couple of hours. The homework problems are usually either more difficult problems relating to the material presented or expansions on the material presented. The programming assignments are usually extensive enough to require at least four or five hours. The programming assignments build on the material presented and usually involve implementing the concepts from the material. In addition, some project assignments are suitable for term projects or Master's-level thesis projects (none are Ph.D. dissertation material).

If any errors are found in this text, please send them directly to us at the following address:

Kim W. Tracy
Bell Labs
Lucent Technologies, Inc.
2000 North Naperville Road
Naperville, IL 60566-7033
tracy@cs.stanford.edu

Please consult the W. H. Freeman World Wide Web site for on-line locations of the programming code: http//www.whfreeman.com/.

SUPPLEMENTS

An Instructor's Manual and accompanying diskette, which contain the solutions to many of the programming assignments, is available to adopters.

ACKNOWLEDGMENTS

We acknowledge the students who have taken our course and given us exceedingly valuable feedback on the text and the exercises. Their feedback has helped to clarify numerous sections of the text.

We also thank the following people for reviewing various drafts and providing valuable feedback:

John Bagley, Lucent Technologies
Ron Brachman, AT&T Labs
Daniel Chester, University of Delaware
Steve Crook, Z. S. Associates
Martha Evens, Illinois Institute of Technology
Peter Greene, Illinois Institute of Technology
Syed Hussein, Motorola Corp.
Daniel Kopec, United States Coast Guard Academy
Karen Owen, Lucent Technologies
Paul Nagin, Hofstra Univeresity
Gordon Novak, University of Texas at Austin
Babu Ranganathan, Allen, Booz and Hamilton
Sid Scott, Lucent Technologies
Janice Searleman, Clarkson University
Bart Selman, AT&T Labs
Michelle Swiatek, Lucent Technologies
Gregg Vesonder, AT&T Labs
Eugene Wallingford, University of Northern Iowa
Reid Watts, NCR
Michael Weintraub, Boston University

In addition, we thank Jim Coplien, Brian Kernighan, Jim Kowal, and Jeff Ullman for valuable insight on book publishing and for-matting. Kim Tracy's management at Bell Labs (now a division of Lucent Technologies, Inc.) has been supportive of this work, and in particular, he thanks Matt Merges, Dan Fyock, Jim Weichel, and Sid Scott for their support.

We also thank the helpful folks at Computer Science Press, including our original editor, Burt Gabriel, and our current editors, Richard Bonacci and Penny Hull, for their patience and help in the long process of creating this book.

Borland International was helpful in providing a copy of their C++ compiler for use in testing the software in this text.

1

ARTIFICIAL INTELLIGENCE: DEFINITION AND SCOPE

Artificial intelligence

is the science of

making machines do

things that would

require intelligence if

done by [people].

MARVIN L. MINSKY

1.1 ARTIFICIAL INTELLIGENCE AS A SCIENCE

We shall present artificial intelligence (AI) to be a field of computer science even though AI is studied and applied in many other fields, including psychology, linguistics, mathematics, and philosophy (Figure 1.1). Indeed, the creation of artificially intelligent agents[1] requires knowledge of these other domains. In this vein, Genesereth and Nilsson (1987) defined AI as the study of intelligent behavior. The definition by Charniak (1985), however, suits our present purposes best: *Artificial intelligence is the study of mental faculties through the use of computational models.*

A test for comparing the behavior of AI agents with human intelligence was proposed by Alan Turing and is discussed in Section 1.6. Some people suggest that AI agents that pass Turing's test exhibit intelligence. Of course, Charniak's definition avoids the problem of defining the term *intelligence,* for which no complete, operational definition has yet been determined. His definition uses the term *mental faculties* to refer to the high-level mental processing tasks that are done by people (or other beings) and include some of the most challenging areas of AI such as vision, language, learning, deduction, planning, and speech. It turns out that some of the most difficult functions to mimic with a computer program are these mental faculties that appear to come so easily to humans (and even other animals).

---

[1] Artificially intelligent agents are programs or machines that can act intelligently by using their knowledge.

FIGURE 1.1

Overlap of the
field of artificial
intelligence with
other fields of study

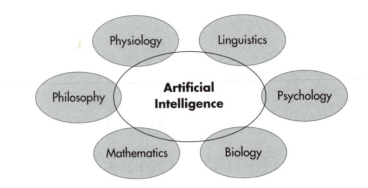

FIGURE 1.2

The arithmetic
dimension of
intelligence

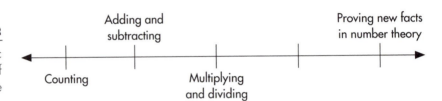

Basically, AI is concerned with the production of functional computational models. Whereas other fields such as psychology are more concerned with theoretical questions about how human mental faculties work, AI is concerned with creating programs and machines that can actually perform those high-level mental processing tasks. We will focus on the concepts and techniques that are used to create these computational models of intelligence.

Even though intelligence is difficult to define explicitly, it can be visualized as a multidimensional space, with different aspects of intelligence lying along the axes of the various dimensions. An arithmetic dimension of intelligence might begin with the ability to count and proceed to the abilities to add, subtract, multiply, divide, and so forth (Figure 1.2). Physical dexterity might also be considered a form of intelligence. It is not directly comparable to arithmetic intelligence, so it is classified as another dimension of intelligence.

Using Charniak's definition of artificial intelligence, we will focus on the concepts and techniques that are used to create computational models of intelligence.

1.2 PROBLEM SOLVING AND AI

The discipline of artificial intelligence is largely focused on the need to solve certain types of problems such as developing a plan of action, finding the best next move in a chess game, or finding a proof of a proposed theorem in calculus. As a result, much of the formalism in AI deals with the different strategies and techniques used to solve the various types of problems. Although one mechanism that can effectively solve all problems has not yet been developed, many different techniques now facilitate the problem-solving process.

Programs that are written in traditional programming languages (such as Pascal or C) can be characterized as well-defined sequences of statements that are designed to solve specific, well-constrained problems. Conversely, AI programs are characterized by well-defined structures that represent knowledge relating to a broad range of problems. Because AI programs tend to use search techniques to find acceptable solutions to the particular, broadly defined problem at hand, much of the research and development in AI has been devoted to discovering efficient and versatile search techniques.

Traditional programs can also be characterized as structured assignment statements; that is, traditional programs generally provide control mechanisms (DO loops, IF statements, and so on) that control the sequence of assignment statement executions. AI programs, however, are usually structured around the problem data and techniques that control the execution of the program using the problem data. This focus has led to a major effort to improve knowledge representation so that knowledge can be accessed efficiently and consistently. Logic is used as the basis for expressing many AI techniques and concepts, because it is the most highly developed language for expressing problem-solving formalisms.

1.3 CURRENT APPLICATIONS OF AI

The application areas described in this section are not the only areas in which AI can be applied, because, by definition, AI should be applicable to any aspect of intelligent behavior. However, the following areas are those in which AI has been successfully applied and are still the focus of active research.

1.3.1 Expert Systems

Expert systems are the most famous and widely used of all AI technologies. They are built from the production system paradigm (see Chapter 8) and encapsulate knowledge for specific domains. Expert systems are most applicable to domains that have problem spaces with clear boundaries.

4

An expert system solves problems within its specific domain by using the encapsulated expertise. Early examples of expert systems are medical diagnosis systems (e.g., MYCIN), tools for geological analysis (e.g., PROSPECTOR), and tools for analyzing mass spectrographic data (e.g., DENDRAL). More modern examples of expert systems are tools that act as doctors' assistants for medical diagnosis (e.g., as PUFF), that help monitor tedious problems and sift through data (e.g., IDES, a security monitor), or that assist with larger problems, such as developing large software systems (e.g., LASSIE).

1.3.2 Games

Games represent relatively small problems that are characterized by clear rules and are usually easy to represent symbolically. These characteristics make games excellent testing beds for artificial intelligence concepts and techniques. As a result, many game programs have been aided by AI research and vice versa. Chess programs have proliferated over the years and are now reaching grand master proficiency levels. These programs have been used to test methods for searching for solutions, for recognizing "interesting" board positions, and for studying how experts view problems.

1.3.3 Machine Learning

Machine learning[2] is currently a very active area of artificial intelligence research. The goal of this research is to enable knowledge-based programs to increase their knowledge by learning. An early example of learning is found in Samuel's checkers program (Samuel, 1963, 1967), which learned to improve its play by using a relatively simple strategy of adjusting weights that were maintained internally. It also retained "interesting" board patterns for future use. An interesting board pattern might be one that was guaranteed to produce a "win" or one that should be avoided because it was likely to produce a "loss." Even with only this simple strategy, Samuel's program was successful.

Researchers learned from Samuel's checkers program, too, because current work in learning includes learning by using examples, by making generalizations from specific instances, and by discovering interesting patterns or theorems.

---

[2] Learning, in this context, could more aptly be called artificial learning because it involves the development of AI agents that can learn new information. However, the terms *learning* or *machine learning* are most common and will be used in this text for consistency.

1.3.4 Natural-Language Understanding and Generation

Natural-language understanding and generation focuses on the recognition and production of human speech and writing. Research in artificial intelligence has focused on natural-language recognition for two reasons. First, many general problems in AI parallel those involved in recognizing natural language, for example, encoding imprecise knowledge into some formalism. Second, the ability to recognize natural language is beginning to produce many new technologies, such as effective machine translation and voice-activated typewriters. Sentences such as "Bilbo saw Frodo with a telescope" are ambiguous without further context. Frodo might have the telescope, or Bilbo might have it. Natural-language recognition tries to resolve such ambiguities by examining the context of the statement.

Natural language can now be artificially generated, but when we try to make the speech (or text) sound natural, the problems that arise are similar to those occurring in natural-language recognition.

1.3.5 Neural Networks

Neural networks are modeled after human brains. The components of a neural network are linked together in a network and function in a manner similar to that of human neurons. Neural networks have been quite successful in solving some problems, such as recognizing patterns or classification. Typical applications are adaptive noise cancellation on phone lines (see Anderson and Rosenfeld, 1988, p. 125), risk evaluation for claims and mortgage applications, and recognition of defective parts (such as fan motors—see O'Reilly, 1989) or particular conditions (like an explosives sniffer—see Doherty, 1989).

A neural network is usually "trained" by a set of known examples for which the correct answers are known. After it has been "trained," examples for which the solutions are not known are presented. For example, we might create a neural network to distinguish between faces of people on the basis of their age, which could be either less than or more than 50 years. The output of the neural network is a classification: "yes" if the person is over 50, "no" if he or she is younger than 50. To train the neural network, we would gather photographs of people of known ages and then present the examples to the neural network as training examples. With each training example, the parameters inside the network would be adjusted to make sure that it could properly classify the example. Of course, the more training examples presented, the more likely it would be that the neural network would correctly classify an unknown example. Neural networks have been amazingly successful at this type of classification problem.

Once a neural network has been trained, it is usually fairly accurate. It is not *always* correct, however; and generally we are unable to recognize a wrong answer (unless we already know the correct one). We can, however, test the network with a new set of examples with known answers (examples that were not included in the training set) and thereby measure its accuracy. For many applications, a 95% accuracy rate is fine. In the detection of fraudulent insurance claims, for instance, a neural network that can detect 95% of the cases of fraud is still much better than any other automated technique.

1.3.6 Planning

Planning is the development of a sequence of actions to achieve a predefined goal. Planning is often associated with robots that are limited to a discrete set of actions. For example, a plan to satisfy one's hunger might involve sending a robot out to get some food. The robot's plan might include the following actions (assuming the robot can perform these actions):

1. Ask what you would like to eat.
2. Assemble list of items (including money!).
3. Get in car.
4. Find closest McDonald's on the map.
5. Determine shortest path to that McDonald's.
6. Drive to McDonald's, using path.
7. Get out of car.
8. Go into McDonald's.
9. Go to counter.
10. Order food.
11. Pay for food.
12. Wait for food to be delivered to your position.
13. Pick up food.
14. Leave McDonald's.
15. Put food in car.
16. Drive car back to starting position.
17. Bring in food.

Planning usually strives to develop plans that are both effective and efficient. One of the difficulties in planning for a robot involves timing. The robot must develop its plan within a limited period. For example, if a robot is being attacked by another robot, it must develop its plan for defense quickly. Otherwise, the beleaguered robot may be destroyed.

1.3.7 Robotics and Vision

Robotics involves all aspects of controlling a robot's behavior, including moving appendages, moving itself, seeing objects, assembling objects, and planning for a goal. Controlling robotic movement involves knowledge of statics and dynamics to control the movement of each appendage. It turns out to be rather difficult to develop robots that walk on only two legs, because the robot must balance itself on the two legs while moving them.

Vision and pattern recognition are primarily concerned with interpreting patterns and extracting meaning from visual images or other data. One of the fundamental problems of vision is trying to reliably identify objects from imperfect images. Consider the problem of identifying a human face. Humans are very good at identifying other human faces even though the subject may have aged many years. Vision programs are not, however, as good at identifying specific human faces or determining what features should remain constant as someone ages. An example of pattern recognition is a program that identifies different types of whales from sonar data patterns. The program may have difficulty distinguishing between a blue whale and a humpback whale, but it should be able to distinguish between a killer whale and a gray whale, simply because the gray whale is by far the larger of the two species.

1.3.8 Theorem Proving

The automatic proving of mathematical theorems has long been an area of artificial intelligence research. The ability to reason automatically (that is, to prove facts from other facts already known) is a very important part of most AI systems, which often must deduce facts from the limited information that is stored in their knowledge base. In fact, most AI systems usually draw conclusions on the basis of imperfect or incomplete knowledge.

Many theorem provers have been implemented, yet very few are used heavily because of their slowness. Problems in theorem proving include developing programs that can prove complex facts efficiently and discovering facts that are worth trying to prove. It makes little sense for a theorem prover to prove hundreds of useless facts (such as that "mice are furry," "mice are small," "mice are furry and small," etc.).

For interesting reading on human theorem proving and problem solving, see the books by Polya (1945) and Solow (1990).

1.4 AI TECHNIQUES: AN EXAMPLE

The *N*-Queens problem requires the player (Pearl, 1984) is to place *N* queens on an $N \times N$ board so that no queen can attack another according to the rules of chess. Recall that a queen can move any number of spaces either horizontally, vertically, or diagonally from its current position. Figure 1.3 shows a solution to the 8-Queens problem. To solve this problem, we will use heuristics to speed the process of finding a solution. **Heuristics** are guesses at how "good" a move will be.

We will also adopt the strategy of positioning a queen in each row, one row at a time. That is, we first place a queen in row 1, then one in row 2, . . . , making sure at each step that the constraints of the problem are not violated. Furthermore, we can pick the position in each row such that we have the best chance of finding positions for later rows. This strategy is applicable simply because there is no solution that can place more than one queen in any given row or column. Using this strategy, we can apply heuristic values to the positions in the next row in an attempt to pick the cells that are most likely to be part of a solution.

Consider the intermediate board position that is shown in Figure 1.4: The dashed lines indicate the cells that can be attacked from the three queens already positioned. We are now ready to choose a position for the fourth queen in the fourth row. Only three positions within this row are not yet in the lines of attack; they are marked A, B, and C. Now we can use a heuristic function to aid us in selecting position A, B, or C for example, determining the total number of unattacked cells that would remain as a result of selecting either A, B, or C. Let's call this heuristic H_1. If we pick A and draw in the lines for it, we get the result shown in the following formula and Figure 1-5:

FIGURE 1.3

A solution to the 8-Queens problem

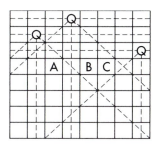

FIGURE 1.4

An intermediate
attempt to solve the
8-Queens problem

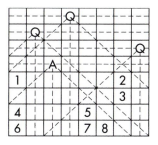

FIGURE 1.5

Picking A results in
eight unattacked cells

$H_1(A) = 8$

If we pick B or C, we get

$H_1(B) = 9$
$H_1(C) = 10$

Because we suspect that the higher the number of unattacked cells remaining, the more choices for positions of future queens, we pick C and then repeat the process for the next row. The usefulness of this heuristic depends on whether it actually helps to pick positions for queens that lead us quickly to the solution. If we continue to use this particular heuristic, we will get to a solution in this particular example. However, this heuristic will not always lead to a solution to the N-Queens problem. In Exercise 1-13, you will have a chance to develop other heuristics.

The heuristic H_1 is not guaranteed to work, because it only looks at the next row and may fail to pick a position that leads to a solution. If it does fail, we may have to back up (backtrack) to a previous point in the search for a solution and try a position other than the one with the highest heuristic value.

This example illustrates several important concepts that appear many times throughout this book:

- Applying an unguaranteed heuristic to guide the search for a solution. This method helps to narrow the search for a solution so that we need not blindly try every possible choice. If the heuristic is useful, then we should find a solution much more quickly than by using a blind search.

- Careful selection of a problem representation (the grid, etc.). Without an appropriate and accurate representation of a problem, we may not have the ability to solve the problem at all. If we pick the wrong representation, the problem might be unsolvable.

- Picking a clear strategy for solving the problem. For this problem, we picked a strategy of putting one queen in each row, from the top down. Other strategies for solving this problem might be less efficient. For example, we could randomly place N queens on the $N \times N$ board and then try to "fix" them, that is, move the queens from their initial random positions until we found a solution, but that approach would be very inefficient.

1.5 SOME RESEARCH PROJECTS IN AI

One of the most interesting (and controversial) research projects in artificial intelligence was originally conducted by Doug Lenat and his team at the Microelectronics and Computer Technology Corporation (MCC). The project, now at Cycorp, Inc., is called *Cyc*, for en*cyc*lopedia (see Lenat, 1990, and Guha, 1990). The goal of the Cyc project is to encode common-sense knowledge in a form that can be used by other systems. The Cyc project applies many of the theoretical issues that are described in this book and will be presented as a case study in Chapter 12.

There has been a resurgence of interest in AI techniques in the areas of information management, of filtering, and of collective use of information from various sources. The volume of data available is growing so rapidly that it has become unmanageable. AI techniques designed to summarize and to filter information are turning out to be quite useful for providing a smaller set of information that can be absorbed. The field of Knowledge Discovery in Databases (KDD) is described in Chapter 12. In addition, the use of agent-oriented programming to ferret out information that is likely to be useful to the agent's owner is also becoming more prevalent. The use of agent-oriented programming as an extension of object-oriented programming also is described in Chapter 13.

1.6 PHILOSOPHICAL CONCERNS IN AI

Philosophy has long been concerned with the possibility and implications of creating artificially intelligent agents. This section describes both a method of evaluating AI programs and some doubts that genuine intelligence can be created in computing machines.

One of the earliest tests for AI was proposed by Alan Turing and is called the Turing test. (For an accessible, partial copy of Turing's famous paper on this test, see Hofstadter, 1981. The complete paper can be found in Turing, 1950.) The Turing test involves a human evaluator, an AI agent, and another human, as shown in Figure 1.6. The evaluator, who is isolated from both the proposed artificially intelligent agent and the other human, sends messages to both the AI agent and the other human. The intent of the test is to determine whether the evaluator can reliably distinguish between and identify the proposed AI agent and the other human on the basis of their replies. If the evaluator cannot reliably distinguish between replies from the AI agent and replies from the other human, then the AI agent is considered intelligent by Turing's definition. (See Shapiro, 1987, for more on the Turing test.)

The Turing test, however, has its critics, who charge that

- It assumes that the intelligence of an artificial agent is comparable to human intelligence, rather than allowing nonhumanlike intelligence also to be considered.

- It presumes a form of intelligence that manipulates symbols (i.e., messages) but does not allow for other forms of intelligence, such as physical dexterity.

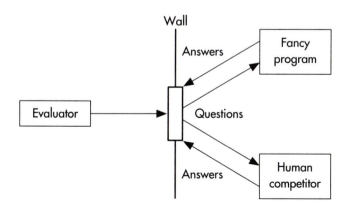

FIGURE 1.6

The Turing test

- It may play on the human evaluator's natural tendency to anthropomorphize the actions of the AI agent (i.e., attribute beliefs, goals, etc., to the AI agent) and thus cause the evaluator to think that the AI agent is behaving intelligently.

But, despite these criticisms, no other operational test for intelligence has yet replaced the Turing test.

Another criticism of the Turing test and of AI in general, is known as the Chinese room experiment (John Searle's paper on this experiment is included in Hofstadter, 1981). Searle's Chinese room experiment consists of a room in which Searle is present; three sets of Chinese writings, which are labeled "script," "story," and "questions"; a set of rules, which are written in English and labeled "program." Searle has no understanding whatsoever of Chinese, so to him the characters in the three sets of Chinese writings could be any arbitrary symbols. The English rules instruct Searle to use the Chinese "script" and "story" as input to generate strings of Chinese characters in response to Chinese "questions." Let's say that Searle becomes so proficient at applying the rules that his output (i.e., answers to the "questions") appear to be answers to questions about the "story." In fact, his answers are so good that they appear to be well-formed Chinese answers to the "story." Does Searle now understand Chinese? Searle claims that he still does not understand a single word of Chinese and is simply following the rules that were given to him. Searle also claims that the rules do little to explain human understanding of Chinese (or of the story), because the rules work even though Searle does not understand any Chinese.

A philosophical question is generated by the Chinese room experiment, namely, If a program that could perform the translation work that Searle was doing in the experiment existed, would the program be intelligent in any sense? Clearly, such a program would appear to have some understanding of Chinese because it would appear to "understand" the stories written in Chinese. Searle, however, argues that because he did not understand Chinese, then neither could the program, even though it might exhibit behavior that mimics understanding. Nevertheless, we could argue that the system is exhibiting intelligent behavior and therefore could be considered intelligent (see Exercises).

1.7 PROGRAMMING PARADIGMS FOR AI

A programming paradigm provides a unique way of modeling the world and writing programs to solve problems within that model. The field of artificial intelligence has used many paradigms; and many of the paradigms popular in other fields of computer science have originated from AI research. There are four commonly used programming paradigms for artificial intelligence:[3] logic programming, functional programming, rule-based programming, and object-oriented programming. Each paradigm is represented by programming languages that support programming based on that paradigm.[4]

Each paradigm is well suited to different types of problems, and artificial intelligence researchers have not chosen any one of them as the best. In fact, each can be used to simulate the other three. Most programming systems tend to offer features from several paradigms. for example, many rule-based programming environments offer object-oriented programming features.

These four paradigms are not the only programming paradigms that exist. Others are parallel programming, data flow, visual programming, and procedural programming paradigms. Experimental computer scientists continue to research and try new paradigms that may prove useful in a particular field of study, or in general.

We will use C++ for most of our examples, primarily because C++ and object-oriented programming are suitable to AI programming and their use is becoming widespread. We also expect that object-oriented languages will continue to be used in the future for AI programs, because many of these programs are embedded in traditional software systems.

The primary programming languages of artificial intelligence are currently Prolog (programming in logic) and LISP (list processing). LISP is more widely used in the United States, whereas Prolog is widely used in Europe and Japan. Other more specialized languages are also available, such as OPS5 (Official Programming System, Version 5), which is designed for expert systems. Still other languages, such as MRS (Metalevel Reasoning System), are well designed for expressing advanced topics.

1.7.1 Logic Programming

Logic programming uses structures from logic as the basis of a programming language and environment. All statements in the language are written to represent statements in logic. The most well-known examples of this paradigm are programs written in the programming language Prolog. Prolog stands for "*pro*grammation *log*ique" in French and not surprisingly translates to "logic pro-

---

[3] These paradigms are used by other fields of computer science, particularly object-oriented programming.

[4] One programming language may support several paradigms, and a programmer may choose not to program within the best-supported paradigm of a programming language.

gramming." Prolog uses statements in logic and a theorem prover that can prove goals, given a set of statements.

1.7.2 Functional Programming

Functional programming uses the theory of mathematical functions as the basis for programming. In pure functional programming, all statements are written as functions. The best-known example of a programming language that supports this paradigm for AI is LISP. LISP, which stands for *list* processing, has the basic data structure of a list in which everything is represented, including programs themselves.

1.7.3 Rule-Based Programming

Rule-based programming is similar to logic programming in that it is based on structures from logic, and programs are generally written as statements in logic. Rule-based programming, however, has more restrictions than logic programming. They are usually associated with rule-based expert systems and are written in a specialized language that is tuned to work well with the rule-based programming paradigm. Rule-based languages such as the Official Programming System, Version 5 (OPS5) are focused around IF-THEN rules. Other, more modern examples of rule-based programming environments are ProKappa, ART/IM, and CLIPS. These rule-based programming environments offer many other features that enhance the usefulness of the system, including features such as uncertain reasoning.

1.7.4 Object-Oriented Programming

Object-oriented programming (OOP) uses objects and classes of objects as its formalism for organizing programs. The programming language SmallTalk, from Xerox PARC, is an object-oriented programming language (OOPL) that helped define most of the formalisms of classes, objects, messages, and inheritance. These terms will be discussed at length in later chapters. We will use the C++ programming language, which is usually termed a *hybrid OOPL* because it is not purely object-oriented. C++ is immensely popular, however, and provides a sufficient mechanism for describing object-oriented programming.

1.8 SUMMARY

Artificial intelligence is a rapidly changing field and is focused on the production of intelligent machines. In striving to reach this goal, we must understand what intelligent behavior is and how machines can emulate that behavior. This chapter outlines many application areas, each of which can be considered a field of study in its own right.

1.9 REFERENCES

Several excellent books provide a good introduction to the field of artificial intelligence. They are *The Handbook of Artificial Intelligence, Volumes 1–4* (Barr, 1981, 1989); *Introduction to Artificial Intelligence* (Charniak and McDermott, 1985); *The Encyclopedia of Artificial Intelligence* (Shapiro, 1987); and *Artificial Intelligence, Structures and Strategies for Complex Problem Solving* (Luger and Stubblefield, 1993). Other good introductions to AI are Russell (1995), Ginsberg (1993), and Rich (1991).

For an excellent book on the history of computing and intelligent machines, see Kurzweil (1990), *The Age of Intelligent Machines.*

1.10 EXERCISES

Warm-up Exercises

1.1. Criticize Charniak's definition of AI as "the study of mental faculties through the use of computational models." Develop your own definition and defend it.

1.2. Human intelligence is measured in many ways, from IQ tests to the grades that we receive in school. Consider a program that is able to consistently score at the genius level on IQ tests. Would you consider such a program "intelligent"? Why or why not? Would the program be considered an AI program by our definition?

1.3. Compare Rich's quote (Rich, 1991), "AI is the study of how to make computers do things which, at the moment, people do better," to Charniak's definition. Which do you prefer? Why?

1.4. Describe your own criteria for considering computer software to be "intelligent."

1.5. Does research into the physiological structure and function of biological systems have any relation to or insight for the engineering of AI programs? Justify your answer.

1.6. List and discuss three potentially negative effects that the further development of AI techniques may have on society.

1.7. List and discuss three potentially positive effects that the further development of AI techniques may have on society.

1.8. Many researchers are enthused about the development of microscopic machines that can perform simple tasks. Miniature motors, switches, and other devices are being designed for incorporation into machines that will be able to do things such as traverse the human bloodstream. Given such devices, one can imagine using them to destroy cancerous cells or to perform other specialized tasks. How could artificial intelligence be used to make these devices more useful in the future?

1.9. Artificial life is a multidisciplinary field that studies how to create lifelike characteristics in software and hardware. Researchers are studying features such as reproduction, instinctive behavior, and mimicking simple animals' behavior. Consider, for example, the ability to create an artificial mouse that behaves as a real-life mouse would in every way. How could such an artificial mouse be used? What could be done (in terms of AI) that could make the artificial mouse more useful?

1.10. Criticize three of the following statements:

a. Truly intelligent programs will not be reliable because they can "decide" not to give the correct answer.

b. Intelligent systems must be at least as intelligent as humans attempting the same task.

c. All programs are eventually run as deterministic algorithms. Therefore, no program can truly learn new knowledge.

d. Intelligence is in the eye of the beholder and cannot be pinned down in a program.

d. For a program to be capable of learning something, it must first be capable of being told it.

1.11. One response to the Chinese room experiment is to claim that Searle himself may not understand the Chinese story and Chinese questions, but the entire system (the room, the rules, Searle, the Chinese writings) does. Do you agree? Why or why not?

1.12. Most of the AI community disagrees with Searle's argument for fundamental reasons. Using your current knowledge of AI, try to identify some of those reasons.

Homework Exercises

1.13. For the N-Queens problem,

a. Determine a new heuristic function that uses the same strategy of picking one row at a time.

b. Determine a new strategy for solving the problem other than those mentioned in this chapter. Pick a new heuristic for this new strategy.

1.14. Think of two areas in the software development process in which an AI program might be useful. One example is using an AI program to evaluate the portability of a piece of software.

1.15. The Smart House project is a multicorporation project to design homes with high-technology features, such as a data network, security system, and integrated controls for appliances. Think of two desirable features that might be feasible with AI technology.

1.16. How might AI technology apply to the following problems?

a. Searching through terabytes of customer information trying to find out which customers' buying habits had changed in the last few weeks.

b. Trying to determine what resources (out of thousands) on a network would be able to solve your request for purchasing the newest book on AI.

1.17. Solve (in whatever way you can) the following classic AI problem:

Three missionaries and three cannibals come to a river. A boat on their side of the river can be used by either one or two persons. How should they use this boat to cross the river in such a way that cannibals never outnumber missionaries on either side of the river?

Try to find a schedule of crossings that gets them all across in a minimal number of crossings.

1.18. Given your current understanding, what programming paradigm (out of those identified in the chapter) would you use for the following problems and why?

a. The development of a real-time system to detect the dialing of a cellular telephone call

b. The development of a library of reusable routines to support development of intelligent, database applications

c. The development of a data-filtering mechanism that tries to determine whether a problem may be beginning to occur by looking at raw data

d. The development of a program to assess English sentences for proper grammar

e. The development of a system that can produce mathematical proofs dealing with set theory

1.19. A thermostat can be considered to have some intelligence. After all, it makes decisions to turn the heater or air conditioner on or off.

a. Using **IF-THEN** rules, give a complete definition of a thermostat's function. One of the rules might be the following:

if room_temperature > setting + 5°, then turn_on_air

Be careful to design your rules so that only one rule is applicable at any given temperature.

b. Do you think that a thermostat should be considered intelligent?

1.20. For each of the following sentences, determine what an AI agent must know to do the task described.

a. Understand the sentence

b. Agree or disagree with the sentence

c. Decide that such a statement or conclusion is needed for the current situation (for example, in part (i), what do we need to know to determine whether or not John Wayne's acting ability is in question?)

   i. "John Wayne was a good actor."

   ii. "This is a high-quality muffin."

   iii. "The *Star Trek* TV series is not true to life."

Programming Exercises

1.21. The Sears Tower in Chicago contains a network of elevators for use in moving throughout the 110-story building. Some are express elevators that stop only on particular floors. Others are local elevators that serve only a portion of the floors. The express elevators move at the rate of 1 second per floor, the local elevators move at 5 seconds per floor, and the service elevators move at 10 seconds per floor. The problem is to find the quickest route from any floor to any other. Consider the network shown in Table 1-1 (the network in the actual Sears Tower differs).

Write a program in a conventional programming language (e.g., C, Pascal, Modula 2, ICON) to solve this problem, given a starting floor and an ending floor from 1 to 110. Your output should list the elevators used and the intermediate floors on which stops or transfers were made.

How difficult would it be to modify your program to handle an arbitrary elevator network and an arbitrary number of floors?

Elevator	Type	Floors Accessible
1	Express	1 and 106
2	Express	1 and 50
3	Express	1 and 80
4	Express	30 and 80
5	Local	1–40
6	Local	30–70
7	Local	60–100
8	Service	100–110

TABLE 1.1

An elevator network

2

OBJECT-ORIENTED DESIGN

OOP (object-oriented

programming) is

really AI.

DANIEL BOBROW,
OOPSLA, 1991

2.1 USING OBJECTS IN AI SYSTEMS

Although object-oriented programming is only one of the available paradigms for artificial intelligence, it is a powerful paradigm widely used in other areas of computer science. Object-oriented languages such as the Common LISP Object System (CLOS) and SmallTalk have long been associated with AI programming; and several other object-oriented programming languages, including C++ and Eiffel, are now being used in AI studies. Many of the ideas present in object-oriented design are also common in AI systems. For example, frame-based systems (to be discussed in Chapter 7) have many characteristics of objects. Semantic networks (also in Chapter 7) embody concepts such as inheritance and a class (or type) hierarchy.

This chapter describes what an object-oriented design is and sets the framework for how to use object-oriented features of a language such as C++ or CLOS. Writing a program in CLOS or C++ does not necessarily make the design of that program object-oriented, however, because the programmer can continue to use a functional or procedural paradigm that is also supported by those languages.

Although this chapter focuses on notation and terminology for object-oriented design, it is just a tutorial and not intended to be complete. For a more complete description of object-oriented analysis and design, see Booch (1994), Shlaer and Mellor (1992), and Coad and Nicola (1993).

2.2 OBJECTS—A PROGRAMMING PARADIGM

Object-oriented programming (OOP) provides a framework that programmers can use to support goals such as modularization of systems, reusability of source code, and testable systems. Object-oriented analysis and design (OOA and OOD) provide methods for analyzing problems and framing them in terms of objects, so that OOP can be used to build the system.

Booch (1994) defines an object as follows (emphasis ours):

> An object has state, behavior, and identity; the structure and behavior of similar objects are defined in their common class; the terms **instance** and **object** are interchangeable.

An object is a unique instance of a particular object class. For example, a dog named Rufus could be considered as an object in the class "schnauzer." "Rufus" refers to the specific object, and "schnauzer" refers to the object class. A particular ceramic figurine of a frog could be considered to be an object in the class "pre-Colombian artifact." Objects have a particular identity, one or more states and associated properties, and behaviors. An object's identity distinguishes it from all other objects. For example, for Rufus, his identity is what makes Rufus distinguishable from other schnauzers. We need some way to tell that this dog is "Rufus." It is not necessarily by using the name Rufus. The mailperson may call Rufus "Butch," but he is still the same dog and the same object. We may have to use an indentifier other than a name, as there may be many Rufuses in our world. For example, we might use "K9-205c" or "Dog with the white belly" to uniquely identify Rufus.

Rufus may have states of "sleeping," "running," and "eating." Rufus can be in only one of these states at any given time, but other schnauzers may concurrently be in another state different from Rufus's state. The state of an object not only includes the dynamic properties of an object but also includes the static properties of an object. For example, the fact that his name is currently "Rufus" and that he has hair are components or Rufus's state.

The behavior of an object includes how the object acts and reacts. For example, what does Rufus do when he receives a command of "sit"? What does Rufus do when he is in a state of "hungry"? Answers to these questions are part of the definition of Rufus as an object.

2.2.1 The Object-Oriented Paradigm

The object-oriented paradigm has several central concepts used to support the definition and development of object-oriented systems:

objects

classes and class hierarchy

abstraction

encapsulation

inheritance

modularity

2.2.2 Objects

Central to a good object-oriented design is the care taken in choosing and defining objects. Objects should represent an important idea, actor, or thing that is needed to solve the problem at hand. For example, if we need to solve the problem of what Rufus will eat next, then Rufus is an important actor in this problem. Rufus's owner may be another important actor in the problem. But Rufus's dog house will probably not be an important object in solving this problem. The concept of being hungry may also be an important idea that we need to have defined as an object with characteristics and expected behaviors. The Booch notation for an object representing "Rufus" is an irregular shape enclosed within a solid line; within the irregular shape, the name of the object appears above a line and the object's attributes are listed below the line (Figure 2.1).

2.2.3 Classes and Class Hierarchy

A class is a group of similar objects. A primary function of the class designation is to group together objects that have similar behaviors and structures. Booch's (1994) definition of a class,

A class is a set of objects that share a common structure and a common behavior.

implies that an object is just an instantiation of a class. The class for Rufus may be the class of all schnauzers. The "schnauzer" class defines all characteristics that are common to schnauzers, such as

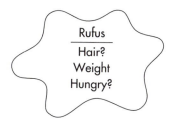

FIGURE 2.1

Rufus object

their expected size, color, and behavior. Furthermore, the schnauzer class may be a **subclass** of a "dog" class. This dog class will define all characteristics that are common to dogs. Class **hierarchy**—a division of general groups into smaller, more specific groups—helps to isolate common characteristics and behaviors of a class in the hierarchy.

The class hierarchy in Figure 2.2 shows how Rufus is an instantiation of the schnauzer class and how the schnauzer class is an instantiation of the dog class. The dashed-line shape encloses a class definition, and the arrows point to the classes in which an object's characteristics are defined.

2.2.4 Abstraction

Abstraction (the process) is a way of focusing only on those characteristics of an object that we care about—the essential characteristics. By defining objects on the basis of their interfaces with other objects, we can ignore many of the details that make each object work internally. For the object called Rufus, we only care about how Rufus interacts with and appears to his surroundings. We do not need to know how Rufus accomplishes the digestion of

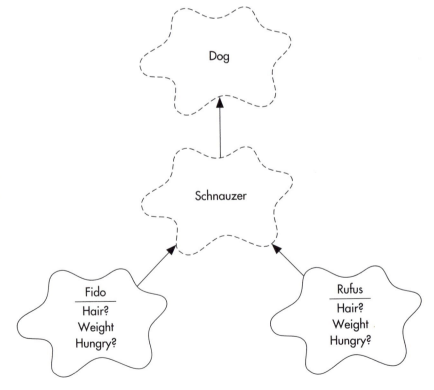

FIGURE 2.2

Dog class hierarchy

his food or how fast his hair grows. Booch (1994) defines an abstraction (the result of the process called abstraction) as follows:

> An abstraction denotes the essential characteristics of an object that distinguish it from all other kinds of objects and thus provide crisply defined conceptual boundaries, relative to the perspective of the viewer.

Objects provide this sort of abstraction (the result) by explicitly declaring a public interface and hiding details that are not relevant to users of that interface.

2.2.5 Encapsulation

Encapsulation is a process that is closely related to and works with the process of abstraction. Whereas abstraction is a technique that provides a distinct object boundary, **encapsulation** is the technique that hides everything else. It allows us to separate the internal implementation of an object from its interface. This separation allows us to change the implementation without affecting the interface and allows the implementation to be protected from those who use the object and its interface.

2.2.6 Inheritance

Inheritance is the acquisition of characteristics from the classes and class hierarchy to which an object belongs. Figure 2.2 shows an example of single inheritance. Rufus inherits from the schnauzer class all characteristics that are unique to schnauzers, and the schnauzer class inherits characteristics that are unique to dogs. Furthermore, Rufus inherits characteristics from the dog class via the schnauzer class. So Rufus will inherit characteristics such as barking and four legs from the dog class.

The more general case is that of multiple inheritance. Suppose we have a cat named Fluffy. Fluffy is a cat, but Fluffy is also a pet. In fact, Fluffy may be a house pet. We could place Fluffy's definition within the class hierarchy shown in Figure 2.3. Here we have Fluffy inheriting characteristics from the class house_pet and also from the class cat. House_pet will inherit characteristics from the more general class of pet. And cat will inherit characteristics from the more general class of mammal. Fluffy will inherit some characteristics like "being domesticated" from the pet class and others like "has hair" from the mammal class.[1]

---

[1] Many OOP languages require an object to be a member of exactly one class and allow multiple inheritance only among classes.

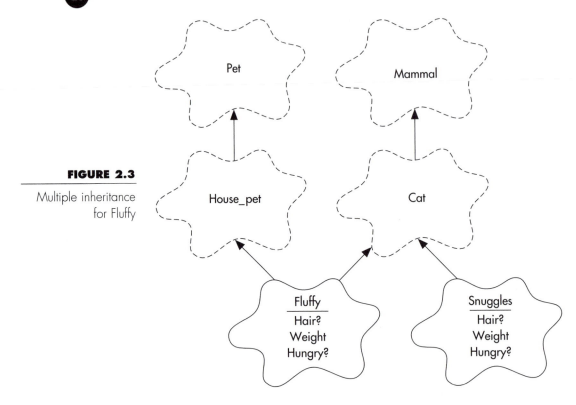

FIGURE 2.3

Multiple inheritance
for Fluffy

With multiple inheritance, there is the possibility that conflicting characteristics can be inherited from different classes. In the Fluffy example, we might have defined the characteristic of "being domesticated" for the pet class but also might have defined the characteristic of "being wild" for the mammal class—because most mammals are wild. Then when we ask whether Fluffy is wild or domesticated, we cannot tell by looking at the parent classes. We would have to explicitly define Fluffy as domesticated and either override one of the other inherited characteristics or provide a mechanism that resolves the ambiguity when Fluffy is accessed.

Inheritance of characteristics is one example of how the notion of hierarchy is used in an object-oriented design. A class hierarchy is one kind of "is a" hierarchy of specialization and generalization relationships. But we can also define objects as being made up of parts, or component objects. This technique is called aggregation and produces what is called a "part of" hierarchy. An example of aggregation is shown in Figure 2.4, where the relationships between the objects Fluffy, Fluffy's paws, and Fluffy's head are represented by using a line with a filled-in circle between each component object and the whole object.

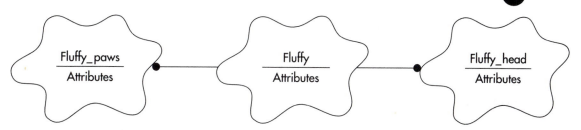

FIGURE 2.4

Aggregation of
Fluffy's parts

2.2.7 Modularity

Modularity is a property of a multicomponent system in which
the components are independent but compatible with one another.
The intent of modularity is to decompose a system into modules
that are loosely coupled, so that internal changes to one module are
localized and apply only to that module. However, the modules
should be able to work together as a cohesive whole to solve the
problem at hand. Encapsulation supports the localization of
changes, and abstraction helps to enforce the cohesive design.

2.3 MICRO DEVELOPMENT PROCESS

Booch defines a process for creating object-oriented systems called
the Micro Development Process, which we shall use here. This
process is primarily used for small projects that have only a few
people involved in the design and development. For larger projects,
a more robust process is needed.

The Micro Development Process has five primary steps:

1. Identification of the classes and objects and their appropriate
   levels of abstraction, to define the scope of the problem
2. Identification of how these classes and objects should behave
   and what their attributes are
3. Identification of the relationships between these classes and
   objects
4. Specification of the interface of the objects and classes, and
   implementation of the interface
5. Refinement of the system by repeating Steps 1 through 4.

2.4 NOTATION

To describe the algorithms and object-oriented designs in this text,
we will use class and object diagrams as described by Booch (1994).

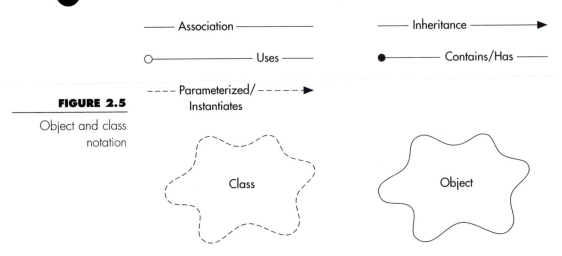

FIGURE 2.5

Object and class notation

We have already been using his notation throughout this chapter, but Figure 2.5 provides a complete summary of the notation we will use to represent class and object hierarchies and relationships.

2.5 SUMMARY

Object-oriented analysis grew out of the merger of systems analysis and design with the new features and requirements of an object-oriented approach to problem solving. In this chapter we introduce the terminology and notation that we will use throughout the text. The notation is primarily based on that of Booch (1994). Object-oriented design is well suited for AI applications and can help produce large, complex systems.

2.6 REFERENCES

Object-oriented analysis and design is presented in many excellent texts. In particular, we recommend books by Booch (1994), Shlaer and Mellor (1992), and Coad and Nicola (1993).

Meyer (1988) describes object-oriented design and uses the Eiffel programming language. Object-oriented programming with C++ is the topic of Wiener and Pinson (1988).

A survey of object-oriented tools for artificial intelligence is covered in Tello (1989).

2.7 EXERCISES

Warm-up Exercises

2.1   An object has identity, states, and behaviors. Define a set of objects and classes for the game of chess. Be sure your objects meet our definition. Do all of your objects have a physical counterpart (for example, does each player object represent a real person)?

2.2   Consider the following definitions for an object. Criticize these definitions and compare them to the one quoted earlier in this chapter.

An **object** is a bundle of data plus the operations that can be performed on that data.

An **object** is a variable declared to be of a specific class (Wiener and Pinson, 1988).

Each **object** is characterized by its own set of attributes and by a set of operations that it can perform. (McGregor and Sykes, 1992).

An **object** is a person, place or thing. When brought to life, it knows things and does things.

2.3.   Consider the following definitions for a class. Criticize these definitions and compare them to the one quoted earlier in this chapter.

A **class** is a description that applies to each of some number of objects.

A **class** is a grouping of objects together, based on common characteristics (Coad and Nicola, 1993).

A **class** is a "generalized" object.

A **class** is a set of objects that share a common conceptual basis (McGregor and Sykes, 1992).

A **class** definition describes the behavior of the underlying abstract data type by defining the interface to all the operations that can be performed on the underlying type (Wiener and Pinson, 1988).

2.4.   Suppose your adviser wants to create an AI program that will find "interesting" articles in journals. Define a set of objects that would be needed to solve this problem.

Homework Exercises

2.5. For Exercise 2.4, define an object-oriented design, using the notation from this chapter. List all classes and objects, their relationships, and any aggregations.

2.6. Based on Rumbaugh et al. (1991), Booch (1994) defines a **link** relationship between objects as follows: A link defines a "physical or conceptual relationship between objects." For example, you may have a controller object that influences another object. Or you may have one object on top of another. Define the link relationships between your objects defined in Exercise 2.5.

2.7. Consider the possibility of cycles in a class hierarchy, that is, a closed loop formed by the arrows that define subclass to superclass relationships for a given system.

   a. Can a class be a subclass of itself? In other words, does it make sense for a class to inherit properties from itself? Why or why not?

   b. Should any cycle in a class hierarchy be legal?

2.8. Classes are the primary focus of object-oriented design. Why does Booch outline them with dashed irregular lines rather than with solid lines, like objects?

2.9. The methodology proposed here (the Micro Development Process) is iterative. AI systems (even non-OO ones) are often developed in an iterative fashion. Speculate why AI systems often require an iterative methodology to develop a working system. Give an example of an AI system where an iterative methodology would be very helpful.

Programming Exercises

2.10. Investigate the language SmallTalk and determine its object-oriented characteristics. Write in SmallTalk a short program that will create the Fluffy class hierarchy shown in Figure 2.3. Define attributes at each level of the hierarchy and then create a Fluffy object. Print all attribute values for Fluffy, including those that are inherited.

2.11. Do Exercise 2.10, except use the Eiffel programming language.

2.12. Do Exercise 2.10, except use the CLOS programming language.

2.13. Do Exercise 2.10, except use the Ada programming language.

3

C++ AS AN AI TOOL

It is not a bad definition of man to describe him as a tool-making animal. His earliest contrivances to support uncivilized life were tools of the simplest and rudest construction. His latest achievements in the substitution of machinery, not merely for the skill of the human hand, but for the relief of the human intellect, are founded on the use of tools of a still higher order.

CHARLES BABBAGE

3.1 C++ PROGRAMMING FOR AI

Object-oriented programming is based on the concepts of abstract data types, class hierarchies, and inheritance. An **abstract data type** is a programming unit that includes a data type and an associated set of operations. It is implemented as a class in C++. When used properly, abstract data types keep the implementation of and access to data types hidden from other parts of the program. Such limited access localizes the effects of changes made to routines related to a specific data type.

C++ is an object-oriented language that implements these concepts. It is primarily an extension of the C programming language, but, unlike C, it includes object-oriented constructs for classes and data-hiding. This chapter provides a brief introduction to C++'s object-oriented features but does not provide complete details of the language. For partial syntax and more examples of C++, see Appendix A. See also books by Ellis and Stroustrup (1990), Stroustrup (1991), and Lippman (1989), which are more general C++ references.

Object-oriented programming provides an excellent structure for AI problems. Through the use of classes, AI programs can be written around the data types relevant to the problem. Most AI programs solve a problem by using the data at hand, so the creation and use of abstract data types fit naturally into AI programs. In this text, C++ is used for all algorithms, to illustrate the ability of object-oriented programming to meet the demanding needs of AI programs. However, C++ is not as directly suited to symbolic computation as other programming languages, such as LISP or Prolog. Nevertheless, class libraries that simulate LISP[1] or Prolog can quickly be built.

---

[1] See Coplien (1994) for a chapter on how LISP-like memory management can be accomplished with C++.

A strong motivation for using C++ for AI programs is its suitability for use in large software systems. Many AI programs are part of a larger software system and must interface with it. When the AI programs are in the same language as or a language similar to that of the overall system (the system may be in C), the linking is greatly facilitated. Furthermore, use of C++ can improve the performance of AI algorithms, which can be very slow when implemented in languages such as LISP or Prolog.

3.2 OBJECTED-ORIENTED CONSTRUCTS IN C++

An object in the C++ programming language is listed within a class, which defines the internal data structures of its members. A class also completely defines the interaction of each object with programs that use it. This definition includes what parts of the object are visible outside of the object (**public**), what procedures can be performed on this object (**methods**)[2], and how objects are created and initialized (by **constructors**). Data structures that are not visible outside of the class are called **private.** To invoke a procedure on an object, a message is sent to the object. A **message** can be viewed as a request to the object to perform an action and should not be concerned about how the action is performed.

The following sample program illustrates the use of classes in C++. The program will print out Hello World! when we run it. Of course, we did not need to use a class for such a simple program, but it shows how classes are accessed and defined in C++.

The file Example1.h gives the definition of the class to be used, a class called Example. Within the class definition, we have private and public data and methods. One special method, called the **constructor,** is used to generate new objects of the class, and it has the same name as the class itself. In this program, the constructor is defined by Example() {hidden_data_1 = 0;} ;. Another special method, called a **destructor,** is indicated by ~Example(); and is used to remove objects from memory. In addition, we have defined some **protected** data. Protected parts of the class are accessible by derived classes, which will be discussed in Section 3.4.2.

```
// A sample C++ class definition
// file example.h
//
#include <stream.h>
```

---

[2] C++ programmers may use different terminology, such as **member functions** for methods and **derived class** for subclass.

```
// A comment
/* Another comment style */
class example

{
  private:
    int hidden_data_1;
    float hidden_2;
  protected:
    int data_accessible_to_derived_class;
  public:
    char public_data[80];
    void function_1();
    char *function_2();
    example() { hidden_data_1 = 0; } ; // Constructor
    ~example(); // Destructor
} ;
```

A second file, Example1.cpp, contains the implementation of the class described in the file Example1.h. It includes the definitions of the two functions of our sample class: Function_1 does nothing but return; Function_2 returns a pointer to a string, which always has a value of Hello World!.

```
// Implementation of methods for simple class
// file example1.cpp
#include "example1.h"
//
void example::function_1()
// What a dull function!
// It does exactly nothing!
{
}
//
char *example::function_2()
// This function is much better!
// It actually returns a value.
{
  return "Hello World!" ;
}
```

A third file, Prog1.cpp, is the main program for our sample. It creates Data, which is an object of the class Example and is used to call Function_2() to return the string Hello World! We then use the stream cout to direct the string to standard output.

```
// Test program for class example
// This program is a convoluted "Hello World" program.
// It uses a sample class to illustrate the basics of
// classes in C++.
// file prog1.cpp

#include "example1.h"
main()
{
  example data;
  char *char_pointer;
  char_pointer = data.function_2();
  cout << char_pointer;
}
```

In this example, we have partitioned the program into three distinct parts:

1. A class description file. This file contains the definition, but not the implementation, of the class. It is usually named by the class name, followed by .h, as in Example1.h.

2. A class implementation file. This file contains the implementation of any functions that were not defined in the description file. It will include the description file so that it can be compiled separately from any programs that use it. The name of the file is usually the class name followed by .cpp, as in Example.cpp. The practice of separating the description from the implementation is very similar to the way in which packages in Modula-2 are defined (see Wirth, 1988).

3. A main program file. This file includes the source code for the main program, and its name is followed by .cpp, as in Prog1.cpp.

The convention of splitting programs and classes into files with the names just described is followed throughout this text.

3.3 C++ PROGRAM FOR AN AI AGENT

An application of object-oriented techniques is to define a class that implements artificially intelligent agents. Such an AI agent naturally has private data and functions that are only accessible by the agent. It also has functions to interact with the outside world. The following file is a simple example of a class definition of an agent that has functions to answer questions put to it by a user. It answers the questions on the basis of the current contents of its memory. To load its memory, we have provided the agent with the capability of learning (being told) new facts.

```
// This file defines a class for an AI agent.
// The agent answers questions about facts given it.
// file agent.h
//
#include "memory.h" // File that defines the class
// Memory
#include "name.h" // File that defines the class Name
class agent
{
  private:
    memory agent_mem; // Class Memory that defines
    // the memory
    name agent_name; // Class Name that defines names
    int age; // Age of the agent
    remember(char *fact); // Adds a fact to memory
    forget(char *fact); // Deletes a fact from memory
//
  public:
    agent(char *name) {age = 0}; // Agent
    // constructor
    char *ask(char *question); // Ask the agent a
    // question
    void tell(char *fact); // Tell the agent a fact
    void negate(char *fact); // Tell the agent
    // not(fact)
    ~agent(); // Agent destructor
};
//
// Insert your favorite robot definition here.
```

The implementation of the class has not been included, because it depends on the purpose of the agent and how it is expected to reason and add knowledge to its knowledge base.

The ability to hide data and methods from other classes and programs gives us the ability to completely localize data and methods to the agent. This feature allows us to simulate the reasoning process of the agent without affecting the programs that use it. We can then substitute a different reasoning process without directly affecting any of the programs that communicate with the agent. By using this isolation technique, we could simulate a precise interface with a robot that only accepts a small set of commands. The separation of these two program components allows us to experiment with the robots reasoning process even before the robot is built!

3.4 FEATURES OF THE C++ PROGRAMMING LANGUAGE

The C++ programming language provides several useful extensions to the C programming language. This section provides a brief overview of these features.

3.4.1 Generic Classes

The purpose of generic classes is to allow the same class definition to be used with objects of different types. A generic class can save time and effort. If we need to sort the elements of lists of integer numbers, real numbers, and character strings, then we would like to have a class that can sort lists of all these data types. With a single class definition, we can write functions like Sort only once. The following example is intended only to introduce the structure of C++ programs and is not indicative of a robust implementation of lists.[3] This program does not use objects as list elements.

```
// These classes define a singly linked list and
// its nodes.
//
// file list.h.
//
#include <stream.h>
//
// typedef defines the type of function that will
// be used to sort the list. It should return a
// positive value if the elements are out of order.
//
typedef int (*compare)(char *, char *);
class list_node
//
// This class specifies a generic node in the list.
// The size of the list node contents is not
// specified and is allocated dynamically as items
// are inserted in the list. All nodes are expected
// to be of the same size, however. The size is
```

---

[3] For the search library, a more extensive and efficient list class for AI search is developed. See Chapter 5 and Section 3.5 for a description of the class that uses C++ templates. Templates support the notion of generic classes in an elegant fashion.

```
// specified in the class list.
//
{
  friend class list;
  //
  // This statement means that the class list can
  // modify the private data of class list_node.
  //
  private:
    list_node *next; // Pointer to the next node
    // in the list
    char *contents; // Allocated dynamically
};
class list
{
  private:
    list_node *head; // Pointer to the head of
    // the list
    int size; // Size of contents in bytes
    void clear_list(); // Delete nodes in list
    compare comp_function; // Pointer to compare
    // function
  public:
    // The constructor, which takes two arguments.
    // The first argument is the size of the
    // contents in a node and the second is a
    // pointer to the function used to compare the
    // contents for sorting.
    //
    list (int siz, compare cf)
    {
      head = 0;
      size = siz;
      comp_function = cf;
    }
    //
    // Insert an item in the list
    //
    void insert(char *record);
    //
    // Return a pointer to the first element of
    // the list
    //
    char *destructive_car();
    //
```

```
      // Return the first element of the list as a
      // full list_node
      //
      list_node *car();
      //
      // Return a pointer to a list that is all of
      // the list except for the first element.
      // Similar to the LISP
      // cdr
      //
      list *cdr();
      //
      // Sort the list, using the comp_function
      //
      void sort();
      //
      // Destruct or remove the elements of the list
      //
      ~list() {clear_list();}
} ;
```

The class List_node has the class List as a class. This association allows the class List to access the private data of the class List_node. Friend classes are usually used for only two reasons: The classes are intimately linked (as in the list example) or direct access to private data is needed to improve performance. In most other cases, friend classes should not be used because they compromise the integrity of the data abstraction defined by the class.

The preceding program also demonstrates the notion of a destructor. Destructors are used to explicitly deallocate the memory space used by an object of a class. Here the destructor is defined by ~List(). Destructors are defined by a tilde, ~, followed by the class name.

The file List.h defines the interface to the list class. It defines all the methods that can be applied to objects of the class. It does not include the implementation of those methods; they are included in the following file, List.cpp.

```
// This file implements the class List
// by defining its methods.
// file list.cpp
//
#include "list.h"
//
void list::insert(char *record)
{
```

```
  list_node *temp;
  temp = new list_node;
  temp -> contents = new char[size];
  for (int i = 0; i < size; i++)
    temp->contents[i] = record[i];
  if (head != 0)
    temp->next = head;
  else
    temp->next = 0;
  head = temp;
  return;
}
char *list::destructive_car()
{
  if (head == 0)
    cout << "Error in destructive car: empty list";
  else
  {
    char *return_val;
    return_val = new char[size];
    for (int i = 0; i < size; i++)
      return_val[i] = head->contents[i];
    delete head->contents;
    head = head->next;
    return return_val;
  }
}
list_node *list::car()
{
  if (head == 0)
    cout << "Error in car: empty list";
  else
  {
    char *return_contents;
    list_node *return_val;
    return_val = new list_node;
    return_contents = new char[size];
    for (int i = 0; i < size; i++)
      return_contents[i] = head->contents[i];
    return_val->contents = return_contents;
    return_val->next = 0;
    return return_val;
  }
}
list *list::cdr()
```

```
{
  list *return_list;
  return_list = new list(size, comp_function);
  return_list->head = head->next;
  return(return_list);
}
void list::clear_list()
{
  list_node *start = head;
  if (start == 0) return;
  do
  {
    list_node *current = start;
    start = start->next;
    delete current->contents;
    delete current;
  } while (start != 0);
}
void list::sort()
//
// Sort, using supplied compare function
//
// This is a bubble sort; a slow n**2 algorithm.
//
{
  int did_switch; // Used to determine whether
  // nodes were swapped
  int n = 0; // The number of nodes in the list
  int num_pairs; // The number of pairs to be
  // checked
  list_node *current; // The current node being
  // considered
  list_node *previous; // The node previous to the
  // current one
  list_node *temp; // Used in swapping nodes
//
// Determine the length of the list
//
  for (current = head; current != 0; current =
                                     current->next)
    n = n+1;
//
// Do the compares and switches
//
  if (n < 2) return;
```

```
      did_switch = 1;
      for (num_pairs = n 1; did_switch; num_pairs)
      {
        did_switch = 0;
        current = head;
        previous = head;
        for (int j = 0; j < num_pairs; j++)
        {
          //
          //Use the pointer to the compare function
          //If true, then exchange nodes
          //
          if ((*comp_function )(current->contents,
                current->next->contents)
          {
          temp = current->next->next;
          if (current == head)
          {
            head = current->next;
              previous = head;
            }
            else
            {
              previous->next = current->next;
              previous = previous->next;
            }
            current->next->next = current;
            current->next = temp;
            did_switch = 1;
            }
          else
          {
            previous = current;
            current = current->next;
          } //end if
        } //end inner for
      } //end outer for
      return;
    } //end sort
```

The Sort method defines a bubble sort by using a function that is passed from the main program. The main program passes a pointer to the function, and the Sort method uses it to compare the contents of each node. If the function passed returns a value greater than zero, then the nodes are not in order with respect to one another.

The main program creates a list of integers and passes a function that can be used to compare integers. This program is completely independent of the implementation of the list. If the class List were changed to allow a more efficient list structure, such as storing the list in a heap, the main program would only have to be relinked rather than recompiled.

```cpp
// This file tests the sort program on lists.
// file main.cpp
#include "list.h"
//
int compare_ints(char *int1, char *int2)
{
  int *i1;
  int *i2;
  i1 = (int *) int1;
  i2 = (int *) int2;
  return (*i1 > *i2);
}
main()
{
  list int_list(sizeof(int), compare_ints);
  int *value;
  int i = 1, j = 2, k = 0, l = 4, m = 50, n = 3;
//
  int_list.insert((char *) &i);
  int_list.insert((char *) &j);
  int_list.insert((char *) &k);
  int_list.insert((char *) &l);
  int_list.insert((char *) &m);
  int_list.insert((char *) &n);
//
  int_list.sort();
//
  cout << "The values are:" ;
  for (int current = 0; current < 6; current++)
  {
    value = ( int *) int_list.destructive_car();
    cout << *value << "";
  }
  cout << "\n";
  int_list.~list();
}
```

3.4.2 Derived Classes and Inheritance

Derived classes are an important feature of C++. They allow classes
to use constructs already created by other classes. One common
usage of the technique is to produce a class that is more specialized
than its parent. In the following example, a class Stack for objects
of data type float is produced from the parent class of a generic list.

```cpp
// This file defines a class Stack for data of type
float.
// The class Stack is derived from the generic
class List.
// file stack.cpp
//
#include "list.h"
//
// A compare function is needed to create the list.
// It is not used for the stack, because stacks
// should not be sorted.
//
int float_comp(char *i, char *j)
{
  float *fi;
  float *fj;
  fi = (float *) i;
  fj = (float *) j;
  return(*fi > *fj);
}
class float_stack: private list
{
  public:
    void push(float rec) {list::insert((char *)
                                        &rec);}
    float pop() {return *((float *) list::
                          destructive_car());}
    float_stack(): list(sizeof(float),float_comp) {}
};
main()
{
  float m,n,o,p;
  float_stack stack;
  n = 20.3;
  m = 0.1;
  o = 2.5;
  p = 200.98;
```

```
stack.push(m);
stack.push(n);
stack.push(o);
stack.push(p);
cout << "The values are:" ;
for (int i = 0; i<4; i++)
   cout << stack.pop() <<"" ;
cout << "\n";
}
```

Derived classes are simple to create and much less prone to error than a completely new class. From the generic class List we can define derived classes for lists of all types: queues of any type, or stacks of any type. Using the Sort operator, we can ensure that the list is always sorted after any insertion in a derived class.

Derived classes inherit the protected items of a parent class and can access them freely. However, they do not inherit private items.

A derived class can have other classes derived from it, thereby producing a class hierarchy.

3.4.3 Overloaded Operators and Functions

The ability to overload operators and functions in C++ is useful for object-oriented programming and artificial intelligence programming. For example, if we define a "pick-up" operator, we could pick-up many different sorts of objects. An operator or a function is overloaded if its arguments or parameters can assume different types. The various types are reflected in the design of the operator or function. For example, if we say Unify(X,Y), where X and Y are clauses in logic, then the function Unify is designed to logically unify clauses (described in Chapter 4). However, when X and Y are literals, then the function Unify is designed to unify logical literals.

3.4.4 Polymorphism and Virtual Functions

An interesting feature of C++ that allows for binding of methods during run time (rather than at the time of compiling) is the virtual function. Polymorphism allows a programmer to send a message to an object, without being concerned about how the action will be accomplished. We have been using polymorphism, but only at compile time.

A virtual function allows a more flexible form of polymorphism to occur at run time, because the programmer can place a pointer to an object of a parent class that is used to reference the virtual function. The pointer can then be changed at run time to point to derived classes with functions of the same name as the virtual function. When the pointer is then used to point to the function, the method in the derived class is used. Wiener and Pinson (1988) provide an excellent introduction to virtual functions.

3.4.5 Additional Features

The following features are explicitly supported in the C++ programming language but not as easily done in the C programming language. They are useful but not critical to object-oriented programming. For more detail, see Ellis and Stroustrup (1990). When appropriate, these features are used in this text.

Anonymous unions. Unions allow storage to be shared between two or more fields, for conservation of memory usage. Unions without a name can be used anywhere that a field or variable can be defined.

Comments. C++ allows comments of the form // to indicate a comment that extends to the end of the line. C-style comments with delimiters /* and */ can still be used.

Constant declarations. The Const specifier can be used to ensure that an entity is used as a constant and that its value is not changed within its scope. The parameter of a function can be declared as Const to ensure that the function treats the parameter as a constant.

Default values for function parameters. Trailing parameters in a C++ function can be assigned default values. This feature allows the function to be called with fewer than the total number of parameters, with the missing parameters being assigned their defaults.

Enumerated types. The name of an enumeration is a type in C++. This restriction allows an enumerated type to be fully enforced by the compiler.

Explicit type conversion. Types should be converted explicitly. C++ allows the name of a type to be used to convert data from one type to another. For example, Int i = (Int) m; will convert **M** from whatever type it is to an integer and assign it to i.

Function parameter type specification. C++ allows the programmer to specify the type of parameters passed to the function. For example,

```
void function_name(int parm1, float parm2)
{
// Function contents would be here.
return;
}
```

Local declarations. C++ permits declarations within blocks, much like Algol-68. This feature allows for storage to be used only within that block and freed when the block is exited. It also helps to keep the declaration of a variable closer to its point of use, which makes the program easier to read. As an example, we can use the following code to declare a variable to be used only within the for loop:

```
For (Int counter = 10; Counter > 0; Counter--).
```

New and delete operators. New and Delete operators are added in C++ to allow for easier allocation and deallocation of memory space in the heap.

Reference parameters in a function. C++ can pass parameters to a function by reference rather than by forcing the calling routine to pass the address of the parameter. This action is specified as follows:

```
//Passing parameters by reference
void square_it (int &value)
{
  value = value * value;
  return;
}
```

The function will square its parameter. For example,

```
int k = 10;
square_it(k);
cout << k;
```

will output 100.

Scope qualifiers. The scope qualifier operator, ::, is used to access a global variable when a local variable has the same name. For example, suppose that we had the following code:

```
// Using the scope qualifier
int i = 2000;
for (int i = 1; i < 10; i++)
{
  cout << ::i << "";
}
```

This code will print out 2000 ten times.

Stream library. The classes Cin, Cout, and Cerr are included in C++ for standard input, standard output, and standard error. The operators associated with these classes can be overloaded so that programmer-defined classes can easily direct objects to and from streams.

Struct and class names are types. The names of classes and structs are types. Rigorous type checking is performed on classes and structs.

Unspecified number of parameters for functions. A C++ function can be defined to have an unspecified number of parameters. This feature allows complete flexibility in the parameters passed to the function but disables the type checking of the parameters.

3.5 DEFINING A C++ CLASS LIST TEMPLATE

In Chapter 5, we will design a search class that uses the following definition of class List. The key feature of this class is that we allow list nodes to be of different types. To allow this, we will use C++s class template feature to simplify the design.

The file Bnode.h defines a base List class that the List class uses to inherit its basic attributes. The file List.h defines the list class using C++ templates. The code is available in the electronic file distribution. It is not described here because of the complexity of the code.

3.6 SUMMARY

The C++ programming language provides a structured environment built on the foundation of the C programming language. The primary feature added to C is C++s implementation of classes and associated object-oriented structures (including inheritance). C++s support of object-oriented programming helps support the development of large software systems.

Object-oriented programming provides an excellent structure for developing artificial intelligence programs and systems. In addition, it helps to simplify the interface to more traditional systems, particularly those written in C++.

3.7 REFERENCES

The C++ programming language was developed at AT&T Bell Labs as an extension to the C programming language in the early 1980s primarily by Bjarne Stroustrup (see Stroustrup, 1986). The intent was to add object-oriented functionality to the C programming language while still supporting programs written in C. The definition of the C++ programming language continues to be refined as more experience is gained with the language.

There are many excellent texts describing C++. Most assume some knowledge of the C programming language. If you know C, a good book to start learning C++ is *An Introduction to Object-*

Oriented Programming and C++ by Wiener and Pinson (1988). Other good C++ references are Lippman (1989), Hu (1989), and Ellis and Stroutstrup (1990). For a book detailing advanced usage of C++, see Coplien (1991). This book contains a chapter that describes how to emulate symbolic processing, such as that used in the LISP programming language.

To effectively use C++, you need a manual for the particular version that you wish to use. Stroustrup (1986, p. 9) gives an excellent list of heuristics for use in writing programs in C++. He suggests when it is appropriate to define a new class for your program. First of all, you must define the concepts that are required to solve the problem. Then you must examine each concept defined. If you can think of the concept as a separate idea, define a class for it. If you can think of the concept as a separate entity, then make it an object of a class. If two classes have something important in common, then define a base class that includes the commonalities. Stroustrup suggests that your base class should be nearly universal.

If you do not know C, then two references that introduce this language are Kernighan and Ritchie (1978) and Bronson and Menconi (1988).

3.8 EXERCISES

Warm-up Exercises

3.1. Define a class in C++ for sets of integers. Be sure to allow members of the set to be sets. Define the private data, public data, and the function prototypes that are allowed. Do not implement the methods.

3.2. Implement the functions of Union, Intersection, and the Boolean function Member to test whether an element is in the set.

3.3. Write a C++ function to flatten an object of type set. That is, the routine must make a single set out of a nested set. The following are a few examples of how your flatten should work:

```
flatten([a,[b,[c,d]]]) = [a,b,c,d]
flatten([[[],[],[a]]) = [a]
flatten([a,b,c]) = [a,b,c]
```

3.4. Write a C++ function to determine the length of a list and add the function to the class List.

3.5. Write a C++ function to reverse the elements of a list.

3.6. Design a C++ class that defines the set of Fibonacci numbers defined by

$$f_1 = 1$$
$$f_2 = 1$$
$$f_n = f_{n-1} + f_{n-2} \qquad \text{for } n > 2$$

You must determine what operations make sense for Fibonacci numbers and implement them.

Homework Exercises

3.7. In Exercise 3.6 you were asked to write a routine to compute the nth Fibonacci number. Analyze your algorithm to determine its running time. If your algorithm is not $O(n)$, then write another routine that works in $O(n)$ time.

3.8. Use C++ to solve the water jugs problem:

There are two jugs, one holding three and the other five gallons of water. There are a number of things that can be done with the jugs: They can be filled, emptied, and dumped one into the other either until the poured-into jug is full or until the poured-out-of jug is empty. Devise a sequence of actions that will produce four gallons of water in the larger jug. (*Hint:* Use only integer values of water.)

3.9. Write a quicksort function in C++ for lists of integers. Use it to replace the bubble sort used in the definition of the class List. Baase (1988) contains a discussion of quicksort.

3.10. Using a class derived from the class List, define a class for queues. You may need to modify the class definition of List to add more functionality.

Programming Exercises

3.11. Use C++ to do the Sears Tower program in Exercise 1.21. Be sure to make your program general enough to handle an arbitrary tower and an arbitrary network of elevators. The actual Sears tower has 103 elevators.

3.12. Write a C++ program to solve the stable marriage problem from Sedgewick (1988):

Suppose there are N men and N women who want to get married. Each man has a list of all the women in his preferred order, and each woman likewise has a list of the men in preferred order. The problem is to find a set of marriages that is stable.

A set of marriages is unstable if two people who are not married to each other both prefer each other to their spouses. For example, suppose there are two men, *A* and *B*, and two women, *X* and *Y*, such that A prefers X to Y, X prefers A to B, and Y prefers B to A. The pairs of marriages *A–Y* and *B–X* is unstable.

Your program should have as input lists of preferences and produce as output a stable set of marriages, that is, one that is not unstable. A theorem from graph theory proves that this ordering is always possible. Test the program on the following five men and five women, with their associated preferences:

Person	Preference list
abraham	chena tammy zia ruth sarah
benjamin	zia chena ruth sarah tammy
chuck	chena ruth tammy sarah zia
david	zia ruth chena sarah tammy
eli	tammy ruth chena zia sarah
zia	eli abraham david benjamin chuck
chena	david eli benjamin abraham chuck
ruth	abraham david benjamin chuck eli
sarah	chuck benjamin david abraham eli
tammy	david benjamin chuck eli abraham

The above data should be read from a file called TEST.DAT. Your program should read the first line of the data to determine what *N* will be. In this case, *N* is five. You may assume that each name is delimited by a space and that the input is valid. Your program should be tested on other sets of data.

4

LOGIC: A FOUNDATION FOR ARTIFICIAL INTELLIGENCE

A mathematician is

a machine for

turning coffee into

theorems.

PAUL ERDÖS,
quoted in
R. Kurzweil, 1990

4.1 THE ROLE OF LOGIC IN AI

Logic is used in AI to describe its theoretical concepts. It is applicable to for this purpose because logicians, through repeated attempts to define reasoning formally, have developed techniques and notation for the reasoning process. Much of this work has been done by formalizing mathematical reasoning and the process of proving theorems. This chapter describes the basic logical foundations for automated theorem proving; in-depth coverage of logic for deduction is covered in Chapter 6. The techniques used for automated theorem proving are covered in Chapter 9; and more advanced uses of logic for the purposes of AI are described in Chapter 12.

Logic has been a critical part of mathematics for centuries, but it has been formalized only in the last two centuries. In *Foundations of Arithmetic*, Frege (1884) created a language that is now called first-order predicate logic and is the subject of most of this chapter. Another important tool for AI was provided by Whitehead and Russell (1913), who attempted to give to mathematics an explicit foundation built on a specific set of axioms. In doing so, they designed a set of formal operations for use in deriving theorems from axioms. This important work contributed to the development of automated theorem provers and checkers and the standard notation of mathematical logic. Alfred Tarski (1956) later created a theory of formal semantics that linked logical expressions to specific meanings. Today, work continues in expanding the use of logic in both mathematics and computer science.

Although logic is used to formalize and prove the correctness of particular methods of reasoning, it is often subsequently replaced by a simpler and more efficient mechanism. The full expressiveness of logic is not needed for every AI program, and implementing it would introduce inefficiencies.

4.2 PROPOSITIONAL LOGIC

Propositional logic is a formal mathematical system of logic used to reason about the world. As we will see in this chapter, propositional logic is quite limited in the concepts that can be expressed with it. First-order predicate logic is an extension of propositional logic and has more expressive power. It is discussed in sections 4.3 and 4.4.

4.2.1 Introduction to Propositional Logic

Propositional logic provides a mechanism for formally representing knowledge and inference mechanisms. This book provides only a short introduction. For more complete coverage, see Barnier and Chan (1989) or Manna and Waldinger (1985). An interesting, popular book by Hofstadter (1979) also delves into some of the intricacies of logic.

Table 4.1 defines the fundamental symbols that we will use. They are defined again later in the text, when they are used. The basic element of any logic is the **statement.** A statement in a two-valued logic is defined by the following properties:

- It consists of a string of symbols that are legal in the language of the logic in which the statement is expressed.
- It is a well-formed formula by the rules of the logic.
- It has only one truth value, either true or false.

TABLE 4.1

Fundamental symbols of logic

Symbol	Meaning
$\wedge$	Logic and
$\vee$	Logic or
$\rightarrow$	Logical implication or "implies"
$\neg$	Logical not
$\equiv$	Logical equivalence
$\forall$	Universal quantifier or "for all"
$\exists$	Existential quantifier or "for each"

The last property is the restriction that makes such logics two-valued. If we allow more than *true* and *false* as truth values, then we have defined a multivalued logic.

Suppose that I say in English, "I am the President of the United States." If we relax the rule that a statement must be a well-formed formula, this expression would be a statement because it has a definite truth value of *false*. But if I say, "This statement is a lie," then the expression would not be a statement, because it cannot be assigned a truth value and still make sense. If we assume that the expression is *true*, then the statement is a lie and therefore *false*, which negates our assumption. If we assume that the expression is *false*, then the statement is not a lie and is *true*, which also negates our assumption. This is known as Russell's Paradox.

For propositional logic, statements are formed by using the following rules to generate well-formed formulas (WFFs):

a. A propositional symbol (or atom), which represents a fact, is a WFF.

b. If A is a WFF, then $\neg A$ is a WFF.

c. If A and B are WFFs, then $(A \vee B)$, $(A \wedge B)$, and $(A \rightarrow B)$ are WFFs.

d. If A and B are WFFs, then $(A \equiv B)$, their equivalence, is a WFF.

e. *true* and *false* represent constant propositional symbols that represent constant truth and falsehood, respectively. They are WFFs.

$(A \vee (A \wedge B))$ is a WFF, yet $(A \vee B \rightarrow C)$ is not. We will relax the requirement of parentheses when the meaning of the WFF is clear from context or when associative laws apply.

The preceding rules define the **syntax** of legal statements in propositional logic. The **semantics,** or meaning, of statements is defined by the interpretation of a WFF and by the meanings of the connectives ($\vee$, $\wedge$, and $\rightarrow$). An **interpretation** of a propositional logic statement is defined as follows:

Given a propositional logic WFF A, let $P_1, \cdots, P_n$ all be symbols in A. I, an interpretation of A, is an assignment of truth values (true or false in a two-valued logic) to each of $P_1, \cdots, P_n$.

The meaning of the connectives can be defined by a **truth table,** which is a table that lists all possible combinations of truth values (where T is an abbreviation for *true* and F an abbreviation for *false*) (see Table 4.2). If there are two propositions, then there are four rows or 2^2 rows in the truth table, as illustrated in Table 4.1. In general, there are 2^n rows in the truth table for n propositions. If we

TABLE 4.2

Propositional logic
operator definitions

A	B	$\neg A$	$A \vee B$	$A \wedge B$	$A \rightarrow B$	$A \equiv B$
T	T	F	T	T	T	T
T	F	F	T	F	F	F
F	T	T	T	F	T	F
F	F	T	F	F	T	T

had a logic with three possible values (say true, false, and maybe), then we would have 3^n rows in a truth table. Consider the following set of propositions:

P: Mice like cheese.
Q: The moon is made of cheese.
R: There are mice on the moon.

We might be interested in the possible truth value of $P \wedge (Q \vee R)$, which can be expressed by a truth table with eight (2^3) rows:

P	Q	R	$(P \wedge (Q \vee R))$
T	T	T	T
T	T	F	T
T	F	T	T
T	F	F	F
F	T	T	F
F	T	F	F
F	F	T	F
F	F	F	F

Three of the possible eight interpretations produce a true value.

4.2.2 Definitions for Propositional Logic

The concept of **logical consequence** is important in identifying facts that can be added to an existing set of facts without contradicting any of the existing set of facts. Given WFFs $A_1, \cdots, A_n$, C is a logical consequence of $A_1, \cdots, A_n$ if and only if for every interpretation, I, in which $A_1, \cdots, A_n$ are all true, then C is also true. For example, R is a logical consequence of $R \vee B$ and $\neg B$.

Any WFF that is *true* in every interpretation is defined as **valid** (for example, $A \vee \neg A$). Any WFF that is *false* in every interpretation is defined as **unsatisfiable** (for example, *false* or $A \wedge \neg A$). A WFF

R	B	R ∨ B	¬B	¬R	((R ∨ B) ∧ ¬B) → R	((R ∨ B) ∧ ¬B) ∧ ¬R
T	T	T	F	F	T	F
T	F	T	T	F	T	F
F	T	T	F	T	T	F
F	F	F	T	T	T	F

TABLE 4.3

R is a logical consequence of ¬B and R ∨ B

that is true for some interpretation is defined as **satisfiable** (for example, $A \rightarrow B$). Thus if C is a logical consequence of $A_1, \cdots, A_n$, then $(A_1 \wedge A_2 \wedge \cdots \wedge A_n) \rightarrow C$ is valid and $(A_1 \wedge A_2 \wedge \cdots \wedge A_n \wedge \neg C)$ is unsatisfiable. An example of these definitions is given in the Table 4.3. Note that when both $R \vee B$ and $\neg B$ are *true*, R is also *true*, which makes it a logical consequence of them.

4.2.3 Use of Propositional Logic

Propositional logic can be used to represent knowledge and reasoning methods. For example, the statement, "If it is snowing, then the road is slick," can be expressed as $S_1 \rightarrow S_2$. S_1 stands for "it is snowing," and S_2 stands for "the road is slick." If you knew that "it is snowing," or S_1, then you could conclude that "the road is slick," or S_2. This method of reasoning is called **modus ponens** and is expressed symbolically as

$S_1 \rightarrow S_2$	Given fact
S_1	Given fact
S_2	Result of applying modus ponens

Disjunctive syllogism is another simple inference method. This method is used when you have statements of the form $A_1 \vee A_2$ and $\neg A_1$ and conclude A_2 from them. Application of this method allows us to conclude from the two facts "Elsie is a cow or a bull" and "Elsie is not a bull" that "Elsie is a cow."

Translating knowledge into propositional logic is not necessarily simple or even unique. For example, again consider the statement, "Elsie is a cow or a bull." This statement could be translated to propositional logic and made more precise as $(C \wedge \neg B) \vee (\neg C \wedge B)$ to indicate that Elsie cannot be both a cow and a bull.

Given a database of facts that includes a statement that is unsatisfiable, one can conclude anything. Therefore, this situation should be avoided. Anything can be concluded from such a statement because *false* → *A* is valid for any WFF *A*. Consider the following example, where nonsense is deduced from nonsense:

If pigs can fly, then I'm a monkey's uncle.	A valid statement of the form *false* → *A*
Pigs fly.	A false statement that we have assumed.
I'm a monkey's uncle.	Our incorrect deduction.

One could argue that the preceding example is not always nonsense. It does assume that the proposition "pigs can fly" is equivalent to *false*, but, strictly speaking, the interpretation depends on the meaning of the statement "pigs can fly" and the environment in which it is being interpreted.

4.2.4 Equivalent Forms for Propositional Logic

Equivalent forms of logical expressions are sets of expressions that have the same truth tables; therefore they can be substituted for one another. The dual of one of these equivalences is also an equivalence. A **dual** is created by replacing all ∨s with ∧s, and all ∨s with ∧s in formulas that contain only ∧, ∨, or ¬ (Table 4.4). If the formula contains the constant *true*, then it must be replaced with *false*, and every occurrence of *false* must be replaced by *true*.

Sets of equivalent forms can be shown to be equivalent by showing that their truth tables are equivalent. Equivalent statements can be replaced by one another in larger statements to simplify the expression or to prove a statement.

TABLE 4.4

Equivalent forms for propositional logic

Equivalence	Dual	Property name
$\neg(\neg P) \equiv P$	$\neg(\neg P) \equiv P$	Double negation
$(P \lor Q) \equiv (\neg P \to Q)$	Not directly derivable*	
$\neg(P \lor Q) \equiv (\neg P \land \neg Q)$	$\neg(P \land Q) \equiv (\neg P \lor \neg Q)$	DeMorgan's Laws
$P \lor (Q \land R) \equiv (P \lor Q) \land (P \lor R)$	$P \land (Q \lor R) \equiv (P \land Q) \lor (P \land R)$	Distributive Laws
$P \land Q \equiv Q \land P$	$P \lor Q \equiv Q \lor P$	Commutative Laws
$((P \lor Q) \lor R) \equiv (P \lor (Q \lor R))$	$((P \land Q) \land R) ((P \land (Q \land R))$	Associative Laws
$P \lor \neg P \equiv true$	$P \land \neg P \equiv false$	
$P \lor (P \land Q) \equiv P$	$P \land (P \lor Q) \equiv P$	
$(P \to Q) \equiv (\neg Q \to \neg P)$	Not directly derivable.	

* To apply the rules for creating duals, we first need to convert the → to the other operators.

4.2.5 Limits of Propositional Logic

For the purposes of artificial intelligence, propositional logic is rather limited. For example, using propositional logic to represent statements with an infinite (or very large) number of objects is very difficult. Consider the statement "All grains of sand are either brown or black." If we also know that "This grain of sand is not brown," we should be able to conclude that "This grain of sand is black." With our limited form of propositional logic, however, we would need a statement for every grain of sand in the world. The concept of existence, as in the statement "Some grains of sand are black," is also difficult to express with propositional logic without giving each black grain of sand a name and asserting that it is black.

Another limitation of propositional logic is that it provides no concept of a function or any sort of relationship between objects. Predicate logic addresses both of these limitations by introducing the notion of quantifiers and variables for use within statements.

4.3 PREDICATE LOGIC

First-order predicate logic (FOPL) is a formal mathematical system of logic that uses predicates in place of the propositions used in propositional logic. **Predicates** are statements about objects in the universe of discourse that can either be *true* or *false*. **Objects**[1] are things in the universe about which we wish to prove facts.

4.3.1 Introduction to Predicate Logic

Predicate logic is basically an extension of propositional logic. It is also sometimes called the predicate calculus. We usually try to limit our use of predicate logic to first-order predicate logic. Logics of a higher order are much more complicated and are used only when they are absolutely needed. "First-order" refers to the use of variables in predicate logic statements. It means that variables can represent only objects within domains and cannot range over other entities, such as predicates. Second-order predicate logic allows variables to vary over predicates.

4.3.2 Syntax for Predicate Logic

The terms defined in this and the following section are used throughout the text. The following forms of expressions are used in FOPL:

---

[1] These objects are not to be confused with the objects used in object-oriented programming. This definition of object is specific to FOPL; OOP objects are programming constructs and can represent the objects described in this section.

- A **constant** is a specific member of some domain of objects. Constants are represented either by lowercase letters from the beginning of the alphabet or by words that begin with a lowercase letter; for example, *a, b, cat.*

- A **variable** is an unspecified member of some domain of objects. Variables are usually represented either by uppercase letters from the end of the alphabet or by words that begin with an uppercase letter; for example, *X, Y, Z, Smart_alecs.*

- A **function** assigns a combination of members from one set of domains to a member of another domain (called the **range**). Functions are represented by lowercase letters and words that begin with a lowercase letter, with their arguments following in parentheses; for example, *f(X,Y,Z)* or *sum(X,Y).*

- The **arity of a function** is the number of arguments (for parameters) that the function has. If two functions have the same name but different arities, then they are different functions— for example, *sum(x,y)* is a function of arity two.

- A **predicate** maps a combination of members from a set of domains to truth values. They can be viewed as functions with a range that consists of the set {*true, false*} . They are represented either by uppercase letters or by words that begin with an uppercase letter, with their arguments following in parentheses; for example, *Is_a(tracy,professor)* or *Part_of(wheel,car).* Predicates can represent properties of domain members as in *Big(bear).* They can also represent relationships between domain members as in *Part_of.* The number of arguments for a particular predicate is called the **arity of the predicate.** Predicates that have the same name but different arities are distinct. For example, *Merged(X,Y)* is distinct from *Merged(X,Y,Z).*

- A **quantifier** is a construct used to denote the scope and character of variables in FOPL statements. FOPL has two quantifiers to define the meaning of variables within a statement. They are ∀ (universal quantifier) and ∃ (existential quantifier). ∀X. means "interpret the statement that follows for all values of X in the domain of objects." ∃X. means "interpret the following statement for one or more values of X in the domain of objects."[2] Thus ∃X.($Cow(X)$ → $Name(X,elsie)$) means "for some X, if X is a cow, then X has the name Elsie." A quantifier has **scope;** that is, it only applies to the part of the statement that follows it. Scope can be represented by a parenthesized expression. For example,

---

[2] Often read "there exists an X" or "for some X."

$$\forall X.(Person(X) \rightarrow \exists Y.Parent\_of(Y,X))$$

means "for each X, if X is a person, then a Y exists such that Y is the parent of X." In this example, the $\exists$ quantifier applies only to the $Parent\_of(Y,X)$ portion of the statement.

- A **sentence** in FOPL is a well-formed formula that has a truth value of *true* or *false* and is generated by the following rules:

  a. *true* and *false*, as constant truth values, are sentences.

  b. A single predicate with its arguments is a sentence.

  c. If A is a sentence, then $\neg A$, its negation, is also a sentence.

  d. If A_1 and A_2 are sentences, then $(A_1 \wedge A_2)$, $(A_1 \vee A_2)$, and $(A_1 \rightarrow A_2)$ are also sentences.

  e. If A_1 and A_2 are sentences, then $(A_1 \equiv A_2)$, their equivalence, is also a sentence.

  f. If X is a variable and A is a sentence, then $\forall X.A$ and $\exists X.A$ are also sentences.

  All these rules are similar to the rules for forming propositional logic WFFs, except the last rule, which introduces quantifiers to the logic language.

- An **atomic sentence** is a sentence consisting of only a constant truth value or a predicate with nonvariable arguments. For example, *Slow(pokey)*, *true*, and *Merged(att,ncr)* are all atomic sentences.

4.3.3 The Semantics for Predicate Logic

It is important to be able to determine the truth value of a given FOPL sentence. An **interpretation** of a statement in FOPL defines the truth value of a sentence by tying the variables and constants to specific objects in chosen domains. An interpretation of a sentence is found by doing the following actions:

a. Choose an object domain.

b. Assign each constant a particular value from its domain.

c. Assign each unquantified variable a particular value from its domain. (In this text, most of the variables are explicitly quantified).

d. Assign each function a mapping from the domains of its arguments to the domain of its value.

---

[3] Occasionally, if two variables have the same scope, they will appear adjacent to each other, with no intervening dot between them. They will still have a dot after them to delimit them from the statement.

TABLE 4.5

Part of an interpreta-
tion for $\forall X\exists Y.P(X,Y)$,
defining P

X Y	a	b
a	T	F
b	F	T

e. Assign each predicate a mapping from the domains of its arguments to a truth value.

For example, for the FOPL statement $\forall X\exists Y.P(X,Y)$,[3] one interpretation is found by picking a domain $D = \{a,b\}$ and by defining P to be a predicate of arity two by Table 4.5. Another interpretation of the same statement would be to let the domain D be the positive integers and define P in such a way that Y is a successor to X (that is, $X + 1$). Then the statement would say that every positive integer has a successor.

4.3.4 Examples of Predicate Logic

Let us see how FOPL can be used for knowledge representation. Consider the following examples.

- Translating "Normal birds can fly" to FOPL might yield

$$\forall X.(\neg Abnormal(X) \wedge Bird(X) \rightarrow Flies(X))$$

That is, if an object is a bird and is not abnormal, then it can fly. You might also translate this statement to

$$\forall X.(Bird(X) \rightarrow Flies(X))$$

and handle the special cases in another way.

- Expressing "All cats love milk" in predicate calculus might result in

$$\forall X\forall Y.((Cat(X) \wedge Milk(Y)) \rightarrow Loves(X,Y))$$

But

$$\forall X\forall Y.((Cat(X) \wedge Milk(Y)) \wedge Loves(X,Y))$$

expresses a very different meaning. The latter statement means that everything is a cat, and everything loves milk, using the same interpretation of "Love," "Milk," and "Cat."

- "Some birds fly" can be expressed as

$$\exists X.(Bird(X) \land Flies(X))$$

But if we had said

$$\exists X.(Bird(X) \rightarrow Flies(X))$$

we would lose the fact that flying birds exist. This second version would be true even if no birds exited at all and a nonflying object did exist. For example, consider X = "horned toad." $Bird(X)$ is false, but so is $Flies(X)$, but $Bird(X) \rightarrow Flies(X)$ is true!

- To express "For each problem, there is a solution," one could use the FOPL statement

$$\forall X \exists Y.(Problem(X) \rightarrow Solution(Y,X))$$

- To express "Nobody loves everyone," we could say

$$\neg \exists X \forall Y.(Loves(X,Y)) \equiv \forall X \neg \forall Y.(Loves(X,Y)) \equiv \forall X \exists Y.\neg(Loves(X,Y))$$

FOPL also can be used to construct a proof of a conclusion. At this point we have no formal proof procedures, so the proof uses informal inference rules. We will discuss formal inference rules later in this chapter.

Suppose we have the following two statements about quacks (people who impersonate medical doctors):

A_1:   Some patients like all doctors.

A_2:   No patient likes a quack.

From these statements, we would like to conclude that

C: No doctor is a quack.

C intuitively follows from the following reasoning process. We know that no patient likes a quack and that some of these same patients like all doctors. So any doctor is liked by some patient. Because that patient does not like quacks, the doctor is not also a quack.

Our assertions and conclusion can be expressed in FOPL as

$$A_1: \quad \exists X.(Patient(X) \wedge \forall Y.(Doctor(Y) \rightarrow Likes(X,Y)))$$
$$A_2: \quad \forall X.(Patient(X) \rightarrow \forall Y.(Quack(Y) \rightarrow \neg Likes(X,Y)))$$

$$C: \quad \forall Y.(Doctor(Y) \rightarrow \neg Quack(Y))$$

The following argument illustrates the proof of this statement.

Because A_1 is true for some domain members, we can pick one for which it is true and call that member p_1. This action gives us the following two facts:

$$Patient(p_1)$$
$$\forall Y.(Doctor(Y) \rightarrow Likes(p_1,Y))$$

A_2 is true for all domain members, including p_1, so in addition to the preceding fact we now have another fact:

$$\forall Y.(Quack(Y) \rightarrow \neg Likes(p_1,Y))$$

Now pick any arbitrary Y, and call it y_1. If this y_1 is a doctor, then we know that $Likes(p_1,y_1)$. If this y_1 is also a quack, then we would get a contradiction ($\neg Likes(p_1,y_1)$). Therefore, for this case ($Doctor(y_1)$), y_1 cannot also be a quack. Because y_1 was an arbitrary choice, we can say that our conclusion is true for all Y or $\forall Y.(Doctor(Y) \rightarrow \neg Quack(Y))$.

4.4 INFERENCE IN PREDICATE LOGIC

The proof in the preceding section is very similar to proof procedures you might see in mathematics. But because it depends on developing a convincing argument that does not follow any particular structure, it can be checked only by other humans. Our aim here is to develop inference rules and proof procedures in such a way that proofs can be generated automatically in FOPL and checked for correctness.

4.4.1 Definitions Used in Inference

Inference is the process of deducing new facts from facts that are already known. The ability to deduce new facts to expand our knowledge is crucial to AI applications. The following definitions are necessary for further discussion of formal inference methods.

- An **inference rule** is a rule that acts on existing statements to produce new statements. An inference rule should usually produce statements that logically follow from the existing statements, but it is not required to do so.

- A **theory** is the set of all statements that are provable from a particular set of axioms. Different sets of axioms may be used to define a theory; each set is called a **model of the theory**. Being a model of the same theory means that it must be possible to prove the same set of facts (i.e., the same theory) from each set of axioms. For instance, in set theory, one might choose to use the **axiom of choice,**[4] but many other axioms have been shown to produce the same set theory. A theory usually includes associated inference rules, either explicitly or implicitly. Any sound inference rules can be used with the theory, but the choice of inference rule may determine what facts are provable in the theory.

- C **logically follows** from a set of statements (call them $A_1, A_2, \cdots, A_n$) if and only if for every interpretation $A_1 \wedge A_2 \wedge \cdots \wedge A_n \rightarrow C$ is *true*. The FOPL statement *"true"* logically follows from any nonnull set of sentences. If C logically follows from a set of sentences, then it is called a **logical consequence** of that set of sentences. For example, if φ is a sentence that logically follows from a database of facts Δ (which form a theory), then we write $\Delta \models \varphi$. The symbol denoting logical consequence is $\models$.

- C is **provable** from a set of facts if a finite sequence of steps (constituting a proof) exists that deduces C from the set of facts. Each step should be an application of an inference rule that is associated with the theory. If φ is provable from a set of facts Δ, then we write $\Delta \vdash \varphi$. The symbol denoting provability is $\vdash$.

- A **proof procedure** is a set of specific inference rules with an algorithm for applying them to set of sentences in order to produce a proof of a new sentence. Resolution is one example of a proof procedure that will be covered in Chapter 6.

- A sentence is **satisfiable** if an interpretation exists for which it is *true*.

- A sentence is **unsatisfiable** if no interpretation exists for which it is *true*.

- A sentence is **valid** if it is *true* for every interpretation.

- A set of sentences is **inconsistent** if they are not all satisfiable simultaneously.

- A set of sentences is **consistent** if they are all satisfiable simultaneously.

---

[4] The axiom of choice basically states that, given a nonempty set of elements (either of finite or infinite cardinality), an element can be chosen from the set. Not all mathematicians agree that this axiom should be assumed to be true.

- An inference rule is **sound** if every expression it produces logically follows from the set of sentences that the inference rule is applied to.

- An inference rule (or set of rules) with its accompanying proof procedure is **complete** if it can produce every expression that logically follows from the set of sentences that the inference rule(s) are applied to.

4.4.2 Inference rules for FOPL

The following inference rules can be used with FOPL. All the inference procedures are sound, but none of them is complete. In other words, they all produce new sentences that are logically implied by the sentences that are used, but some valid sentences in FOPL cannot be proved by using these rules alone. For the following inference rules, the conditions for the inference rule appear above the horizontal line (that is, what must be true in order to apply the rule). The lowercase Greek letters represent legal FOPL sentences. Below the line are the new sentences that can be deduced. An abbreviation for each rule is provided for reference in proving theorems in FOPL.

- **Modus Ponens** Inference Rule (MP)

$$\frac{\varphi \to \chi}{\chi}$$

For example, if we know $Turtle(pokey) \to Slow(pokey)$ and $Turtle(pokey)$, we can conclude $Slow(pokey)$.

- **Modus Tollens** Inference rule (MT)

$$\frac{\varphi \to \chi}{\neg \varphi}$$

In this case, if we know $Turtle(pokey) \to Slow(pokey)$ and $\neg Slow(pokey)$, then we can conclude $\neg Turtle(pokey)$.

- **And Elimination** Inference rule (AE)

$$\frac{\varphi \wedge \chi}{\varphi}$$

$$\chi$$

If we know *Turtle*(*pokey*) ∧ *Slow*(*pokey*), we can conclude that *Turtle*(*pokey*) and *Slow*(*pokey*).

- **And Introduction** Inference Rule (AI)

$$\frac{\varphi \quad \chi}{\varphi \wedge \chi}$$

This rule is the inverse of And Elimination. In this case, if we know *Turtle*(*pokey*) and *Slow*(*pokey*), we can deduce that *Turtle*(*pokey*) ∧ *Slow*(*pokey*).

- **Universal Instantiation** Inference rule (UI)

$$\frac{\forall v.\varphi}{\varphi_{v/\tau}}, \text{ where } \tau \text{ is any term}$$

Instantiation means to replace a variable with a specific object. This rule is used to replace an existential quantifier by a function that contains no other variables in the sentence. For example, if we knew that ∃*X*∀*Y*.(*Parent_of*(*X*,*Y*)), we could deduce ∀*Y*.(*Parent_of*(*parent*(*a*),*Y*)). This process is discussed as part of the resolution proof procedure (see Chapter 6) and is called **skolemization.** The notation of v/τ means that for every occurrence of the variable v, we substitute the term τ. For example, if we have the statement of ∀*X*∀*Y*.(*Loves*(*X*,*Y*)), we can substitute occurrences of *X* with a specific term (such as *barney*) to get ∀*Y*.(*Loves*(*barney*,*Y*)).

The Universal Instantiation rule reasons from the general to the specific. If we know that a statement is *true* for all elements in a domain, it must be true for a specific element in that domain. For example, if we know ∀*X*.(*Turtle*(*X*) → *Slow*(*X*)), we can substitute pokey for *X* and deduce *Turtle*(*pokey*) → *Slow*(*pokey*). In general, we can substitute a term for a universally quantified variable, as long as that term does not use any variables that are used within the statement and results in an object of the domain. For example, we could also substitute *mother*(*pokey*), where *mother* is a function that produces the mother of *pokey*.

- **Existential Instantiation** Inference rule (EI)

$$\frac{\exists v.\varphi}{\varphi_{v/\pi(v_1,v_2,\cdots,v_n)}}, \text{ where } \pi \text{ is aa new function and } v_1,v_2,\cdots,v_n \text{ are the unquantified variables in } \varphi \text{ excluding } v$$

4.4.3 Axiom Schemata for FOPL

Some FOPL sentences are valid purely because of their logical form. Such sentences are called **logical axioms.** There are an infinite number of these, however, and they can be expressed more realistically as **axiom schemata,** which can be instantiated to a particular logical axiom. These axioms are used in developing proofs in FOPL. These axioms are used in conjunction with the inference rules to generate steps in a proof. The placeholders in axiom schemata can be any FOPL sentence; here they are represented by lowercase Greek letters. the following schemata are taken from Genesereth and Nilsson (1987) and are only some of the possible valid schemata. More complete lists of schemata can be found in Manna and Waldinger (1985, 1989).

- The **Implication Introduction** axiom schema (II) is used to infer implications. If we know ϕ, it can be inferred that $\varphi \rightarrow \phi$. This is given by the axiom schema

$$\phi \rightarrow (\varphi \rightarrow \phi)$$

  Using this axiom schema, if we know that *Turtle*(*pokey*) (ϕ), then we can deduce that *Pig*(*pokey*) $\rightarrow$ *Turtle*(*pokey*) (i.e., $\varphi \rightarrow \phi$), because we already know that *Turtle*(*pokey*) is *true* and whether *Pig*(*pokey*) (i.e., φ) is *true* or *false* does not matter.

- The **Contradiction Realization** axiom schema (CR) allows us to use the contradiction that is produced by assuming a statement to deduce its negation.

$$(\varphi \rightarrow \neg\phi) \rightarrow ((\varphi \rightarrow \phi) \rightarrow \neg\varphi)$$

  For example, if we assume $\forall X.(Turtle(X) \wedge \neg Turtle(X))$ (φ) and from this we can conclude both $\neg Turtle(hare)$ ($\neg\phi$) and $Turtle(hare)$ (ϕ), then we know that $\neg\forall X.(Turtle(X) \wedge \neg Turtle(X))$ ($\neg\varphi$) must be *true*.

- The **Universal Distribution** axiom schema (UD) allows us to distribute universal quantifiers through implication.

$$(\forall v.(\phi \rightarrow \varphi)) \rightarrow ((\forall v.\phi)) \rightarrow (\forall v.\varphi))$$

  For example, if we know $\forall X.(Turtle(X) \rightarrow Has\_a(X,shell))$ ($\forall v.(\phi \rightarrow \varphi)$), then we can deduce that $(\forall X.(Turtle(X)) \rightarrow (\forall X.Has\_a(X,shell))$. The first statement says that if X is a turtle, then X has a shell. The second says that if everything is a turtle, then everything has a shell.

- The **Universal Generalization** axiom schema (UG) allows us to universally quantify variables that are not contained in a statement, unless the variables are bound by another quantifer.[5]

$$\phi \rightarrow \forall v.\phi, \text{ where } v \text{ is bound or does not occur in } \phi$$

For example, if we know $\forall X.(Turtle(X))$, we can conclude $\forall Y \forall X.(Turtle(X))$, because Y does not occur within the statement.

- The **Universal Instantiation** axiom schema (UI_2) reflects the same idea as the inference rule of universal instantiation. Using this schema, we would not have to use the inference rule but could include this axiom schema instead.

$$(\forall v.\phi) \rightarrow \phi_{v/\tau}, \text{ where } \tau \text{ is any term}$$

- The **Implication Distribution** axiom schema (ID) allows us to distribute one implication over another. If ϕ implies that φ implies χ, then if ϕ implies φ, it also implies χ.

$$(\phi \rightarrow (\varphi \rightarrow \chi)) \rightarrow ((\phi \rightarrow \varphi) \rightarrow (\phi \rightarrow \chi))$$

Using these axiom schema and the inference rules, we can develop formal proofs for theorems in FOPL. Each step in our proofs should be an application of one of these inference rules or an instance of an axiom schema.

4.4.4 Applications of the FOPL Inference rules

We use the inference rules and axiom schema to develop formal proofs of FOPL theorems. For example, let's try to deduce that Elsie the cow eats grass, given the following axioms:

$$A_1: \quad \forall X.(Jersey(X) \rightarrow Cow(X))$$
$$A_2: \quad \forall X.(Cow(X) \rightarrow Eats(X,grass))$$
$$A_3: \quad Jersey(elsie)$$

From these axioms and the inference rules, we arrive at the following proof for $Eats(elsie,grass)$:

---

[5] A **bound variable** is one that is within the scope of a quantifier that restricts it. **Unbound variables** are those that are not within the scope of a relevant quantifier. For example, the statement $P(X)$ contains the unbound variable X.

1. $Jersey(elsie) \rightarrow Cow(elsie)$ UI_1, A_1
2. $Cow(elsie)$ $MP, 1, A_3$
3. $Cow(elsie) \rightarrow Eats(elsie, grass)$ UI_1, A_2
4. $Eats(elsie, grass))$ $MP, 2, 3$

Another example (from Genesereth and Nilsson, 1987) is to prove $P \rightarrow R$ from the sentences $P \rightarrow Q$ and $Q \rightarrow R$. This example uses the axiom schemata in conjunction with the rules of inference for a proof in propositional logic. It is proved as follows:

1. $P \rightarrow Q$ Given
2. $Q \rightarrow R$ Given
3. $(Q \rightarrow R) \rightarrow (P \rightarrow (Q \rightarrow R))$ II
4. $(P \rightarrow (Q \rightarrow R))$ 2,3,MP
5. $(P \rightarrow (Q \rightarrow R)) \rightarrow ((P \rightarrow Q) \rightarrow (P \rightarrow R))$ ID
6. $(P \rightarrow Q) \rightarrow (P \rightarrow R)$ 4,5,MP
7. $P \rightarrow R$ 1,6,MP

Truth tables are an acceptable proof procedure for statements in propositional logic but are not generally usable for FOPL proofs. Truth tables fail because, if a FOPL statement has any variables in it, then the variables could introduce an infinite number of interpretations. A truth table essentially checks all interpretations, but obviously it cannot list an infinite number of them.

4.5 SUMMARY

This chapter introduces first-order predicate logic. Understanding formal logic is fundamental to building reasoning systems. Even if your system does not use formal logic, it is important to understand the types of conclusions your system can reach and when the reasoning mechanism can break down. Chapters 6, 9, and 12 discuss other logical systems and inference mechanisms that deal with specific problems.

4.6 REFERENCES

Logic and artificial intelligence are linked in several texts. The best reference on the use of logic in AI is Genesereth and Nilsson's *The Logical Basis of Artificial Intelligence* (1987). Schöning's *Logic for Computer Scientists* (1989) provides a good reference.

For a theoretical foundation of logic for computer programming, see Manna and Waldinger (1985, 1989). More references on logic and theorem proving will be given in Chapters 6 and 12. For some interesting (although highly mathematical) references on linking model theory, logic, algebra, and computer science, see Burris and Sankappanavar (1981) and Pratt (1985). Collections of interesting papers on logic are contained in Nagel (1962) and Van Heijenoort (1967).

4.7 EXERCISES

Warm-up Exercises

4.1 Let P and Q denote the following predicates:

$P(X)$: X is a right triangle with one angle of 30 degrees.

$Q(X)$: X is a right triangle with one leg that is half the hypotenuse.

Write a statement in predicate logic to reflect the following theorem, using P and Q as above.

If every X that is a right triangle with one angle of 30 degrees is a right triangle with one leg that is half the hypotenuse, then every X that is a right triangle but does not have a leg equal to one-half of its hypotenuse is not a right triangle with one angle of 30 degrees.

4.2 What problems would be encountered in attempting to represent the following statements in FOPL? It should be possible to deduce the final statement from the others. (Problem adapted from Rich and Knight, 1991.)

- Otis only likes to eat Chinese food.
- It's safe to assume that a restaurant in Dayton, Ohio, serves only American food unless you are explicitly told otherwise.
- The Olive Garden restaurant in Dayton usually serves Italian food.
- People don't do things that will cause them to be in situations they don't like.
- Otis doesn't go to the Olive Garden in Dayton very often.

4.3 Which of the following are statements in some two-valued logic? If the expression is not a statement, explain why.

a. $0 = 3$

b. 4 divides 38

c. This statement is false.

d. $\forall X \exists Y.(X + Y = X)$

4.4 Which of the following statements are valid in propositional logic?

a. $((P \to Q) \land (Q \to R)) \to (P \to R)$

b. $(P \land Q \to R) \to (Q \to (P \to R))$

c. $((P \to Q) \land \neg P) \to \neg Q)$

d. $(P \to Q) \to (\neg Q \to \neg P)$

4.5 Prove that Modus Ponens is sound for propositional logic.

4.6 **Abduction** is an inference rule that infers P from $P \to Q$ and Q. Show that abduction is not sound in propositional logic.

4.7 Prove that implication is transitive in propositional logic. That is, show that

$$((P \to Q) \land (Q \to R)) \to (P \to R)$$

4.8 Suppose there are two robots, R_1 and R_2. R_1 operates under the assumption that the world is flat and has edges. R_2 operates under the assumption that the world is round and has no edges. Describe several differences that result from the theories by which R_1 and R_2 operate. In other words, state several facts that are provable by one robot and not the other.

4.9 Russell's Paradox actually used the statement "Consider a set A, which is defined to be the set of all sets that are not members of themselves." Then ask the question "Does A contain itself?" Show how this yields a paradox.

Homework Exercises

4.10 Use predicate logic to solve the following problem.

Three persons are shown three red hats and two black hats. They are seated in chairs placed in single file and blindfolded. A hat is placed on each person's head, the remaining hats are hidden, and the blindfolds are removed. One at a time, each person is asked to guess the color of the hat on his own head.

The person who sits in the third chair is asked first. He confesses that he does not know the color of his hat, even though he can see the hats on the heads of his two companions. the second person, who can see only the hat of the person in front of him, also admits that he cannot guess his color. The first person, who can see no hats at all, says that he knows the color of his hat, and he is indeed correct. What color is the first person's hat?

4.11 Use predicate logic to solve the following problem.

The natives of a remote section of Chicago are all members of either one of two tribes, *South-siders* or *North-siders*. To a non-Chicagoan, they look exactly alike. But the members of the *North-siders* tribe always tell the truth, and the members of the *South-siders* tribe always lie. To this section of Chicago came an explorer, who met three natives.

"Of what tribe are you?" the explorer asked the first native.

"Rush and Division," replied the native. (The native actually says, "I am *North-siders*" or "I am *South-siders*," but you cannot understand it. Only other natives understand.)

"What did he say?" asked the explorer of the second and third natives, both of whom spoke English.

"He says he is *North-siders*," said the second.

"He says he is *South-siders*," said the third.

To what tribes did the second and third natives belong?

4.12. Use predicate logic to solve the following problem.

Smith, Jones, and Robinson are the pilot, copilot, and navigator on a plane, but not necessarily in that order. Riding the plane are three passengers with the same last names. We know the following facts:

• Passenger Robinson lives in Los Angeles.

• The copilot lives in Omaha.

• Passenger Jones long ago forgot all the math he ever knew.

• The passenger with the same name as the copilot lives in Chicago.

• The copilot and one of the passengers, a top mathematician, attend the same poker games.

• Smith beat the navigator at billiards.

Match the names of the crew members to their jobs.

4.13 For each of the following three sentences, give an interpretation that makes that sentence false but makes the other two sentences true.

a. $\forall X \forall Y \forall Z.(P(X,Y) \wedge P(Y,Z) \rightarrow P(X,Z))$

b. $\forall X \forall Y.(P(X,Y) \wedge P(Y,X) \rightarrow X = Y)$

c. $\forall X \forall Y.(P(a,Y) \rightarrow P(X,b))$

4.14 Give a formal proof of the sentence $\forall X.(P(X) \rightarrow R(X))$ from the premises $\forall X.(P(X) \rightarrow Q(X))$ and $\forall X.(Q(X) \rightarrow R(X))$. Provide a clear justification for each step, using some already known fact, that the variables are clearly quantified and in that it is FOPL.

4.15 Prove that the dual of a valid propositional logic statement is unsatisfiable.

4.16 Is each of the following sentences unsatisfiable, satisfiable, or valid?

a. $P \rightarrow P$

b. $P \rightarrow \neg P$

c. $\neg P \rightarrow P$

d. $\exists X.(P(a) \rightarrow P(X))$

e. $\forall X.(P(a) \rightarrow P(X))$

f. $P \equiv \neg P$

g. $P \rightarrow (Q \rightarrow P)$

h. $[(\exists X \forall Y.P(X,Y) \rightarrow \forall X \exists Y.P(X,Y)) \wedge$
$(\forall X \exists Y.P(X,Y) \rightarrow \forall X \forall Y.P(X,Y))] \rightarrow$
$[\exists X \forall Y.P(X,Y) \rightarrow \forall X \forall Y.P(X,Y)]$

4.17 Show that the inference rules given in Section 4.4 are not complete; that is, find a valid statement that cannot be deduced by using the inference rules listed there.

4.18 Prove that a WFF of propositional logic that contains only the $\equiv$ is valid if and only if each propositional constant occurs an even number of times. For example, $(P \equiv Q) \equiv (P \equiv (Q \equiv P))$ is not valid because P occurs an odd number of times.

4.19 Consider the problem of representing an often-true stereotype in FOPL. For example, how would you represent a statement that is often thought to be true, such as "Doctors have bad handwriting"? What would have to be done to allow this statement to be used to infer other facts? What care must be taken to ensure that the cases where it is not true are recognized?

4.20 A WFF in propositional logic that contains three distinct propositional constants, will have $2^3 = 8$ rows and $3 + 1$ columns in its truth table. In general, each WFF in propositional logic with n distinct propositional constants can be described by a truth table of 2^n rows and $n + 1$ columns.

a. Given any truth table of order n, $n \geq 1$ (that is, of 2^n rows and

$n + 1$ columns), give algorithms for constructing a WFF (containing at most n distinct propositional constants) that matches the truth table given and is a WFF of the following forms:

i. Conjunctive normal form (i.e., a conjunction of disjunctions of literals)

ii. Disjunctive normal form (i.e., a disjunction of conjunctions of literals)

b. Apply your algorithms to the following table to produce WFFs.

X	Y	Z	Value
true	true	true	true
true	true	false	false
true	false	true	true
true	false	false	false
false	true	true	true
false	true	false	true
false	false	true	false
false	false	false	true

Programming Exercise

4.21 Write a procedure to verify whether the input is a legal predicate logic statement by using the syntax defined in Section 4.3.2.

HEURISTIC SEARCH

5.1 SOLVING PROBLEMS WITH SEARCHES

Search (and, more specifically, heuristic search) is a powerful method for solving classes of problems that can be represented as a set of different problem states. The idea is to begin at an initial state and progress through intermediate states until at least one goal state is found—a goal state being defined as a state that sufficiently solves the problem. The *N*-Queens problem described in Chapter 1 was solved by using a heuristic search method. A **heuristic** is a rule of thumb that helps to solve a problem but is not guaranteed to provide a solution. You use a simple heuristic whenever you search for a parking space—look for empty spaces. If you adopt a greedy heuristic, you try to park in the most desirable space. But this more restrictive heuristic is, of course, not guaranteed to get you a parking space. Another simple heuristic involves thumping watermelons with your finger to test their ripeness. A dull sound is supposed to indicate that the melon is ripe. Any other sound indicates that it is not ripe. This heuristic is also not guaranteed to work.

A search proceeds from a set of initial states until a goal state is found. Operators are used to determine the possible next states. The set of all possible states is called the *children of the state*. How we get from the initial state to the goal state is done in many different ways, depending on the problem. Sometimes the aim is to find a solution (or goal state) as quickly as possible. At other times, the aim is to find all solutions (or goal states) to the problem. Our search strategy describes how we use known facts and goals to find a solution path. Two familiar strategies of searching for a solution path are often used. The first is the **data-driven** approach, where we start from facts that are known and then search for a goal state. We used a data-driven approach in the *N*-Queens problem. We started with an initial state and then searched for any goal state; in other words, we started with the initial state and no particular goal in mind. The second is the **goal-driven** strategy. It searches from a potential goal and tries to find a path to the known facts. If we had taken a goal-driven approach to the *N*-Queens problem, we would have started with a particular goal (say, the one in Figure 1.2) and then tried to find a path back to an empty board. A data-driven approach is also sometimes called **forward chaining,** because we are using known facts to proceed toward a goal. A goal-driven approach is sometimes called **backward chaining.** These strategies are illustrated in the context of expert systems in Chapter 8.

5.2 A HEURISTIC SEARCH EXAMPLE: HILL CLIMBING

In a heuristic search, we use a heuristic function to choose which children of a state are most likely to be on a solution path to the goal. Hill climbing is a method of heuristic search that is based on the notion of local optimization. Hill-climbing heuristics are usually taken to be **irrevocable,** that is, heuristics that allow no backtracking to try alternative solutions. For example, suppose we want to climb a mountain as quickly as possible, so we apply the heuristic of always climbing the steepest adjacent slope. Application of this method may get us stuck on a minor peak and not to the top of the mountain. Thus this search method does not always produce a solution.

Let us use a hill-climbing heuristic to solve the 8-Puzzle, which is a simple game with eight tiles and an empty space, all arranged in a three-by-three square. Tiles may only be moved horizontally or vertically into the empty space. The goal of the game is to order the tiles in ascending order according to the numbers written on them. In the goal state, the tiles should be ascending in the clockwise direction, with the tile labeled "one" occupying a corner. The center tile must be empty. The initial state can have the tiles in any position. This game and the heuristics used to solve it are discussed in Nilsson (1980).

Suppose we start with the initial state shown in Figure 5.1 and wish to end with the goal state shown in the same figure. The heuristic function we will use is the negative of the number of tiles that are out of place. For our initial state, that number is -4; for our goal state, it is 0.[1] To solve this puzzle, we evaluate all possible

---

[1] In later sections we generally define heuristic functions to be positive values, that is, estimates of the cost to reach a goal.

FIGURE 5.1

An initial state (a) and a goal state (b) for this instance of the 8-Puzzle

2	8	3
1	6	4
7		5

(a)

1	2	3
8		4
7	6	5

(b)

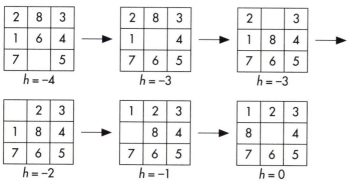

FIGURE 5.2

Hill-climbing solution to the 8-Puzzle

moves at the given state to determine which move best improves our heuristic. If no moves improve it (or if further moves fail to keep it equal), then we quit. Otherwise, we pick the move that increases the heuristic the most.

It is easier to view the moves at any point in this game in terms of "moving the empty space," even though it is the tiles that must actually be moved. Thus, in our initial state, the empty space can move right, left, or up. As noted earlier, in the initial state, we have four tiles that are not in their proper positions, so the value of the heuristic is -4. If we move the empty space up, the heuristic value would be -3, an improvement. If we choose to move the empty space to the right, then the heuristic would be -5. If we choose to move it to the left, the heuristic would also be -5. Thus we choose to move the empty space up.

Figure 5.2 shows the application of the heuristic in choosing moves. This heuristic function works for this particular instance of the 8-Puzzle, but it does not solve the problem in general. Suppose that we had the initial and goal states shown in Figure 5.3. In this case, any move of the blank space lowers the value of the heuristic, so we must quit—and fail to find a solution. Because a hill-climbing heuristic always attempts to improve the value of the heuristic and is irrevocable, it can easily get stuck at a local maximum of the heuristic function—as this example proves.

FIGURE 5.3

Alternative initial (a)
and goal (b) states
for the 8-Puzzle

1	2	5
	7	4
8	6	3

(a)

1	2	3
	7	4
8	6	5

(b)

5.3 STATE SPACE SEARCH

Problems that can be defined in terms of initial, intermediate, and goal states can be represented graphically. Such representations must be described in formal terms that allow us to express them in code.

5.3.1 Definitions

A **state space** is the complete set of all initial, intermediate, and final steps in solving a problem. Each state must define an identifiable point in the search for a solution. For the N-Queens problem (see Chapter 1), the state space includes the empty chess board, any board with one Queen in one or more rows, and a solution with a single Queen in each row. Thus there are $1 + \Sigma_{i=1}^{8} 8^i$ states in the state space for the 8-Queens problem. Only some of these states are solutions to the problem, and many of them are not part of any solution path. Some of the intermediate states already have two queens that can attack each other. Usually, because of the large size of the state space, we generate only those states that might be part of a solution. To generate new states from the existing ones, we use **operators.** For example, in the N-Queens problem we considered only those moves that were still potentially part of some solution and did not consider those that allowed the newly added queen to be attacked by a queen already placed on the board. Here, the operator generates only valid states.

We can also define subspaces within the state space. The **reachable search space** is the portion of the state space that can be reached from an initial state by the repeated application of operators. The **search space** is the portion of the state space that is searched in solving a particular instance of a problem.

A **solution** can be defined as a sequence of operators that transforms an initial state to a goal state. It is important to consider the entire path from an initial state to a goal state, because the path itself may be used in evaluating the solution. For instance, if our aim is to find the shortest path to the solution, then we need to retain all solution paths so that we can compare their lengths.

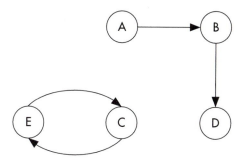

FIGURE 5.4

A digraph

We will represent search path through the search space either as trees or as **directed graphs** (**digraphs;** see Figure 5.4). In both cases, the initial states will be at the top of the graph. Edges of the digraph correspond to the application of operators to generate new states. In this representation, a solution will be a path from an initial state to a goal state. We use a digraph representation in order to take advantage of graph search algorithms.

5.3.2 Applications of State Space Search Methods

Certain types of problems can be solved by using a state space search. Suppose we wanted to parse an input string of 0s and 1s. We have sentences (represented by S) in our language that are defined by the rules[2]:

$$S \rightarrow 01$$
$$S \rightarrow 0S$$
$$S \rightarrow 1S$$

So, given a string of 0s and 1s, can we determine whether it was produced by these grammar rules? To express this problem in terms of a state space search problem, we need to define the parameters of the search.

Parameter	Definition
state	a string, using members of {0,1,S}
state space	set of all strings using {0,1,S}
goal state	S
initial state	the input string of 0s and 1s

---

[2] These rules represent replacing the left-hand side by the right-hand side. So "$S \rightarrow$ 01" means that if we had "$1S$" we could apply the rule to get "101".

Parameter	Definition
operators	$01 \rightarrow S$
	$0S \rightarrow S$
	$1S \rightarrow S$
	$SS \rightarrow S$

We use the operators to rewrite portions of the input string to produce a new string that contains an S instead. This new string represents our new state.

Or suppose we want to color the states in a map of the United States, but we don't want neighboring states to be the same color. If we wish to solve the map coloring problem by using a state space search, then we need the following definitions.

Parameter	Definition
state	any partially colored map
state space	set of all partially colored maps
goal state	any state where no two adjacent regions have the same color and all regions are colored
initial state	uncolored map
operator	application of a color to a region of the map

A third problem we might want to solve by using a state space search is the monkey and bananas problem:

A monkey is in a room with some bananas hanging from the ceiling of the room. A box in the room can be pushed by the monkey. The monkey cannot reach the bananas from the floor, but he can reach them if he stands on the box and if the box is under the bananas. The monkey can climb onto the box. How does the monkey get the bananas?

For this problem, we can represent a state by a vector that contains four variables: the position of the monkey, the position of the box, whether the monkey is on or off the box, and whether the monkey has the bananas or not. The initial state exists when the position of the monkey is at a, the position of the box is at b, the position of the bananas is at c, the monkey is off the box, and the monkey does not have the bananas. We can represent this initial state as (a,b,OFF,NOHAS). The goal state is to have the monkey and the box in the same position as the bananas, with the monkey on the box with the bananas—or (c,c,ON,HAS). For operators, we have

Operator	Result of applying operator
goto(P)	monkey moves to position P:(X,Y,OFF,Z) $\Rightarrow$ (P,Y,OFF,Z)
push(P)	monkey pushes box to position P:(X,X,OFF,Z) $\Rightarrow$ (P,P,OFF,Z)
climb	monkey climbs onto box:(X,X,OFF,Z) $\Rightarrow$ (X,X,ON,Z)
grab	monkey grabs the bananas:(c,c,ON,NOHAS) $\Rightarrow$ (c,c,ON,HAS)

For this problem, we would not want to include the entire state space. It makes little sense to consider all the different positions to which the monkey can move, only those that help solve the problem. We can simplify the problem by grouping states together on the basis of some property and then searching this new state space. Figure 5.5 shows how we could group the states on the basis of the values of the variables. By using this state space, we can ignore those states that do not influence our solution to the problem. This generalized state space is called a **state schema** representation of the problem.

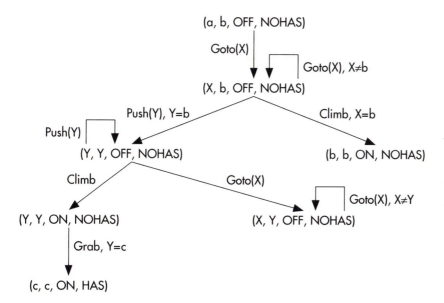

FIGURE 5.5

State schema representation for monkey and bananas problem

5.3.3 Defining a State Space in C++

Throughout the description of the search algorithms and the C++ source code we use several search-related terms. We represent each state in the search space as a **node** in a tree or more generally in a directed graph. Nodes are related to one another: if we are at one node we can determine the possible nodes to move to (using operators) and the set of possible nodes we can move to are called **children** of the node. The previous state we were in before a given node is called the **parent** of that node. A child of a node may be referred to as the **successor** of that node. The process of determining the possible children of a node is called **expansion** of that node. The number of children created for a node is called the **branching factor** for the node. The starting state (or first node in a search space) is called the **root** of the search tree or graph. Nodes with no children are **leaf nodes.** A **tree** is set of nodes where each node has only one parent (except the root has none), there are no cycles (no node has a child of a parent or earlier ancestor), there is a single root, and every node is related to at least one other node in a parent or child relationship. A graph does not have these restrictions.

In performing a search we also may maintain lists to keep track of the current state of the search. We will use a list called **OPEN** to refer to nodes that are newly generated children that have not yet been expanded. The nodes on the OPEN list are those nodes representing the current boundary of the search space. We will also use a list called **CLOSED** to refer to nodes that have been "visited" and have been expanded to determine their children.

We need a framework for describing a state space in the C++ programming language, one that defines the necessary interface and elements of a search space. However, it will always need to be updated to reflect a particular search space. Two classes within this framework are defined: Search and Node. The class Search contains all the necessary information for describing a state. The class Search will be used to keep track of states in the search algorithms. Class Node defines a state in the search space.

The following file contains a framework for describing a state space in C++:

```
//file: search.h
/*    Search

The base class Search defines a skeleton search
class from which the actual search classes such as
DepthGraph are derived. This means that Search
should never (have to) be used for direct deriva-
tion!
```

Essentially, this class implements two linked lists
of Node * objects: OPEN and CLOSED. OPEN contains
nodes that are ready for expansion and CLOSED
contains nodes that already have the expansion
procedure applied to them.

Every class that is (indirectly!) derived from
Search must pass the start node, the goal node,
and the number of operators to the constructor of
Search (or rather, to the search class derived
from Search).

Note: The objective of add() is to add a new node
to the list. It is used by those classes that are
directly derived from Search, like DepthGraph.
*/

```
#ifndef _search_H_
#define _search_H_
#include <stdio.h>
//#include "list.h"
#include "nodes.h"
//
class Search
{
  public:
    Search(int numop, Node *start, Node *goal);
      virtual ~Search();
      virtual int is_goal(const Node *);
    int generate();
      void display() const;
      IntrList<Node> *get_sol();
      Node *get_goal() const;
      virtual void set_startnode(Node *);
      void set_goalnode(Node *);
      void clear();
  private:
    Node *solve();  // Actual search engine in
                       combination with add()
    virtual int add(Node *) = 0;  // Adds node to
                                      open
      void print_sol(Node *) const;
    int num_op;    // Number of operators to be used
      Node *goalnode,    // User-specified goal node
        *solgoal;  // Found goal node
  protected:  // Protected because several classes
```

```
                            need access through add()
          SortedIntrList<Node> open,
                   closed;
} ;
#endif

//file: nodes.h
#ifndef _nodes_H_
#define _nodes_H_
#include <stdio.h>
#include <stdlib.h>
#include "array.h"
#include "list.h"


/*    Node
The base class Node is derived from class ListNode
and defines basic states that will be generated
during the search process.

In other words, it defines the (abstract, since
we're dealing with a base class) objects that the
search space consists of. Every class that is
derived from Node must have the following func-
tions:
do_operator(): generates and returns one successor,
               i.e., a new state, when operator n
               is applied. Returns NULL when opera-
               tor n cannot be applied.
or expand():   returns a linked list of successors
               (the linked list must be built by
               using the Node *next field). This
               function is an alternative for
               do_operator(), either one has to be
               implemented!
equal(): determines if 2 objects are the same, must
         return 1 if true and 0 if false.
display(): displays the object.

Note that the virtual function eval() that is used
to determine the order of objects is not actually
used in class Node; therefore it just returns 1 (it
can't be pure virtual because is it called in
solve()). For a real usage of this function see
class BEST_Node and UNI_Node.
*/
```

```
class Node : public ListNode
{
  public:
    Node();
      Node *clone() const;
    void setparent(Node *);
    Node *getparent() const;
      virtual int operator==(const Node &) const = 0;
      virtual int operator<(const Node &) const;
      // not pure virtual since it's only needed in
      // shortest path search
      virtual void display() const = 0;
    virtual Node *do_operator(int);
      virtual IntrList<Node> *expand(int);
        // both of these not pure virtual since
        // either may be implemented
  private:
    Node *parent;   // to trace solution path
};
class DepthNode : public Node
{
  public:
    DepthNode();
    unsigned getdepth() const;
    void setdepth(unsigned);
  private:
    unsigned depth;

};
/*    UniNode
The base class UniNode is derived from class Node
and defines a special kind of nodes: nodes that
will be generated during the search process of a
uniform cost search. These nodes will be placed in
an ordered list; the order of 2 nodes is determined
by eval() based on their 'g-values'.

G is a cost associated with the node: it's a mea-
sure of the cost of getting from the start node to
the current node. This value is computed by com-
pute_g().
*/
class UniNode : public Node
{
  public:
```

```
    UniNode();
    int operator<(const Node &) const;
    int get_g() const;
    void set_g(int);
  private:
  int g;        // cost of getting from the start
  node to this node
};
/*     BestNode
The base class BestNode is derived from class
UniNode, which in turn is derived from class Node.
Class BestNode defines a special kind of nodes:
nodes that will be generated during the search
process of a best first search. These nodes will be
placed in an ordered list; the order of 2 nodes is
determined by eval() based on their 'f-values'.

G (see unode.h) and F are costs associated with the
node. G is a measure of the cost of getting from
the start node to the current node and F the sum
of G and H, the estimated cost of getting from the
current node to the goal node. These values are
computed by compute_g() and compute_h() respective-
ly.
*/
class BestNode : public UniNode
{
  public:
    BestNode();
    int operator<(const Node &) const;
    int get_f() const;
    void set_f(int);
  private:
    int
      f;      // f is g + h
};

/* . AONode
Class AONode defines nodes that will be generated
in an AND-OR search process. It is derived from
class Node. AONode is a base class for class ORNode
and ANDNode and should never be used for direct
derivation.
*/
enum TypeOfNode { OR, AND };
```

```
enum NodeStat { Unsolvable, Solved, Undef };
class AONode : public Node
{
  public:
      AONode();
      AONode(int);
      void incn_left();
      AONode *clone() const;
    virtual TypeOfNode gettype() const = 0;
    virtual int get_nsucc() const = 0;
      virtual AONode *getsucc(int = 0) const = 0;
      virtual void setstatus(NodeStat) = 0;
    virtual NodeStat getstatus() const = 0;
      virtual int setsolved(AONode *) = 0;
      virtual int setunsolvable() = 0;
  protected:
    NodeStat status;    // Solved, Unsolved or Undef
    int n_left;
    /* number of successors left to be solved (AND
       node), or: number of successors that may be
       still be solved (OR node) */
};
/*    AndNode
Class AndNode is derived from class AONode. It must
be used in an AND-OR search when a set of subprob-
lems, i.e, a set of new nodes, is generated that
ALL have to be solved. In this case the user should
create an AndNode, by new AndNode(), and pass every
node representing a subproblem to this AndNode:
AndNode::addsucc(some_ornode)). Alternatively, an
AndNode may be created by calling the second con-
structor: new AndNode(no_of_nodes) and then the
successor nodes may be passed by calling
AndNode::setsucc(n, node_n).
*/
class AndNode : public AONode
{
  public:
      AndNode();
      AndNode(int n_nodes);
      TypeOfNode gettype() const;
      void setstatus(NodeStat);
    NodeStat getstatus() const;
      int setsolved(AONode *);
      int setunsolvable();
```

```
        AONode *getsucc(int) const;   // get successor
                                         n from succlist
    int get_nsucc() const;
        void setsucc(int, AONode *);   // set successor
                                        n in succlist to...
        void addsucc(AONode *);   // add a successor
                                             to succlist
        void display() const;
      int operator==(const Node &) const;
   private:
      static TypeOfNode type;     // is this an AND
                                      node or OR node?


    PtrArray<AONode> succlist;   // this node's
                                        successors
};
/*  OrNode
    Class OrNode is derived from class AONode, which
    in turn is derived from class Node. It is used in
    the process of an AND-OR search and should be
    used in conjunction with class AOSEARCH_. Nodes
    that are meant to be generated in an AND-OR
    search should be derived from class OrNode.
*/
class OrNode : public AONode
{
  public:
       OrNode();
    TypeOfNode gettype() const;
    int get_nsucc() const;
      AONode *getsucc(int n) const;
      void setstatus(NodeStat);
    NodeStat getstatus() const;
      int setsolved(AONode *);
      int setunsolvable();
    private:
      static TypeOfNode type;     // is this an AND
                                       node or OR node?
        AONode *succ;       // this node's successor
};
class BackNode : public ListNode
{
  public:
    BackNode();
    virtual int operator==(const BackNode &) const
```

```
    = 0;
    virtual BackNode *do_operator(int);
    virtual BackNode *expand_one(int);
      // both of these not pure virtual since
      // either may be implemented
    virtual void display() const = 0;
    BackNode *clone() const;
  private:
    int last_op;
};
#endif
```

5.4 DEPTH-FIRST AND BREADTH-FIRST SEARCHES

Two frequently used search methods are depth-first search and breadth-first search. Depth-first searches immediately go as deep into the search space as possible in hopes of finding a solution quickly. Breadth-first searches try all branches at one level before proceeding deeper into the search tree. The first solution that a breadth-first search finds will be the solution with the shortest path from the initial state to a goal state.

The algorithms in this section work for binary trees and also for general digraphs.

5.4.1 Depth-first Search of a Binary Tree

Figure 5.6 illustrates how depth-first search works on a binary tree. It starts with the root and then visits the left child. It then visits the left child of the left child. The algorithm can be described by the following steps:

1. Mark the current node as visited.
2. If the current node has any children, then do a depth-first search of each child, starting with the left-most one.
3. If the current node is a leaf node, then return.

The depth-first algorithm for diagraphs must have a way of checking nodes that have already been visited. This is usually done by putting all nodes visited onto a CLOSED list.

For implementing depth-first searching methods in C++, we must first define classes that are used in representing graphs, as represented by the following class definitions in the file Graph.h. The search class (such as Breadth Graph) is derived from class

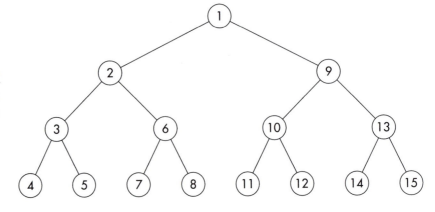

FIGURE 5.6

Depth-first search of a
binary tree

Search and the nodes of the search from class Node. It also contains
the definitions for other graphs that are used in later sections.

```
//file: graph.h
#ifndef _graph_H_
#define _graph_H_
//
#include <stdio.h>
#include "search.h"
#include "bisearch.h"
#include "node.h"
//
/*      BreadthGraph
This class implements a breadth first search algo-
rithm, by generating a search GRAPH. It is derived
from class Search.
*/
class BreadthGraph : public Search
{
  public:
    BreadthGraph(int op, Node *start = NULL, Node
                                   *goal = NULL);

    int add(Node *);
} ;
/*      DepthGraph
This class implements a depth-first search algo-
rithm, by generating a search GRAPH. It is derived
from class Search.
*/
```

```
class DepthGraph : public Search
{
  public:
    DepthGraph(int op, Node *start = NULL, Node
                                   *goal = NULL);
    int add(Node *);
    void setdepth(unsigned);
    unsigned getdepth() const;
  private:
    unsigned maxdepth;
} ;
/*    BiBreadthGraph
This class implements a bidirectional breadth-first
search algorithm, by generating two search GRAPHs.
It is derived from class BiSearch.
*/
class BiBreadthGraph : public BiSearch
{
  public:
    BiBreadthGraph(int op, Node *start = NULL,
                           Node *goal = NULL);
    int add(IntrList<Node> *, IntrList<Node> *,
                                      Node *);
} ;
/*    BiDepthGraph
This class implements a bidirectional depth first
search algorithm, by generating two search GRAPHs.
It is derived from class BiSearch.
*/
class BiDepthGraph : public BiSearch
{
  public:
    BiDepthGraph(int op, Node *start = NULL,
                         Node *goal = NULL);
    int add(IntrList<Node> *, IntrList<Node> *,
                                      Node *);
} ;
/*    Best
This class implements a best-first search algorithm.
It is derived from class Search and processes nodes
of class BestNode (see bnode.h) on the program
disk. Classes that are derived from class BestNode
should have the following functions:
  compute_g(): To compute the G-value of a node
  compute_h(): To compute the H-value of a node.
```

```
*/
class Best : public Search
{
  public:
    Best(int op, Node *start = NULL,
                            Node *goal = NULL);
        void set_startnode(Node *);
    int add(Node *);
    virtual int compute_g(const Node *) = 0;
    virtual int compute_h(const Node *) = 0;
} ;
/*    UnicostGraph
This class implements a uniform cost search algo-
rithm, by generating a search GRAPH. It is derived
from class Search. Classes that are derived from
class UnicostGraph should have the following func-
tion:
  compute_g() : computes the G-value of a node.
*/
class UnicostGraph : public Search
{
  public:
    UnicostGraph(int op, Node *start = NULL,
                            Node *goal = NULL);
    int add(Node *);
    virtual int compute_g(const Node *) = 0;
} ;
#endif
```

The following C++ code implements the functions required for a depth-first search of a graph.

```
//file: dnode.cpp
#include "nodes.h"

DepthNode::DepthNode()
{
  depth = 0
}
void DepthNode::setdepth(unsigned d)
{
  depth = d;
}
unsigned DepthNode::getdepth() const
{
```

```
    return(depth);
}


//file: gdepth.cpp
#include "graph.h"
/*    DepthGraph
The constructor passes the start node, the goal
node, and the number of operators to Search.
*/
DepthGraph::DepthGraph(int op, Node *start,
                                    Node *goal)
   :Search(op, start, goal)
{
maxdepth = 0;
}
//
void DepthGraph::setdepth(unsigned d)
{
  maxdepth = d;
}
//
unsigned DepthGraph::getdepth() const
{
  return(maxdepth);
}
/*    ADD
Adds a node to the search GRAPH only if it's not
already in the GRAPH
ADDED: depth-bound check
*/
int DepthGraph::add(Node *succ)
{
  if (maxdepth)
  {
    unsigned depth;
      DepthNode *par,
           *dsucc = (DepthNode *)succ;
  par = (DepthNode *)dsucc->getparent();
    depth = par->getdepth() + 1;
      if (depth >= maxdepth)
        return(0);
    dsucc->setdepth(depth);
  }
  if (!closed.lookup(succ) && !open.lookup(succ))
  {
```

```
      open.addtohead(succ);
      return(1);
   }
   return(0);
}
```

5.4.2 Limiting the Depth-first Search

A variant of depth-first search is known as **bounded depth-first search.** This variant helps to keep the search from getting too deep in the search tree or following an infinite path. The bound limits the depth of the search to levels in the tree that are less than or equal to this bound. For example, if the bound were five, then only the first five levels of the tree would be searched. We can use the notion of bounded depth-first search to create an iterative depth-first algorithm. This method increases the bound by one at each iteration and again tries a bounded depth-first search.

5.4.3 Depth-first Search of a General Digraph

A depth-first search of a general digraph works in a similar way. You first mark the current node as visited and then perform a depth-first search on all children. In a general digraph, however, one may revisit nodes or never reach certain nodes. In the digraph shown in Figure 5.7 we were able to visit all nodes when beginning at the top. We did revisit many nodes.

FIGURE 5.7

Depth-first search of a digraph and resulting search tree. The numbers indicate the order in which the nodes are visited.

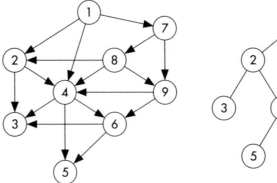
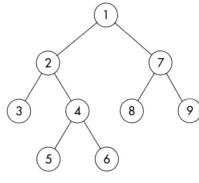

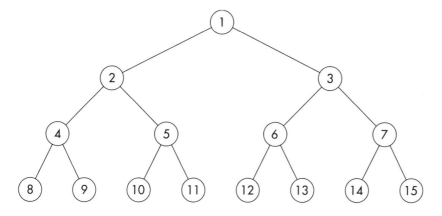

FIGURE 5.8

Breadth-first search of
a binary tree

5.4.4 Breadth-first Search of a Binary Tree

Figure 5.8 shows the order in which nodes are visited by a breadth-first search in a binary tree. Instead of visiting new-found children first, we visit any previously known children first. For the binary tree, we search the tree ply (level of the tree) by ply.

The following code implements a breadth-first search of a graph in the C++ programming language. It assumes that a state space has been defined for the problem being solved by the algorithm.

```
//file: graph.h
#ifndef _graph_H_
#define _graph_H_

#include <studio.h>
#include "serxh.h"
#include "bisearch".h"
#include "nodes.h"

/*     BreadthGraph
  This class implements a breadth first search
  algorithm, by generating a search GRAPH. It is
  derived from class Search.
*/
class BreadthGraph : public Search
{
  public:
    BreadthGraph(int op, Node *start = NULL,
             Node *goal = NULL); int add(Node *);
};
/*     DepthGraph
```

This class implements a depth first search algorithm, by generating a search GRAPH. It is derived from class Search.
*/
```
class DepthGraph : public Search
{
  public:
    DepthGraph(int op, Node *start = NULL,
                              Node *goal = NULL);
    void setdepth(unsigned);
    unsigned getdepth() const;
  private:
    unsigned msxdepth;
};
```
/*   BiBreadthGraph
This class implements a bidirectional breadth first algorithm, by generating two search GRAPHs. is is derived from class BiSearch.
/*
```
class BiDepthGraph : public BiSearch
{
  public:
    BiDepthGraph(int op, Node *start = NULL,
                              Node *goal = NULL);
    int add(IntrList,Node> *, IntrList<Node> *,
                                        Node *);
```
/*   BiDepthGraph
This class implements a bidirectional depth first search algorithm, by generating two search GRAPHs. It is derived from class BiSearch.
*/
```
class BiDepthGraph : public BiSearch
{
  public:
    BiDepathGraph(int op, Node *start = NULL
                               *goal = NULL);
    int add(IntrList,Node> *, IntrList<Node> *,
                                       Node*);
};
```
/*   Best
This class implements a best first algorithm. It is derived from cladss Search and processes nodes of class BestNode (see bnode.h). Classes that are derived from class BestNode should have the following functions:

```
  compute_g() : to compute the G-value of a node.
  compute_h : to compute the H-value of a node.
*/
class Best : public Search
{
  public:
    Best(int op, Node *start = NULL,
                            Node *goal = Null);
  void set_startnode(Node *);
  virtual int compute_g(const Node *) = 0;
  virtual int compute_h(const Node *) = 0;
};
/*    UniCostGraph
This class implements a uniform cost search algo-
rithm, by generating a search Graph. It is derived
from class Search. Classes that are derived from
class UnicostGraph should have the following func-
tion:
  compute_g() : computes the G-value of a node.
*/
classf UnicostGraph : public Search
{
  public:
    UnicostGraph(int op, Node *start = NULL, Node
*goal = NULL);
  int add(Node *);
  virtual int compute_g(cons Node *) = 0;
};
#endif

//file: breadth.cpp
#include "graph.h"
/*    BreadthGraph
The constructor passes the start node, the goal
node, and the number of operators to Search.
*/
BreadthGraph::BreadthGraph(int op, Node *start,
                                  Node *goal)
  :Search(op, start, goal)
{
}
/*    ADD
Adds a node to the search GRAPH only if it's not
already in the GRAPH
*/
```

```
int BreadthGraph::add(Node *succ)
{
  if (!closed.lookup(succ) && !open.lookup(succ))
// If successor is neither on CLOSED nor OPEN,
// add it to the Tail of OPEN.
  {
    open.addtotail(succ);
    return(1);
  }
  return(0);
}
```

5.4.5 Breadth-first Search of a General Digraph

For a general digraph, we search all children before proceeding deeper into the graph. Figure 5.8 shows how such a breadth-first search works. As in the depth-first search algorithm for digraphs, we may revisit nodes or never visit some nodes. In Figure 5.9 several nodes are revisited, but all are found by using the algorithm.

5.4.6 Choosing Between Depth-first and Breadth-first Search

Depth-first search and breadth-first search examine the search space in different orders. As a result, they behave differently and are more appropriate for different types of problems. One important characteristic of breadth-first search is that it will find the shortest solution path, because it always takes the shortest path from the start node to any node. Therefore, when a solution is found, it has been reached by the shortest path to it. If we do not need the shortest path to a solution but want to find a solution quickly, then depth-first search may prove to be better. Because a depth-first

FIGURE 5.9

Breadth-first search of a digraph with resulting search tree. The numbers indicate the order in which the nodes are visited.

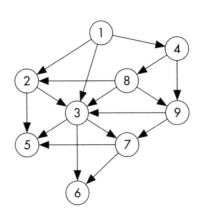
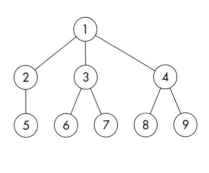

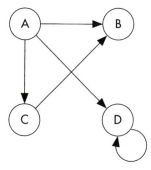

	A	B	C	D
A	0	1	1	1
B	0	0	0	0
C	0	1	0	0
D	0	0	0	1

FIGURE 5.10

A digraph and its adjacency matrix

search dives deeply into the search space quickly, it is likely to arrive at terminal nodes more quickly. Goal nodes are usually terminal nodes, so depth-first search is more likely to find them quickly.

If we use an adjacency matrix representation for a directed graph, then in the worst case a depth-first search will have to examine every element of the adjacency matrix. An **adjacency matrix** is a two-dimensional matrix where each cell of the matrix represents two nodes connected with an arc (Figure 5.10). If we call the number of vertices V, then the amount of time the algorithm takes is $0(V^2)$. The open space used by a depth-first search is determined by the maximum size of OPEN. In the worst case, we have to go to the deepest leaf node in the search tree. If we are N levels deep and each node along the path has an average of B children, then the OPEN list could contain as many as N × B entries.

For a breadth-first search, the time complexity in the worst case is the same as that for a depth-first search. However, the space usage of a breadth-first search can be much higher than that for a depth-first search. At any given time, the number of nodes on the OPEN list can be the number of children at a particular level of the tree. Now, if the branching factor is high, the number of nodes at deeper levels can quickly become unwieldy and exhaust the available space, because the amount of space used is an exponential function of the branching factor. If the average branching factor is B. then at the nth level of the tree we will have B^n nodes on the OPEN list.

5.5 BEST-FIRST SEARCH

Best-first search uses a heuristic function to guide the search rather than simply following the structure of the state space graph, as depth-first and breadth-first searches do. A best-first search may at times behave like a depth-first search and at other times like a breadth-first search. As a result, a best-first search takes on characteristics of both, depending on the heuristic function employed.

Viewed simply, the best-first search algorithm is just like the depth-first and breadth-first algorithms, except that the OPEN list is ordered, not on the basis of the location of each node, but on the basis of the heuristic value of each node. More specifically, the best-first search algorithm (Pearl, 1984) is

1. Put the start node on a list, called OPEN, of nodes that have not been expanded to successor states.
2. If OPEN is empty, exit with failure; no solution exists.
3. Remove from OPEN a node n at which f (the evaluation function) is minimum and place it on a list, called CLOSED, to be used for expanded nodes.
4. Expand node n, generating all its successors.
5. If any of n's successors is a goal node, exit successfully.
6. For every successor n' of n,
   - Calculate $f(n')$.
   - If n' was neither on the OPEN list nor on the CLOSED list, add it to OPEN. Assign the newly computed $f(n')$ to NODE n'.
   - If n' already resided on THE OPEN LIST or THE CLOSED LIST, compare the newly computed $f(n')$ with the value that was previously assigned to n'. If the old value is lower, go to next step. If the new value is lower, substitute it for the old n'. Also, if the new value is lower and the node n' was on the CLOSED list, move it back to OPEN.
7. Go to step 2.

Figure 5.11 shows a simple case where the values of the heuristic function are fixed and noted beside each node. The graph is searched by a best-first search in the order indicated by the labels "A" to "I." $g(x)$ is the length of the path from the start node (here A) to the current node. So, $f(E) = 4$ plus $g(E) = 1$. So, $f(E) = 4 + 1 = 5$.

So, if we consider all leaf nodes as potential goals, node H looks the best at this point, according to best-first search.

The following C++ algorithm implements a best-first search (actually, an Algorithm A (see Section 5.6.3) search, using a predefined search space class). The search space class must include a definition of the heuristic function and the current path length from the start state to each state expanded thus far.

```
//file:bnode.
#include "nodes.h"
```

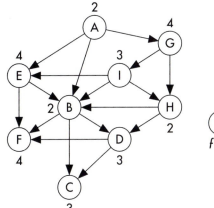 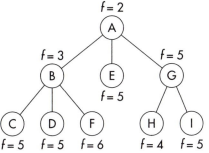

FIGURE 5.11

Best-first search, using heuristic values

```
/*      BestNode
The constructor sets the node's F-value and G-value
to 0.
*/
BestNode::BestNode()
{
   f=0
}
/*      GET_F
Return F-value of node.
*/
int BestNode::fet_f() const
{
   return(f);
}
/*      SET_F
Set F-value of node.
*/
void BestNode::set_F(int val)
{
   f=val;
}
Determines the order of two nodes based on their f-
values, i.e., if node A has got a lower f-value
than node B this means that node A ranks before B
(nodes are ordered in order of ascending f-values
because a lower f-value means that the node is
closer to the goal).
*/
```

```
int BestNode::operator<(const Node &other) const
{
//return(f<((BestNode &)other).get_f());
    return(f<((BestNode &)other).f);
}
//file: gbest.cpp
#include "graph.h"
/*      BestNode
The constructor passes the start node, the goal
node, and the number of operators to Search.
*/
Best::Best(int op, Node *start, Node *goal)
  :Search(op, start, goal)
// This way the G- and F-values of the start node
// won't be computed,
// but this is not a problem.
{
}
void Best::set_startnode(Node *start)
{
  ((BestNode *)start)->set_f(compute_h(start));
  open.insert(start);
}
/*      ADD
```

This function examines each node that it is offered
and decides whether or not it should be added to
OPEN. First, it fills in the node's G- and F-values
by calling compute_g() and compute_f(). Next, it
tries to look up this node on the OPEN list and on
the CLOSED list. If the node is already on OPEN but
its F-value is worse than that of the older node
(this comparison is made by eval()), then it can
simply be thrown away. If its F-value is better,
the older node will be thrown away (by
remove_found()), and the new node will be added to
the OPEN list (by insert()). The same goes if a
node is found to be already on the CLOSED list. A
node that is neither on OPEN list nor on CLOSED
list can simply be added to OPEN (by insert(),
which creates an ordered list).

```
*/
int Best::add(Node *succ)
{
  BestNode
      *parent,
```

```
      *old = NULL,
      *bsucc = (BestNode *)succ;
   int g;
//
   parent = (BestNode *)bsucc->getparent();
//
   g = parent->get_g() + compute_g(bsucc);
/*
A node's G-value is composed of the overall cost so
far, i.e., the cost of getting from the start node
to the parent of this node and the added cost of
getting from the parent to this node.
*/
   bsucc->set_g(g);
//
   bsucc->set_f(g + compute_h(bsucc));
/*
A node's F-value consists of its G-value and the
value returned by the heuristic function
compute_h().
*/
   if ((old = (BestNode *)open.lookup(succ))
                                             != NULL)
   {     // Node already on OPEN list
     if (*bsucc < *old)  // New node better
     {
       open.remove_found(DoDel);  // Remove &
                                      destroy old node
       open.insert(bsucc);  // Add this node to
                                the graph
       return(1);
     }
     return(0);
   }
   if ((old = (BestNode *)closed.lookup(succ))
                                             != NULL)
   {     // node already on CLOSED LIST
     if (*bsucc < *old)  // New node better
     {
       closed.remove_found(DoDel);  // Remove & des-
                                        troy old node
       open.insert(bsucc);
       return(1);
     }
     return(0);
```

```
    }
// Node on neither OPEN nor CLOSED lists
    open.insert(bsucc);
    return(1);
}
```

5.6 EVALUATING HEURISTIC FUNCTIONS AND SEARCH ALGORITHMS

So far, we have not discussed what makes one heuristic search method better than another. To choose effectively between different heuristic methods, we need to evaluate them somehow, and we also need to know whether a particular heuristic function is guaranteed to find an optimal solution or any solution at all. With these goals in mind, we will define several formal properties of heuristic functions and a class of heuristic search algorithms known as A^* algorithms (see Section 5.6.3).

5.6.1 Evaluation Functions to Guide the Search

Usually, we want the search to find a low-cost path to a solution; that is, we want to find a solution in a small number of steps. To do this, we need to include each new node on the OPEN list, keep track of how deep the new node is in the tree, and calculate what the cost is in getting from the start state to this state. We also need to consider how close the node is to a solution or what we guess the cost will be to get to a solution through that state. So our evaluation function, $f(n)$, is the sum of the two parts:

$$f(n) = g(n) + h(n)$$

where $g(n)$ is the cost of getting from the start node to node n. and $h(n)$ is our heuristic estimate of the cost of getting from node n to a goal state. The sum of $g(n)$ and $h(n)$ can be viewed as our current heuristic estimate of the cost of a solution path through node n. On the basis of this definition, $h(n) \geq 0$ for all n, with $h(n_{goal}) = 0$. This type of evaluation function can be used to guide our best-first search and to aid our analysis and comparison of different heuristics.

Instead of using a measurable cost for $g(n)$ and $h(n)$, such as the amount of resources required to move a robot between positions, we can substitute the length of the path. Using the length of the path makes sense when the cost associated with traversing one link

Board 1 (h=5, g=0, f=5):

1	4	2
7	8	3
	6	5

Board 2 (h=4, g=1, f=5):

1	4	2
	8	3
7	6	5

Board 3 (h=3, g=2, f=5):

1	4	2
8		3
7	6	5

Board 4 (h=3, g=3, f=6):

1		2
8	4	3
7	6	5

Board 5 (h=2, g=4, f=6):

1	2	
8	4	3
7	6	5

Board 6 (h=1, g=5, f=6):

1	2	3
8	4	
7	6	5

Board 7 (h=0, g=6, f=6):

1	2	3
8		4
7	6	5

FIGURE 5.12

Using an evaluation function to solve the 8-Puzzle

in the search space is approximately the same as that for any other link. For example, for $g(n)$, we can use the shortest path from the start node to n. For $h(n)$, we can use our best guess of the length of the shortest path from n to a goal state. The algorithm that uses a best-first search with this type of evaluation function is called **Algorithm A.**

Suppose we apply this kind of evaluation function to the 8-Puzzle shown in Figure 5.12. For each state n, we define

$h(n)$ = number of tiles out of place in state n

$g(n)$ = the length of the path from the start state to n

Figure 5.12 shows only the solution path; that is, states that are not chosen are not shown. In the initial state there are five tiles out of place, and the path to the initial state is zero in length. At each point in the search space, we have several tiles that we could move. We can pick the **best** alternative by picking the state with the lowest f value. Thus we have $f(1) = 5 + 0 = 5$. As we get deeper in the search space, $g(n)$ increases, so states higher in the tree have lower $f(n)$ values than do states lower in the tree. Use of a $g(n)$ that grows rapidly causes the best-first search to behave more like a breadth-first search, because it causes those states higher in the tree to have a lower $f(n)$ value.

To compare evaluation functions, we define $f^*(n)$ to be the actual, optimal cost of a solution that passes through node n.

$$f^*(n) = g^*(n) + h^*(n)$$

$g^*(n)$ is the actual optimal cost from the initial node to node n, and $h^*(n)$ is the actual optimal cost of a path from node n to a solution. $h^*(n)$ can be viewed as a perfect heuristic function, in that it always chooses the correct node next and guides the search to a solution as quickly as possible. Although an actual f^* is usually impossible to determine because it requires complete knowledge of the search space, evaluation functions that can approach it are better than those that cannot.

5.6.2 Evaluation of Best-first Search

In the worst case, best-first search can search all the nodes before it finds a solution, just as depth-first and breadth-first searches did. If it applies a good heuristic, however, it should have to examine only a small portion of the reachable space. The space complexity can be as bad as a breadth-first search because in the worst case our heuristic can force our best-first search to actually be a breadth-first search. (This worst-case scenario occurs when $g(n)$ is very high and overwhelms $h(n)$.) The space used can also be as small as that used in a depth-first search. (This best-case scenario occurs when $h(n)$ is very high, overwhelms $g(n)$, and is the same for all nodes at each level of the search tree.) However, you can expect that, generally, best-first search will use a larger amount of space for the OPEN list than a depth-first search will use. In other words, how a best-first search behaves in time and space depends on its heuristic. A best-first search is a blend of depth-first and breadth-first searching, and it uses a heuristic function to determine which is more appropriate.

5.6.3 Formal Properties of Heuristic Functions and Search Algorithms

We can define the formal properties of heuristic functions and search algorithms. On the basis of these definitions, we can classify heuristic functions and algorithms. Then, if we know the type of the heuristic function or algorithm, we can guarantee that it will perform at a certain level. In general, we desire heuristic functions that will guide us to solutions as quickly as possible

An algorithm is said to be **complete** if it terminates with a solution when one exists. At a minimum, we want our search algorithms to be complete. Being a complete algorithm says nothing of the algorithm's efficiency or effectiveness. A simple breadth-first search is complete. However, if we use a hill-climbing method where we allow no backtracking, then the algorithm is not complete because we are not guaranteed to find a solution.

A search algorithm is **admissible** if it is guaranteed to find a path of minimal cost (i.e., an optimal path) to a solution, if a path exists. A heuristic function is admissible if $h(n) \leq h^*(n)$, where $h^*(n)$ is actual optimal cost, for all n.

A heuristic function, $h(n) \geq 0$, for all n, is said to be **monotone** if it satisfies the following constraints:

$h(n) \leq c(n,n') + h(n')$, where n' is a descendant of n

(also often expressed as $h(n) - h(n') \leq c(n,n')$

and

$h(n_{goal}) = 0$ for each n_{goal} that is a goal state

where $c(n,n')$ is the actual minimal cost of going from n to n'. The cost of getting from a node to itself is assumed to be 0, and this assumption yields the second condition: goal states must evaluate to zero. The monotone characteristic of a heuristic function ensures that a heuristic is locally consistent with the arc cost between nodes.

A heuristic function h_1 is said to be more informed than heuristic function h_2 if both are admissible and $h_1(n) \geq h_2(n)$ for every nongoal node n. In other words, a more informed heuristic is one that is more effective in finding a solution and searches a smaller portion of the search space. Remember that an admissible heuristic was one that was guaranteed to find an optimal solution if one exists. If we can use a heuristic with equal or higher $h(n)$s, then we should find that solution more quickly, because our heuristic is telling us more reliably which direction to proceed. If the heuristic values get too large, then the heuristic is no longer admissible.

5.6.4 A* Algorithm

The A^* algorithm uses the A algorithm of best-first search with a more specific evaluation function:

$f(n) = g(n) + h(n)$, where
$g(n)$ = the cost of the current path from the start node to n
$g(start\_node) = 0$
$h(n)$ = an underestimate of $h^*(n)$ and admissible
$h(start\_node) = 0$

We will use the properties of heuristics and algorithms defined in the preceding section to analyze the A^* algorithm. Note that we also assume that each node has a finite number of children.

First we want to show that A^* is complete. To do this, we need to show that A^* terminates with a solution whenever a solution exists. If we restrict ourselves to finite graphs. we know that A^* terminates simply because each new node expansion adds new links to the traversal tree. These added links represent newly added acyclic paths, which will eventually be exhausted. Note that nodes reopened from the CLOSED list represent new paths, because we only reopen a node when a strictly cheaper path exists to it. To show that A^* is complete, we must show not only that it terminates but also that it terminates with a solution. We return with a failure only when the list OPEN is empty. If a solution path exists, OPEN cannot become empty before the solution is found. If it did, there would be a last node on the solution path (call it n') that had no successors and that had been expanded. This contradicts our assumption that n' is on a solution path, because every node on a solution path (except goal nodes) must have at least one successor also lying on a solution path.

A^* is admissible. This proof is left as an exercise (see Exercise 5.11).

An A^* algorithm guided by a monotone heuristic finds optimal paths to all expanded nodes. For a proof of this statement, refer to Pearl (1984). This result guarantees that, at any point in the search, our partial solution paths are of the lowest cost.

A property of monotone heuristics when used by the A^* algorithm is that it causes the sequence of f values of chosen nodes to be nondecreasing. (This characteristic led to the name "monotone.") To prove this statement, let n_2 be expanded immediately after n_1. If n_2 was on the OPEN list while n_1 was expanded, then $f(n_1) \leq f(n_2)$ is true because n_1 was selected over n_2. Let $c(n_1,n_2)$ be the cost of the path from n_1 to n_2. If n_2 was not on OPEN, then n_2 must be a new entry to OPEN. This conclusion means that n_2 is a successor of n_1, for which $g(n_2) = g(n_1) + c(n_1,n_2)$ and for which monotonicity also applies:

$$f(n_2) = g(n_1) + c(n_1,n_2) + h(n_2) \geq g(n_1) + h(n_1) = f(n_1)$$

This result shows that the sequence of f values cannot decrease.

For two A^* algorithms with heuristics h_1 and h_2, if h_2 is more informed than h_1, then the search space of h_2 is a subset of that used by h_1, except for nodes that are equal h_1 and h_2 values. A proof of this statement appears in Pearl (1984). A direct result of this theorem is that the more informed the heuristic we use with A^*, the more efficient the search will be.

5.7 COMBINING SEARCH METHODS

We can combine the different search methods in order to more effectively solve some problems with large reachable search spaces. In this section we will discuss different ways of combining the three search methods: best-first search, depth-first search, and hill-climbing search. For large problems, it may be difficult to use pure best-first search because of the large space needs of the algorithm. To get some benefit from best-first search, however, we can combine it with depth-first search. Figure 5.13 shows two ways to combine

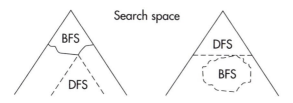

FIGURE 5.13

Alternative ways of combining depth-first search (DFS) and best-first search (BFS) for large search spaces

them. In the left half of Figure 5.13, a best-first search is used to begin the search and to find a good starting point for a more efficient, depth-first search, which can then begin at the most promising node found by the best-first search. This method will work reasonably well if a best-first search can indeed yield a good starting point for the depth-first search. For example, consider the problem of information retrieval from a vast amount of information (say, data scattered all over the worldwide web). Suppose we have the task of finding information (say, we are looking for U.S. census data on the number of students that are attending U.S. universities but are not U.S. citizens) that we know is contained in one site; our problem is finding the correct site. Once we find the site, we can do a complete search of it for the specific information needed. So, if we do a best-first search for the site, then we can do a depth-first search of the information itself.

In the right half of Figure 5.13, a depth-first search is used to find the best point from which to start our best-first search. This approach is useful if we can identify the overall best starting point for a best-first search. Suppose we have a problem for which we first determine where to begin the search; and once we get there, we then need to employ heuristics to find what we need. To solve this problem, we might first use a depth-first search of the upper levels and then begin exploring (using best-first search) from that point.

Another way to combine the two search methods is to do a depth-first search in which each element of the depth-first search is a best-first search (Figure 5.14). This method would be appropriate for a very large search space. Heuristics can be used to explore the space first, but because the space is so large, the best-first search can be restarted as better nodes are identified. In other words, if one of these best-first searches fails to produce a better end point, then we can backtrack to a previous, second-best starting point from a previous best-first search, essentially nesting the best-first searches in a depth-first search.

Another method that is sometimes useful is to combine a hill-climbing search with best-first search, similar to the combined search method shown in Figure 5.14. The idea is to keep only the most promising node (pure hill-climbing search) or to keep several

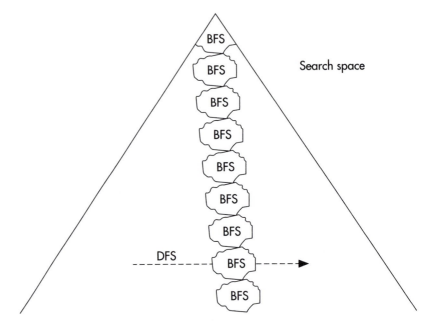

FIGURE 5.14

Intermingling depth-first search (DFS) and best-first search (BFS)

promising nodes (so some limited backtracking can be done) and to do a best-first search from that point. If illustrated, this combination method would look like that in Figure 5.14 except that hill-climbing search would replace DFS and little backtracking would be done.

5.8 GAME TREES AND α–β PRUNING

Games are an excellent application of heuristic search methods. Games that involve multiple players are more complicated than simple, one-person games. The primary additional complexity is due to the addition of unpredictable opponents who wish to win at your expense.

If the game has a small reachable search space that can be completely searched, then we can analyze the game's search space to try to win. The minimax procedure is used for this type of game. A variant of minimax is used when the reachable search space is too large. This variant is called α–β pruning and uses heuristics to approximate the minimax procedure and to prune the search space.

5.8.1 Minimax Procedure

The minimax procedure assigns to each node of the search space a value based on the path to winning and losing nodes. One player is

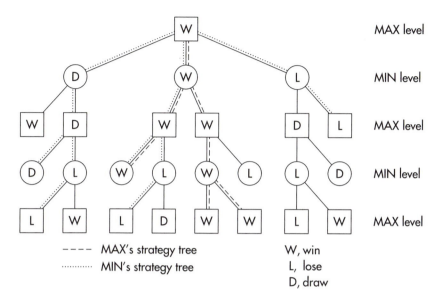

FIGURE 5.15

Using the minimax algorithm to determine game strategy

called MAX. MAX's objective is either to maximize his score or to win. The other player is called MIN. MIN is trying to minimize MAX's score or to force MAX to lose. If we (MAX) assume that our opponent (MIN) has complete knowledge of the search space, this assumption simplifies our usage of the minimax procedure, because we can assume that all MIN's moves are designed to minimize MAX's score.

For example, Figure 5.15 shows a complete search tree for a small hypothetical game. In this particular game, there is no score—only win, loss, or draw. Particular plies (or levels) of the search space are labeled as either MIN or MAX nodes; these labels indicate whose move it is at that point in the search. The leaf nodes indicate whether it is a loss or win for the player MAX. We evaluate internal nodes of the search space on the basis of whose ply they are on: MIN's or MAX's. If they are on MIN's level, then MIN has control over them and will pick the move that is worst for MAX. To evaluate a MIN node, we simply take the minimum value of all its children nodes. Here, for the lowest left-most terminal node, its parent is a MIN node, so it gets the minimum value of the terminal nodes, or an "L" for loss. To evaluate a MAX node, we can take the maximum of its children because MAX has control over which move is made and can maximize MAX's chances.

In Figure 5.15, the strategies of the two players are indicated by dashed and dotted lines. MAX's strategy is to traverse that portion of the search space that terminates in a win. MIN's strategy is to force a loss if possible. Note that MIN's strategy must include a choice for all branches where MAX chooses the move. This is why all three branches from the start node are included. The same is also true for MAX in that when MIN has control, MAX's strategy must include all branches that MIN might take.

5.8.2 α–β Pruning

Minimax pursues all branches of the search space, including those that could be pruned by using a more intelligent algorithm or a well-informed heuristic. α–β pruning improves the efficiency of searching for two-person games. The basic idea behind an α–β search is to perform a depth-first search and to use two values produced during the search (α and β) to prune future branches of the search space. α and β are the scores of parent nodes based on the scores of child nodes that have been examined so far. The α value is associated with nodes within MAX's control. The β value is associated with nodes within MIN's control. The α value can never decrease, and the β value can never increase. a is the value that indicates the worst that MAX can score, assuming that MIN does its "best" with the same knowledge of the search space that MAX has. Similarly, the β value indicates the best that MAX can score with MIN doing its "best." Suppose we are at a MAX node with an α value of 10 (Figure 5.16). Then MAX need not consider any child nodes with a value of less than or equal to 10, because they will not help to further maximize MAX's score. Similarly, if we are at a MIN node with a β value of 10, then MIN need not consider any child nodes with a value of 10 or greater because they will not help to minimize MAX's score. The following rules state in a formal way when we can prune branches:

FIGURE 5.16

α–β pruning

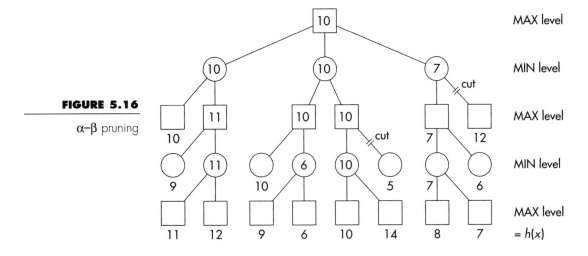

- We do not need to search a branch below a MIN node that has a β value less than or equal to the α value of any of its MAX ancestors.
- We do not need to search a branch below a MAX node having an α value greater than or equal to the β value of any of its MIN ancestors.

The implementation of the α–β algorithm in C++ is included in the search library.

5.9 REPRESENTING LOGIC PROBLEMS

Various graphical devices can be used to help us solve logic problems. AND/OR graphs are one of these devices. Representing logic problems as a state space search is another.

5.9.1 Using AND/OR Graphs

In a pure state space search, we treat the search as one problem. But in a search using AND/OR graphs, we break down the overall problem into subproblems. These subproblems also can be broken down into further subproblems until they are no longer decomposable.

Figure 5.17 shows the two types of links that make up AND/OR trees. An AND node is denoted by placing an arc between the edges of the graph. This notation indicates that the two child nodes must both be solved in order to solve the parent. For the example shown in Figure 5.17 we must solve both the P node and the Q node in order to solve the $P \wedge Q$ node. An OR node is indicated by the absence of such an arc. The OR notation means that solving one child is sufficient to solve the parent. In Figure 5.17 the OR notation indicates that we need only solve the P node or the Q node in order to solve the $P \vee Q$ node.

Figure 5.18 shows how a more complex expression can be represented as an AND/OR tree. This approach is not a pure state space search, because each node does not represent a complete description

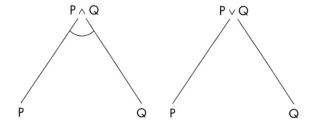

FIGURE 5.17

AND/OR graph elements

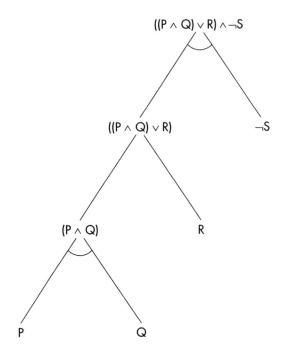

FIGURE 5.18

AND/OR graph
example for
$((P \wedge Q) \vee R) \wedge \neg S$

of the progress in solving the problem. This type of representation is known as a **problem-reduction representation** of the problem.

5.9.2 Representing Logic Problems for a State Space Search

We can describe the problem of trying to satisfy a propositional logic statement in terms of a state space problem. We will consider problems that can be completely stated by using rules of the form $P_1 \wedge P_2 \wedge \cdots \wedge P_n \to C$ or $P_1 \vee P_2 \vee \cdots \vee P_n \to C$ and associated propositional facts. This concept can be easily expanded to more general forms of these rules. We can represent the state space by having each state represent a conjunction of problems. The operators are

- If one of the conjuncts (call it P) requires us to solve all of $P_1, P_2, \cdots, P_n$, then the new state replaces P with $P_1, P_2, \cdots, P_n$. (We use this operator when we have a rule such as $P_1 \wedge P_2 \wedge \cdots \wedge P_n \to P$.)
- If one of the conjuncts (call it P) requires us to solve one of $P_1, P_2, \cdots, P_n$, then we have n successor states, with each $P_i \leq 1 \leq i \leq n$) replacing P in one of the successor states.

The goal state is a conjunction of problems, all of which are known to be solved. The initial state is the overall unsolved problem.

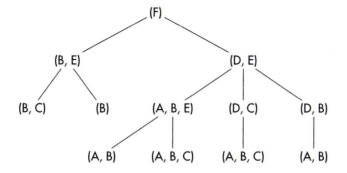

FIGURE 5.19

State space
representation for
propositional logic

This approach is illustrated by the search space in Figure 5.19 where conjunctions of problems are denoted by a set of problems in parentheses. We assume the following facts:

$$B \vee C \rightarrow E$$
$$A \wedge B \rightarrow D$$
$$D \wedge E \rightarrow F$$
$$B \wedge E \rightarrow F$$
$$A \wedge B \wedge C$$

and A, B, and C are known to be true. We want to solve problem F, so we apply the operators to develop the search space in Figure 5.19.

The figure shows that if we can solve F by using the left branch, then we can solve the problem simply by solving B. If we follow the right branch, then we can solve F by following any subbranch. If A, B, and C are true (and in two cases we need only A and B), then we can state that F has been shown.

A search of this type is also supported by the included search library by using the "AOSearch" components contained in the program files.

5.10 SEARCH IN C++

A set of search classes in C++ has been designed to make AI search algorithms easier to handle in C++. These classes are defined and applied in this section.

5.10.1 C++ Search Library

The design of the C++ search library centers on two sets of classes:

1. *Search graphs.* These classes define the graphs, and problem graphs are derived from the search graph classes.
2. *Node definitions.* This set of classes defines the nodes of the search graph in terms of each problem state.

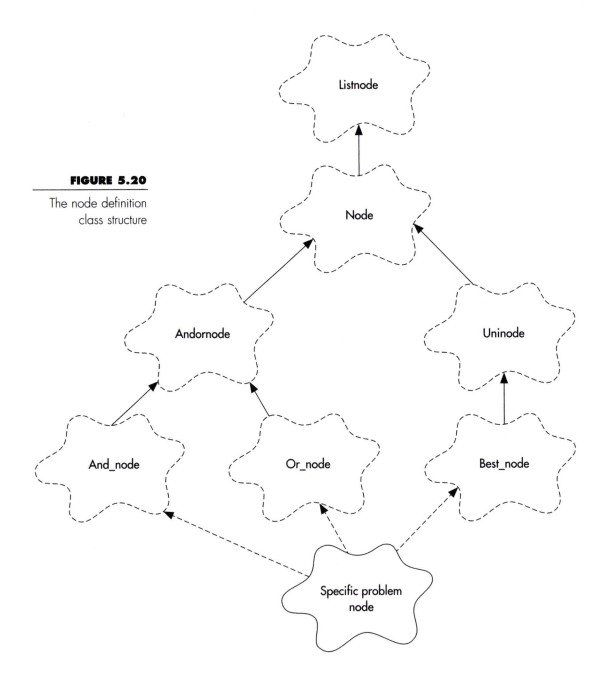

FIGURE 5.20

The node definition class structure

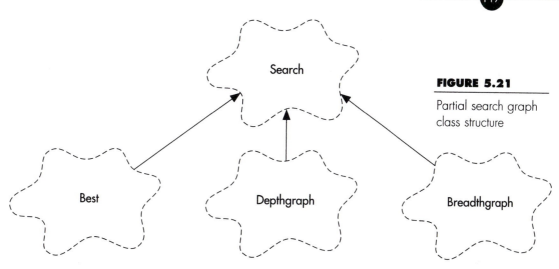

FIGURE 5.21

Partial search graph
class structure

Figures 5.20 and 5.21 summarize the node definition class structure
for the class library included with this text. A specific problem node
will be an object of one of the node classes, depending on the type
of problem.

5.10.2 Solving the 8-Puzzle with a C++ Program

Using the class libraries, we can solve the 8-Puzzle with several different search strategies. The following program solves the 8-Puzzle
by using depth-first search.

```
//file: 8puzzle.h
#include <stdio.h>
#include "graph.h"
/*
In this exercise we solve a "real" 8-puzzle. We're
interested in more than the position of the empty
tile; we want to know exactly which tiles have to
be moved to transform the start configuration into
the goal configuration.
*/
/*     PNODE
Class PNode defines objects representing a board
configuration.
*/
class PNode : public DepthNode
{
  public:
```

```
      PNode(const char *, int empty_x, int empty_y);
      PNode(const char *, int, int, int, int);
// Implementation of virtual functions
      int operator == (const Node &) const;
      void display() const;
      Node *do_operator(int);
  private:
      PNode
        *do_left() const,
        *do_right() const,
        *do_up() const,
        *do_down() const;
      int compare_board(const char [3][3]) const;
      int
        x,  // Coordinates of empty tile
        y;
      char
        board[3][3];  // Array to represent board
                         configuration
} ;
//
class Puzzle : public DepthGraph
{
  public:
    Puzzle(PNode *start, PNode *target);
} ;
```

The rest of the code for the 8-Puzzle best-first search in C++ is given below.

```
//file: 8puzzle.cpp
#include "8puzzle.h"
//
Puzzle::Puzzle(PNode *start, PNode *target)
  :DepthGraph(4, start, target)
{
}
/*     PNODE
Initializes a PNode object.
*/
PNode::PNode(const char *b, int empty_x, int
empty_y)
{
  char *p = *board;
  int i;
```

```
  for (i = 0; i <= 8; i++)
    *(p + i) = *(b + i);
  x = empty_x;
  y = empty_y;
}
/*    PNode
Initializes a new configuration using its "parent"
configuration. First copies the old board and then
swaps the two tiles that are on old_x, old_y and
new_x, new_t respectively.
*/
PNode::PNode(const char *b, int old_x, int old_y,
                            int new_x, int new_y)
{
  char *p = *board;
  int i;
  for (i = 0; i <= 8; i++)
    *(p + i) = *(b + i);
  board[old_x][old_y] = board[new_x][new_y];
  board[new_x][new_y] = 0;
  x = new_x;
  y = new_y;
}
/*    DISPLAY
Displays a board configuration.
*/
void PNode::display() const
{
  int row, col;
  for (row = 0; row < 3; row++)
  {
    for (col = 0; col < 3; col++)
      printf("%d ", board[row][col]);
    putchar('');
  }
  putchar('');
}
/*    EQUAL
Determines whether two nodes (i.e., two board posi-
tions) are the same. First, the x- and y-coordi-
nates of the empty tile are compared and next, if
necessary, the two boards themselves.
*/
int PNode::operator == (const Node &other) const
{
```

```
    const PNode &pnother = (PNode &)other;
    if (x != pnother.x && y != pnother.y)
        return(0);
    return(compare_board(pnother.board));
}
/*    COMPARE_BOARD
Compares the current board configuration with
another. Could have used memcmp() here.
*/
int PNode::compare_board(const char bo[3][3]) const
{
    const char
      *p = *board,
        *b = *bo;
    int
      i;
    for (i = 0; i <= 8; i++)
      if (*(p + i) != *(b + i))
        return(0);
    return(1);
}
/*    DO_OPERATOR
Applies operator n to the current configuration,
i.e. it moves the empty tile (by calling one of the
do_..() functions); this operator results either in
a new board configuration or in NULL, if the opera-
tor can't be applied.
*/
Node *PNode::do_operator(int index)
{
    switch(index)
    {
      case 0:
        return(do_down());
      case 1:
        return(do_up());
      case 2:
        return(do_right());
    }
    return(do_left());
}
PNode *PNode::do_left() const
{
```

```
  if (!y)
    return(NULL);
  return(new PNode(*board, x, y, x, y - 1));
}
PNode *PNode::do_right() const
{
  if (y == 2)
    return(NULL);
  return(new PNode(*board, x, y, x, y + 1));
}
PNode *PNode::do_up() const
{
  if (!x)
    return(NULL);
  return(new PNode(*board, x, y, x - 1, y));
}
PNode *PNode::do_down() const
{
  if (x == (2))
    return(NULL);
  return(new PNode(*board, x, y, x + 1, y));
}
int main()
{
  char
    start[3][3] = {
          {1, 3, 4} ,
          {8, 0, 2} ,
          {7, 6, 5} ,
          } ;
  char
    goal[3][3] = {
          {1, 2, 3} ,
          {8, 0, 4} ,
          {7, 6, 5} ,
          } ;
  Puzzle
    puzzle(new PNode(*start, 1, 1),
                      new PNode(*goal, 1, 1));
  if (puzzle.generate())
      puzzle.display();
  return(1);
}
```

5.11 SUMMARY

In this chapter, state space search is defined and several different algorithms for searching the state space are presented. The most important of these algorithms for artificial intelligence is best-first search. Best-first search allows us to apply heuristic functions that are designed to help us find a solution quickly. We also discussed some properties of heuristic functions that can be used to compare them with one another.

Heuristic search provides a powerful mechanism on which many of the AI methods discussed in this text are based. Later chapters use this foundation of searching to build algorithms for planning, production systems, natural language processing, and other AI problems.

5.12 REFERENCES

Heuristic search has been an area of interest in artificial intelligence for as long as AI has been practiced. The need for searching a problem space is fundamental to most areas of AI, including planning, theorem proving, and game playing. One of the best references in this area is Pearl (1984). Other references are Nilsson (1980), Pearl (1983), and Pearl (1988).

To review search algorithms and techniques further, see an algorithms text such as Baase (1988) and Sedgewick (1988). Analysis of many search algorithms is contained in Knuth (1973b).

5.13 EXERCISES

Warm-up Exercises

5.1 Can the heuristic used in Chapter 1 for the 8-Queens problem be used in an A^* algorithm (i.e., is it admissible)?

5.2 Determine whether depth-first or breadth-first search would be preferable for solving each of the following problems. Justify your answers.

   a. Finding a needle in a haystack.

   b. Finding the original reference to the word "wombat."

   c. Finding out if you have an ancestor who was part of a royal family.

   d. Finding out if you have an ancestor who was part of the Danish royal family.

   e. A program for examining sonar readings and interpreting them, e.g., telling a large submarine from a small submarine from a whale from a school of fish.

f. An expert system that will help a human find bugs in software from a set of defined specifications.

5.3 For the examples given in Exercise 5.2, determine whether a goal-driven or a data-driven search is preferable and why.

5.4 Consider using best-first search for each of the problems given in Exercise 5.2. If best-first search is feasible, give a short description of the states that you would use and of a search heuristic that you think would be better than a blind search. Are all your heuristics admissible?

5.5 The sliding-tile puzzle consists of three black tiles, three white tiles, and an empty space in the configuration shown in the accompanying figure.

B	B	B		W	W	W

The puzzle has two legal moves with associated costs. A tile can move into an adjacent empty location. This move has a cost of 1. A tile can hop over one or two other tiles into the empty position. This move has a cost equal to the number of tiles jumped over. The goal is to have all the white tiles to the left of all the black tiles. The position of the blank is not important.

a. Propose a heuristic for solving this problem and analyze it with respect to admissibility and monotonicity.

b. Propose a second heuristic and compare its informedness to your first one.

5.6 Perform minimax and α–β pruning of the tree shown in the accompanying figure. When doing minimax, assume that this is the complete game tree. When applying α–β pruning, assume that all leaf nodes may actually have further nodes below them and that the values given are only heuristic values.

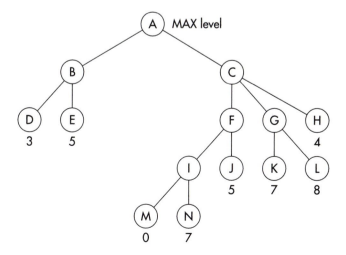

5.7 Why do game-playing programs usually work from a current state to a goal, rather than backward from a goal? Give a property of a game that might suggest using a backward strategy?

5.8 Define an algorithm for heuristically searching AND/OR graphs. Note that all descendants of an AND node must be solved in order to solve the parent. Thus in computing heuristic estimates of costs to a goal, the estimate of the cost to solve an AND node must be at least the sum of the estimates to solve the different branches. Use this algorithm to search the accompanying graph. The start node is *A*.

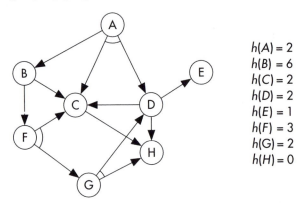

$h(A) = 2$
$h(B) = 6$
$h(C) = 2$
$h(D) = 2$
$h(E) = 1$
$h(F) = 3$
$h(G) = 2$
$h(H) = 0$

5.9 Give a simple example that shows whether the heuristic function *h* can return values that are so high that the best-first search will not necessarily find the optimal solution.

Homework Exercises

5.10 You are explaining the problem of searching for a move in chess to a physics student. Your physics friend notices that the algorithm needs to find the maximum of some function (i.e., the move that is best for you) and suggests that you should simply differentiate the function, set the result to zero, and solve. Explain why this will not work.

5.11 Prove *A** is admissible. Hint: The proof should show that

   a. During its execution, there is always a node on OPEN that lies on an optimal path to the goal.

   b. If there is a path to a goal, A* will terminate by finding the optimal path.

5.12 Does admissibility imply monotonicity of a heuristic? If so, prove it. If not, what additional constraints on the heuristic are needed?

5.13 Discuss ways to improve a heuristic during a search. You would like to use information gained during the search to make better choices of states to expand. This involves modification of how the heuristic is calculated.

5.14 Draw out the complete state space for the missionaries and cannibals problem given in Chapter 1. You may assume that the repeated states will be detected and cut off so that their successors will not be investigated. (However, do put the repeated state itself in the tree, marked as such.) For each state, label it by using Ms and Cs to show where everyone is. Develop a possible heuristic. Is it admissible?

5.15 Prove that, when given two monotone heuristics, h1 and h2, the heuristic $max(h_1,h_2)$ is also a monotone heuristic.

5.16 Let G be a connected graph, and let v be a vertex in G. Let TB be a depth-first search tree formed by doing a depth-first search of G starting at v. Let T_B be the breadth-first search tree formed by doing a breadth-first search of G starting at v. Is it always true that $depth(T_D) \geq depth(T_B)$? Give a clear argument or a counterexample.

5.17 Show that a monotone heuristic is also admissible.

5.18 Suppose that we start out the 8-Puzzle with one of the following start states:

8	3	4
	1	2
7	6	5

3	8	4
	1	2
7	6	5

Use our heuristic of the number of misplaced tiles to help guide us to a solution for both start states. How well does our heuristic perform in finding a solution from these start states? Does it work better for one start state than the other? Why?

5.19 Many start states of the 8-Puzzle are not solvable. How many possible start states are there? How many of all possible start states are unsolvable?

Programming Exercises

5.20 Write a program to return the solution path generated by a best-first search, depth-first search or breadth-first search for a 16-Puzzle problem (same as the 8-Puzzle, except on a 4×4 board.) If you choose a best-first search, use either the heuristic mentioned in this chapter or create a new one. Note: The reachable search space of this problem is very large.

5.21 Implement the Knight's Tour Problem on an 8×8 chess board. The output of your program will be a list of the spaces that the Knight lands on in the order in which it lands on them, beginning with its initial position. The problem is to start a Knight on a space and then using legal Knight's moves, land on every space on the board exactly once. For consistency, use numbers for the board positions as follows:

1	2	3	4	5	6	7	8
9	10	11	12	13	14	15	16
17	18	19	20	21	22	23	24
25	26	27	28	29	30	31	32
33	34	35	36	37	38	39	40
41	42	43	44	45	46	47	48
49	50	51	52	53	54	55	56
57	58	59	60	61	62	63	64

The output should simply be some permutation of the numbers 1 through 64.

In your C++ program, use heuristic search to make the program more efficient.

You may pick the starting position of the Knight to be any position that you like (which may in fact help you get to a solution quicker). However, your solution should work with any starting position. You may use any of the search pruning methods or heuristics that we have discussed and are welcome to come up with new ones that may help solve the problem more quickly. You will have to extend the search library to support the α–β pruning algorithm.

You should allow a parameter to be passed to your program, indicating the starting position.

5.22 A variant of the Knight's Tour Problem given in Exercise 5.24 is to require that the Knight end on the same space that it started on. Rewrite your program to force the Knight to form this "Hamiltonian circuit." Does the heuristic you used in Exercise 5.24 work?

5.23 Write a C++ program to solve the missionaries and cannibals problem by using heuristic search. Use a best-first search algorithm with an appropriate heuristic. Your program must be general enough to handle n missionaries and n cannibals. Your program must take n as a parameter. Here is a statement of the generalized missionaries and cannibals problem:

> n missionaries and n cannibals are standing on the left bank of a river. There is a small boat to ferry them across with enough room for only one or two persons. They wish to cross the river. If ever there are more missionaries than cannibals on either side of the river, the missionaries will convert the cannibals. Find a series of ferryings to transport safely all the missionaries and cannibals across the river without exposing any of the cannibals to conversion.

Express your solution as a series of crossings of the form: [MM,MC,CC]. The first element of the list are the people on the left bank (here two missionaries). The second element are those in the boat (here a missionary and a cannibal). Every crossing that is part of the solution should be printed and no crossings that are not part of the solution should be printed. The third element are those on the right bank (here two cannibals). Your solution should not repeat states.

5.24 Apply the α–β search procedure given in the search library on the following two-player game, Number Tic-Tac-Toe:

1	2	3
4	5	6
7	8	9

The board is a square Tic-Tac-Toe diagram (see accompanying figure). One player uses the even numbers between 1 and 9 ({2,4,6,8}) and the other player uses the odd numbers ({1,3,5,7,9}). The odd-number player has one extra number and always goes first, placing one of his numbers on any square. The second player follows in turn, and so on. Each player may use each of his numbers only once. The object is for each player to make a row of three numbers in any direction (vertically, horizontally or diagonally), the sum of which is 15. The player that succeeds in doing so first wins the game.

Your program should use the numbering scheme for the squares given in the accompanying figure. That is, if your program moves by placing 8 in the upper, left-hand corner of the board, then you print out "My move is number 8 in square 1." If the program wins, print out "I win." If the player wins, print out "You win." Ask for input for each player's move by asking "In what square do you wish to place which number?" Your program should accept answers of the form "3,7" to indicate that you wish to place number 7 in square number 3 (the upper, right-hand corner). Your program should give the player the option of playing either odd numbers or even numbers by asking, "Do you wish to play odd? y/n".

Your program should always attempt to win the game whenever possible.

5.25 Apply a best-first search procedure to the following two-player game, *Three-Men Morris:*

Each player has three pieces. One player has white pieces and the other has black pieces. The player with the white pieces moves first by placing a piece at any of the line intersections in the accompanying figure. The players take turns until all pieces have been placed on the board. Only one piece may occupy any given intersection at a particular time. Pieces are then moved on the board. A piece may only be moved to an adjacent intersection or a connecting line. The player that first completes a line of three of his pieces (either vertically, horizontally, or diagonally) wins the game.

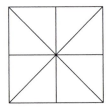

Your program should ask whether the player wishes to play white or black. A player enters moves in the form "U,M" to indicate the wish to place or move a piece to the upper line, middle intersection. The first and second parameter can be in {U,M,L} , to mean "upper," "middle," and "lower," respectively. Display the program's moves in the same format. Your program should try to win and not allow a player to place an illegal move.

5.26 Write a program in C++ to solve the *N*-Queens problem described in Chapter 1, using the C++ search routines and best-first search.

Projects

5.27 Rewrite the search library included with this text in the Eiffel programming language.

5.28 Rewrite the search library included with this text in the SmallTalk programming language.

5.29 Write a C++ program that will implement the Go board game and find a heuristic that will beat at least a beginning player. (*Note:* This game is particularly hard to find good heuristics for and is considered much harder to produce a world-class program for than is chess.}

5.30 Write a C++ program to play solitaire. Investigate any known heuristics and employ best-first search. You program should use a definable heuristic. Your game should use the rules as defined by the default MS/Windows® Solitaire game. So you would first deal the cards that are in random order. You would then decide (on the basis of your heuristic) which card to play. You may need multiple heuristics to successfully play the game. For example, one heuristic might be to play a card if it is the only playable card. Using this heuristic, you will clearly need another heuristic to handle the case when there are multiple cards that can be played during a current state of the game. Using the MS/Windows program, do a scientific study to determine how your program does compared to real players (i.e., give the same problem set to your program and to a set of players and compare your programs score to the players average score).

5.31 Write a C++ program to play checkers. Investigate known heuristics and employ best-first search. Your program should use a definable heuristic and work quickly and beat most players.

LOGIC: A FOUNDATION FOR INFERENCE

"Today I feel no

wish to demonstrate

that sanity is

impossible."

ALDOUS HUXLEY,
1946

6.1 RESOLUTION: A PROOF PROCEDURE

In this chapter we introduce a popular technique for proving facts in first-order predicate logic (FOPL), a technique called **resolution.** Variants of this automated theorem proving technique are part of many systems, including the programming language Prolog. In Chapter 8 we present an expert system that operates much like Prolog, and in Chapter 9 we present a theorem prover that uses a variant of resolution. See Chapter 4 for a discussion of the use of propositional logic and predicate logic to prove theorems in logic.

Resolution is an inference rule that can be used for generating proofs in FOPL. It is based on a simple inference rule that can be implemented in a computer program and can automatically prove (or disprove) assertions from a set of give facts (Figure 6.1). This procedure requires that all axioms used in the proof be converted to a standard form, the clausal form.

The process of building a resolution proof for a statement requires the following steps:

1. Convert all axioms to clausal form.

2. Convert the negation of the statement that is to be proved to clausal form.

3. Apply the resolution procedure until the empty clause is produced, indicating a contradiction. The resolution procedure is generally as follows:

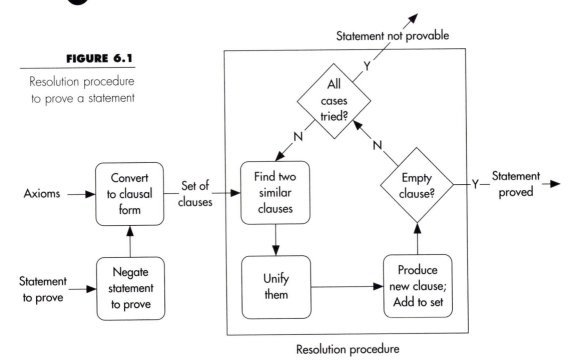

FIGURE 6.1

Resolution procedure
to prove a statement

a. Find two similar terms in different clauses.

b. Make the two terms represent the same term (that is, **unify** them). One should be positive and the other negative.

c. Produce a new clause that includes all terms except those that are used to match the clauses.

d. If the empty clause is not produced after all possible resolutions have been tried, then the statement is false.

This procedure is actually **binary resolution**, because only two terms are used in finding clauses for use in each resolution step. The form of resolution that is described here uses the negation of what is to be shown in order to produce a contradiction. This technique is called **proof by refutation** and is similar to proof by contradiction, which is commonly used in mathematics.

6.1.1 Clausal Form

The first step in resolution is to convert all axioms and the negated goal to **clausal form,** which is a simplified form of FOPL that contains literals and clauses. A **literal** is an atomic sentence or the negation of an atomic sentence, for example, *Turtle(pokey)* or

¬*Cow*(*elsie*). **Positive literals** are atomic sentences; **negative literals** are negations of atomic sentences. A **clause** is the disjunction of a set of literals, for example, *Turtle*(*pokey*) ∨ ¬*Slow*(*pokey*). A **Horn clause** is a clause with at most one positive literal.

Any FOPL sentence can be converted to clausal form. The following nine-step procedure accomplishes this conversion:

1. *Remove implications* (→) *and equivalences* (≡). Eliminate → by using the fact that φ → φ ≡ ¬φ ∨ φ. Eliminate ≡ by using the fact that φ≡φ is equivalent to (¬φ ∨ φ) ∧ (φ ∨ ¬φ).

2. *Reduce the scope of not* (¬). This conversion is done by using the three equivalences:

   a. ¬(¬φ) ≡ φ

   b. DeMorgan's laws: ¬(φ ∧ φ) ≡ ¬φ ∨ ¬φ and ¬(φ ∨ φ) ≡ ¬φ ∧ ¬φ

   c. ¬∀v.φ ≡ ∃v.¬φ and ¬∃v.φ ≡ ∀v.¬φ

3. *Make variable names unique.* Because variable names are chosen arbitrarily and have no meaning in and of themselves, we can replace them with different names. For this step, we make each variable name unique. For example, if we have the statement ∀X.(*Cow*(X)) ∨ ∀X.(*Turtle*(X)), we can rename the Xs because they really refer to different variables. We would then have ∀X_1.(*Cow*(X_1)) ∨ ∀X_2.(*Turtle*(X_2)).

4. *Move all quantifiers left.* Move all quantifiers to the left of the statement, keeping them in the same order.

5. *Eliminate existential qualifiers.* We eliminate an existential quantifier by replacing it with a function that references a value to which the quantifier refers. If the existential quantifier is not within the scope of any other quantifier, then we can replace the variable references with a constant function. This process is called Skolemization. If it is within the scope of other quantifiers, however, then that variable may depend on those other variables. For example,

$$∀X∃Y.Parent\_of(Y,X)$$

converts to

$$∀X.Parent\_of(mother(X),X)$$

Note that each function that is introduced must have a new function name that does not appear in any of the statements that are being converted. This function is called a Skolem function. If the function is only a constant (no variables) then it is termed a Skolem constant.

A simpler example is $\exists X. Turtle(X)$. This statement would be changed to $Turtle(pokey)$, provided *pokey* has not been used before.

6. *Drop the universal quantifiers.* Because all remaining variables are universally quantified, we can drop them, and any proof procedure can assume that any variable is universally quantified.

7. *Convert the statement to conjunctive normal form.* In this step, we convert the statement to a conjunction of disjunctions of literals. In other words, we convert the statement to a set of disjunctions of literals. These disjunctions must be $\wedge$ed together. This conversion can be done by using the associative and distributive laws of $\vee$ and $\wedge$. One particular rule to use is the following equivalence:

$$\phi \vee (\varphi \wedge \chi) \equiv (\phi \vee \varphi) \wedge (\phi \vee \chi)$$

8. *Separate the conjunctive normal form into clauses.* In this step, we split the conjunctive normal form into clauses by eliminating the $\wedge$ and making each disjunction of literals a separate clause.

9. *Standardize the variables.* We must check the variable names for uniqueness, because each sentence in step 8 may have produced several clauses with identical variable names. In this step we rename variables if necessary, so that all variable names are unique.

The following example (from Genesereth and Nilsson, 1987) uses these nine rules to convert a statement to clausal form:

Initial Statement:	$\forall X.((\forall Y.P(X,Y)) \rightarrow \neg(\forall Y.Q(X,Y) \rightarrow R(X,Y)))$
Step 1	$\forall X.(\neg(\forall Y.P(X,Y)) \vee \neg(\forall Y.\neg Q(X,Y) \vee R(X,Y)))$
Step 2	$\forall X.((\exists Y.\neg P(X,Y)) \vee (\exists Y.Q(X,Y) \wedge \neg R(X,Y)))$
Step 3	$\forall X.((\exists Y.\neg P(X,Y)) \vee (\exists Z.Q(X,Z) \wedge \neg R(X,Z)))$
Step 4	$\forall X \exists Y \exists Z.(\neg P(X,Y) \vee (Q(X,Z) \wedge \neg R(X,Z)))$
Step 5	$\forall X.(\neg P(X,f_1(X)) \vee (Q(X,f_2(X)) \wedge \neg R(X,f_2(X))))$
Step 6	$\neg P(X,f_1(X)) \vee (Q(X,f_2(X)) \wedge \neg R(X,f_2(X)))$
Step 7	$(\neg P(X,f_1(X)) \vee Q(X,f_2(X))) \wedge (\neg P(X,f_1(X)) \vee \neg R(X,f_2(X)))$
Step 8	$(\neg P(X,f_1(X)) \vee Q(X,f_2(X)))$
	$(\neg P(X,f_1(X)) \vee \neg R(X,f_2(X)))$
Step 9	$(\neg P(X_1,f_1(X_1)) \vee Q(X_1,f_2(X_1)))$
	$(\neg P(X_2,f_1(X_2)) \vee \neg R(X_2,f_2(X_2)))$

When converting a FOPL statement to clausal form, rules may be skipped if they do not apply to the particular statement.

6.1.2 Substitution

The resolution procedure uses substitutions to unify terms. In other words, substitutions are used to make two expressions equal. A **substitution** is a set of associations between variables and terms that satisfies the following conditions:

1. Each variable in a substitution can be replaced by only a single term. A term is either a constant, a function, another variable, or a composition of functions.
2. None of the terms that is being used by the substitution contains any variable that is being replaced in the substitution. This is called the *occurs check* in the resolution procedure.

For example, the substitution

$$\{X/house\_of(Y),Z/mother(W)\}$$

would replace all occurrences of the variable X with $house\_of(Y)$ and all occurrences of Z with $mother(W)$. The following are not substitutions:

$$\{X/f(X)\} \ \{X/f(Y),Y/aconstant\}$$

Let

$$\sigma = \{X/Z,Y/mother(Z)\}$$

Applying σ to the clause $P(X,Y) \vee Q(Z)$ yields $P(Z,mother(Z)) \vee Q(Z)$. The notation used to indicate that substitution σ has been applied to a clause P_1 is $P_1\sigma$.

Substitutions can be composed with one another to produce other substitutions. Applying the result of the composition produces the same result as applying both substitutions. A **composition** of two substitutions is a substitution that is equal to applying the first substitution followed by the second substitution. This fact is expressed as $P(\sigma_1 \circ \sigma_2) = (P\sigma_1)\sigma_2$. The composition $\sigma_1 \circ \sigma_2$ is found by applying σ_2 to the terms of σ_1 and then adding the terms of σ_2 to it. More formally, if

$$\sigma = \{X_1/t_1,...,X_n/t_n\}$$

σ_1	σ_2	$\sigma_1 \circ \sigma_2$
$\{X/f(W),Y/b\}$	$\{W/a,Z/c\}$	$\{X/f(a),Y/b,W/a,Z/c\}$
$\{Y/f(a,X),Z/b\}$	$\{W/g(Z)\}$	$\{Y/f(a,X),Z/b,W/g(\hat{Z})\}$[1]
$\{Y/X,Z/b\}$	$\{X/Y,W/c\}$	$\{Z/b,X/Y,W/c\}$
$\{X/a,Z/f(Y)\}$	$\{Y/c,X/b\}$	$\{X/a,Z/f(c),Y/c\}$

TABLE 6.1

Examples of substitution compositions

[1] Note that in order for this to remain a substitution, the variable $\hat{Z}$ must be distinct from the variable Z that is being replaced in the substitution.

and

$$\sigma_2 = \{Y_1/s_1,...,Y_n/s_n\}$$

then

$$\sigma_1 \circ \sigma_2 = \{X_1/t_1\sigma_2,...,X_n/t_n\sigma_2,Y_1/s_1,...,Y_n/s_n\}$$

with the removal of any element of the form $X_j/t_j\sigma_2$ for which $t_j\sigma_2 = X_j$, and any element Y_i/s_i for which $Y_i \in \{X_1,...,X_n\}$. For example,

$$\{W/g(X,Y)\} \circ \{X/a,Y/b,Z/c\} = \{W/g(a,b),X/a,Y/b,Z/c\}$$

Another example, where the conditions apply for the removal of elements, is

$$\{X/Y,Z/b\} \circ \{Y/X,Z/g(a,b,c)\} = \{Y/X,Z/b\}$$

$Z/g(a,b,c)$ does not apply in the composition because Z/b supercedes it and replaces all Z occurrences. Table 6.1 presents more examples of substitution compositions.

6.1.3 Unification

A unifier is defined in terms of substitutions; that is, a **unifier** of two literals is a substitution that makes the two literals identical. More formally, σ is a unifier of literals P_1 and P_2 and only if $P_1\sigma = P_2\sigma$. The task of unification is to find a substitution that unifies two given literals. Table 6.2 presents examples of unifiers for pairs of literals. The first pair of literals actually has many possible unifiers. For example, Y and Z did not need to have c assigned to them. The second and third pairs, however, are more general because they do not unnecessarily bind variables to values. For resolution, we want the **most general unifier** (MGU) for each pair of literals that we unify. The MGU of

Literal 1	Literal 2	Unifier(s)
$P(X,b,Y)$	$P(a,W,Z)$	$\{X/a,W/b,Y/c,Z/c\}$
		$\{X/a,W/b,Z/Y\}$
		$\{X/a,W/b,Y/Z\}$
$P(f(X),Y)$	$P(f(a),b)$	$\{X/a,Y/b\}$
$P(f(a,X),X)$	$P(f(Y,b),c)$	None

TABLE 6.2

Unifiers for pairs of literals

literals P_1 and P_2 (let's call it σ) is a unifier for P_1 and P_2 ($P_1\sigma = P_2\sigma$) and for any other unifier, λ; and there is a substitution β such that

$$P_1\lambda = (P_1\sigma)\beta$$
$$P_2\lambda = (P_2\sigma)\beta$$

When the MGU of P_1 and P_2 is used, any other unifier can be simulated by composing some substitution with the MGU.

An algorithm for computing the MGU, taken from Genesereth and Nilsson (1987), follows. For a complete theoretical background on unification and proofs of correctness, see Manna and Waldinger (1989).

```
Recursive Procedure Mgu (x,y)
  Begin x=y → Return(),
    Variable(x) → Return(Mguvar(x,y)),
    Variable(y) → Return(Mguvar(y,x)),
    Constant(x) or Constant(y) → Return(False),
    Not(Length(x)=Length(y)) → Return(False),
    Begin i ← 0,
      g ← [],
    Tag i=Length(x) → Return(g),
      s → Mgu(Part(x,i),Part(y,i)),
      s=False → Return(False),
      g ← Compose(g,s),
      x ← Substitute(x,g),
      y ← Substitute(y,g),
      i ← i + 1,
      Goto Tag
    End
  End

  Procedure Mguvar (x,y)
    Begin Includes(x,y) → Return(False),
      Return([X/Y])
    End
```

This procedure computes the MGU, if it exists. If the MGU does not exist, the procedure returns the result *false*. The predicate Variable is *true* for variables, and the predicate Constant is *true* for constants. The Length of an object is the number of arguments a function or predicate has. Part(x,0) is the function or predicate name[2] of *X*, with the arguments being Part(x,1) to Part(x,n). Substitute applies its second argument, which is a substitution, to its first argument, which is an expression. Compose returns the composition of the substitutions that are passed as arguments. Includes is *true* if the variable that is passed is contained in the expression that is passed.

6.1.4 Resolution Procedure

Given a set of statements in clausal form, we look for two literals in different clauses that are unifiable and related by negation, that is, one is the negation of the other. Thus, if we find two clauses C_1 and C_2, of the form

$$C_1: P_1 \vee A_1 \vee A_2 \vee A_3 \dots$$
$$C_2: \neg P_2 \vee B_1 \vee B_2 \vee B_3 \vee \dots$$

and if P_1 and P_2 are unifiable, then we can resolve these two clauses to produce

$$R: (A_1 \vee A_2 \vee A_3 \vee B_1 \vee B_2 \vee B_3 \vee \dots)\sigma$$

where σ is the MGU of P_1 and P_2. *R* is called the **binary resolvent** of C_1 and C_2. We can show that the *R* is a logical consequence of C_1 and C_2. This assertion means that resolution is sound.[3] However, resolution is not complete, because not everything that logically follows can be proved by using resolution. But resolution can be shown to be complete if we add the negation of what we wish to prove, and that is exactly what is done to produce a proof by refutation.[4]

The process of resolution using a refutated goal involves five steps:

1. Add the negated goal, in clausal form, to the set of clauses that is to be used in the proof.

---

[2] The predicate or function name is also called a **function**.
[3] As defined in Chapter 4, "sound" means that everything proved using resolution logically follows.
[4] Factoring must also be added to the procedure. See Genesereth and Nilsson (1987) for an explanation of factoring.

2. Determine two clauses with literals that unify, one positive and one negative.

3. Produce a new clause by resolving the two clauses found.

4. Continue this process until an empty clause is found, representing a contradiction. This will occur when we resolve clauses that contain only one literal.

5. Use the substitutions that were found during the unification process to produce any bindings for variables that are necessary for the proof. **Bindings** are the assignment of values to a variable.

Chapter 9 presents more detailed information on how to implement, control, and speed up resolution theorem proving.

6.1.5 Examples

One interesting example of resolution comes from Genesereth and Nilsson (1987). In this example from set theory, we have two axioms:

$$\forall X \forall S \forall T.(X \in S \wedge X \in T \equiv X \in S \cap T)$$
$$\forall S \forall T.(\forall X.(X \in S \to X \in T) \equiv S \subseteq T)$$

The first axiom defines set intersection and the second defines subsets. Our goal is to prove from these the fact

$$\forall S \forall T.(S \cap T \subseteq S)$$

That is, our goal is to show that the intersection of two sets is a subset of either of the sets.

Converting the axioms to clausal form, we get

Axioms	Resulting clauses
$\forall X \forall S \forall T.(X \in S \wedge X \in T \to X \in S \cap T)$	$X \notin S \vee X \notin T \vee X \in S \cap T$
$\forall X \forall S \forall T.(X \in S \wedge X \in T \leftarrow X \in S \cap T)$	$X_1 \notin S_1 \cap T_1 \vee X_1 \in S_1$
	$(X_2 \notin S_2 \cap T_2) \vee X_2 \in T_2$
$\forall S \forall T.(\forall X.(X \in S \to X \in T) \to S \subseteq T)$	$f(S_3,T_3) \in S_3 \vee S_3 \subseteq T_3$
	$f(S_5,T_5) \notin T_5 \vee S_5 \subseteq T_5$
$\forall S \forall T.(\forall X.(X \in S \to X \in T) \leftarrow S \subseteq T)$	$\neg(S_4 \subseteq T_4) \vee X_4 \notin S_4 \vee X_4 \in T_4$

The negated goal in clausal form is $\neg(A \cap B \subseteq A)$. Putting this in resolution proof form yields

Item	Clause	Resolvent
1	$X \notin S \vee X \notin T \vee X \in S \cap T$	Axiom
2	$(X_1 \notin S_1 \cap T_1) \vee X_1 \in S_1$	Axiom
3	$(X_2 \notin S_2 \cap T_2) \vee X_2 \in T_2$	Axiom
4	$f(S_3,T_3) \in S_3 \vee S_3 \subseteq T_3$	Axiom
5	$f(S_5,T_5) \notin T_5 \vee S_5 \subseteq T_5$	Axiom
6	$\neg(S_4 \subseteq T_4) \vee X_4 \notin S_4 \vee X_4 \in T_4$	Axiom
7	$\neg(A \cap B \subseteq A)$	Negated goal
8	$f(A \cap B,A) \in A \cap B$	4,7
9	$f(A \cap B,A) \notin A$	5,7
10	$f(A \cap B,A) \in A$	2,8
11	[ ]	9,10

For the example about doctors and quacks used in Chapter 4, we have the following axioms and desired conclusion in FOPL:

$$A_1: \exists X.(Patient(X) \wedge \forall Y.(Doctor(Y) \rightarrow Likes(X,Y)))$$
$$A_2: \forall X.(Patient(X) \rightarrow \forall Y.(Quack(Y) \rightarrow \neg Likes(X,Y)))$$
$$C: \forall Y.(Doctor(Y) \rightarrow \neg Quack(Y))$$

Converting these expressions to clause form yields

$A_1: Patient(a)$
$A_1: \neg Doctor(Y_1) \vee Likes(a,Y_1)$
$A_2: \neg Patient(X_2) \vee \neg Quack(Y_2) \vee \neg Likes(X_2,Y_2)$
$\neg C: Doctor(b)$
$\neg C: Quack(b)$

A resolution proof using the negated conclusion and the axioms is

Item	Clause	Resolvent
1	$Patient(a)$	A_1
2	$\neg Doctor(Y_1) \vee Likes(a,Y_1)$	A_1
3	$\neg Patient(X_2) \vee \neg Quack(Y_2) \vee \neg Likes(X_2,Y_2)$	A_2
4	$Doctor(b)$	$\neg C$
5	$Quack(b)$	$\neg C$
6	$Likes(a,b)$	4,2

Item	Clause	Resolvent
7	¬*Patient*(*a*) ∨ ¬*Quack*(*b*)	6,3
8	¬*Patient*(*a*)	5,7
9	[ ]	8,1

6.2 REASONING WITH UNCERTAINTY

Representing uncertainty about knowledge and then using that uncertain knowledge to make inferences is a necessity for many problems. Very often information is far from certain yet still contains useful knowledge. For example, if the local TV weather person predicts that there is an 80% chance of more than two inches of snow tomorrow, then that is useful information because I know that I need to prepare for snow. If, however, the station predicts a 1% chance of more than 10 inches of snow falling, then it is not clear that I should prepare for snow.

Using multiple sources of uncertain information is even more tricky. For example, if one stock broker predicts that my Apple Computer stock is going to go up by 10 points in the next month and another stock broker predicts that Apple will decline by two points in the next month, then combining that information may be difficult. It may be that one stock broker is much better than another and I should ignore the second stock broker's opinion. It could also be that the first stock broker is an excellent stock broker but knows nothing about Apple Computer and is very uncertain about her prediction. Worse yet, both stock brokers may be certain of their predictions, and both may turn out to be completely wrong. Even in this simple example, it is not always clear how to merge information with different certainty values.

6.2.1 Bayes's Rule

Fortunately, probability theory can be applied to the task of deducing the probabilities of outcomes. Bayes's rule is helpful in working with conditional probabilities.

Conditional probability theory is used to define probabilities of propositions that depend on the truth of other propositions. For example, we might express the following conditional probability:

A ≡ Calvin received an A in calculus
B ≡ Calvin cheated on the final in calculus

$\Pr(A|B) \equiv$ Probability that if Calvin cheated on the final, then he gets an "A"

$\Pr(B|A) \equiv$ Probability that if Calvin gets an A, then he cheated on the final

So, if $\Pr(B|A) = 1$, then it is certain that Calvin cheated on the final to get an A.

Bayes's Rule, which helps manipulate and calculate conditional probabilities, is

$$\Pr(B|A) = \frac{\Pr(A|B)\Pr(B)}{\Pr(A)}$$

An *if-then* rule can be stated as a conditional probability. If the conditions (the *if* part) C are met, then the hypothesis (the *then* part) is true. So to express uncertainty about a rule, we can assign a probability to $\Pr(H|C)$. To express the likelihood of the hypothesis given the likelihoods of the conditions, we need to find $\Pr(H)$. If we know $\Pr(C)$ and $\Pr(H|C)$, then using Bayes's rule, we can find $\Pr(H)$—assuming we can also get the probability of $\Pr(C|H)$, which is the probability that given the hypothesis to be true, the conditions will also be true.

Suppose we want to use two pieces of knowledge to infer a third such as the rule,

if the memory is failing ∧ the operating system does not detect the failure
then we will get unexplained application failures

This rule expresses a conclusion (unexplained application failures) that will be true only if each of the conditions is true. Each of the conditions may be true with a certain level of probability. We might think that part of memory is failing because we smell ozone and one of the memory chips looks darker than the others. As a result we might estimate the chance of the memory having failed to be 80%. We might also be able to guess at the probability that the operating system would not detect the failure. But note that the probability that the operating system will not detect the problem is conditional on there being a memory failure. We could estimate this probability to be high for a PC operating system such as MS/DOS, say, 70%. Given that we have one condition at 80% and the other at 70%, what is the likelihood that we will get unexplained application failures? We can combine these probabilities with Bayes's rule. If we define A as "the memory is failing" and B as "the operating system does not detect the failure," then we can express the event as

$$\Pr(A) \wedge \Pr(B|A) = \Pr(B|A) \frac{\Pr(A|B)\Pr(B)}{\Pr(A)} = \frac{(.8)(.7)}{.8} = .7 = 70\%$$

This equation says that the probability of B given A is the same as when we also have A true. We then solve $\Pr(B|A)$ using Bayes's rule. Note that we also assume that assuming B (that no error is detected) has no effect on A. So, we can say that the probability of unexplained application failures is 70%.

Now, we might also not be quite sure about the rule itself. That is, even if we have memory failures that go undetected by the operating system, then we may not always get unexplained application errors. So the rule itself might have a certainty of applying of only 60%. Given this, we can apply Bayes's rule again, because the rule itself can be expressed as a conditional probability. Given the conditions of the rule, the hypothesis of the rule is true with some probability. That is, if we call C the conditions of the rule (which we calculated to have a probability of 70% together), and H the hypothesis of unexplained application failures, then we have

$$\Pr(H|C) = .6 = \frac{\Pr(C|H)\Pr(H)}{\Pr(C)} = \frac{(.7)\Pr(H)}{.7} = \Pr(H) = .6$$

This equation states (in computing the conditional probability of $\Pr(C|H)$) that if H is true, then the $\Pr(C)$ is the probability of an OS-undetected memory failure, which was originally estimated at 70%. So the probability of unexplained application failures happens to be the same as the probability of the rule being valid.

6.2.2 Certainty Factors

Another inference method involves certainty factors and is used in the medical diagnosis expert system called MYCIN. A **certainty factor** is an expression of the probability of an expression being true. Instead of using probabilities directly, MYCIN uses certainty factors that range from –1 to +1. A certainty factor of –1 says a proposition is known to be false, whereas a value of +1 says that a proposition is known to be true. A value of 0 says that the truth value is completely uncertain. For a conjunction of propositions, the system chooses the minimum (MIN) of the certainty factors (CF) to represent the entire clause. For example, if we have $a \wedge b \wedge c \wedge d \rightarrow e$, the certainty factor of $a \wedge b \wedge c \wedge d = \text{MIN}\{CF(a), CF(b), CF(c), CF(d)\}$. The idea is that we cannot be any more certain of the truth of the entire set than of its weakest link, the minimum value. The implication is handled differently. It is defined as

$$CF(a) = c$$
$$CF(a \rightarrow b) = d$$
$$CF(d) = \begin{bmatrix} c > 0, c \times d \\ 0, otherwise \end{bmatrix}$$

The idea here is that if the certainty of our conditions are tending toward false, then we should not use them to satisfy our rule.

If we have a disjunction, then we need to include the cases in which they are both either true or false. So, for $CF(a \vee b)$, with $CF(a) = c$ and $CF(b) = d$, we have three cases:

If $c > 0$ and $d > 0$, then $CF(a \vee b) = c + d - cd$
If $c < 0$ and $d < 0$, then $CF(a \vee b) = c + d + cd$

If c and d are of opposite signs, then $CF(a \vee b) = \dfrac{a + b}{1 - \min(|a|, |b|)}$

Suppose we want to create a rule that allows us to identify friendly dogs:

$A \equiv$ dog is wagging its tail
$B \equiv$ dog is not showing teeth maliciously
$C \equiv$ dog is lying on its back
$D \equiv$ dog is not asleep
$E \equiv$ dog is alive

So our rule for identifying friendly dogs is

$(A \wedge B \wedge E) \vee (C \wedge D \wedge E) \rightarrow$ the dog is friendly

For a given situation, we might assign certainty factors as

$CF(A) = .8$ (it's usually easy to tell, but not always!)
$CF(B) = .5$ (the dog is showing some teeth, but probably not with evil intent)
$CF(C) = .6$ (whoops, the dog is on its side—does that count?)
$CF(D) = 1.0$ (that I can tell)
$CF(E) = 1.0$ (well, it's wagging its tail!)

To calculate the certainty factor for each conjunctive portion of the conditions, we take the minimum of .8, .5, and 1.0 to get .5 and the minimum of .6, 1.0, and 1.0 to get .6. For the portion of the disjunctive formula that applies when both disjuncts are positive, we get a value of .5 + .6 − .3 = .8. So, in this case we are 80% certain that the dog is friendly.

The certainty factor approach is a simple mechanism that works relatively well but is usually replaced by a more complete probabilistic approach such as the application of Bayes's rule or the use of Bayesian networks.

6.2.3 Bayesian Networks

A **Bayesian network** is a diagram that shows the conditional relationships of propositions in the current problem. For example, the degree of friendliness of a dog might have an effect on other propositions, such as the likelihood of it being petted. This condition might also have an effect on the likelihood that you will talk to the owner. It might also have an effect on whether or not you make it to the next meeting. This complicated situation can be represented by simple diagrams like that shown in Figure 6.2.

Figure 6.2 also includes two causes for the friendliness of the dog: the dog is well fed and it has a caring owner. It could also be the case that the fact that owner is caring might also increase the likelihood that the dog is well fed, a situation that would imply another arrow from "Caring owner" to "Well-fed dog." These diagrams can become quite complex, but they explicitly show where there are dependencies between different propositions and they speed up the propagation of probabilities.

Bayesian network diagrams can be parsed by using graph algorithms and interpreted by using probability theory.

FIGURE 6.2

A simple Bayesian network about dogs and owners

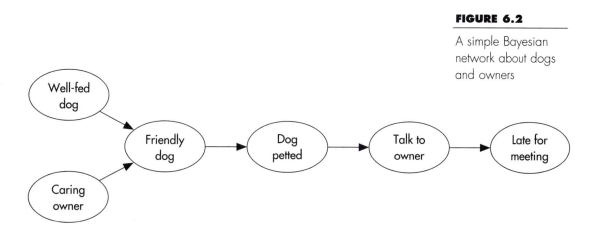

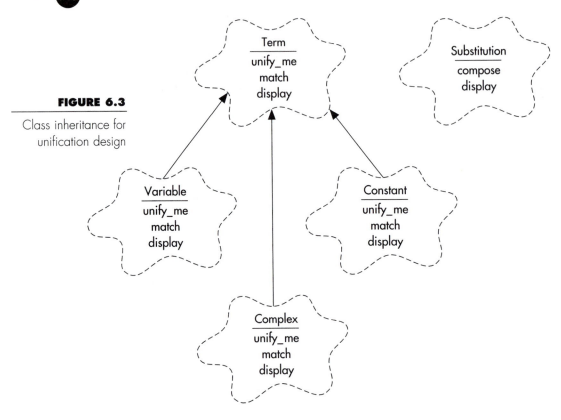

FIGURE 6.3

Class inheritance for
unification design

6.3 DESIGN OF AN OBJECT-ORIENTED SYSTEM FOR LOGIC

Suppose we want to design an object-oriented system to support the
unification of logical terms, as described in the preceding sections.
First, we need to identify the key objects involved in unification.
There are two: terms to represent the logical expressions to be unified and substitutions to create the unifier for the terms. Next, we
must represent logical expressions in terms of their component
parts. We begin by defining a base class for all logical terms. Then
we will define specialized types of logical terms, to inherit those
common properties (Figure 6.3).

Another important design decision is the user interface for unification. We decided to focus on the interface for "complex" terms
that contain variables. That is, the user of these classes will create
objects of the "complex" class and then try to find the substitution
that is the most general unifier for them. The unification classes
can then help form the basis for other systems that depend on the
use of logic terms, such as expert systems (discussed in Chapter 8),

theorem-proving systems (discussed in Chapter 9), and planning systems (discussed in Chapter 10).

6.4 USING C++ FOR LOGIC

To use the C++ programming language for FOPL, we need to build up classes that describe objects in the domain. We will illustrate this process by defining a class for clauses and then presenting a unification algorithm that uses that class.

6.4.1 Defining Classes for Unification

Two classes will be used for unification: a Substitution class and a Term class. The Substitution class is used to define substitutions (Section 6.1.2). The Term class defines objects, which will be unified. For this program, complex objects are predicates with any number of parameters.

The following code implements the interfaces defined for the classes Substitution and Term, including the classes Var (for variable terms), Constant (for constant terms), and Complex (for compound terms). This definition follows the overall design described in Section 6.3.

```
//file logic.h
#ifndef _LOGIC_H_
#define _LOGIC_H_

#include <stdio.h>
#include <stdlib.h>
#include <string.h>
#include <ctype.h>
#include <iostream.h>
#include "xstring.h"
#include "array.h"

/*
 * TermType is used for runtime type information
 * to determine if pointers or references to
 * derivatives of class Term are of the same type.
 */
enum TermType {Var_T, Constant_T, Complex_T};

/* Forward declaration. */
class Substitution;
```

```
class Var;

/*
 * Class Term is a base class common to class Var,
 * Constant and Complex. This base class is needed
 * so that (pointers to) objects of each of these
 * types can be stored in the same container class.
 * The actual type of an object is determined by
 * gettype(). Matching and unification of two Term
 * objects is done by match() and unify_me()
 * respectively.
 */
class Term
{
  public:
      virtual ~Term();
      virtual TermType gettype() const = 0;
      virtual int unify_me(const Term &,
                           Substitution &) const = 0;
      virtual int match(const Term &) const = 0;
      virtual Term *dup() const = 0;
      virtual void display(ostream &) const = 0;
      virtual const Term *get_realvalue(const
                           Substitution &) const = 0;
      virtual int occurs_in(const Var *) const;
      Term *clone() const;
      int operator==(const Term &other);
};


/*
 * Class Var represents variables. Variables must
 * be expressions of the form "X1" and "Y5", i.e.,
 * one capital letter and an integer. If the
 * integer is 1 it may be left out, so "X" is
 * equivalent to "X1". The capital letter is
 * treated as a sign and the integer as the sign's
 * alue. An array is used to keep track of the
 * highest value of each sign so that variables can
 * easily be updated to a "fresh" value.
 * During unification the substitution of variables
 * is not actually carried out. Instead, if a
 * variable X is to be replaced by term T, this
 * information is saved in an environment list, and
 * every occurence of X will be treated as if it
 * were T. Information from the environment list,
```

```
 * i.e., the actual value of a variable, is
 * retrieved by function get_realvalue().
 */
class Var : public Term
{
  public:
      Var(const char *);
      TermType gettype() const;
      int unify_me(const Term &, Substitution &)
                  const;
      int match(const Term &) const;
      Term *dup() const;
      void display(ostream &) const;
      void update();
      const Term *get_realvalue(const Substitution &)
                                   const;
      private:
      int val;
      char name;
      static TermType type;
      static unsigned int vartable[26];
};


/*
 * Class Constant represents constants. Constants
 * are strings and as such each Constant object
 * contains a String object.
 */
class Constant : public Term
{
  public:
      Constant(const char *);
      TermType gettype() const;
      int unify_me(const Term &, Substitution &)
                  const;
      int match(const Term &) const;
      Term *dup() const;
      void display(ostream &) const;
      const Term *get_realvalue(const Substitution
                                   &) const;
  private:
      String val;

      static TermType type;
};
```

```
/*
 * Class Complex represents predicates, i.e.,
 * expressions of the form "man(X)", "f(a, b(Y2))".
 * A predicate is regarded as a combination of a
 * functor and its arguments: variables, constants
 * and other predicates. The functor is represented
 * by a String object and the arguments by a list
 * to pointer of objects to Term objects:
 * PtrList<Term>.
 */
class Complex : public Term
{
  friend ostream &operator<<(ostream &, const
  Complex &);
  public:
      Complex();
      Complex(const char *);
    Complex &operator=(const Complex &);
      Complex &operator=(const char *);
      int operator==(const Complex &) const;
      int operator!=(const Complex &) const;
      Complex *clone() const;
      int unify(const Complex &, Substitution &)
              const;
      void apply_subst(Substitution &);
      void update_vars();
      void update_vars(Substitution &);
      void display() const;
      int notempty() const;
  private:
      TermType gettype() const;
      int match(const Term &) const;
      int unify_me(const Term &, Substitution &)
              const;
      Term *dup() const;
      const Term *get_realvalue(const Substitution &)
                          const;
      int occurs_in(const Var *) const;
      void display(ostream &) const;
      void parse_string(const char *);
      char *read_body(char *, char *);
      void parse_error(char *, char *, char *);

      String functor;
    PtrArray<Term> arguments;
```

```
        static TermType type;
};


/*
 * Class Binding represents bindings: pairs of
 * variables and values that the variables are
 * bound to. Bindings are stored in a Substitution
 * object.
 */
class Binding
{
   friend ostream &operator<<(ostream &, const
                                    Binding &);
   friend Substitution;
   public:
       Binding(const Binding &);
       Binding(const Var &, const Term &);
       ~Binding();
     Binding &operator=(const Binding &);
       int operator==(const Binding &) const;
       Binding *clone() const;
       void replace_binding(Binding *);
   private:
     Var *first;
       Term *second;
};


/*
 * Class Substitution represents substitutions:
 * collections of bindings. Class Substitution
 * therefore contains a list of Binding objects:
 * PtrList<Binding>.
 */
class Substitution
{
   friend ostream &operator<<(ostream &, const
                                  Substitution &);
   public:
       int operator==(const Substitution &) const;
       int operator!=(const Substitution &) const;
       Substitution *clone() const;
       int is_empty() const;
       int compose(const Substitution &);
       void update(const Substitution &);
       void clear();
```

```
        void add_binding(const Var &, const Term &);
        const Term *get_bound(const Var &) const;
    private:
        int occurs_in(const Var *) const;

        PtrArray<Binding> bindings;
};

#endif
```

The following code implements the methods defined for the classes Substitution and Term, including the classes Var (for variable terms), Constant (for constant terms), and Complex (for compound terms). This implemenation follows the design described in Section 6.3.

```
//file logic.cpp
/*
 * The unification algorithm follows the design of
 * Fitting "First-Order Logic and Automated
 * Theorem Proving": if a binding is found for two
 * terms the substitution will not actually be
 * caried out. Instead, if the variable X is to be
 * replaced by term T, every occurence of X will be
 * treated as if it were T. These bindings, i.e.,
 * pairs of X/T, are saved in an environment list.
 * Every time a variable is encountered, this list
 * is checked to determine the "real" value of the
 * variable. The environment list also serves as
 * the solution to the unification process because
 * when the unification process ends, it will
 * represent the substitution that will unify both
 * terms. In one important respect we don't follow
 * Fitting: every binding that is added to the
 * environment list is composed immediately.
 */

#include "logic.h"

/*
 * static variables used to determine the type of
 * the each logic class.
 */
TermType Var::type = Var_T;
TermType Constant::type = Constant_T;
TermType Complex::type = Complex_T;
```

```
/*
 * Every object of type Var is treated as a sign
 * (a capital letter) with a value. To keep track
 * of the highest value used for each sign a
 * static array is used.
 */
unsigned int Var::vartable[26] = {0,0,0,0,0,0,0,0,
0,0,0,0,0,0,0,0,0,0,0,0,0,0,0,0,0,0};

Term::~Term()
{
}

Term *Term::clone() const
{
  return(dup());
}
int Term::operator==(const Term &other)
{
  return(match(other));
}

/*
 * occurs_in() makes sense only for objects of type
 * Complex object, in case of Var and Constant
 * object the result is always false.
 */
int Term::occurs_in(const Var *) const
{
    return(0);
}

/*
 * This routine parses and creates a Var object. A
 * variable consists of a capital letter and a
 * number. The capital letter is used as a sign
 * whose value (the number) is stored in an array.
 * When a new value for a sign is introduced, the
 * array is updated accordingly. This procedure
 * makes it possible to introduce a simple
 * "variable updating" routine, update_vars(), used
 * to make the variables in a term unique.
 */
Var::Var(const char *str)
{
```

```
      name = *str;

    val = atoi(str + 1);
    if (val > vartable[name - 'A'])
        vartable[name - 'A'] = val;
}

TermType Var::gettype() const
{
  return(type);
}



/*
 * Get_realvalue() determines the actual value/type
 * of a variable: whenever a variable is bound to
 * a new value, the binding is not applied
 * immediately but stored in the substitution. This
 * routine checks if the variable is part of the
 * substitution. If it is, the new value of the
 * variable is returned; if not, the variable
 * itself is returned.
 */
const Term *Var::get_realvalue(const Substitution
                                    &subst) const
{
  const Term *ret = subst.get_bound(*this);
  return(ret ? ret: this);
}


int Var::unify_me(const Term &other, Substitution
                  &subst) const
{
  const Term *one, *two;

  /*
   * Get the real value of the variable, i.e., the
   * value that the variable is bound to, in the
   * substitution. Because this may be a different
   * type, it may be necessary to call unify_me()
   * again.
   */
  one = get_realvalue(subst);
  if (one->gettype() != Var_T)
      return(one->unify_me(other, subst));
```

```
   /*
    * Because the second term may be of type Var,
    * also get its real value.
    */
   two = other.get_realvalue(subst);

   /* If there's a direct match, no substitution is
    * needed.
    */
   if (one->match(*two))
       return(1);

   /*
    * At this point the unification will succeed
    * unless the variable is part of the second
    * term, i.e., perform the occurs check.
    */
   if (two->occurs_in((Var *)one))
       return(0);

   /* Update the substition with the new binding. */
   subst.add_binding(*(Var *)one, *two);
   return(1);
}

int Var::match(const Term &other) const
{
  if (other.gettype() != type)
      return(0);
  return((((Var &)other).name == name) &&
                     (((Var &)other).val == val));
}
Term *Var::dup() const
{
  return(new Var(*this));
}

void Var::display(ostream &stream) const
{
  stream << name;
  if (val)
      stream << val;
}

/*
```

```
 * Update() updates the variable by increasing the
 * array entry of the sign (the capital letter)
 * associated with the variable and assigning this
 * value to the Var object.
 */
void Var::update()
{
  vartable[name - 'A']++;
  val = vartable[name - 'A'];
}


Constant::Constant(const char *str)
{
  val = str;
}


TermType Constant::gettype() const
{
  return(type);
}


const Term *Constant::get_realvalue(const
Substitution &subst) const
{
  /* The real value of a Constant object is the
  /* object itself. */
  return(this);
}


int Constant::unify_me(const Term &other,
                       Substitution &subst) const
{
  const Term *two;

  /*
   * Because the second term may be of type Var,
   * get its actual value, i.e., the value that the
   * variable is bound to in the substitution.
   */
  two = other.get_realvalue(subst);

  /* If there's a direct match, no substitution is
   * needed. */
  if (match(*two))
      return(1);
```

```
  /* Unification succeeds only if the second term
   * is a variable. */
  if (two->gettype() == Var_T)
  {
      subst.add_binding(*(Var *)two, *this);
      return(1);
  }
  return(0);
}

int Constant::match(const Term &other) const
{
  return((other.gettype() == type) && (((Constant &)
                               other).val == val));
}

Term *Constant::dup() const
{
  return(new Constant(*this));
}

void Constant::display(ostream &stream) const
{
  stream << val;
}

Complex::Complex()
{
}

Complex::Complex(const char *str)
{
  parse_string(str);
}

Complex &Complex::operator=(const Complex &other)
{
  if (this != &other)
  {
    functor = other.functor;
    arguments = other.arguments;
  }

  return(*this);
}
```

```
Complex &Complex::operator=(const char *str)
{
  arguments.clear(DoDel);
  parse_string(str);
  return(*this);
}

int Complex::operator==(const Complex &other) const
{
  return(match(other));
}

int Complex::operator!=(const Complex &other) const
{
  return(!match(other));
}

TermType Complex::gettype() const
{
  return(type);
}

const Term *Complex::get_realvalue(const
Substitution &subst) const
{
  /* The real value of a Complex object is the
  /* object itself. */
  return(this);
}

/*
 * Unify() serves as the interface function for
 * unifying two objects of type Complex.
 */
int Complex::unify(const Complex &other,
                   Substitution &subst) const
{
  if (!unify_me(other, subst))
  {
     subst.clear();
     return(0);
  }
  return(1);
}
```

```
int Complex::unify_me(const Term &other,
                      Substitution &subst) const
{
  const Term *two;
  Complex *c_two;
  int arity;

  /*
   * Because the second term may be of type Var,
   * get its actual value, i.e., the value that the
   * variable is bound to in the substitution.
   */
  two = other.get_realvalue(subst);

  /* If there's a direct match, no substitution is
   * needed. */
  if (match(*two))
      return(1);

  /*
   * If the second term is a variable and if it
   * does not occur in the current term,
   * unification succeeds.
   */
  if (two->gettype() == Var_T && !occurs_in((Var
                                             *)two))
  {
      subst.add_binding(*(Var *)two, *this);
      return(1);


  /* If the second term is a constant, unification
   * fails. */
  if (two->gettype() == Constant_T)
      return(0);

  /*
   * Because the second term is neither a variable
   * nor a constant, it must be of type Complex.
   * First determine if the functor and arity match
   * and next try to unify the arguments.
   */
  c_two = (Complex *)two;
  arity = arguments.getsize();
```

```
        if ((c_two->functor != functor) ||
                    (c_two->arguments.getsize() != arity))
            return(0);

      /*
       * Call unify_me() recursively to check if the
       * arguments of both terms can be unified.
       */
      for (int i = 0; i < arity; i++)
      {
          if (!arguments[i]->unify_me(*c_two->
                                    arguments[i], subst))
              return(0);
      }
      return(1);
}

int Complex::match(const Term &other) const
{
    if (other.gettype() != type)
        return(0);

    Complex &c_other = (Complex &)other;

    /* Check if the functors match. */
    if (c_other.functor != functor)
        return(0);

    /* Compare the arguments of both objects to each
    /* other. */
    return(arguments == c_other.arguments);
}

Complex *Complex::clone() const
{
    return(new Complex(*this));
}

Term *Complex::dup() const
{
    return(new Complex(*this));
}

void Complex::display(ostream &stream) const
{
```

```
  int arity = arguments.getsize();

  stream << functor << "(";
  if (arity)
  {
      arguments[0]->display(stream);
      for (int i = 1; i < arity; i++)
      {
        stream << ", ";
        arguments[i]->display(stream);
      }
  }
  stream << ")";
}

ostream &operator<<(ostream &stream, const
                    Complex &complex)
{
  complex.display(stream);
  return(stream);
}

void Complex::display() const
{
  cout << *this;
}

int Complex::notempty() const
{
  return(arguments.getsize());
}

/*
 * Occurs_in() is the implementation of the occurs
 * check: it checks if the Complex object contains
 * the supplied Variable.
 */
int Complex::occurs_in(const Var *var) const
{
  int arity = arguments.getsize();

  for (int i = 0; i < arity; i++)
  {
      /*
       * If the argument is itself a Complex object,
```

```
    * call occurs_in() on it recursively.
    */
   if (arguments[i]->gettype() == Complex_T)
   {
     if (arguments[i]->occurs_in(var))
         return(1);
   }
   /* If the argument matches the variable the
    * occurs check succeeds. */
   else if (arguments[i]->match(*var))
           return(1);
 }
 return(0);
}


/*
 * Apply_subst() applies a substitution to Complex:
 * update those variables in the Complex that are
 * bound to a new value in the substitution.
 */
void Complex::apply_subst(Substitution &subst)
{
  const Term *val;
  int i, arity = arguments.getsize();

  for (i = 0; i < arity; i++)
  {
    /*
     * If the argument is a variable, determine if
     * it is bound in the substitution. If so, the
     * variable is deleted and replaced by a copy
     * of the term that the variable is bound to.
     */
    if (arguments[i]->gettype() == Var_T)
    {
        val = subst.get_bound(*(Var *)arguments[i]);
          if (val)
          {
          delete(arguments[i]);
          arguments[i] = val->dup();
          }
    }
    /*
    /* If the argument is itself of type Complex
      *also call apply_subst() on it recursively.
```

```
       */
     else if (arguments[i]->gettype() == Complex_T)
        ((Complex *)arguments[i])->apply_subst(subst);
   }
}


/*
 * Update_vars() updates all variables in Complex,
 * i.e., it makes the variables unique. The original
 * and new values of the variables are stored in
 * the subsitution supplied. The substitution may
 * then be used to update other terms that (may or
 * may not) contain the same variables, which must
 * be bound to the same new values. Note that
 * normally the substitution supplied to this
 * function will be empty. But this is not
 * mandatory. If there are already bindings present
 * in the substitution, they will be used to update
 * the variables in the Complex object, i.e., the
 * same procedure used in apply_subst() will be
 * applied. This comes in handy in case these
 * functions must be combined when some of the
 * variables must be replaced by the bindings in
 * the substitution and others must be updated (for
 * an example of this use of update_vars(), see the
 * STRIPS planner).
 */
void Complex::update_vars(Substitution &subst)
{
  const Term *term;
  int i, arity = arguments.getsize();

  for (i = 0; i < arity; i++)
  {
      /*
       * For every variable in the arguments list,
       * check it if is already part of the
       * substitution. If it is not, the variable
       * must still be updated and a new binding
       * consisting of OldVar/NewVar is added to
       * the substitution. If it is, the variable
       * has already been updated and must only be
       * replaced by its new value.
       */
    if (arguments[i]->gettype() == Var_T)
```

```
      {
        term = subst.get_bound(*(Var *)arguments[i]);
        if (!term)
        {
          Var old = *(Var *)arguments[i];
          ((Var *)arguments[i])->update();

             subst.add_binding(old, *arguments[i]);
        }
        else
        {
          delete arguments[i];
          arguments[i] = term->dup();
        }
      }
      /*
       * If the argument is itself of type Complex
       * call update_vars() on it recursively.
       */
      else if (arguments[i]->gettype() == Complex_T)
        ((Complex *)arguments[i])->update_vars(subst);
  }
}

void Complex::update_vars()
{
  Substitution subst;
  update_vars(subst);
}

Binding::Binding(const Var &t1, const Term &t2)
{
  first = (Var *)t1.dup();
  second = t2.dup();
}

Binding::Binding(const Binding &other)
{
  first = (Var *)other.first->dup();
  second = other.second->dup();
}

Binding &Binding::operator=(const Binding &other)
{
  if (this != &other)
```

```
  {
    delete first;
    delete second;

    first = (Var *)other.first->dup();
    second = other.second->dup();
  }
  return(*this);
}

Binding::~Binding()
{
  delete first;
  delete second;
}

int Binding::operator==(const Binding &other) const
{
  if (!first->match(*other.first))
      return(0);
  return(second->match(*other.second));
}

Binding *Binding::clone() const
{
  return(new Binding(*this));
}

/*
 * Replace_binding() determines if the current
 * binding must be updated with the information
 * contained in another binding and, if true,
 * performs the update. For example, if the current
 * binding is X/Y and the other binding is Y/a,
 * the current binding is updated to become Y/a.
 */
void Binding::replace_binding(Binding *bind)
{
  /*
   * If the variable of the current binding is
   * bound to an object of type Complex, this
   * object may contain variables that must be
   * updated with the binding information of the
   * other binding. To do this, a temporary
   * substitution will be created consisting of the
```

```
    * information in the other binding, and this
    * substitution is applied to the Complex object
    * by calling apply_subst().
    */
   if (second->gettype() == Complex_T)
   {
       Substitution s;

       s.add_binding(*bind->first, *bind->second);
       ((Complex *)second)->apply_subst(s);
   }
   /*
    * To determine if the other binding contains new
    * binding information, the variable of the
    * current binding must match the variable of the
    * other binding. If true, the current binding is
    * updated by replacing the value the variable is
    * bound to with the new value from the other
    * binding.
    */
   else if(second->match(*bind->first))
   {
     delete(second);
     second = bind->second->dup();
   }
}
ostream &operator<<(ostream &stream, const
                    Binding &bind)
{
  bind.first->display(stream);
  stream << "/";
  bind.second->display(stream);
  return(stream);
}


int Substitution::operator==(const Substitution
                              &other) const
{
  if (bindings.getsize() != other.bindings.getsize())
      return(0);

  for (int i = 0; i < bindings.getsize(); i++)
      if (other.bindings.find(bindings[i]) < 0)
          return(0);
  return(1);
```

```
}

int Substitution::operator!=(const Substitution
                              &other) const
{
  return(!(*this == other));
}

Substitution *Substitution::clone() const
{
  return(new Substitution(*this));
}

int Substitution::is_empty() const
{
  return(bindings.getsize() == 0);
}

/*
 * Add_binding() adds a new Var/Term pair to the
 * substitution. Two things must be done: a new
 * binding consisting of Var/Term must be created
 * and added to the substitution, and existing
 * binding information must be updated with the new
 * information supplied by this new binding.
 */
void Substitution::add_binding(const Var &var,
                               const Term &term)
{
  /* Create a new binding consisting of Var/Term. */
  Binding *bind = new Binding(var, term);
  /* Update existing bindings where necessary. */
  for (int i = 0; i < bindings.getsize(); i++)
      bindings[i]->replace_binding(bind);

  /* Add the new binding to the other bindings. */
  bindings += bind;
}

/*
 * Compose() composes two substitutions. Before the
 * actual composition can take place, two things
 * must be checked. If {X/Y} is a binding in the
 * first substitution, X must not be bound to a
 * different value, e.g., {X/a}, in the other
```

```
 * substitution. If this check fails, the
 * subsitutions are incompatible. The second check
 * is a kind of occurs check: if the first
 * substitution contains a binding A {X/g(Y)} and
 * the second substitution contains a binding
 * B {Y/f(X)}, composition is not possible because
 * of the recurrence of X in the second half of
 * binding B.
 */
int Substitution::compose(const Substitution &other)
{
  const Term *term;
  int i;

  for (i = 0; i < bindings.getsize(); i++)
  {
      /*
       * Determine if the other substitution
       * contains a binding for this variable.
       */
    term = other.get_bound(*(Var *)bindings[i]->first);

      if (term)
    {
       /*
        * It does. Check if the two values for the
        * variables are identical (check 1).
        */
       if (!bindings[i]->second->match(*term))
          return(0);
       }
       else
       {
       /*
        * They are not. Check if the variable occurs
        * in the second half of any of the bindings
        * of the other substitution (check 2).
        */
       if (other.occurs_in((Var *)bindings[i]->first))
          return(0);
     }
  }

  /*
   * Perform the composition, but take care not to
```

```
         * include any bindings from the other
         * substitution that are already part of the
         * current binding.
         */
      for (i = 0; i < other.bindings.getsize(); i++)
          if (bindings.find(other.bindings[i]) < 0)
          add_binding(*other.bindings[i]->first,
                             *other.bindings[i]->second);

      return(1);
    }


    /*
     * Update() performs a limited form of composition.
     * Its main use is to update substitutions like
     * {X/Y} with other substitutions like {Y/a} (so
     * that {X/Y} becomes {X/a}). It cannot be used to
     * update substitutions like {X/f(Y)} and {Y/a}. It
     * differs from compose() in two respects: it does
     * not add the new binding, e.g., {Y/a}, to the
     * current substitution and it does not perform the
     * "occurs check", so be careful when calling this
     * routine.
     */
    void Substitution::update(const Substitution &other)
    {
      const Term *term;
      int i, numbind = bindings.getsize();

      for (i = 0; i < numbind; i++)
      {
          if (bindings[i]->second->gettype() == Var_T)
          {
            /*
             * Determine if the other substitution
             * contains a binding for this variable. If
             * it does, the old value for the variable
             * is deleted and replaced by the new one.
             */
            term = other.get_bound(*(Var *)
                                    bindings[i]->second);
            if (term)
            {
                delete bindings[i]->second;
                bindings[i]->second = term->dup();
```

```
            }
          }
        }
}


/*
 * Occurs_in() checks if a variable is part of any
 * of the bindings that the substitution consists of.
 */
int Substitution::occurs_in(const Var *var) const
{
  int numbind = bindings.getsize();

  for (int i = 0; i < numbind; i++)
      if (bindings[i]->second->occurs_in(var))
          return(1);

  return(0);
}


/*
 * Get_bound() checks if a variable is part of the
 * substitution and, if true, returns the term that
 * is it bound to.
 */
const Term *Substitution::get_bound(const Var
                                      &term) const
{
  int i, numbind = bindings.getsize();

  for (i = 0; i < numbind; i++)
  {
      if (bindings[i]->first->match(term))
      return(bindings[i]->second);
  }
  return(NULL);
}


ostream &operator<<(ostream &stream, const
                    Substitution &subst)
{
  int numbind = subst.bindings.getsize();

  stream << "(";
```

```
    if (numbind)
    {
        stream << *subst.bindings[0];
        for (int i = 1; i < numbind; i++)
            stream << ", " << *subst.bindings[i];
    }
    stream << ")";
    return(stream);
}

void Substitution::clear()
{
  bindings.clear(DoDel);
}


/*
 * Parsing routines, including a limited and
 * primitive form of error checking. Examine at
 * your own risk.
 */
void Complex::parse_string(const char *str)
{
  char tmp, *foo, *p;

  if (!(foo = strdup(str)))
  {
        puts("Complex::Complex() - Out of memory");
        exit(0);
  }

  for (p = foo; *p && isalpha(*p); p++)
        ;
  if (!*p)
        parse_error("Unexpected end of term", foo, p);
  if (*p != '(')
      parse_error("Unexpected character", foo, p);

  tmp = *p;
  *p = '\0';
  /* Initialize functor. */
  functor = foo;

  *p = tmp;
  /* Initialize arguments. */
```

```
    read_body(foo, p + 1);
    delete(foo);
}

char *Complex::read_body(char *str, char *pos)
{
  Term *term;
  char c, *p, *start, *space;
  char *end_msg = "unexpected end of term";

  for (p = pos; *p; p++)
  {
     while (*p && isspace(*p))
       p++;
     if (!*p)
       parse_error(end_msg, str, p);
     start = p;

     /* If the term starts with a capital letter,
      * it must be a variable. */
    if (isupper(*p))
      {
         while (*++p && isdigit(*p))
    ;
    if (!*p)
         parse_error(end_msg, str, p);

    if (isspace(*p))
    {
         space = p;
         while (*++p && isspace(*p))
            ;
         if (!*p)
            parse_error(end_msg, str, p);
         if (*p != ',' && *p != ')')
            parse_error("unexpected character",
                          str, p);
         c = *space;
         *space = '\0';
         term = new Var(start);
         *space = c;
    }
    else
    {
         if (*p != ',' && *p != ')')
```

```
                    parse_error("digit expected", str, p);
            c = *p;
          *p = '\0';
          term = new Var(start);
          *p = c;
    }
}

/* Otherwise it must be a constant or complex. */
else
{
  while (*++p && isalpha(*p))
        ;
  if (!*p)
      parse_error(end_msg, str, p);

  /* Found a complex? */
  if (*p == '(')
  {
    Complex *cp = new Complex;
      /* term = new Complex(str, start, p); */
      c = *p;
      *p = '\0';
      cp->functor = start;
      *p = c;
      p = cp->read_body(str, p + 1);
    if (!*p)
          parse_error(end_msg, str, p);
      if (*p != ')')
          parse_error(") expected", str, p);
      else
          p++;
      term = cp;
  }

  /* Otherwise it must be a constant. */
  else
  {
    if (!*p)
          parse_error(end_msg, str, p);
    if (isspace(*p))
    {
          space = p;
          while (*++p && isspace(*p))
              ;
```

```
                    if (!*p)
                        parse_error(end_msg, str, p);
                    if (*p != ',' && *p != ')')
                        parse_error("unexpected character",
                                        str, p);
                    c = *space;
                    *space = '\0';
                    term = new Constant(start);
                    *space = c;
                }
                else
                {
                    if (*p != ',' && *p != ')')
                            parse_error("character or digit
                                            expected", str, p);
                    c = *p;
                    *p = '\0';
                    term = new Constant(start);
                    *p = c;
                }
            }
        }

        arguments += term;
        if (!isspace(*p) && *p != ',')
            return(p);
    }
}

void Complex::parse_error(char *msg, char *str,
                                char *pos)
{
    int i = pos - str;

    printf("%s\n", str);

    while (i-)
        putchar(' ');

    if (*pos)
        printf("^ '%c': %s\n", *pos, msg);
    else
        printf("^: %s\n", msg);

    exit(0);
}
```

6.4.2 Unification

The code in the preceding section is a C++ implementation of the most general unifier (mgu) algorithm described in Section 6.1.3, including the complex and substitution classes. The implementation given in the preceding section has unification algorithms for terms of each data type: variable, constant, and complex (i.e., compound). Much of the code given in that implementation is to help in parsing the character strings that form logic clauses. Once the parsing is done, however, we can then write relatively simple programs to actually unify expressions. The following short C++ main program illustrates how these routines are used.

```
//file (from description file for logic)
#include "logic.h"

void main()
{
  Complex a,
    b("f(g(Y), f(g(a), Z))"),
    c("f(X11, g(b))"),
    d("f(a, Y1234)"),
    e("g(a)"),
      f(b);

  Substitution s, s2, s3;

  cout << a << "   " << f << "\n";
  /*
   * Outputs:
   * ()   f(g(Y), f(g(a), Z))
   */

  a = "f(X, f(X, Y))";

  cout << a << "\n" << b << "\n" << a.unify(b, s) ↵
                                 << "\n";
  /*
   * Outputs:
   * f(X, f(X, Y))
   * f(g(Y), f(g(a), Z))
   * 1
   */

  cout << s << "\n";
  /*
```

```
  * Outputs:
  * (X/g(a), Y/a, Z/a)
  */

a.apply_subst(s);
cout << a << "\n";
/*
  * Outputs:
  * f(g(a), f(g(a), a))
  */

cout << (a == b) << " " << (a == a) << "\n";
/*
  * Outputs:
  * 0 1
  */

c.unify(d, s2);
s3 = s2;
cout << s2 << " " << (s == s) << " " << " " <<
                (s == s2) << " " << s3 << "\n";
/*
  * Outputs:
  * (X11/a, Y1234/g(b)) 1  0 (X11/a, Y1234/g(b))
  */

cout << e << "\n";
/*
  * Outputs:
  * g(a)
  */
e = d;
cout << e << " " << d << "\n";
/*
  * Outputs:
  * f(a, Y1234) f(a, Y1234)
  */
}
```

6.5 SUMMARY

In this chapter we introduce the resolution proof procedure and reasoning with imprecise knowledge. Resolution is a popular proof procedure that is incorporated in many automated theorem-proving systems because it is relatively easy to translate into a working program. We also present a method of encoding logic statements and a way of unifying them by using an object-oriented design and then C++. Once built in C++, the unification mechanism provides a basis from other procedures used later in this text, including a resolution-based theorem prover, a Prolog-like interpreter, and a planner.

6.6 REFERENCES

See Chapter 4 for a list of general references on the use of logic in AI. Resolution is extensively covered in Genesereth and Nilsson (1987) and Chang and Lee (1973). Shafer and Pearl (1990) provides an excellent set of papers on reasoning with uncertainty.

6.7 EXERCISES

Warm-up Exercises

6.1. Construct an example to show that composition of substitutions is not commutative; that is, show $\phi(\sigma_1 \circ \sigma_2) \neq \phi(\sigma_2 \circ \sigma_1)$.

6.2. Construct an example to show that resolution (without including the negated goal) is not complete. Using the example you just constructed, show how it can be shown by adding the negated goal.

6.3. What can be done with propositions that have certainty factors of zero assigned? Is there any useful inference that they can be involved in? Is so, give an example. If not, explain why.

6.4. Should propositions with a certainty factor of zero be allowed to be entered in the knowledge base? Why or why not?

6.5. Create a Bayesian network for the following propositions:
I studied for the exam.
I passed the exam.
I attended every class.
I read the textbook.
I took notes.
I did not sleep in class.
I got an A in the course.
I understood the concepts presented in the course.
The instructor was easy to understand.
The instructor understood the material.
The instructor did not sleep in class.

Homework Exercises

6.6. Use resolution to solve homework problem 4.10, the hat problem.

6.7. Use resolution to solve homework problem 4.11, the tribe problem.

6.8. Use resolution to solve homework problem 4.12, the plane problem.

6.9. Prove that composition of substitution sets is associative. In other words, show that $\phi(\sigma_1 \circ (\sigma_2 \circ \sigma_3)) = \phi((\sigma_1 \circ \sigma_2) \circ \sigma_3)$.

6.10. The following story is quoted from Niklaus *Wirth's Algorithms + Data Structures = Programs*.

> I married a widow (let's call her *W*) who has a grown-up daughter (call her *D*). My father (*F*), who visited us quite often, fell in love with my step-daughter and married her. Hence my father became my son-in-law, and my step-daughter became my mother. Some months later, my wife gave birth to a son (S_1), who became the brother-in-law of my father, as well as my uncle. The wife of my father, that is, my step-daughter, also had a son (S_2).

Using FOPL, create a set of expressions that represent the situation in the above story. Add expressions defining basic family relationships such as the definition of father-in-law. Use modus ponens on this system to prove the conclusion that "I am my own grandfather." Also use resolution to prove the same statement.

6.11. Determine whether the members of each of the following pairs of expressions unify with each other. If they do, give the most general unifier. If they do not, give a brief explanation.

a. *Color(tweety,yellow)* and *Color(X,Y)*

b. *Color(tweety,yellow)* and *Color(X,X)*

c. *Color(hat(postman),blue)* and *Color(hat(Y),X)*

d. *R(f(X),b)* and *R(X,Z)*

e. *R(f(Y),Y,X)* and *R(X,f(a),f(V))*

g. *Loves(X,Y)* and *Loves(Y,X)*

6.12. Find the most general unifier of the set {*P(X,Y,Z)*, *P(W,U,W)*, *P(a,U,U)*}. Note that you need to generalize the algorithm to handle more than just two literals at once.

6.13. Prove that resolution is refutation complete; that is, prove that the procedure of including the negated goal is complete.

6.14. Heads I win; tails you lose. Use resolution to show that I win. What assumptions must you make to make resolution usable? What commonsense knowledge did you use to determine what assumptions were reasonable? (Problem adapted from Genesereth and Nilsson, 1987.)

6.15. Express Fermat's last theorem in predicate logic. (Fermat's last theorem states that, for each natural number n, there exist natural numbers a, b, and c such that $a^n + b^n = c^n$, for $n > 2$.)

   a. Attempt to prove this theorem by using resolution.

   b. What problems are there in trying to prove this statement by using any of the methods discussed in this chapter?

6.16. Fluffy is a cat or Fluffy is not a cat. Fluffy is a cat. Use resolution to show that Fluffy is not "not a cat."

6.17. A substitution σ is called **idempotent** if $\sigma \equiv \sigma \circ \sigma$. Show that the MGU algorithm produces a most general unifier that is idempotent.

6.18. Suppose that σ_1 is an idempotent most general unifier for terms t_1 and t_2 and σ_2 is any most general unifier. Show that $\sigma_2 = \sigma_1 \circ \sigma_2$.

6.19. Examine the definition of certainty factors and determine whether they have a basis in probability theory. If they do, show how the rules are valid by using probability theory. If only some of the rules are valid, show why the valid ones are valid in probability theory and why the others are not valid.

6.20. Compute the probability of the hypothesis in the following rule (with probability .9 of being a valid rule):

if many ants are in your garden (Probability = .6) and

your garden is near your house (Probability = .7) and

your house is not completely sealed (Probability = .9) and

your house has not been sufficiently sprayed with pesticides (Probability = .6)

then your house will have ants inside

Programming Exercises

6.21. Write a C++ program using logic.h to unify the expressions in Exercises 6.11 and 6.12.

6.22. Modify logic.h and logic.cpp to find multiple unifiers rather than just the most general unifier.

Projects

6.23. Write a C++ program to convert a FOPL statement to clausal form. Your program should take statements of the following form and return a list of clauses:

(foreach X)(forall Y).((p(X) and (q(Y) or r(X)) implies s(Y))

Your program can assume that the statement is fully parenthesized and that the above statement represents all keywords that will be input (*foreach, forall, and, or,* and *implies*). Your program should implement the procedure given in this chapter, and you may wish to use the C++ class structure for terms given in this chapter.

7

KNOWLEDGE REPRESENTATION

Any mechanically embodied intelligent process will be comprised of structural ingredients that a) we as external observers naturally take to represent a propositional account of the knowledge that the overall process exhibits, and b) independent of such external semantical attribution, plan a formal but causal and essential role in engendering the behaviour that manifests that knowledge

BRIAN SMITH, 1985

7.1 FORMS OF KNOWLEDGE REPRESENTATION

The representation of knowledge is central to the development of an AI system. We must somehow represent relevant knowledge in a form that the AI system can manipulate. Unless a system has encoded knowledge, it cannot possibly be called intelligent. But the knowledge must be carefully encoded so that it fits the problem domain being considered. Operations such as inference of new facts or knowledge can be made more efficient by tuning the knowledge representation to the problem.

Because there are many different types of problems for which efficient knowledge representation schemes are needed, many schemes have been developed and continue to be used widely. Each different scheme of knowledge representation has its own particular benefits and drawbacks. For example, first-order predicate logic (FOPL) is capable of representing very wide ranges of knowledge in many ways. As a result of the expressive power of FOPL, the same piece of knowledge can be expressed in many different ways.

7.1.1 Some Forms of Knowledge Representation

Knowledge can be encoded in many different ways. We can encode knowledge directly in FOPL. Or knowledge can be encoded indirectly in a procedural representation of knowledge. **A procedural representation of knowledge** encodes *how* something is done by actually performing the knowledge it encodes. A program written in Prolog implements knowledge with the help of a procedural interpretation. Logic programming, when rigorously defined, is independent of a procedural interpretation and encodes knowledge directly in logical form. Representations of knowledge that are independent of a procedurial implementation are called **declarative representations of knowledge.** A square root function written in Pascal contains the knowledge necessary to implement square roots. However, that knowledge is not explicit and would be difficult to use to derive additional properties of the square root function. The ability to shoot an arrow into a bull's eye at 100 meters requires knowledge of how to physically perform this feat. But expressing this type of knowledge is difficult because the action requires the interaction of eyesight and many muscles and nerves. The knowledge that robots need to shoot an arrow into a bull's eye would have to be expressed in some way to allow the robot to perform at the same level.

A popular form of knowledge representation is a semantic network, which is a web of concepts linked together by relationships between the concepts. There are many types of semantic networks with a similar basic structure. Consider the semantic network in Figure 7.1, which describes how a shoe salesperson sells shoes. It consists of semantic nodes representing concepts (in this example, they are all nouns) and links between those concepts. The links (arrows) indicate relationships between the concepts. This example centers on the concept of selling and has a direct object, "shoes" (shoes are being sold), and an indirect object, the "Customer" (to whom the shoes are being sold). The "Salesperson" (in this case, "Ralph") uses his "voice" and "smile" as instruments in selling the shoes.

FIGURE 7.1

Semantic network representation of selling shoes

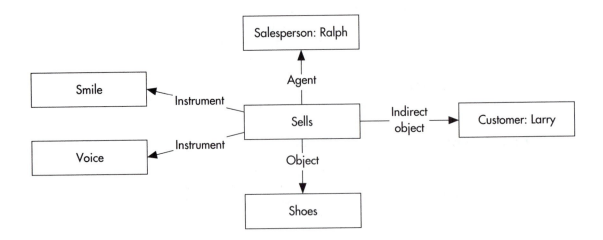

Other representations have different ways of encoding knowledge. Frames use a structure consisting of objects, which have slots to represent characteristics of the object. For example, consider a frame designed to express the concept of a person talking to another person (Figure 7.2). Although we can use a general structure to handle most cases of a person talking to another, each instance of this concept will have specific values for the various fields in the frame, such as who is talking, loudness, language spoken, and the person being talked to.

Another representation that has a more detailed structure is the script.[1] Scripts are a how-to guide for responding to a given situation. For example, a Fast-Food script might describe how to act when we visit a fast-food restaurant for a meal (Figure 7.3). In the script, we are expected to order something, pay for it, eat it, and leave.

This chapter introduces many of the key concepts of knowledge representation. Further detail is contained in later chapters: Chapter 11 contains more detail about interpreting natural language representations. Chapter 12 contains advanced topics for representing knowledge by using logic. Chapter 13 contains a detailed description of the Cyc project, which is concerned with the task of representing a large of amount of knowledge.

Name	Person_speaking
Isa	Act
Properties	Takes_time loudness who_talking language . . .
Defaults minute	Takes_time = 1 loudness = 1 decibels who_talking = Joe language = English

FIGURE 7.2

Frame representation of one person talking to another

---

[1] The definitions for the actions (called ACTs) in scripts are given later in this chapter.

Script:	Fast_Food	**Scene 1: Entering**
		C PTRANS C into restaurant
Track:	Eat_inside	C PTRANS C to counter
Props:	Counter	**Scene 2: Ordering**
	Food = F, Money,	C MBUILD Choice of Food, F
	Trash, Table, Can	C MTRANS 'I want F' to O
		C ATRANS Money to O
Roles:	Customer = C	C MBUILD Where to Sit
	Owner = O	C PTRANS to table
	Cook = K	C Move to C to sitting position
Entry Conditions:		**Scene 3: Eating**
C is hungry		C INGEST F
C has money		C MOVE C to standing position
		C MTRANS Trash to can
Results: C has less money		**Scene 4: Leaving**
C is not hungry		C PTRANS C to out of restaurant
O has moremoney		

FIGURE 7.3

Fast-food restaurant script

7.1.2 Components of Knowledge Representation

Sowa (1995) identifies three components of knowledge representation:

1. Logic provides the formal structure for knowledge representation and rules of inference.
2. Ontology defines the kinds of things that can exist and their interrelationships in some application domain.
3. Computation provides a method of implementing in a computer program the representation and inference mechanisms.

Sowa defines logic as "any declarative language that can be used to describe a subject and support inferences about it." As such, it includes not only first-order predicate logic (FOPL) but also techniques such as semantic networks, frames, scripts, and object-oriented models. Other specialized knowledge representation languages are CLASSIC, KIF, and CycL.

Ontology defines the kinds of things that can exist in the knowledge representation mechanism; it is usually represented as a hierarchy. An ontology functions much like an object-oriented class hierarchy, in which subclasses inherit properties from their superclasses. A simple example of such a hierachy is shown in Figure 7.4:

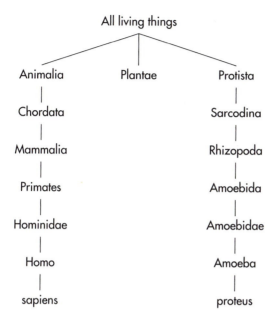

All living things

Animalia   Plantae   Protista

Chordata   Sarcodina

Mammalia   Rhizopoda

Primates   Amoebida

Hominidae   Amoebidae

Homo   Amoeba

sapiens   proteus

FIGURE 7.4

Partial ontology for living things

the hierarchy of kingdom, phylum, class, order, family, genus, and species for human beings and for amebas.

The ability to perform computation by using a computer program distinguishes knowledge representation from a philosophical description of knowledge. This area of study includes the development of mechanisms that ensure that computations are feasible and, we hope, efficient. In other words, there must be computable mechanisms such as compilers and interpreters that can use the knowledge represented and the inference mechanisms to produce usable knowledge.

7.2 DIFFICULTIES IN KNOWLEDGE REPRESENTATION

Representing knowledge presents many difficulties, partly because there are many different types of knowledge that need to be represented. The rules for the game of checkers can be represented quite easily by using IF-THEN rules. However, representing the knowledge required to shoot a bull's eye would be better done some other way.

Another difficulty stems from the necessity of representing knowledge in a form that can be used for inference and for adding new knowledge. The previously mentioned square-root function written in Pascal is an example of a representation that is very difficult to infer new knowledge from or add new knowledge to.

Third, some knowledge is inherently difficult to encode. It seems so obvious that no one has bothered to formalize it. Take, for example, the fact that cats shed their fur. How do we represent this piece of information so that we can infer that their fur will end up in the carpet or that we can control their shedding by periodically brushing them? This problem is not an easy one and its solution usually depends on deciding how the knowledge will be used well in advance of encoding it. It is often difficult to encode the relationships between a new piece of knowledge and an existing base of knowledge. Again, regarding the fact that cats shed their fur, we need to link this fact to other facts so that we can tell which cats we are talking about, when this occurs, and what the characteristics of their fur are.

7.2.1 Frame Problem

The **frame problem** is the problem of representing things that do *not* change when a rule is applied. Consider, for example, the problem of a robot that moves objects in a room. In the room is a table next to the window. The table has a lamp on it. Suppose we have a rule that is of the form "IF Object(X) and Position(X,P) and P ≠ Q and Push(X,Q), THEN Position(X,Q)." Then if we attempt to push the table, we do not know whether we are changing the position of the lamp or not. We need to define somehow that the position of the window is still the same after the move and the position of the lamp depends on the position of the table. Axioms that define what does not change are called **frame axioms**. We must define frame axioms for each action that may potentially change the value of each predicate that we have defined. If we have N predicates and A actions, then we would have to define $N \times A$ frame axioms.

7.2.2 Granularity

When representing a set of facts, the granularity of that representation must be chosen. (As we will see in *Cyc*, several granularities must be dealt with.) The **granularity** is the level of detail in the representation. For example, if we wish to represent the contour of a particular beach, we can represent it by the position of each individual grain of sand. However, such a detailed representation makes it computationally difficult to determine properties such as where a sand castle might be. Suppose instead that we represent the beach by a contour map and contour lines that represent multiples of six inches. Using this representation, we are more likely to be able to find sand castles. Expanding on the contour map representation, we can vary the granularity of our representation by changing the sensitivity of the contour lines. If we choose contour lines with a sensitivity of one-tenth of an inch, then we could potentially find breathing holes produced by sand crabs. However, by increasing the sensitivity, we would also increase the amount of computation required. In general, we want the granularity to be as general as possible for the types of problem solving that we propose to do.

7.2.3 Conflicting Inheritance

The inheritance of information from other pieces of knowledge is a highly desirable property for a knowledge representation scheme (Figure 7.5). Let's say we have a piece of knowledge that represents "Fluffy is a cat." But we do not want to have to encode everything about what it means to be a cat along with this piece of knowledge. What we would like to do is to inherit that knowledge from the knowledge that represents "cat." That is, we could infer that "Fluffy has fur" because cats have fur and Fluffy is an instance of a cat. Furthermore, we would not want to have to encode everything about what it means to be an animal in our representation of "cat." So we would want "cat" to inherit knowledge from "animal." If we know that animals are living, then we should be able to use our inheritance mechanisms to infer that "Fluffy is living." However, suppose that Fluffy is no longer living. We want to have some mechanism to describe what Fluffy's state is when it is different from what we would get from inheritance. That is, we need some mechanism to also specify exceptions. Some of the mechanisms are discussed in Section 7.4.

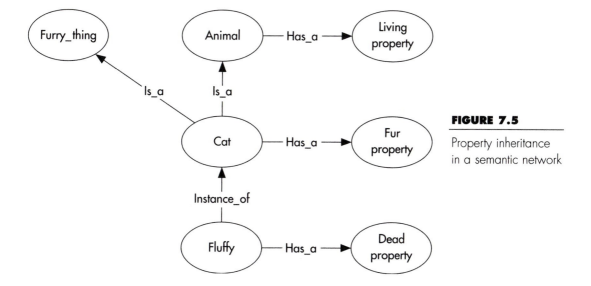

FIGURE 7.5

Property inheritance in a semantic network

7.3 PREDICATE LOGIC

Predicate logic gives us a lot of flexibility when assigning a predicate to a piece of knowledge. Recall that an interpretation of a predicate logic statement is defined by assigning values to the predicates, constants, and functions, values that yield a truth value of the statement. As a result, we are free to pick any names for our predicate that we choose. However, if we are to use FOPL for knowledge representation, we need to assign a meaning to predicate names themselves in order to represent new pieces of knowledge. We must take care to be consistent, because FOPL is not concerned with name consistency and will not catch inconsistencies.

FOPL attempts to be truth preserving in its operations. But, as we will see in later representations, this is not always possible. When we try to represent natural language, for instance, we are not as interested in the truth of the statement as we are in the meaning is of what was said.

FOPL is very useful in theoretical discussions of issues in knowledge representation and in proving the correctness of inference mechanisms for different formalisms, because of the rigorous nature of its inference rules and its solid, extensive theory. FOPL is well abled to express IF-THEN rules. For example, if we were expressing the rules needed to diagnose a computer hardware fault, we might have something like

$$Memory\_read\_result(fail) \rightarrow Problem\_is(memory)$$
$$\forall X.(Io\_fault(X) \rightarrow Problem\_is(channel\_error))$$
$$Smoke\_in\_computer\_room \rightarrow Problem\_is(fatal\_problem)$$

Most rule-based expert system languages use an IF-THEN approach for defining their rules.

We can also represent inheritance with Isa relations and Instance relationships. An object is defined to be an Instance of another when there exists a chain of Isa relationships to the other. For example, if "Fluffy" Isa "cat" and a "cat" Isa "animal," then "Fluffy" is an Instance of animal. This representation can be formalized with the following FOPL statements:

$$Instance(fluffy, cat)$$
$$Isa(cat, animal)$$
$$\forall X \forall Y.(Isa(X,Y) \rightarrow Instance(X,Y))$$

These formalization methods allow us to express the knowledge associated with "cat," "animal," and "fluffy" at their respective levels. For example,

$$\forall X.(X = \textit{fluffy}) \rightarrow \textit{Weight}(X,\textit{six\_pounds}))$$
$$\forall X.((X = \textit{fluffy}) \rightarrow \textit{Color}(X,\textit{calico}))$$
$$\forall X.(\textit{Instance}(X,\textit{cat}) \rightarrow \textit{Number\_feet}(X,\textit{four}))$$
$$\forall X.(\textit{Instance}(X,\textit{cat}) \rightarrow \textit{Has}(X,\textit{fur}))$$
$$\forall X.(\textit{Instance}(X,\textit{animal}) \rightarrow \textit{Living}(X))$$

In an object-oriented language such as C++ or SmallTalk, being an instance of a class is very much like being an Instance here. In fact, many knowledge representation systems are now being written in object-oriented programming languages.

One often-mentioned drawback of FOPL is that equivalent forms of the same statement are hard to recognize and seem unnatural. For a rule like

$$\forall X.(\textit{Bird}(X) \rightarrow \textit{Flies}(X))$$

we can write an equivalent statement such as

$$\forall X.(\neg \textit{Flies}(X) \rightarrow \neg \textit{Bird}(X))$$

by using the contrapositive form. However, it is hard to recognize quickly that this second form contains the same information as the first. An inference rule like resolution requires a standard clausal form and therefore requires us to put our statements in a form that may be difficult to recognize as equivalents of the original statements.

7.3.1 Knowledge Interchange Format

The Knowledge Interchange Format (KIF) knowledge representation language was created to meet the need for a common language for the interchange of knowledge between different applications. It is hoped that this or another common language can be used to support the interchange of knowledge so that applications around the world can share and use the knowledge of other applications.

KIF provides mechanisms for expressing general FOPL statements, for expressing knowledge about knowledge (like the ontology used), and for specifying inference rules (including nonmonotonic rules, which are explained in Chapter 12). For example, the axiom of regularity can be expressed in KIF as

```
(forall (?s)
  (=> (not (empty ?s))
  (exists (?u) (and (member ?u ?s) (disjoint ?u
?s)))))
```

This same axiom can be stated in FOPL as

$$\forall S.(\exists U.(U \in S \wedge (U \cap S = \varnothing)) \to (S \neq \varnothing))$$

or in English as "every nonempty set has an element with which it has members in common" For example,

$$S = (\{a,b\}, \varnothing, \{c\})$$

is such a set as

$$U = \{c\} \cap S = \varnothing$$

See Genesereth and Fikes (1992) for more details on the syntax and semantics of KIF.

7.3.2 CLASSIC

CLASSIC is a knowledge representation system that uses many of the ideas we have discussed, including frames and FOPL. CLASSIC (and its predecessor, KL-ONE[2]) centers on what it calls **concepts,** which are FOPL-like statements that use the following partial syntax (in Extended Backus-Naur Form, EBNF; see Section 11.2.1 if you are not familiar with EBNF) given in Resnick et al. (1991):

```
<concept-expr> ::= (AND <concept-expr>⁺) |
(ALL <role-expr> <concept-expr>) |
(AT-LEAST <positive-integer> <role-expr>) |
(AT-MOST <non-negative-integer> <role-expr>) |
(SAME-AS <attribute-path> <attribute-path>) |
. . .
```

Suppose we use CLASSIC to define a concept of HEALTHY-VEG-ETARIAN (also in Resnick et al., 1991):

```
(AND PERSON
  (AND (ALL food HEALTHY)
    (ALL food PLANT)))
```

This example shows how we can easily restrict an existing concept of **PERSON** on the basis of his characteristics (here all his food is a plant and is also healthful). Note that CLASSIC uses LISP-like parenthesized expressions.

---

[2] Also described as a frame-based system because it can be thought of as a network of concepts and relations.

The CLASSIC language is used in many real-world systems throughout AT&T Corporation, Lucent Technologies, and other organizations. One important trade-off that CLASSIC makes is in expressiveness. It is not as powerful as general FOPL, primarily because of efficiency reasons and the desire to use CLASSIC in real-life systems.

CLASSIC supports inference mechanisms to classify concepts into ontologies and methods for subsumption of concepts. On the basis of the definitions of concepts, CLASSIC can arrange them into a "subsumption hierarchy" rather than requiring the users to specify them. As a result, CLASSIC is useful for organizing large sets of concepts that can be represented by characteristic features.

7.4 SEMANTIC NETWORKS

7.4.1 Basic Principles

Semantic networks make up a general class of graph-based representations that typically represent knowledge as interconnected nodes, which are linked by labeled arrows. Various types of semantic network representations differ in the names that are allowed for links and nodes. As a result, different inference mechanisms must be used to interpret the various types of representations.

Consider Figure 7.6, which shows a partial semantic network for two marsupials. This network has four types of links: Is_a, Instance_of, Has_a, and Can. An Is_a link indicates that one concept is a subset[3] of another. In the figure, a wombat is a subset of (or a kind of) marsupials. A Has_a link indicates that one concept has a property that is embodied in another concept. Instance_of links represent when a node is a specific member of a particular concept. In the figure, a marsupial has the property of a pouch in which it bears its young. A Can link indicates that one concept has the ability to perform another concept. Here, animals are able to move themselves from place to place and are able to breathe.

Inheritance of properties in this type of semantic network is derived by following a chain of Is_a links. Any property of the last link in the Is_a chain that is indicated by a Can or a Has_a link can be inherited. For example, we can follow the Is_a chain from "Jumper" through "Kangaroo" and "Marsupial" and end at "Animal". The three properties of "Animal" can be inherited by "Jumper." That is, we can infer that "Jumper" has a "Living Property" by using using inheritance.

---

[3] An Is_a link is the same type of relationship as a subclass to superclass relationship in an OO model. An Instance-of link is the same type of relationship as that of an OO object to its defining class or classes.

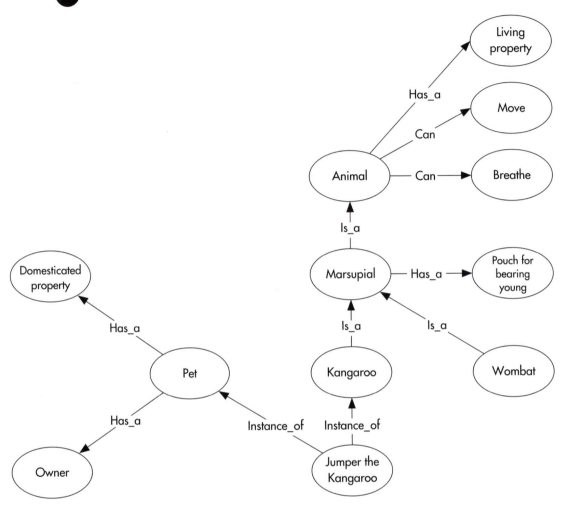

FIGURE 7.6

Semantic network for
selected marsupials

Because "Jumper" also Is_a "pet," we can also infer that "Jumper"
Has_a "Ownership Property" and is owned by some individual.

If we wish to override the inheritance of properties within a semantic network, then we need to specify exceptions to the general rule.
One way of doing this is to specify exceptions at the appropriate level
in the network. Suppose that "Jumper" is not owned by anyone in particular because he escaped from his previous (unknown) owner.
However, "Jumper" is still a pet, although one looking for a new owner.
In this instance, we would attach the information that "Jumper"
Has_a "Unowned Property." Thus, when we refer to the semantic net,
we should first examine all the properties at the lowest level. If no
value for the property is found, we proceed to ancestors in the
Is_a/Instance_of hierarchy. This mechanism works as follows: When

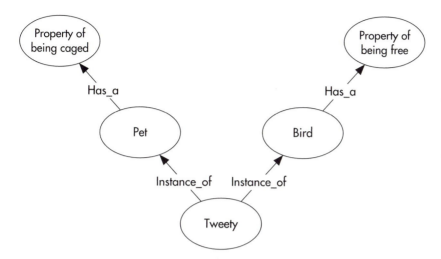

FIGURE 7.7

Multiple inheritance
and clashing
properties

searching for a property for an object, we first examine whether the property (or its negation) can be found directly attached to the object. If not, then we move up one level in the Is_a/Instance_of hierarchy and check to see whether the property can be found there, and so on.

A particular object may have two ancestors at the same level with conflicting properties. For example, in Figure 7.7, "Tweety" is an Instance_of both "pet" and "bird". However, if we have stipulated that birds are free and that pets are caged, then we cannot determine from the semantic network which overrides the other. One way to handle this would be to assign likelihoods to each property and then decide on the basis of the calculated values. Another way would be to define a procedure that would automatically determine which value should be dominant (see Exercises 7.12 and 7.22).

A semantic network is a powerful mechanism for representing knowledge, but it has some shortcomings. One is the lack of a formal syntax. However, this deficiency is easily overcome by introducing more structure into semantic networks, just as we do in conceptual graphs (see Section 7.4.2). Another shortcoming is the lack of formal semantics. In other words, the meaning of a semantic network is a function of the procedures that interpret it. Therefore, the meaning varies from one interpretation procedure to another. Finally, the automatic construction of semantic networks from natural language is difficult. The *efficient* construction of a semantic network from an existing knowledge base is also difficult, because many decisions must be made as to what objects should be types and where properties of objects should be attached to the network.

7.4.2 Conceptual Graphs

A **conceptual graph** is a particular type of semantic network that has a more precise structure for links and nodes. This knowledge representation tool was described by J. F. Sowa (1984, 1995). A conceptual graph is a finite, connected directed graph. It is also a bipartite graph (a term meaning that the removal of any single link results in two subgraphs). A conceptual graph uses nodes (depicted as ellipses) rather than labeled arrows to represent the relationships between concepts (depicted as rectangles). The elliptical relationship nodes are called **conceptual relations** and the rectangular concept nodes are called **concepts**. Concepts can only connect directly to conceptual relations and vice versa (the rule that causes the graph to be bipartite).

In the conceptual graph shown in Figure 7.8, a "Person" named "Harry S. Truman" is described. The elliptical "Name," "Birthplace," and "Former_job" nodes are conceptual relations. The rectangular nodes are all concept nodes. The identifier "Harry S. Truman" should be unique within the concept node "Person," and "Name" conceptual relations should be used to refer to the names that are used to describe an individual.

Types in conceptual graphs. Conceptual graphs use a separate type hierarchy to handle the Is_a relationship. For example, in Figure 7.9 the "absurd type" ($\perp$) is a subtype of everything, and the "universal type: ($\top$) is a supertype of every other type. The **type** of a concept is indicated by the name of the concept node. The type of "Harry S. Truman" is "Person" in Figure 7.8. We can also represent a variable instantiation of a concept by placeholders such as the *X and *Y used

FIGURE 7.8

Conceptual graph representation of Harry S. Truman

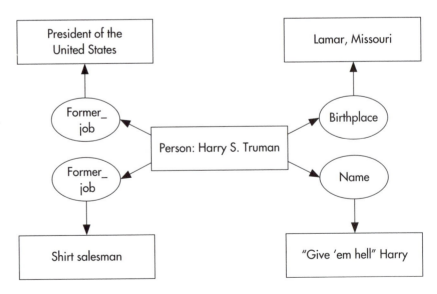

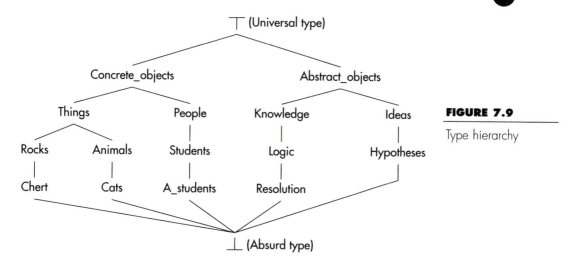

FIGURE 7.9

Type hierarchy

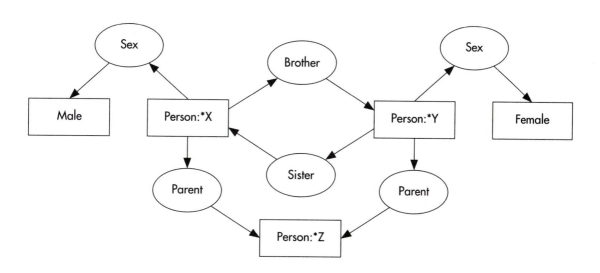

FIGURE 7.10

Conceptual graph representation of the relationships between brother and sister

in Figure 7.10. This figure expresses the proposition that two people are brother and sister if they share the same parent and are of different sexes. It also expresses the proposition that if two people of different sexes share the same parent, then they are brother and sister. As noted earlier, the *X, *Y, and *Z" represent arbitrary instantiations of person. This conctual graph could represent a sentence like "The two people are brother and sister, and they have a common parent." Figure 7.10 could also represent the statement, "I am a brother to my stepsister, because she shares at least one parent with me."

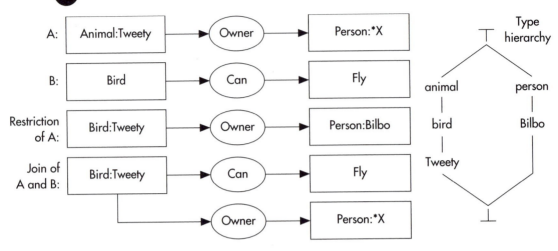

FIGURE 7.11

Restriction and join of
conceptual graphs

Manipulating conceptual graphs. We can perform operations on conceptual graphs, combining and manipulating them to infer new conceptual graphs. Figure 7.11 shows two such operations on two simple conceptual graphs. Graph A states that an animal called Tweety is owned by some person. Graph B states that birds can fly. The third graph is the *restriction* of A, using the type hierarchy given. A **restriction** of a conceptual graph simply replaces a node in an existing graph with an object that is a subtype of the original. In this example we have performed two restrictions at once. First, we replaced the "Animal" in A with "Bird" because "Bird" is a subtype of "Animal." Second, we replaced the "Person:*X" with a specific person, namely, "Bilbo."

The fourth conceptual graph shown in Figure 7.11 is a **join** of two existing graphs. We linked two graphs by a common concept or two concepts in which one is a subtype of the other. In other words, we joined graphs A and B, which have the nodes "Animal: Tweety" and "Bird," by replacing these two nodes with a single node that is the subclass of the two previous nodes: "Bird: Tweety."

The restriction and join operations on conceptual graphs both produce graphs that are **specializations** of the original graphs. That is, the knowledge they represent is less general than the original statements.

We can also **simplify** an existing graph. We can eliminate any duplicate relations without changing the meaning of the graph. A simplication is not a specialization of the original graph as the simplification still represents exactly the same information.

These operations can be reduced to several rules, which may be applied to conceptual graphs:

1. A variable placeholder in a concept can be replaced with a specific value.

2. A concept can be replaced by a subtype as long as the replacement is still consistent with any specifically mentioned instances of this concept.

3. Any duplicate relations can be removed without affecting the value of the graph.

These rules, however, are not rigorous enough to be inference rules. That is, we cannot guarantee the truth of a statement derived by applying these rules, even if the original graphs are known to be true. For example, consider graph A in Figure 7.11. If we replace "*X" with "Frodo," the revised graph will not be true if, in fact, "Bilbo" is the owner.

Representing knowledge about knowledge. Conceptual graphs are very flexible and can be used to specify more complex expressions than we have discussed so far. We can create a macro concept (called a **proposition**) by enclosing a graph within a box and treating it as a single concept. We can then manipulate these higher level concepts just as we manipulated simple objects. This mechanism allows us to work with notions of belief, knowing, negation, and other meta-level concepts. The conceptual graph in Figure 7.12 shows an application of the technique.

FIGURE 7.12

Conceptual graph representation of the concept "Bob believes that Otis and Jane are not brother and sister."

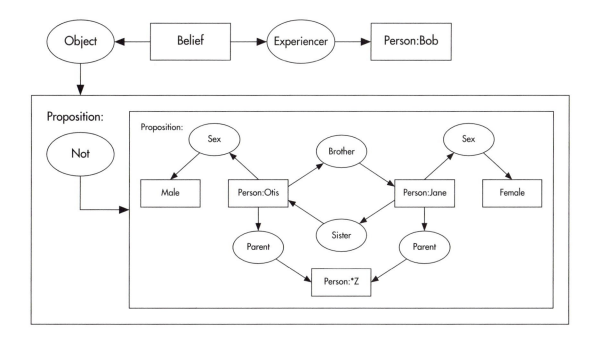

Figure 7.12 shows a conceptual graph that uses the proposition construct twice to express the statement that "Bob believes that Otis and Jane are not brother and sister." The innermost proposition represents the statement that "Otis and Jane are brother and sister." The next-level proposition expresses the negation of the first proposition. Finally, the outer construction represents Bob believing the larger proposition.

In Section 7.7 we will explain how this mechanism can be used to express agent knowledge and belief.

7.4.3 Using C++ to Represent Semantic Networks

Semantic networks are easy to represent in C++. To represent the semantic network shown in Figure 7.6, we can use the following C++ statements as a framework.

```
class pet
{
  public:
    owner_type p_owner;
    property_type domesticated;
};
class animal
{
  public:
    property_type living;
    void move();
    void breathe();
};
class marsupial:public animal
{
  public:
    pouch_type pouch;
};
class kangaroo:public marsupial
{
  public:
    kangaroo();    //Constructor
    ~kangaroo();    //Destructor
};
class wombat:public marsupial
{
  public:
    wombat();    //Constructor
    ~wombat();    //Destructor
};
```

```
class kangaroo_pet:public kangaroo, public pet
{
  public:
    kangaroo_pet();
    ~kangaroo_pet();
};
main()
{
  kangaroo_pet jumper();
}
```

Note that we can directly support multiple inheritance with C++. We must add a class (here kangaroo_pet) to allow objects to be created that inherit properties from both classes. Note that Can links are represented as member functions, Is_a links are represented as a class hierarchy, and Has_a links are represented as attributes. Instance-of links are represented as objects (Jumper is created as an object of the Kangaroo class).

7.5 REPRESENTING NATURAL LANGUAGE

The representation of natural language (both spoken and written) is one of the most difficult problems of AI, primarily because the meaning of a portion of natural language is dependent on an understanding of the context of the sentence. And we must also understand references in the sentence to assumptions and commonsense knowledge. In addition to these complexities, we also need to be able to recognize irony, sarcasm, and other indirect meanings beyond those of the actual statement. Consider, for example, the following headline from the *Chicago Tribune* sports page: "Celtics happy there's a Ford in their present." This statement is actually referring to a new manager (named Ford) and not a new Ford car. To someone who is familiar with sports activity at that time, this play on words makes perfect sense. However, to someone who knows nothing about sports or who is unfamiliar with the Celtics or Ford, the statement makes little sense.

Although natural language representation and translation are very difficult, even partial solutions to this problem can have widespread application. The understanding and representation of natural language can lead to programs that read and understand all the newspapers of the world. The program could then be asked questions about the news or even summarize the news that is relevant to a particular individual. Instead of using computer keyboards as our primary input mechanisms, we could use natural language. Such natural language interaction would allow most of the population to use computers. It is not difficult to imagine many more applications in which the understanding and representation of natural language would have a high payoff.

Because of its importance, many attempts have been made to represent and understand natural language. One approach is to define some **semantic primitives,** which are defined as indivisible pieces of meaning in natural language. The most widely known and successful of these approaches is known as **conceptual dependency theory**.

We will address the problems associated with natural language processing again in Chapter 11.

7.5.1 Conceptual Dependencies

One approach to representing natural language is to use a fixed set of primitive constructs to which most natural language ideas can be translated. The idea is to represent the meaning of the sentence independently of the language so that a canonical form can be produced for all sentences that have the same meaning. Schank and Colby (1973) defined a set of primitive actions and dependencies that have been used with some success.

The sentence in Figure 7.13 is a typical example of how conceptual dependencies are used to encode meaning. In this example there are two primitive acts (called ACTS). One is "PTRANS" (standing for "physical transfer"), which indicates the change in location (indicated by "l") of an object. The second is "INGEST," which indicates the ingestion of an object by an animal. The "o" indicates the object case relation. That is, "Crumpets" is related to INGEST by being the object of ingestion. The "f" indicates future tense (will eat), and the "D" indicates the direction case relation (from the plate to his mouth).

There are four **primitive** conceptual categories out of which dependency structures can be built. They are

Primitive	Description
ACT	Action
PP	Object (picture producer)
AA	Modifier of action (action aider)
PA	Modifier of PP (picture aider)

A set of primitive ACTs appeared in Rich and Knight (1991). The following list of primitives is not necessarily the complete set. You may

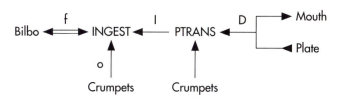

FIGURE 7.13

Conceptual dependency representation of the sentence "Bilbo will eat the crumpets from the plate."

find in translating other sentences that a new primitive is desired. However, for most cases, the following primitives should be sufficient.

Act	Description
ATRANS	Transfer of an abstract relationship (e.g., give)
ATTEND	Focusing of a sense organ toward a stimulus (e.g., smell)
PTRANS	Move an object (e.g., jump)
EXPEL	Expulsion of something from an animal (e.g., sweat)
GRASP	Grasping of an object by something (e.g., grab)
INGEST	Ingestion of something by an animal (e.g., eat)
MBUILD	Building new information out of old (e.g., plan)
MOVE	Movement of a part by its owner (e.g., wave)
MTRANS	Transfer of mental information (e.g., tell)
PROPEL	Application of physical force to an object (e.g., push)
SPEAK	Production of sounds (e.g., yell)

7.5.2 Case Frames

One semantic network approach to representing natural language is based on the structure of English verbs. The network is built around the verb of a sentence and uses links from the verb to the other parts (nouns) of the sentence. This mechanism is called a **case frame**. Some case frame relationships are agent, instrument, location, object, and time. These same relationships are also used in the conceptual dependency approach discussed earlier.

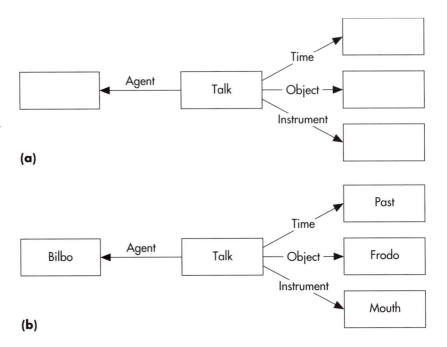

FIGURE 7.14

(a) Stored case frame for the verb "talk." (b) Case frame representation of the sentence "Bilbo talked to Frodo."

The case frame method works by storing case frames for each verb that might be used and then referring to them when that verb is found. For example, in reading the sentence "Bilbo talked to Frodo," we would refer to the case frame for "talk" and then fill in the rest of the links according to our predetermined case frame for "talk." An example of this method is shown in Figure 7.14.

Once the case frame representation of a sentence has been generated, it is effectively independent of the original language. The same case frame representation can represent several similar sentences. Figure 7.14 might also represent "Bilbo chatted to Frodo," for instance.

7.6 FRAMES AND SCRIPTS

7.6.1 Frames

A **frame** is a defined object with a predetermined structure. We can link these frames together in a network representation much like semantic networks, except that each object is a frame. Each frame contains **slots,** which are placeholders for values in that particular frame. The slots can have default values, procedures that determine the values, or values that must be specified by the user. Languages such as C++, CLASSIC, and KL-ONE support this type

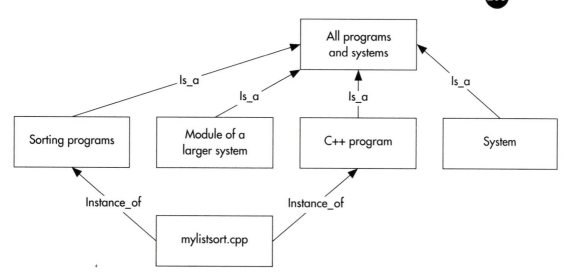

FIGURE 7.15

Partial frame network representing a C++ program

of frame network; Figure 7.15 shows how we might represent a C++ program with frames.

Inheritance works much the same way for a frame network as it did for semantic networks. Is_a links are followed to determine inherited values from ancestors of the frame in question. A particular instance (here "mylistsort.cpp") will have values for the slots that are derived from the frames of which it is an instance. So, we will derive the slots and their default values for "mylistsort.cpp" from those defined in the "sorting programs" and "C++ program" frames. Our program might also be an instance of other frames (such as "System" or "Module of a larger system"), and it would then need to get more slots and values from those frames also.

Frames can be represented by an object-oriented language that uses class definitions for frames and slots. This representation is, in fact, almost exactly the same as a class hierarchy diagram. See Section 7.8 for some object-oriented approaches to frames.

7.6.2 Scripts

Scripts are a sequence of related events or actions intended to provide a structured context for reasoning about events or planning actions. More simply, they can be viewed as instructions for how to behave in a predefined situation, just as a script for a play does.

Scripts are composed of the following elements:

- **Name**   The name of the script is used to refer to the script as a whole. In the script shown in Figure 7.16, the name is "class_attend."

FIGURE 7.16

Script representation
for attending a class

Script:	Class_attend	**Scene 1:** Entering S PTRANS S into class S MOVE S to desk P PTRANS P into class
Track:	University	
Props:	Blackboard = B Handouts = H Desk Trash Homework	**Scene 2:** Lecture P ATRANS H to S and OterStudents S ATRANS homework to P P MTRANS Lecture_Contents to S S MTRANS QUestions to P P MTRANS Answers to S (option: if test go to Scene 3, otherwise, Scene 4)
Actors:	Student = S OtherStudents Instructor = P	
Triggers:	S is registered Today is class	**Scene 3:** Testing P TRANS Test to S S MOVE Pencil to answer questions S ATRANS Test to P
Results:	S has handouts P has no handouts S has work to do	**Scene 4:** Leaving (option: if H not worth keeping then S ATRANS H to Trash) S PTRANS S to out of classrooom

- **Track**   The track contains more information about the script than is contained in the name itself. In the script in Figure 7.16, track is "University," to distinguish this script from other scripts that might have the same name but represent, say, "High School" class attendance.

- **Triggers**   Triggers are the conditions that must be met for the script to be used. In Figure 7.16, the triggers are registration for the class, ability to attend the class, today is the scheduled day of the class, and others.

- **Results**   Results are the things that have changed when the script is executed. In Figure 7.16, these are having more work to do and receiving or not receiving handouts.

- **Props**   Props are the nonactor elements that play a part in the script. In Figure 7.16, props include handouts and the blackboard.

- **Actors**   Actors are the people or objects in the script that can effect change. In Figure 7.16, yourself, other_students, and the instructor are actors.

- **Scenes**   Scenes are the part of the script; each scene is a list of events and actions. Each scene can be viewed as a subscript that shares the above items with the other scenes of the larger script. The scenes in Figure 7.16 are going_to_class, attending_class, and leaving_class.

- **Related scripts**   Related scripts are those that are similar to this one; if this script fails, the system can pick a related script to try. This field is also used to denote scripts that may be called from the current script.

The actions within the scripts are usually represented by the same primitives used in conceptual dependency theory (see the list in Section 7.5.1).

Scripts are often used for attempting to understand stories within in the domain of the scripts. Most alternatives are laid out in the script, so that using the information in the natural language story, we can pick the more likely alternative.

When we use scripts, we can encounter a problem known as the **match problem**. This is the problem of deciding when to apply the script, especially when several scripts' entry conditions are met. And sometimes it is not possible to determine whether the entry conditions have been met or not, because of the ambiguity of natural language. Let's say we have two scripts, one about attending a university course and another about getting insurance for our car and we attempt to understand the following story:

We drove our car to the university. We registered and today classes are being held. In order to avoid the traffic, we decided to come back another day to get our insurance.

From the story itself, it is difficult to tell whether our car is registered or we are registered in a course. Therefore, it is difficult to tell which script to apply.

Another problem is sometimes called the **between the lines** problem; it is inherent in all programs that attempt to do semantic reasoning. The problem is that much of the knowledge that we need to understand a story is not explicit in the story itself, but is assumed. Take the following example:

Tonight was our class. So we went.

In this simple example we assume that we are allowed to go the class (are registered). The problem is that we are unsure whether we can apply the script, because of the missing information about being registered. Much of the way we interpret natural language depends on our common understanding of the world. Being able to directly interpret natural language will have a high payoff in the possible functionality that automated systems can provide. We will investigate the *Cyc* project in Chapter 13, which is attempting to solve just this problem.

7.7 OBJECT-ORIENTED KNOWLEDGE REPRESENTATION

Many of the knowledge representation mechanisms and languages discussed in this chapter support object-oriented concepts. In particular, the notion of inheritance is common in many representation schemes. Recently, there has been a trend toward reintegrating the concepts of object-oriented design with knowledge representation systems and mechanisms as illustrated by the following sections on object-oriented frames, rules, and data.

One can represent a mechanism such as a semantic network directly in an object-oriented language (see Section 7.4.3). The nodes participating in Is_a links are translated to classes (or instances of a class), and those at the end of Has_a links are encapsulated attributes of the classes related to those nodes. While this approach should produce a highly efficient solution to the particular problem being encoded, it lacks the ability to add nodes to the network without recompilation.

7.7.1 Object-Oriented Frames

An excellent example of merging frames, objects, and rules is the Knowledge representation Object-Oriented Language (KOOL). KOOL is a simple object-oriented language that integrates features of frame-based systems (such as slots) and object-oriented systems (single-parent inheritance). It then supports rules (see Chapter 8) to use the knowledge encoded in objects. See Albert (1988) for more information.

Implementation of a frame-based system in an object-oriented language is illustrated by Schneider's (1988) implementation of FRL in SmallTalk. It defines classes to support a frame system in SmallTalk. The classes are Frame, Slot, Facet, and ValueFacet.

7.7.2 Object-Oriented Rules

Chapter 8 will present several rule-based production systems that use object-oriented (C++) environments. Another approach is to add object definition mechanisms to existing rule-based systems. Hybrid environments (such as those described in Roche, 1988) mix

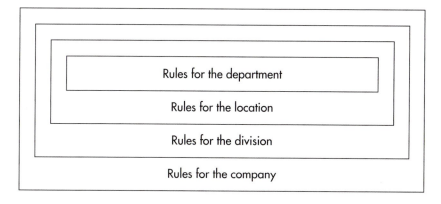

FIGURE 7.17

Rules that apply at different levels of generality but are related

different paradigms. For example, we could combine a frame-oriented knowledge representation scheme with using an object-oriented language inference engine.

Another interesting approach is to transform a rule-based system into a system that uses objects. That is, the rule-based production system is translated into an object-oriented program (see Odeh and Padget, 1993, for one such system).

7.7.3 Object-Oriented Data Models

Several attempts have been made to focus on the data portions of a system and produce object-oriented representations of them. We have classified these representations as **data models**, because their purpose is much like that of logical data models in defining a database. Data models define the structure of data used in a knowledge-based program; or, in other words, they define much of the knowledge base.

One such system is the Tanguy knowledge base management system that is built on top of C++. The intent of Tanguy is to integrate sets, rules, and data definitions in an object-oriented environment. An example of the motivation behind Tanguy is the need for rules to apply at different levels of generality (Figure 7.17). This illustration implies that it would be convenient if the rules could be inherited by objects in a subclass. Then, a rule applying to the entire company would also apply to a specific department. Tanguy supports embedding rules in C++ code that are processed by a precompiler.

Another example of a data model is the Object-Oriented Data Language (OOL), which is designed to produce object-oriented data models for object-oriented database systems. It currently defines classes of data objects and seems suitable for expressing ontologies, similar to those written in the **CLASSIC** knowledge representation language. See Formica, Missikoff, and Vazzana (1991) for more details.

An object-oriented methodology for defining an object-oriented data model for a knowledge-based system is described in Higa et al. (1992).

7.8 SUMMARY

The knowledge representation techniques discussed in this chapter each have their own benefits and drawbacks. FOPL has the benefits of being able to express almost any concept and to support theoretical concerns. Semantic networks have the benefit of expressing how concepts are related to one another in a single network. Semantic networks require decisions about the kinds of links allowed, for consistency. Frames are a way to express structured knowledge, especially knowledge that can be expressed in a hierarchical fashion. Frames fit well with object-oriented programming paradigms. Conceptual dependencies have shown some success in being able to represent natural language by using a small set of primitives and connectives (dependencies). As such, they represent an excellent beginning in solving the complex natural language problem. Scripts have also shown success in interpreting situations (or stories about situations) that have an inherent structure and predictability. The problems of representing imprecise knowledge, belief, and knowing knowledge are still topics of active research.

In general, several conclusions can be drawn about knowledge representation:

- The proper representation scheme is dependent on the problem at hand.
- Each representation scheme has its benefits and drawbacks.
- Introducing an explicit structure helps to simplify the usage of the representation.

7.9 REFERENCES

An excellent textbook covering many aspects of knowledge representation is Sowa (1995). A collection of important papers in the field has been published in Brachman and Levesque (1985). The field is quite active and continues to produce many interesting papers, which are presented at the following conferences: at the *International Joint Conferences on AI* (IJCAI), the *American Association for AI* (AAAI) *National Conferences* (AAAI), and the

Knowledge Representation conferences. CLASSIC is described in Resnick et al. (1991), KIF in Genesereth and Fikes (1992), conceptual graphs in Sowa (1984, 1995), and conceptual dependencies in Schank and Abelson (1977). Specific references to object-oriented approaches to knowledge representation were given in Section 7.8.

7.10 EXERCISES

Warm-up Exercises

7.1. Translate the following frame into English.

Name	Clam
Isa	Invertebrate Mollusk
Properties	hard_shell weight size used_in_food bivalve has_a_shell lives_in
Defaults	weighs(3 Oz) size(3 inches) lives_in(sea)

7.2. Translate the following semantic network into English.

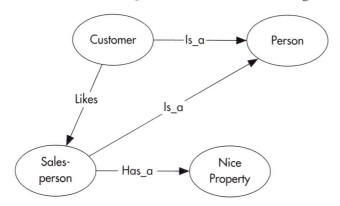

7.3. Translate the following script into English.

Script:	System_Login	**Scene 1:** Find Terminal
		U PTRANS U to Terminall
Track:	UNIX System	U MOVE U to sit
		U MOVE U to typing position
Props:	Keyboard = K	
	Login ID = I	**Scene 2:** Logging in
	Password = P	U MTRANS "Enter" Key
		S MTRANS "Please login"
Actors:	User = U	U MTRANS I to S
	Systems = S	S MTRANS "Password."
		U MTRANS P to S
Triggers:	U hasa valid I on S	
	S is up	**Scene 3:** Working
	U not logged onto S	U execute "Work" Script
Results:	U has done work	
		Scene 4: Logout
		U MTRANS "exit" to S

7.4. Translate the following FOPL statements into English.

$$\forall X.(Person(X) \wedge Lawyer(X) \rightarrow \exists Y.(Represents(Y,X)))$$
$$\forall X.(Person(X) \wedge Champion(X) \rightarrow Eats\_for\_Breakfast(X,wheatees))$$
$$B_{Marius}(B_{Otis}(\forall X.(Cat(X) \rightarrow Fuzzy(X))) \wedge (\exists X.(Cat(X) \rightarrow Fuzzy(X))))$$
$$\wedge\ Fuzzy(fluffy)$$

Homework Exercises

7.5. Translate the representations given in Exercises 7.1 through 7.3 into FOPL.

7.6. Translate each of the following sentences into predicate calculus, KIF, and conceptual graphs:

a. "I would not eat green eggs and ham here or there."

b. "Barbers love to shave."

c. "Barbara Walters is a regular on ABC."

For each sentence, what do you have to assume to make it representable in those three formalisms?

7.7. Specialization of conceptual graphs using *join* and *restrict* is not a truth-preserving operation. Give an example that demonstrates that the restriction of a true graph is not necessarily true.

7.8. Translate the accompanying conceptual graphs into predicate calculus and KIF.

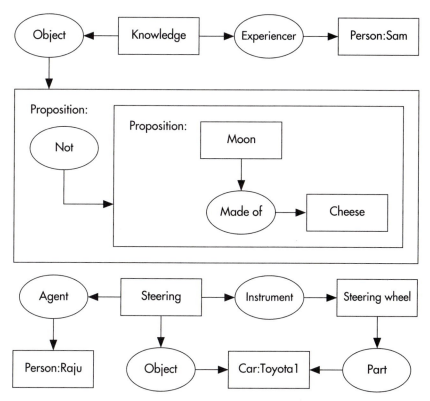

7.9. Translate Figure 7.3 (the script for a fast-food restaurant) into FOPL.

7.10. Develop case frames for the following English verbs:

a. yell

b. see

c. extract

d. bite

If any have multiple meanings (as verbs), generate case frames for all the meanings. Please note any default values for any of the case relationships. For example, for the "bite" case a default instrument might be "teeth."

7.11. Define an appropriate granularity for reasoning about "wood" in the following situations:

a. Reasoning about carpentry problems such as what pieces of wood are appropriate for building a chest of drawers and what cuts need to be made.

    b. Identification of a particular piece of wood as belonging to a particular species, such as elm, oak, or ebony.

    c. A robotic mole program that must distinguish between wood (which it can bore through) and rocks (which it cannot bore through).

7.12. Inheritance can be either simple of complex. Consider the problem of dominant and recessive traits. Dominant traits are always inherited if there are no other competing dominant traits. Recessive traits can only be inherited if no dominant competing traits are present. If there are several competing dominant traits, then any one can be chosen. Using the inheritance mechanism in C++, write a pseudo-code program that solves this problem. Start with a semantic network structure that has Has_a and Is_a links.

7.13. Create a frame representation for large software systems. Your representation should have slots for characteristics of the program (or subprogram) such as number of lines, complexity, subprograms, and parameters.

7.14. Using conceptual dependencies, define a script for the following scenarios.

    a. Taking your dog for a walk.

    b. Writing and debugging a program in C++.

    c. Moving from one residence to another in the same city.

    d. Opening a checking account at a bank.

    e. Robbing a bank.

7.15. Describe a representation that could be used in a program to solve analogy problems like that in the figure on page 213. This class of problems was addressed by T. G. Evans (1968). The representation must be capable of depicting the essential features of size, shape, and relative position. The example is the correct answer C to the problem shown in the figure because it represents the correct relationship of objects, namely, the second object inside the first object.

7.16. Create a semantic network in C++ and design a hasproperty-like inference mechanism that uses Has_a, Can, and Owns links to test whether entities in the network have properties.

7.17. Given a two-dimensional world with polyhedral objects that are defined by their vertices (in order), define a representation of the space such that conflicts with another object (say, a robot) are easily detectable. You may assume that the mobile object is a unit square and moves only in straight lines.

7.18. A buzzword is a word that is used to represent an evolving

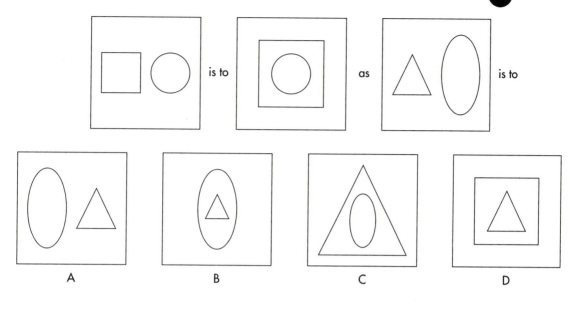

A   B   C   D

concept or goal. Try to represent the following buzzwords in predicate logic.

a. *seamless integration* of software modules

b. *best-in-class* software production facilities

c. *highly reliable* software

For each buzzword, explain how (or if) your definitions would work in helping to interpret advertising documentation for a software product. What happens if your definitions are too specific? Too general?

Figure for
Exercise 7.15

Programming Exercises

7.19. Write a C++ program to translate a semantic network like those in the chapter into **FOPL**.

7.20. Write a full implementation of a semantic network in C++ that uses token passing to make inferences about the network.

7.21. Write a C++ program to solve analogy problems like that used in Exercise 7.15. Use the representation that you defined in that problem. You may assume that the only shapes are those given (square, circle, and triangle) and the only possible relationships are inside, outside, or alone. There are no more than three objects per instance. Read the data for your problem from a file. Your program must prompt for the name of the data file.

7.22. Write a C++ program to use the inheritance mechanism that you defined in Exercise 7.12 that used dominant and recessive traits. Test your program on a family tree model in which the traits of the eldest ancestors have been defined. Determine the properties of the youngest children. Here is a sample list of data:

```
mother(m1,son1).
father(f1,son1).
mother(m2,daughter1).
father(f2,daughter1).
mother(daughter1,gson1).
father(son1,gson1).
trait(f1,blond_hair).
trait(f1,blue_eye).
trait(m1,brown_hair).
trait(m1,brown_eye).
competing_traits([blue_eye,brown_eye]).
competing_traits([blond_hair,brown_hair]).
dominant(brown_eye).
dominant(brown_hair).
```

Your program should prompt for the name of the input file and should print out the traits of the children that have no children (in this case, gson1). If a trait is not declared dominant, then it is a recessive trait.

7.23. Design and write a C++ program to manipulate conceptual graphs. Your system should be able to perform simplifications, restrictions, and joins of conceptual graphs.

7.24. Write a C++ program that can read in a script and use that script to interpret a series of C++ statements in another file. That is, the script will define a C++ program design by outlining the major scenes in the program and alternative paths. The program that you read in will be an instance of the general case defined by the script. The output of your program will be a description of the program's use of the script, for example, scenes used, values defined.

PRODUCTION SYSTEMS

Minds exist in brains and may come to exist in programmed machines. If and when such machines come about, their causal powers will derive not from the substances they are made of, but from their design and the programs that run in them. And the way we will know they have those causal powers is by talking to them and listening carefully to what they have to say.

DOUGLAS
HOFSTADTER, 1981

8.1 INTRODUCTION TO PRODUCTION SYSTEMS

A production system is a computing model that provides the theoretical basis for expert system technology. It uses a rule set and an inference engine to solve problems. Expert systems build on this theory by providing an environment that allows rules to be specified easily and that frees the knowledge engineer from much of the programming task. The idea behind an expert system is that a programmer can encode the knowledge of an expert in a rule set that allows the system to come to the same conclusions as an expert. Expert systems have become successful for many problems, particularly those that can be bounded by a relatively small set of rules.

Consider, for example, the following set of rules:

```
professor(tracy)
teaches(tracy,ai)
course(ai)
if professor(X) and teaches(X,Y) and course(Y)
              then pay(X, 3)
if pay(Y,X2) and X2 > 0 then employee(Y)
```

From these rules, we can deduce that employee(tracy). This notion of using rules to define our knowledge gives us a simple mechanism for solving various complex problems. The remainder of this chapter defines how a production system does this problem solving. Expert systems are widely deployed and have solved a wide variety of problems, such as scheduling, configuration, and diagnosis. Applications of expert systems to areas such as law and medicine have become fields of study in their own right.

8.2 THEORY OF PRODUCTION SYSTEMS

Production systems are based on a simple theoretical model of computation. This model can be used in many ways and applied to many different types of problems.

8.2.1 Production System Procedure

A production system uses a simple cycle: it applies rules and then modifies a global data structure called **working memory**[1] (see Figure 8.1). It starts with an initial **rule base,** which contains all the IF-THEN rules that dictate under what circumstances data in the working memory should change. The working memory can also be initialized by writing in known information for the initial state of a particular instance of the general problem. The system then functions by examining all the rules conditions (the IF parts) and determining which ones are satisfied, given the current working memory contents. The rules whose conditions are met form a set of rules called the **conflict set.** One of these rules is chosen to be applied (or **fired**) by using a **conflict resolution strategy.** The rule is fired and, in the process, updates the working memory (and in some systems, it can also update the rule base!). The

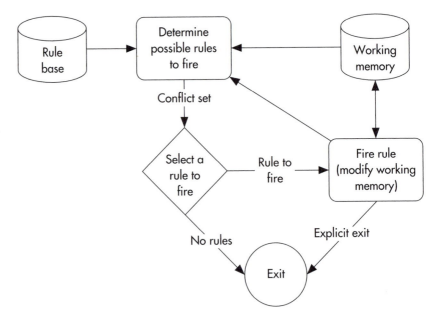

FIGURE 8.1

Production system procedure. The heavier lines indicate the production system cycle.

---

[1] Strictly speaking, this procedure most closely follows the *Official Programming System, Version 5,* OPS/5 production system procedure. See Brownston et al. (1985) for more details on OPS/5.

cycle of picking and firing rules continues until either there are no more rules to fire or an explicit exit is made when a certain rule is fired.

8.2.2 Production System Conflict Resolution Strategies

The heart of a production system is the strategy that is used to pick from the conflict set the rule to fire. Varying the way this is done changes the behavior of the system, sometimes dramatically. The strategy chosen essentially controls the way the search for a solution is carried out. Usually, this strategy is a simple one (such as pick the first applicable rule), but it could be any of the following:

- *First applicable rule.* The strategy of picking the first applicable rule allows the rules to be ordered by the designer of the system, who can then use that order to ensure that the system will terminate and to control which rules fire first.
- *Most complex rule.* The rule with the most conditions may be chosen to fire first because it is the most specific and therefore has used more information from the working set and may arrive at a solution more quickly.
- *Least recently used rule.* The rule that has not been used for the longest period of time may be used to ensure that the maximum number of rules from the rule base are used to solve the problem. This strategy is based on the premise that all the rules are needed.

A rule is not usually refired until the working memory used to satisfy the conditions (the left-hand side, or IF side) has changed. This practice avoids an infinite loop on a single rule.

Typically a production system[2] works by examining the values in the working memory, searching for the matching conditions (left-hand sides) of rules, and then determining which rules have conditions that are met. This method is called a **data-driven** (or **forward-chaining**) approach. Alternatively, an expert system can be asked to show a particular goal (i.e., the termination condition); then the production system can look for right-hand sides of rules that could generate the goal (or parts of the goal). Then the left-hand sides of those rules that lead to the goal are examined to determine which rules would generate their conditions and so forth. This is approach is called a **goal-driven** (or **backward-chaining**) approach.[3]

---

[2] Modern expert system environments usually support both backward- and forward-chaining mechanisms.

[3] Inspired by how the Prolog programming language performs backward chaining. See Clocksin and Mellish (1984) for more details on Prolog.

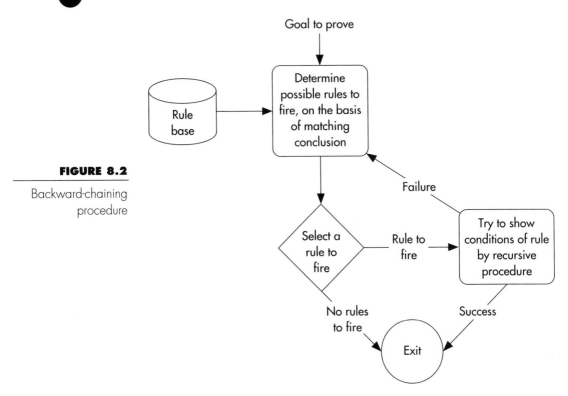

FIGURE 8.2

Backward-chaining
procedure

Figure 8.2 illustrates how backward chaining works. It begins by setting a goal that it would like to show. It then tries to match that goal to the conclusion part (right-hand side) of rules. Only rules that can produce this goal in their conclusions have a chance of proving this goal. It then chooses one of those rules and tries to prove the conditions (left-hand side) of the that rule (if any). It attempts to prove the condition by reentering the procedure. If it is able to prove all the conditions of the chosen rule, then the recursive calls to the procedure will return success and the goal will be proved. If one of the conditions cannot be shown, then one of the recursive calls will return failure and that rule will fail. Then we can try to select another subgoal to show the original goal.

A set of Prolog statements illustrates the backward-chaining process:

```
father(sam).
parent(P)  :- mother(P).
parent(P)  :- father(P).
```

Prolog statements are of the form *conclusion :- conditions*, where :-

can be read as if. The conditions are represented as a list of conjugates separated by commas. These Prolog statements mean that Sam is a father and something is a parent if it is a mother or a father. Variables are represented by uppercase letters. To show the goal parent(sam), we look for rules with conclusions that match the goal. The two parent rules both match the goal (unifying the variable with sam). If we decide to use the first rule fires first strategy, then we try to show mother(sam) with a recursive use of the procedure. However, mother(sam) is not provable (because it does not fit our fact), so the recursive call fails. We then try the second rule with father(sam) as the subgoal in a recursive use of the procedure. This one is provable and matches the fact father(sam). Therefore the recursive call returns true. So the original goal of parent(sam) can return true.

Some problems lend themselves to a data-driven approach. Take, for example, the problem of medical diagnosis. The goal is to determine the underlying pathology that matches the conditions given. We are given a list of specific symptoms. Using a data-driven approach, we would look for rules that have a left-hand side that matches our symptoms and then fire only those rules that apply to this set of symptoms. For the diagnosis problem, we would start by looking at all the rules that identify problems (of any kind) and then trying to determine what other rules must to be satisfied in order to identify any problem. This procedure is likely to involve most of the rules, unless there are only a small set of problems that can be identified or a likely problem can be identified.

Other problems lend themselves to a goal-driven approach, specifically, those in which a precise goal can be specified. Suppose we want to find a path between two points, using a set of data that identifies the positions of obstacles on a large map. Our goal is to get from A to B. We might find that we can move directly from A to B. In most cases, we would not have to use large portions of the data on the map, because we only need the part that is between A and B.

8.2.3 Representing Problems as Production Systems

Problems can be stated in the form of a production system to be solved. To do so, you must specify

- a set of facts, or initial working memory
- a set of rules
- a **termination condition,** which specifies either when a solution has been found or when no solution exists

Example 1. *Simple diagnosis.* We wish to diagnose the cause of a problem with our gas oven. The oven exhibits the following symptoms:

Pilot light is on.

Oven does not heat.

Our termination condition is either a problem has been found that explains our symptoms or all applicable rules have been tried and no problem was found.

We can write rules to diagnose oven problems, such as

Rule 1	if the oven has a pilot light then the oven is a gas oven
Rule 2	if the oven has nongas burners then the oven is an electric oven
Rule 3	if the oven is a gas oven and the pilot light is off then the problem is that the oven is dirty, or the pilot light is faulty, or there is no gas supply
Rule 4	if the oven is an electric oven and the burners do not work then the problem is that the oven is not plugged in, or the fuse is blown, or the power supply has failed
Rule 5	if the oven is an electric oven and the burners do work and the oven does not work then the problem is that theoven heating element has failed
Rule 6	if the oven is a gas oven and the pilot light is on and the oven does not work then the oven is dirty
Rule 7	if the oven is an electric oven and the burners do not work then the problem is that the oven is not plugged in, or the fuse is blown, or the power supply has failed

To solve this problem, we first need to apply Rule 1 (the only rule that applies to our current working memory) to determine whether or not the oven is a gas oven. The fact that it is a gas oven is then written to working memory. Once we know it is a gas oven, we can search for rules that apply; and we find that Rule 6 is the only new rule that applies (the conditions for Rule 1 have not yet changed, so it is not part of the conflict set). We can then determine that the problem is that the oven is dirty. Because we have found a problem, our termination condition is met and we exit the production system.

8.3 EXPERT SYSTEMS AND PRODUCTION SYSTEMS

Although expert systems are based on the production system model, there is usually an **expert system development environment** (sometimes called an **expert system shell**) that provides other capabilities to make the system more maintainable and easier to build. An expert system development environment usually includes the following components:

- **Inference engine.** Executes the procedure of a production system by choosing which rules to fire and by modifying the working memory as the system runs.

- **Explanation subsystem.** Direct support for generating explanations of an outcome of the expert system; provides to a user meaningful explanations as to what rules were applied and why.

- **Rules and knowledge-base editor.** Specialized editor for creating rules and facts to be stored in the rule base.

- **User interface builder.** Support for building user interfaces that are appealing and easy to use; often be the key that determines whether or not the expert system gets used as intended.

- **Knowledge base.** A knowledge base is more general than a rule base and allows the storage of other forms of knowledge.

- **Testing and debugging environment.** Environment that helps find bugs and inconsistencies in a knowledge base; particularly critical for a knowledge base with many interacting rules.

Expert system tools are also beginning to offer support for other, more advanced reasoning techniques, such as nonmonotonic reasoning (see Chapter 12 for more details on these techniques).

Some commercial expert system development environments also are beginning to support object-oriented data types. Usually these systems support a more complex data type, which can be used in the working memory, rather than just the simple data types mentioned here. This support for object-oriented data types is not completely consistent with the object-oriented approach because the functionality of the objects is not embedded in the objects but still is usually represented by separate rules. See Section 8.5 for examples of how rules have been added to object-oriented designs for AI systems in C++.

8.4 APPLICATIONS OF EXPERT SYSTEMS

Production systems (particularly in the form of rule-based expert systems) have been extremely successful. The following sample applications are meant to illustrate the breadth of successful applications.

Expert systems are particularly successful in applications where the following conditions hold:

- The problem area can be scoped well enough to allow the range of input information as well as the set of possible solutions to be defined.
- The required knowledge can be written in the form of rules and does not require the use of other techniques such as modal or nonmonotonic reasoning techniques.
- The problem area is not large (expert systems with more than several thousand rules tend to be hard to maintain and extend).
- Solutions to the problem area are not easily expressed by a traditional algorithm.

The most successful application areas for expert systems have been

- *Diagnosis and repair.* Diagnose the root problem on the basis of symptoms.
- *Medical applications for diagnosis and treatment.*
- *Advisors for complex problem areas.*
- *Classification problems.* Given an input set of data, classify each piece of information into one of many possible categories.
- *Validation problems.* Given a set of rules that must be met (like regulations), determine whether or not the current data set fits them. If not, why not?
- *Planning and scheduling.* Find a suitable plan or schedule on the basis of the constraints of the input data.
- *Configuration problems.* DECs R1, or XCON for VAX system configuration.
- *Decision support.* SRIs Prospector for decision making in mineral exploration.

8.4.1 Diagnosis and Repair

Diagnosis and repair systems attempt to diagnose problems on the basis of incoming symptom information. Some of these systems must filter out thousands of irrelevant messages to determine which ones are valid symptoms for problems within the systems scope.

Generally, these systems must also be able to correlate different symptoms in an attempt to determine whether they relate to a common problem.

Example 2. *GCESS: A symptom-driven diagnostic shell.* This application shell can be used for any applications that use incoming symptoms to diagnose a set of potential problems (Holtzmann and Fischer, 1993). It was built to support a system for the United States Air Force called Guidance and Control Expert System Shell (GCESS), but the intent was to develop a shell that was general enough to be used for other diagnostic applications.

Example 3. *Network diagnostic systems (Pacific Bell).* Networks can provide a challenging and complex environment for diagnosis of problems, so they have been a popular application for expert systems. Pacific Bell has developed expert systems to monitor, repair, and predict faults in the network. A system monitors for significant errors by filtering the incoming messages and looking for only those that indicate serious problems. It has a repair subsystem that is essentially an advisor that maintains expertise on how to fix problems. This approach allows the repair staff to be more effective. The main system has a predictive component that checks system files and notifies personnel of impending problems, even before the problems create error messages.

Example 4. *IMPACT: Network event correlation.* GTE Laboratories developed an expert system shell to perform network alarm correlation in real time (Jakobson, Weissman, and Goyal, 1995). It has been used to build various telecommunications network event correlation applications. It uses a form of reasoning that is called **model-based reasoning** and uses models of the network configuration and models of network elements to do intelligent correlation of alarms coming from the network.

8.4.2 Medical Applications

The medical field has long been the source of many successful expert system applications. Most of the systems pick a specific medical area and the expertise for that can match (or sometimes surpass) human experts in the area.

Example 5. *PUFF.* The purpose of this system is to diagnose pulmonary function disorders by using data from patient respiratory tests. An early version with only 55 rules was tested against medical experts and achieved an outstanding 90 to 100% agreement (Feigenbaum, 1977). A later system used frames and rules to support the rule and knowledge base, and has further evolved into follow-up systems called CENTAUR and WHEEZE.

Example 6. *ONCOCIN.* This system assists oncologists (doctors specializing in cancer) with the management of a treatment regime for cancer patients undergoing structured chemotherapy (Bischoff et al., 1983). ONCOCIN contains a rule base that has knowledge about cancer treatments and drugs and uses that knowledge to critique a physicians treatment plan.

Example 7. *PHEO-ATTENDING.* This expert system critiques a physicians treatment of a patient and recommends and describes other approaches (Miller, Blumenfucht, and Black, 1984). A key feature of this system is its attempt to model conflicting expertise and advice.

8.4.3 Advisors

Maintaining a complex set of knowledge in an expert system that can be used to advise others is a popular use of expert systems. In particular, if the expertise is difficult to acquire or if it is not cost effective for everyone to acquire the expertise, then it might be useful to encode that knowledge in an expert system. Many such expert systems have been developed by using rare experts to produce a highly available expert system.

Example 8. *The DRAIR Advisor.* This system helps in the preparation of Deficiency Report Analysis Information Reports (DRAIRs); Robey, Fink, Venkatesan, Redfield, and Ferguson, 1993. These reports provide U.S. Air Force engineers with an analysis of an airplane items performance history that includes cost and maintenance history. It then recommends improvements for deficient airplane parts. This system integrates the expert system with a large relational database of information relating the parts history.

8.4.4 Classification Problems

Classification problems take a particular input situation and try to determine how to classify that situation. Expert systems function well at this when a set of complex interrelated rules are needed to identify the situation.

Example 9. *The metals analyst.* General Electric Corporation has developed an expert system to identify common metals and alloys on the basis of 212 rules that codify simple properties (such as hardness, color, and density) and the results of simple chemical tests (Anthony, 1985).

Example 10. *FinCEN AI system (FAIS).* This expert system supports the Financial Crimes Enforcement Network (FinCEN), an agency of the U.S. Treasury Department. It evaluates reports of large cash transactions[4] in an attempt to identify money laundering. It functions as an analysts tool to help ferret out previously unknown

---

[4] Banks in the United States are required to report all such transactions over $10,000.

leads that are highly likely to be money laundering. This system also uses an underlying relational database of transaction data and a set of suspiciousness rules to form the core of the expert system.

8.4.5 Validation Problems

Validation involves checking a current input situation to see whether it meets a set of criteria or regulations. Because there are many areas where complex sets of regulations apply or where complex sets of criteria are needed, there are many expert systems of this type.

Example 11. *The GE compliance checker (GECCO).* This expert system is used by the home mortgage industry (Bynum, Noble, Todd, and Bloom, 1995). It supports the underwriting and resale processes for mortgage loans and is now being offered as a commercial product to home mortgage lenders. Loan underwriting is the process of assessing the risk incurred by the lender through evaluation of the subjects assets, property, and other factors that may affect the risk. GECCO makes the underwriting process less subjective and also much easier to improve.

8.4.6 Planning and Scheduling

Example 12. *Unit Commitment Advisor for power-generation scheduling.* Stone & Webster Engineering Corporation has developed an expert system (called the Unit Commitment Advisor to help in determining a schedule (and plan) for a power-generation station. It is used to make decisions such as when to generate power, when to buy power, and when to do maintenance.

Example 13. *DAS: Intelligent scheduling systems for shipbuilding.* Daewoo Shipbuilding Company (a Korean company that builds very large oil carriers and other ships) developed a system called DAewoo Shipbuilding Scheduling (DAS; J. Lee et al., 1995). Ship building involves complex scheduling issues because of customization requirements and time constraints. DAS is interesting because it combines three specialized expert systems to handle particular aspects of the schedule: erection at the docks, curved block assembly, and paneled block assembly. In addition to integrating these three expert systems, the system also uses a neural network for estimates of a tasks effort.

8.5 INTEGRATING RULE-BASED AND OBJECT-ORIENTED APPROACHES USING C++

Because rule-based expert systems have been very successful at solving many problems, many rule-based environments have been built by using C++ as a base. Some of those environments are ILOG Rules, RAL/C++, and R++, each of which takes a different approach to that integration of rule-based programming and C++.

8.5.1 Basic Conflict Between Rule-Based and Object-Oriented Programming

The rule-based programming paradigm is distinctly different from the object-oriented programming paradigm. In particular, there is a philosophical difference that makes rule-based programming difficult to integrate with object-oriented programming.

The rule-based paradigm depends on a separation between the rules (which dictate some of the behavior) and the facts and data of the problem (Figure 8.3a). In fact, this separation is one of the strengths of the rule-based paradigm because it allows the system to use the same rule base to solve many different problems. In the object-oriented paradigm, an objects behavior and data both must be specified as part of the objects class definition (Figure 8.3b). However, rule-based programming can be integrated naturally into the object-oriented paradigm (Figure 8.3c). The object-oriented paradigm can be extended to explicitly support a specific type of behavior, embodied in rules. The input data are objects and the rules are part of those objects. The R++ system described in Section 8.5.4 takes this approach. The approaches described in Sections 8.5.2 and 8.5.3 allow rules to be specified about objects, but in all other respects they function more as a traditional expert system that happens to be written in C++.

Most of the programs in this text use the approach given in Figure 8.3a. That is, we separate the problem-specific data from the object definition so that the O–O programs can handle many variants of the same type of problem. That done, we implement as much of the programs with the object-oriented paradigm as is reasonable while keeping the problem flexibility.

FIGURE 8.3

(a) The rule-based paradigm separates data from behavior. (b) The object-oriented paradigm depends on an integration of data and behavior. (c) Integration of rule-based and object-oriented paradigms.

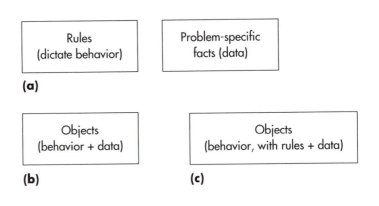

8.5.2 ILOG Rules

The ILOG Rules development environment, sold by ILOG, Incorporated, allows the addition of rule-based modules into C++ applications. This system translates each modules rules into C++ code, which can then be compiled into an executable program. The approach is to allow access to an inference engine written in C++ by a subset of the code. It essentially embeds a traditional expert system inference engine and rule base in a C++ application. It also supports a **Truth Maintenance System** (TMS) to support nonmonotonic reasoning and keeping working memory consistent (see Chapter 12 for more on nonmonotonic reasoning). The following example gives a definition of rules and shows how that definition integrates with objects. Note that the rules are very similar to conventional expert system rules, in particular, the OPS/5 expert system shell syntax.

```
//==================================================
// PLANES RULES BASE⁵
//==================================================
{
#include <iostream.h>
#include <iplanes/movobj.h>
#include <iplanes/fighter.h>
#include <iplanes/awacs.h>
#include <iplanes/missile.h>
#include <iplanes/simul.h>
extern SimSimulator* simulator;
}
(defimplementation MovingObject ()
(
  (heading type {float} )
  (speed type {float} )
  (headingToMatch type {float} )
  (speedToMatch type {float} )
  (state type {SimState} )
  (side type {int} )
  ))
//
(defimplementation Fighter (MovingObject)
(
  (leader type {SimMovingObject*} )
  (enemy type {SimFighter*} )
```

---

[5] Used by permission from ILOG, Inc. These rules are included as part of ILOGs *C++ Software Components Demonstration CD/ROM*, February, 1995.

```
(isControlled type {int}
   reader {?object->isControlled()}
   writer {?object->setControlled(?value)} )
(leaderHeading type {float}  writer {0} )
(leaderSpeed type {float}  writer {0} )
(distanceToLeader type {LeaderDistance} writer {0} )
(deltaHeading type {float}  writer {0} )
(leaderSituation type {SimSituation}  writer {0} )
(fuel type {float}  writer {0} )
(missiles type {int} )
))

(defimplementation Awacs (MovingObject)
  ((headingToPoint type {float}  writer {0} )
   (distanceToPoint type {float}  writer {0} )
   ))

(defimplementation Missile (MovingObject)
  ((target type {SimMovingObject*} )
   (sender type {SimFighter*} )
   (fuelLevel type {int} )
   ))
   .
   .
   .
   .
//————————————————————————————————————
// The ruleset
//————————————————————————————————————

(defruleset Fighting

// ==================================================
// The rules that make an escorter follow its
// leader
// ==================================================

// Standard behavior: go in the leader direction

(defrule catch_up_leader high
  ?p:(Fighter leader<>0)
  ->
  (modify ?p headingToMatch=
          {p->getHeadingToLeader()} )
  )
```

```
// If the plane is before its leader, try to go
// behind. Slow down to make a steep turn in the
// leader direction

(defrule turnToLeader default
  ?p:(Fighter leader<>0 leaderSituation=SimBefore
    heading<>{?p->getHeadingToMatch()} )
  ->
  (modify ?p speedToMatch=SimMinimumSpeed)
  )

// If the plane is far from its leader, but going
// to the leader, then set the maximum speed.

(defrule catchUpLeader1 default
  ?p:(Fighter leader<>0 leaderSituation=SimBefore
    heading={?p->getHeadingToMatch()}
distanceToLeader>=SimFar)
  ->
  (modify ?p speedToMatch=SimMaximumSpeed)
  )
```

The preceding code comes from a game that involves flying a plane and trying not to get shot down. It uses C++ objects (defined in the header files) and rules such as these to give the opponent fighter aircraft some rule-based intelligence. These rules would then be sent through a preprocessor to translate them into C++.

Problem data in working memory is expressed as objects. The integration of object-oriented programming with rule-based programming is accomplished primarily through the objects in working memory.

8.5.3 Rule-Extended Algorithmic Language (RAL/C++)

RAL/C++ is produced by Production Systems Technologies, Incorporated and more tightly integrates object-oriented programming with a rule-based approach.[6] It allows the definition of special objects—working memory elements, rules, and a knowledge source—to support the rule-based portion of the application.

Working memory elements (WMEs) are objects that can be checked for matches with the left-hand side (LHS) of a rule. WMEs can be grouped and structured so that they can be efficiently

---

[6] See Forgy and Hrishenko (1991a,b) and Forgy (1994) for more information on RAL/C++.

matched to the conditions to see which ones are satisfied. Rules have a LHS that checks WMEs to see whether the rule should fire and a right-hand side (RHS) that performs actions, much like a regular C++ function body. Having distinct declarations for WMEs also allows compile-time type checking to ensure that all of the LHSs of rules depend only on objects declared to be WMEs.

A **knowledge source** in RAL/C++ consists of a set of rules, a set of working memory elements, and functions and objects. This structure allows a single application to use multiple knowledge sources and to keep them distinct, and to contain what amounts to multiple expert systems, each with its own rule set and working memory. These component expert systems could then be tuned to work on a subset of the problem and to communicate their results (RAL/C++ has a construct called **channels** to do sharing between knowledge sources.) The following code in RAL/C++ shows the syntax of how rules and WMEs are defined. This example shows only the syntax of RAL/C++.

```
module test_module;
#include fire.h
/* Declare the type of knowledge source */
BaseKsObject test_ks;
/* Declare the WMEs and the rule set */
wmedef Msg
{
  symbol val;
} ;
ruleset test_rset : ∧PrintMsg
*{
test_rule
{
  C1 (Msg val :: str);
->
  delete C1;
  printf(%s, pname(str));
}
} *
```

RAL/C++ also gives the programmer direct control over the conflict resolution strategy by having function that selects a rule that has the conditions of its LHS met by the working memory and another function that explicitly executes the RHS of the rule. RAL/C++ goes a step further than ILOG Rules toward an integrated object-oriented approach. In RAL/C++, both working memory and the declaration of rules and knowledge sources are both explicitly defined as objects.

8.5.4 R++

R++ integrates rules as a new type of class method that specifies rulelike behavior for the object.[7] As such, it more directly integrates rule-based programming into an object-oriented paradigm than either RAL/C++ or ILOG Rules does. Specifically, R++ uses a new element called a **path-based rule,** which has syntax and semantics similar to C++ class functions. Path-based rules are declared as part of a class definition and operate directly on C++ objects. Because they are part of the regular class definition, they also adhere to other object-oriented expectations, such as heritability. The intent is to give C++ programmers a natural way to perform data-driven tasks, such as enforcing object constraints and reacting to important object states.

A simple example of a rule declaration in R++ follows:

```
class Employee
{
protected:
  char*name;
  int salary;
  int years_of_experience;
  Employee*manager;
  .  .  .
  rule paid_too_much;
} ;

rule Employee::paid_too_much {
  Employee*m = manager &&
  m->salary > salary
=>
  cout << name << "is overpaid because they make
            more than their manager" << m->name;
}
```

In this example, we check employees to see whether or not they are overpaid (here, overpayment is found if they earn more than their manager). The program works by checking to see if this rule should be applied any time an object of the class employee changes its data (if either the manager or the salary changes, the rule should be

---

[7] The system is currently an internal prototype within AT&T Labs. See *R++: Adding Path-Based Rules to C++,* by J. Crawford, D. Dvorak, D. Litman, A. Mishra, and P. Patel-Schneider, DRAFT of July 1995. Versions for education and research can be requested by sending electronic mail to r++@eagle.hr.att.com at AT&T. See also AT&T (1995).

checked). It will then print out the name of the employee who is overpaid whenever that object state is met.

The simplicity of R++s approach makes it easy to integrate R++ code into a C++ program. In particular, R++ is an excellent way to enforce constraints for an object-oriented database.

8.6 A C++ PRODUCTION SYSTEM

The Prolog-like, backward-chaining production system described in this section is a simple goal-driven production system written in C++. Its design and implementation take an object-oriented approach, but the resulting rule-based system does not integrate rules and working memory into the object-oriented paradigm. The approach here is to use rules like those in Prolog and to use a Prolog-like inference engine to prove goals. The following Prolog.h file defines Prolog-like facts and rules as subclasses defined within the PrologBase class. These subclasses use the unification algorithms defined in the logic.h file.

```
//file: pclause.h
#ifndef _pclause_H_
#define _pclause_H_

#include <stdio.h>
#include <iostream.h>
#include "logic.h"
#include "list.h"

/*
 * PrologBase defines a common base class for
 * objects of class PrologFact and PrologRule so
 * that they can be stored in the same container
 * class. Also, a pure virtual function match() is
 * defined, which makes matching between a Complex
 * object and an object of one of these classes
 * transparent. If the match succeeds, the
 * substitution that was needed to unify both
 * predicates is returned, together with a set of
 * clauses, if any, that represent new goals that
 * must be satisfied.
 */
class PrologBase
{
  public:
```

```
        virtual ~PrologBase() { };
        int operator==(const PrologBase &) const;
        virtual PrologBase *clone() const = 0;
        virtual void display() const = 0;
        virtual int match(const Complex &matchme,
                        PtrList<Complex> &newgoals,
                        Substitution &subst) = 0;
};


/*
 * Class PrologFact represents facts that may be
 * stored in the Prolog DB. It is little more than
 * a specialization of class Complex.
 */
class PrologFact : public PrologBase, public
                                            Complex
{
  public:
      PrologFact(const char *);
      PrologFact(const PrologFact &);
      PrologBase *clone() const;
      void display() const;
      int match(const Complex &, PtrList<Complex>
                                & , Substitution &);
};


ostream &operator<<(ostream &, const PrologFact &);


/*
 * Class PrologRule represents rule that may be
 * stored in the Prolog DB. Rules consist of a
 * head, an object of type Complex, a body, and a
 * list of Complex objects.
 */
class PrologRule : public PrologBase
{
  friend ostream &operator<<(ostream &, const
                            PrologRule &);
  public:
      PrologRule(const char *);
      PrologRule(const PrologRule &);
      PrologBase *clone() const;
      void display() const;
      int match(const Complex &, PtrList<Complex>
                        & , Substitution &); private:
```

```
      Complex head;
      PtrList<Complex> body;
};

#endif

========================================================

//file prolog.h
#ifndef _prolog_H_
#define _prolog_H_

#include <stdio.h>
#include "pclause.h"
#include "btrack.h"
#include "ptable.h"

class Prolog;

/*
 * Class PrologNode represents nodes in the search
 * tree. It contains the goal stack, binding
 * information, and a reference to the clause that
 * was last visited.
 */
class PrologNode : public BackNode
{
  friend Prolog;
  public:
      PrologNode();
      PrologNode(PtrList<Complex> *);
      ~PrologNode();

      int operator==(const BackNode &) const;
    void display() const;
    BackNode *expand_one(int);
  private:
      PtrList<Complex> *goalstack;
      Substitution subst;
    int lastdone;
};

/*
 * Class Prolog represents the search technique. In
 * this case, as will be expected, a backtracking
```

```
 * algorithm is selected. Functions are defined to
 * enter queries and to extract the
 * results from the search.
 */
class Prolog : public BackTrack
{
  friend PrologNode;
  public:
    Prolog(PrologTable &);
      int is_goal(const BackNode *);
      void set_query(const char *);
      int get_result(Substitution &);
      int get_next_result(Substitution &);
  private:
      static PrologTable *table;
};

#endif
```

The development of the following Prolog-like inference engine was greatly simplified by the earlier development of the unification algorithm and other logic classes.

```
 //file: pclause.cpp
#include "pclause.h"

/*
 * This function is here to keep
 * PtrArray<PrologBase>::find() happy. It is not
 * actually used anywhere (if it were, it should be
 * made pure virtual, and the real definition of
 * this function should be in PrologFact and
 * PrologRule).
 */
int PrologBase::operator==(const PrologBase &)
                                              const
{
  return(0);
}

PrologFact::PrologFact(const PrologFact &other)
      : Complex(other)
{
}
```

```
PrologFact::PrologFact(const char *str)
  : Complex(str)
{
}

/*
 * Match() determines if the Prolog fact matches
 * the specified Complex by unifying the two of
 * them. If they do match, the resulting
 * substitution is stored in subst. Before the
 * actual match is done, a variant of the Prolog
 * fact is created to ensure that "fresh" variables
 * are being used.
 */
int PrologFact::match(const Complex &matchme,
PtrList<Complex> &outgoals, Substitution &subst)
{
  Complex variant = *this;
  variant.update_vars();

  if (matchme.unify(variant, subst))
      return(1);
  return(0);
}
PrologBase *PrologFact::clone() const
{
  return(new PrologFact(*this));
}

void PrologFact::display() const
{
  cout << *(Complex *)this << ".";
}

ostream &operator<<(ostream &stream, const
                                    PrologFact &f)
{
  return(stream << f << ".");
}

PrologRule::PrologRule(const PrologRule &other)
{
  head = other.head;
  body = other.body;
}
```

```
PrologBase *PrologRule::clone() const
{
  return(new PrologRule(*this));
}

/*
 * PrologRule's must be of the form:
 *
 * a(X, Y) :-
 *b(X, Y) &
 *c(X, Y).
 *
 * Note the occurrence of '&' instead of ','. This
 * is because a delimiter is needed other than '&'.
 * Also, don't forget the '.' at the end.
 */
PrologRule::PrologRule(const char *str)
{
  char buf[256];
  char const *p = str;

  p = strstr(str, ":-");
  strncpy(buf, str, p - str);
  *(buf + (p - str)) = '\0';

  head = buf;

  ++p;
  while (isspace(*++p))
      ;
  str = p;

  while ((p = strchr(str, '&')) || (p = strchr
                                        (str, '.')))
  {
      Complex *cplex;

      strncpy(buf, str, p - str);
      *(buf + (p - str)) = '\0';
    cplex = new Complex(buf);
      body.addtotail(cplex);
      if (*p != '.')
          while (isspace(*++p))
                ;
      else
```

```
            break;
        str = p;
    }
}

/*
 * Match() determines if the Prolog rule matches
 * the specified Complex by unifying the head of
 * the rule with the Complex. If the unification
 * succeeds, the resulting substitution is stored
 * in 'subst' and the goals in the body of the
 * rules are updated with the substitution and
 * copied to 'outgoals'. Before the actual match is
 * done a variant of the rule is created to ensure
 * "fresh" variables are being used.
 */
int PrologRule::match(const Complex &matchme,
                      PtrList<Complex> &outgoals,
                      Substitution &subst)
{
  Substitution s;

  /*
   * Create a variant of the head only; the terms
   * in the body will be updated only if the
   * unification succeeds.
   */
  Complex variant = head;
  variant.update_vars(s);

  if (matchme.unify(variant, subst))
  {
    Complex *c;
      PtrListIterator<Complex> iter(outgoals);

      /*
       * Copy the terms in the body to outgoals and
       * update them with the substitutions that
       * were used in creating the variant and in
       * the unification.
       */
      outgoals = body;
      for (c = iter.getfirst(); c; c =
                                iter.getnext())
        {
```

```
            c->update_vars(s);
            c->apply_subst(subst);
        }
      return(1);
    }
  return(0);
}

void PrologRule::display() const
{
  cout << *this;
}

ostream &operator<<(ostream &stream, const
                                    PrologRule &rule)
{
  ROPtrListIterator<Complex> iter(rule.body);
  const Complex *c;

  stream << rule.head << ":-\n";

  stream << "\t" << *iter.getfirst();
  while ((c = iter.getnext()))
      cout << ",\n\t" << *c;

  cout << ".";
}

======================================================

//file prolog.cpp
#include "prolog.h"
PrologTable *Prolog::table;

PrologNode::PrologNode()
{
  lastdone = -1;
}

PrologNode::~PrologNode()
{
  delete goalstack;
}

/*
```

```
 * Note that the argument passed to this function
 * must point to allocated memory.
 */
PrologNode::PrologNode(PtrList<Complex> *solveme)
{
  goalstack = solveme;
  lastdone = -1;

  /*
   * Rename all variables in the goal stack so as
   * to make them unique. Store the original and
   * new values of the variables in the
   * substitution so that the original variables
   * with their bindings can be returned.
   */
  PtrListIterator<Complex> iter(*goalstack);
  for (Complex *c = iter.getfirst(); c; c =
                                   iter.getnext())
     c->update_vars(subst);
}

int PrologNode::operator==(const BackNode &other)
                                              const
{
  const PrologNode &pother = (PrologNode &)other;
  if (!(*goalstack == *pother.goalstack))
      return(0);
  if (!(subst == pother.subst))
      return(0);
  return(lastdone == pother.lastdone);
}

void PrologNode::display() const
{
  cout << subst << "\n";
}

/*
 * The procedure for expanding a PrologNode is
 * fairly simple. The Prolog rules and facts are
 * searched for one that matches the top goal of
 * the goal stack. If any new goals are introduced
 * by this match (this will happen if a rule
 * instead of a simple fact was involved in the
 * match), these goals are placed on top of the
```

```
 * goal stack. Because the new goals are placed on
 * top of the stack, they will be solved before
 * the old goals, which is exactly the way Prolog
 * works.
 */
BackNode *PrologNode::expand_one(int)
{
  Substitution subst_used;
  PtrList<Complex> *newgoals;
  PrologNode *succ;
  Complex *first;

  newgoals = new PtrList<Complex>;

  /* Get top goal from goal stack. */
  first = goalstack->gethead();

  /*
   * Search the Prolog database for a match,
   * starting at the entry next to the one that
   * was last visited.
   */
  lastdone = Prolog::table->findmatch(lastdone + 1,
                    *first, *newgoals, subst_used);

  /* If no match could be found, there are
   * successor nodes. */
  if (lastdone < 0)
  {
    delete newgoals;
    return(NULL);
  }
  else
  {
    PtrListIterator<Complex> iter(*goalstack);
    Complex *c, *d;

  /* Create a successor node. */
    succ = new PrologNode;
    /*
     * The new goals (if any) must be solved before
     * the old goals: place them on top of the
     * successor's stack.
     */
    succ->goalstack = newgoals;
```

```
      /*
       * Copy the old goal stack, minus the first
       * element, which is now solved and must be
       * popped off, to the goal stack of the
       * successor. All variables occurring in the
       * old goals must be updated with the with the
       * new binding information that was obtained
       * from the match with the clause in the Prolog
       * database.
       */
      for (iter.getfirst(), c = iter.getnext(); c; c
                                 = iter.getnext())

    {
     d = c->clone();
      d->update_vars(subst_used);
      succ->goalstack->addtotail(d);
    }

      /*
       * Copy the substitution to the successor and
       * update it with the new binding information.
       */
      succ->subst = subst;
      succ->subst.update(subst_used);
      return(succ);
    }

}

Prolog::Prolog(PrologTable &pt)
  : BackTrack(0)
{
  table = &pt;
}

int Prolog::is_goal(const BackNode *node)
{
  const PrologNode *n = (PrologNode *)node;

  /* The node is a goal node if its stack is
   * empty. */
  return(n->goalstack->getcount() == 0);
}

  /*
```

```
 * Set_query() creates a new goal stack and
 * initializes the search tree.
 */
void Prolog::set_query(const char *str)
{
  PtrList<Complex> *goal;
  PrologNode *start;

  /* Create a new PrologNode and a new goal stack. */
  goal = new PtrList<Complex>;
  goal->addtohead(new Complex(str));
  start = new PrologNode(goal);

  /* Empty the search tree and insert a new start
   * node. */
  clear();
  set_startnode(start);
}

/*
 * Get_result() starts the search process. If a
 * solution is found 1 is returned and 0 otherwise.
 * The bindings that were needed to satisfy the
 * goal, if any, are returned in the supplied
 * substitution.
 */
int Prolog::get_result(Substitution &answer)
{
  if (generate())
  {
      const PrologNode *sol = (PrologNode *)
                                      get_goal();
      answer = sol->subst;
      return(1);
  }
  return(0);
}

/*
 * Get_next_result() restarts the search process
 * and returns the next solution if one could be
 * found.
 */
int Prolog::get_next_result(Substitution &answer)
{
```

```
  if (generate_next())
  {
    const PrologNode *sol = (PrologNode *)
                                      get_goal();
    answer = sol->subst;
    return(1);
  }
  return(0);
}
```

The Prolog-like inference engine and the prolog.h file defining facts and rules can be used to solve the following problem: What are Suzie and Robbie? Note that the syntax of the Prolog-like statements uses & rather than the commas normally used in Prolog. This program represents a simple semantic network with isa and has links.

```
//file: sample2.cpp
#include "prolog.h"

char *clauses[] =
{
    "has(robbie, darkspots).",
    "has(robbie, tawnycolor).",
    "eats(robbie, meat).",
    "has(robbie, hair).",
    "has(suzie, feathers).",
    "flieswell(suzie).",
    "isa(X, mammal):- \
                has(X, hair).",
    "isa(X, bird):- \
                has(X, feathers).",
    "isa(X, carnivore):- \
                eats(X, meat).",
    "isa(X, cheetah):- \
                isa(X, mammal) & \
                isa(X, carnivore) & \
                has(X, tawnycolor) & \
                has(X, darkspots).",
    "isa(X, albatross):- \
                isa(X, bird) & \
                flieswell(X).",
    NULL
};
```

```
int main()
{
   Substitution subst;

   /* Create Prolog database. */
   PrologTable table;

   /* Create search object, passing it to the Prolog
    * DB. */
   Prolog prolog(table);

   /* Fill the Prolog DB. */
   table.addclauses(clauses);

   /* Enter a query and start the search. */
   prolog.set_query("isa(X, Y)");
   prolog.get_result(subst);
   cout << subst << "\n";

   /* Important: clear the substitution. */
   subst.clear();
   while (prolog.get_next_result(subst))
   {
       cout << subst << "\n";
       subst.clear();
   }
   return(1);
}
```

8.7 SUMMARY

This chapter presents the basic theory for a production system, which consists of a working memory, a rule base, and a conflict resolution strategy. An expert system is a fully supported environment based on the production system model. Expert systems have been and continue to be very successful for many different types of problems in many types of environments. Several examples show the breadth of such expert system applications. The chapter also presents current products that are attempting to integrate the rule-based programming paradigm with the object-oriented paradigm.

8.8 REFERENCES

Many references provide a good background for the production system model, including Nilsson (1980) and Shinghal (1992). For other examples of expert system applications, see the *Proceedings of Innovative Applications of Artificial Intelligence* (IAAI) *Conference*. There are other references that provide many ideas and example expert systems such as Smart and Langeland-Knudsen (1986) and Shapiro (1987). More specific references are given throughout this chapter where appropriate.

8.9 EXERCISES

Warm-up Exercises

8.1. Describe the differences in difficulty of writing solutions for the elevator problem of Chapter 1 either in a conventional language or in using a rule-based environment.

8.2. Describe a problem where a goal-driven approach is much better than a data-driven approach.

8.3. Describe a problem where a data-driven approach is much better than a goal-driven approach.

8.4. Describe a problem in the area of software development where a rule-based approach would be appropriate.

Homework Exercises

8.5. Specify a working memory, rules, and a termination condition for a production system to solve the missionaries and cannibals problem as stated in Chapter 1.

8.6. One way to specify a conflict resolution mechanism is to assign what is known as a hill-climbing function value (see Chapter 5) to each state the working memory can assume. The idea is to examine the conflict set and pick the rule that will have the largest positive effect on the functions value. Specify a hill-climbing function for the missionaries and cannibals problem.

8.7. Specify a working memory, rules, and a termination condition for a production system to solve the elevator problem given in Chapter 1.

8.8. Evaluate the differing approaches of RAL/C++, ILOG Rules, and R++ in terms of usability, consistency with the object-oriented paradigm, and simplicity. On the basis of this evaluation, which product would you use to develop an application that has a large rule-based component? Why?

8.9. We noted in the chapter that large rule bases often tend to be difficult to maintain. Why? What complications occur as the rule base gets larger?

8.10. Choose one of the real-life examples given in the chapter and find the reference for it. Read the reference and evaluate how it could be improved to solve a larger set of problems. Also determine other, similar problems for which the approach taken by the example can be directly applied.

8.11. Specify a working memory, rules, and a termination condition for a production system to solve a class-scheduling problem. The system should have rules that can apply to any students needs. Assume that you need to develop a schedule for a student for one semester that maximizes the number of classes she takes that apply toward graduation. The rules should consider prerequisites, what the student has already taken, and what is required to graduate.

Programming Exercises

8.12. Using the C++ production system provided (as given in Section 8.6 or using R++), write a set of rules to solve the elevator problem of Chapter 1. Use the production system structure you defined in Exercise 8.7.

8.13. Modify the C++ production system given in Section 8.6 to use a different conflict resolution strategy. Modify it to use a least recently used rule algorithm. Apply this modified expert system to the 8-Puzzle problem. Also run the original C++ expert system on the same rule set. Are the results the same from the two expert systems?

8.14. Another commercial product, Rete++, produced by The Haley Enterprise, Inc., also integrates rule-based programming with C++. Gather more information about this product (electronic mail at info@haley.com). Investigate how it integrates rule-based programming into the object-oriented programming paradigm. How does it compare with the approaches of ILOG Rules, RAL/C++, and R++?

8.15. Design an expert system, using the C++ expert system shell, to assist football coaches in calling plays. Include in your program rules to handle opposing team strategies, records, and your teams ability to run the plays. For simplicity, consider that there are only 10 offensive plays and 10 defensive plays that either team can call. Also, assume that there is an historical record of how well a given team has played for each pair of the 100 combinations. Assume there are only two teams. The expert system should be able to predict the likely plays that your opponent will call and the best call that you could make in response.

8.16. Some expert system shells allow the right-hand side of rules to modify existing rules or create new rules. The intent is to allow the system to learn new rules and improve itself over time. This, however, can be a dangerous approach and should be done very carefully. Describe some problems that can occur if new rules can be created at run time.

Projects

8.17. Design an expert system that can assist a real estate agent in choosing properties for clients to visit. The system not only should attempt to find properties in the system that match the prospective buyers obvious criteria (cost, location, schools, etc.), but also should consider other factors that might influence a buyers likelihood of liking a property (perhaps marital status, age, temperament). Meet with an experienced real estate agent and extract rules that are likely to work. Also determine the information that can be searched easily in the housing listings.

8.18. Design and implement an expert system to answer questions about the United States Civil War. The program should be able to answer questions about the strategy deployed by generals for any battle of the war. In addition, implement a mechanism that will use previously existing battles to determine what might have happened had generals met in a battle *not* actually fought during the war, for example, Grant versus A. P. Hill at Richmond.

8.19. Design and implement an expert system to count the number of function points[8] in C++ code. You should use the rules that have been developed for counting function points, parse C++ code to look for the information to supply those rules, and then automatically output your function point count. Test your system by finding a person who is experienced in function point counting in C++ and have them count a few of the same examples that you use to test your expert system. Describe the results of your system in terms of performance, accuracy, and ability to replace human function point counters.

---

[8] Function points are a method of measuring the size of a program on the basis of inputs, outputs, files referenced, etc. Refer to *CACM*, February, 1993, Vol. 36, No. 2 and to the *IFPUG Function Point Counting Practices Manual, Release 3.0*, by J. Sprouls and published by the International Function Point Users Group, Westerville, Ohio, 1990

9

AUTOMATED THEOREM PROVING

9.1 THEOREM PROVING METHODS

Automated theorem proving has long been a concern of computer science and AI. However, the use of an explicit set of inference rules and axioms is not solely applicable to the world of mathematical proofs. Any system that depends on the consistency of its knowledge base and on the ability of that base to make deductions also requires a reliable inference mechanism.

Mathematicians may use methods that are not sound for proving a theorem but still come up with valid proofs in the end. They might skip steps or make intuitive leaps in order to construct a proof. Theorem provers do not need to be complete either. Indeed, many existing theorem provers are not complete, but they still can prove many useful results.

Methods that do not depend on domain-specific knowledge are sometimes called **weak problem-solving** methods. These methods contrast with mechanisms that do depend on domain-specific knowledge, such as rule-based expert systems.

At the first conference on Artificial Intelligence, held at Dartmouth in 1956, Newell and Simon discussed a program called the Logic Theorist, which is a deduction system for propositional logic (Newell, 1956). Another very early system was Gelernter's theorem prover for elementary geometry (Gerlernter, 1963). The General Problem Solver is an important descendant of the Logic Theorist and is discussed in Section 9.2.2 (Newell and Simon, 1963a, b).

9.2 MEANS-ENDS THEOREM PROVERS

Means-ends problem-solving methods work by trying to reduce the differences between the goal and the data. The earliest theorem-proving systems were of this type, and means-ends analysis of problems is still useful in other settings but rarely used directly in today's theorem provers. However, many of the strategies and concepts used in these early theorem provers are still used today. The general strategy was to reduce the statements to some sort of canonical form, to apply a set of sound (and usually complete) inference rules, and to use a strategy for applying those rules.

9.2.1 The Logic Theorist

As mentioned earlier, the Logic Theorist (LT) was one of the first theorem provers and was built by Newell and Simon (1956, 1963a). It was able to prove many theorems from the first and second chapters of Whitehead and Russell's 1913 text, *Principia Mathematica*. Newell and Simon were interested in understanding how mathematicians prove theorems, so they developed heuristics to try to model the theorem-proving process. LT proved theorems such as $\neg(P \lor Q) \to \neg P$. The LT operates by reducing the theorem to be proved to an axiom or an earlier proved theorem. It does this by reasoning backward, using three operators:

- *Detachment:* To show a theorem φ, the programs searches for an axiom or theorem of the form $\phi \to \varphi$. If it finds a matching axiom or theorem, it will then try to prove f.
- *Forward chaining:*[1] To show a theorem of the form $\phi \to \varphi$, it searches for an axiom or theorem of the form $\gamma \to \phi$ and then tries to prove $\gamma \to \varphi$.
- *Backward chaining:* To show a theorem of the form $\phi \to \varphi$, it searches for an axiom or theorem of the form $\gamma \to \varphi$ and then tries to prove $\phi \to \gamma$.

These three rules focus first on the goal (the "ends") and attempt to find methods (the "means") for achieving the goal. This is why the LT is a form of means-ends analysis theorem prover. The rules function much like the axiom schema introduced in Section 4.4. The LT uses the three operators in conjunction with substitutions and tautological replacement of terms to attempt to prove statements in

---

[1] These definitions of backward and forward chaining are specific to the Logic Theorist. They are similar in spirit, but the LT uses goal-driven search (or backward chaining), as defined in Section 5.1.

logic. A breadth-first search of the state space and application of the operators are used to generate new states.

9.2.2 The General Problem Solver

Development of the General Problem Solver (GPS; Newell and Simon, 1963b) was motivated by the hope that the technique of trying to eliminate differences could be used to solve problems. Many individuals appear to use such a technique of problem solving. Suppose we are given the task of parking a car. We could solve this problem by trying to eliminate the difference between the current state of the car and the goal of being parked. We first check to see if we are already parked. If we are not, we try to move the car so that it is closer to a parking space and then try to move it into the space. At each step, we compare our current state with the goal state and then try to eliminate a difference between the two. This method of reducing differences between the current state and a goal state is called **means-ends analysis.** This approach is often taken in planning systems (see Chapter 10).

GPS uses **goals, methods,** and **operators.** It develops goals to be used in solving a problem. Goals are of three types:

- *Transformation goals:* To transform one object into another
- *Reduction goals:* To reduce a difference between two objects by modifying one of them
- *Application goals:* To apply an operator to an object

A transformation goal is achieved with a tranformation method, which tries to reduce the difference (by using a reduction goal and a corresponding method) and then tries to recursively transform (with a new transformation goal), the result of the difference reduction into the desired goal. The basic structure for these methods is shown with

```
Transform-method(ϕ, φ)
   Reduction-method(ϕ, φ, ϕ)      //Transforms ϕ into
             ϕ by reducing difference between ϕ and φ
   if ϕ = φ then return(success)
   Transform(ϕ, φ)
Reduction-method(ϕ, φ, ϕ)
   Select untried operator O (if none, fail)
   Application-method(O, ϕ, ϕ) //Transforms ϕ into
                                  ϕ by applying O
Application-method(O, ϕ, ϕ)
   Reduce differences between ϕ and preconditions
          for O by using Reduction-method, if needed
   Produce ϕ by applying O to ϕ (or output of above)
```

| | **Operators** | | | | |
Possible differences	**Honk horn**	**Turn wheel**	**Forward**	**Backward**	**Signals**
Car position			X	X	X
Car direction		X	X	X	X
Car sound	X		X	X	X
Car lights					X

TABLE 9.1

An incomplete difference table for parking a car

A **difference table** is particularly helpful for choosing which operators to apply to reduce given differences. The purpose of the difference table is to identify what changes are possible for a given operator. Suppose we were able to perform the following tasks in a car: honk horn, turn steering wheel, move forward, move backward, turn on signals. We could apply some of them as operators to help us park the car. Honking the horn and turning on the signals do not help us achieve our goal; however, the other operators could help. A difference table can help us quickly identify which operators to use to get us closer to a goal.

Table 9.1, a partial difference table for parking a car, shows possible differences and whether an operator could possibly affect the difference. For example, honking the horn affects the sound a car is making, but it has no effect on the car's position. Driving a car forward or backward can affect the direction the car is moving. For a particular problem, some differences may not be as important as others. In the car-parking problem, the sound and lights are not important to the problem. In general, the differences can be prioritized, as well as the effectiveness of an operator in reducing a difference. This prioritization helps the user identify which operator to try next.

For complex problems, this simple variant of means-ends analysis is not usually very effective, because the differences can be interrelated or the operators create other differences. This simple method also requires a well-formulated goal, which you may or may not have at the outset of trying to solve a more complex problem.

9.3 RESOLUTION THEOREM PROVERS

In Chapter 6 we discussed resolution in terms of an inference rule. In this section we discuss how to use resolution in a theorem-proving system. One of the primary difficulties in implementing a theorem prover that uses resolution is that the number of potential resolutions grows exponentially. This method can create a very large search space and thus make it difficult to prove theorems that are based on a large number of axioms and theorems. However, several general methods allow us to approach this search problem. When building a theorem prover for a particular domain, search strategies can be tuned to the domain at hand by using a best-first search with a well-chosen heuristic.

9.3.1 Search Strategies

Several alternative search strategies can be used to choose from the available clauses to be resolved. When implementing a theorem-proving system for a particular application, one would probably use one or more of the following strategies, as well as a domain-specific heuristic, to produce a best-first search for a particular problem domain.

Unit-preference strategies. A **unit resolvent** is the outcome of an application of resolution in which one of the parent clauses is a **unit clause,** that is, a clause in which there is only one literal. In each application of resolution in which one of the resolvents is a unit clause, we get a clause that is shorter (in terms of the number of literals) than the other parent's. So, if we continue to apply resolution as long as at least one of the resolvents is a unit clause, we will continue to get closer to the empty clause.

Unfortunately, we cannot guarantee that we can prove any statement by using only unit resolvents, because this method is not a complete strategy in and of itself. In fact, normally this strategy is used in conjunction with others in order to produce a complete strategy. If we always use a unit resolvent when possible and some other strategy when we cannot use a unit resolvant, then we are using a **unit-preference** search strategy.

Set of support strategy. The **set of support** strategy is to identify some subset of the input clauses and require that each application of resolution use either one of those clauses or one of their descendants. For example, we could require that each resolution use the clause produced by the negated goal or one of its descendants. This particular application of the set of support strategy focuses attention on the statement that we wish to prove and assumes that it will generate the contradiction. If we choose this strategy (with the set of support being centered on the negated goal), it can be shown that as long as the other input clauses are satisfiable, then our strategy will be complete and always produce a contradiction when one exists (see Wos et al., 1984). This is not surprising, because we would expect the negated goal to be the one that ultimately produces the contradiction when resolved with the satisfiable set of clauses.

Breadth-first and depth-first strategies. We can select a simple breadth-first search of the clauses to find the shortest path to proving the goal. Or we can use Prolog, which uses a depth-first search for finding clauses to try and resolve. Both of these strategies will completely search the space and do not necessarily improve the performance of the resolution procedure. For small problems, however, these strategies can work quickly without the extra overhead that may be produced with the other strategies.

Input strategy. In the **input strategy** we always use one of the initial clauses (including the negated goal) as one of the clauses for each resolution. This strategy is very closely related to the unit resolution strategy. In fact, whenever unit resolution will produce a contradiction so will the input strategy, and vice versa. And, like the unit strategy, this strategy is not complete.

Take, for example, a set of unsatisfiable clauses in which none of the clauses is a unit clause. All clauses have more than one literal. The resolution of two of these clauses will always produce clauses that have at least two literals. Using the input strategy on this set of clauses will never produce the empty clause. But, for the moment, assume that we were able to produce the empty clause with this strategy, that we were able (in the last resolution) to resolve one of the input clauses with a unit clause to produce the empty clause. This thought experiment shows, however, that resolution is not possible, because, to achieve this result, we would also need a unit clause as one of the input clauses. Therefore, this example cannot be shown to be unsatisfiable by the input strategy, even though it is unsatisfiable.

Linear strategy. When we use a **linear strategy,** we choose as one of the resolvents either one of the input clauses or one of the ancestors

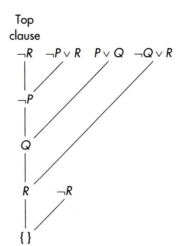

FIGURE 9.1

Using the linear strategy to produce a proof

of the other clause. In that sense, it is a generalization of the input strategy because it allows ancestral clauses to be used in the resolution. This method is called linear resolution, because it produces a proof that is linear in nature (Figure 9.1). The linear strategy can be shown to be refutation complete. The first clause (often called the **top clause**) used in the chain for a linear strategy should be picked so as to be the clause that makes the set unsatisfiable. This is usually the negation of the theorem to be proved. Picking the top clause in this way will guarantee that we will arrive at a contradiction by using it as the top clause, if a contradiction exists.

Ordered strategy. An **ordered strategy** for resolution is a very restrictive strategy for choosing clauses. For this strategy, we treat each clause as an ordered list and only use the first literal of each clause in resolutions. Using an ordered resolution strategy is much more efficient than the other strategies, because we are only searching a small portion of the search space to find potential clauses to resolve. However, this strategy alone is not refutation complete.

The Prolog programming language uses a form of this ordered strategy in its resolution mechanism (along with a depth-first search). However, Prolog requires its clauses to be **Horn clauses**. (A Horn clause is a clause with at most one positive literal.) With this restriction, the resolution mechanism is refutation complete and still very efficient.

Deletion strategies. A **deletion strategy** is a restriction technique in which clauses with a specified property are deleted before they are ever used by the resolution procedure. Because those clauses are deleted as soon as they appear, such a strategy can lead to computational savings.

One such deletion strategy is to remove any clause that contains a **pure literal,** which is a literal that has no complementary literals in the database. For example, if we have a literal $\neg A$ in several clauses but no clauses in the system that contain A, then we can delete all those clauses containing $\neg A$. The reason that we can delete such clauses is that we will never be able to eliminate those literals by using resolution and any clauses produced by resolution would contain that pure literal. Applying this technique to the initial set of clauses is all that is required, because resolution never generates a new pure literal.

Another deletion strategy is **tautology elimination**. A tautology is any clause containing a pair of complementary literals, such as $P(f(a)) \vee \neg P(f(a)) \vee Q(Y)$. It can be proved that removal of such clauses has no effect on the satisfiability or unsatisfiability of the set of clauses. However, we must be careful when applying this strategy to remove only tautologies with exactly complementary literals. That is, the two literals must be equal (except that one is the negation of the other) and not just unifiable. For example, $\neg P(f(Y)) \vee P(f(a))$ is not a tautology.

A third deletion strategy is **subsumption elimination**. A clause ϕ **subsumes** a clause Ψ if and only if there exists a substitution σ such that $\Psi \sigma \subset \phi$. For example, $P(f(a)) \vee Q(Z) \vee R(f(Z))$ subsumes $P(X) \vee Q(Y)$ because we can apply the substitution $\{X/f(a), Y/Z\}$ to the latter to produce a subset of the former. Consequently, we can delete the second clause from the database. This strategy simply says that adding other literals to the clauses is not helpful when the shorter clause subsumes it. It can be shown that the deletion of the subsumed clauses does not affect the satisfiability or unsatisfiability of the set of clauses.

9.3.2 Aids to the Resolution Inference Rule

One alternative resolution method is **hyperresolution.** The forms discussed in the preceding sections can combine only two clauses in each resolution step, a constraint that makes them **binary resolution** methods. However, it is possible to combine more than two clauses in each step, and this technique is called hyperresolution. In hyperresolution, we start with one clause that has several negative literals and resolve it with other clauses in the database that contain matching positive literals. The clause with the negative literals is called the **nucleus** of the hyperresolution, and the clauses with the positive literals are called the **satellites**. Indeed, all literals in the satellite clauses must be positive, even those not involved in the resolution. The clause that results from the hyperresolution must also contain only positive literals.

Hyperresolution is applied in an attempt to get to a contradiction quickly without generating the numerous intermediate steps that might be required by binary resolution. For example, consider the following nucleus:

$$\neg Cat(X) \vee \neg Fluffy(X) \vee Pet(X) \vee \neg Meows(X)$$

The following clauses are the satellites:

$$Cat(rufus)$$
$$Fluffy(rufus)$$
$$Meows(rufus)$$

Using hyperresolution, we can deduce the following clause in one step:

$$Pet(rufus)$$

This outcome would have taken three steps to reach if we had used binary resolution.

Hyperresolution is refutation complete, just as binary resolution is refutation complete.

Another useful tool to aid resolution is known as **demodulation,** which is a method of rewriting terms and clauses so that they take on equivalent forms. In other words, when a new clause is generated, we apply the demodulators to it to reduce it to a canonical form and then add it to the database. For example, we could define the following set of demodulators for family relationships:

$$Equal(mother(mother(X)), grandmother(X))$$
$$Equal(father(father(X)), grandfather(X))$$
$$Equal(father(brother(X)), father(X))$$
$$Equal(mother(brother(X)), mother(X))$$
$$Equal(mother(cousin(X)), aunt(X))$$
$$Equal(sister(mother(X)), aunt(X))$$

We can then replace all occurrences of *mother(mother(bill))* with *grandmother(bill)* in new clauses. Demodulation is used only to replace expressions (e.g., functions and constants, and functions of functions, and so on, but not predicates) with equivalent expressions.

A similar technique is known as **paramodulation,** which replaces terms with equivalent terms and can work in more complex situations. Consider, for example, the following paramodulator:

$$Equal(father(father(frodo)), bilbo)$$

We can apply this paramodulator to *ancestor_of(father(father(X)),X)* to get *ancestor_of(bilbo,frodo)* by using the information contained in the paramodulator. Paramodulation was able to replace *father(father(frodo))* with *bilbo* even though the clause required the substitution of $\{X/frodo, father(father(frodo))/bilbo\}$. Paramodulation allows a nontrivial replacement of variables in both the arguments of the equality predicate (the paramodulator) and the predicate into which the substitution is made. In demodulation, only one argument of the equality predicate is replaced—with the other argument, the equivalent defined in the demodulator.

9.3.3 Resolution with C++

In Section 9.6 we will present a resolution-based theorem prover implementation in C++ that uses the logic classes already introduced to implement a variant of the linear resolution strategy.

9.4 TABLEAU THEOREM PROVERS

An alternative proof method is the **tableau theorem prover,** which uses a table of alternative inference rules. The inference rules in the table use general forms. Usually, the input of a tableau theorem prover is FOPL statements in disjunctive normal form form rather than statements written in a more restrictive form such as clausal form. Many normal forms can be used, depending on the type of inference rules included in the particular tableau.

A tableau theorem prover works by constructing a proof tree, which keeps track of the application of inference rules and of the resulting statements. To prove a given statement, we ask the tableau theorem prover to prove the negation of that statement. The theorem prover then applies the inference rules given in the table until a contradiction is reached, that is, until a given expression and its negation both appear in the same branch of the proof tree (or until a direct contradiction, *false,* appears in the branch of the tree). All branches of the proof tree must be closed for the proof to be complete. This method is called **semantic tableau**, to emphasize the notion that the inference rules in the tableau impose a meaning on the clauses in the tableau by using a rule where one term can be replaced by a new term simply because another exists. The inference rules in a tableau encode some of FOPL's semantics and thereby allow these replacements to be made.

Some resolution theorem provers use the tableau method, although most use clausal form. We can define resolution in terms of several inference rules without using clausal form, but this approach makes resolution more complex to control. For a discussion of resolution through a tableau theorem prover and how to implement it, see Fitting (1990).

9.4.1 Tableau Inference Rules

Fitting (1990) has grouped his tableau inference rules into several categories. The first includes basic inference rules that are used to simplify an expression.

- Tableau inference rule to eliminate double negations:

$$\frac{\neg(\neg Z)}{Z}$$

- Tableau inference rule to reduce $\neg True$ to *False*:

$$\frac{\neg True}{False}$$

- Tableau inference rule to reduce $\neg False$ to $True$:

$$\frac{\neg False}{True}$$

Fitting (1990) also defined reduction rules for conjunctive and disjunctive forms of propositional logic. A **conjunctive form** can be split into two component parts that both logically follow from the conjunctive form. A **disjunctive form** can be split into two component pieces that are "or"ed together. α is used to represent any conjunctive form, and β represents any disjunctive form. Specific α and β forms are defined later, but general inference rules apply to the forms as follows:

- Tableau inference rule for conjunctive forms:

$$\frac{\alpha}{\begin{array}{c}\alpha_1\\\alpha_2\end{array}}$$

- Tableau inference rule for disjunctive forms:

$$\frac{\beta}{\beta_1|\,\beta_2}$$

By the α inference rule, we produce from one expression two new terms, both in the same branch of the tree. By the β inference rule, we produce from one expression two new terms, one assigned to one branch of the proof tree and the other to another branch. Table 9.2 lists the α and β forms to which these rules apply. The α forms are all ultimately some type of conjunction, and the β forms are all ultimately some type of disjunction. By tabulating these forms so that we can recognize them, we can save ourselves the effort of converting the input statements to a normal form, and a clausal form. $(X \uparrow Y)$ is equivalent to $\neg(X \wedge Y)$, and $\uparrow$ is called a **NAND** operator. $(X \downarrow Y)$ is equivalent to $\neg(X \vee Y)$, and $\downarrow$ is called a **NOR** operator.

Conjunctive Form			Disjunctive form		
α	α_1	α_2	β	β_1	β_2
$X \wedge Y$	X	Y	$\neg(X \wedge Y)$	$\neg X$	$\neg Y$
$\neg(X \vee Y)$	$\neg X$	$\neg Y$	$X \vee Y$	X	Y
$\neg(X \rightarrow Y)$	X	$\neg Y$	$X \rightarrow Y$	$\neg X$	Y
$\neg(X \leftarrow Y)$	$\neg X$	Y	$X \leftarrow Y$	X	$\neg Y$
$\neg(X \uparrow Y)$	X	Y	$X \uparrow Y$	$\neg X$	$\neg Y$
$X \downarrow Y$	$\neg X$	$\neg Y$	$\neg(X \downarrow Y)$	X	Y

TABLE 9.2

Rule forms

TABLE 9.3

Universal and
existential form for γ
and δ rules

Universal form		Existential form	
γ	$\gamma(t)$	δ	$\delta(p)$
$\forall X.\phi$	$\phi\{X/t\}$	$\exists X.\phi$	$\phi\{X/p\}$
$\neg\exists X.\phi$	$\neg\phi\{X/t\}$	$\neg\forall X.\phi$	$\neg\phi\{X/p\}$

Fitting (1990) defined other rules to deal with quantification of variables and to allow substitutions of variables by a specific term, much as the Universal Instantiation (UI) and Existential Instantiation (EI) inference rules did in Chapter 4. These rules also group terms into specific forms. A **closed term** is one with no unquantified variables. The forms in these inference rules are universal and existential forms:

- Universal form inference rule:

  $$\frac{\gamma}{\gamma(t)}, \text{ for any closed term } t$$

- Existential form inference rule:

  $$\frac{\delta}{\delta(p)}, \text{ for any new parameter } p$$

The forms that the γ and δ rules work on are defined in Table 9.3.

9.4.2 The Tableau Proof Method

The tableau proof method works by applying the inference rules defined in the preceding section until all branches of the proof are closed. A branch ϕ of a tableau is **closed** if both X and $\neg X$ occur on f for some propositional formula X or if *false* occurs on f. A tableau is closed if all branches of the tableau are closed.

Consider the tableau proof shown in Figure 9.2. Step 1 is the negation of the statement that we wish to prove. Steps 2 and 3 are derived by using an α rule on step 1. Steps 4 and 5 are derived by applying the α rule to step 3. Steps 6 and 7 are from step 5, again using an α inference rule. Steps 8 and 9 are from step 2 by a β rule and therefore produce a split in the tree. Steps 10 and 11 are also generated by applying a β rule to step 4. They also produce a split in the tree.

In this tableau proof, all branches are closed. We must examine three branches: the branch ending in P, the branch ending in S, and the branch ending with $Q \rightarrow R$. The branch ending in P (10) is closed because its negation is present as an ancestor in the tree at step 8.

1. $\neg((P \to (Q \to R)) \to ((P \vee S) \to ((Q \to R) \vee S)))$		
2. $P \to (Q \to R)$		
3. $\neg((P \vee S) \to ((Q \to R) \vee S))$		
4. $P \vee S$		
5. $\neg((Q \to R) \vee S)$		
6. $\neg(Q \to R)$		
7. $\neg S$		
8. $\neg P$		9. $Q \to R$
10. P	11. S	

FIGURE 9.2

A tableau proof of $(P \to (Q \to R)) \to ((P \vee S) \to ((Q \to R)$

The one ending in S (11) is closed because its negation appears as an ancestor at step 7. Finally, the branch ending in $Q \to R$ is closed because its negation occurred in step 6 of the tableau. Therefore, the tableau is closed and is a proof of $(P \to (Q \to R)) \to ((P \vee S) \to ((Q \to R) \vee S))$.

9.5 OBJECT-ORIENTED THEOREM PROVER

In Chapter 8, we presented a Prolog-like production system that could be expanded into a theorem prover application. In this section, we present another approach, using a more direct implementation of resolution. It only works on propositional logic, but it could be expanded, without any change in the high-level approach, to work on first-order predicate logic.

This theorem prover works on propositional logic statements that have already been translated into clauses of literals that are "or"ed together. The prover uses a variant of the linear strategy described earlier, a variant called **ordered linear resolution** because it orders the literals of each clause. So, for example, if "[p, q]" is resolved with "[~q, r]," then it produces "[p, r]." All of these clauses are ordered. This method is based on another method described in detail by Chang and Lee (1973). Their method of using ordered linear resolution preserves completeness of resolution (Figure 9.3).

Chang and Lee (1973) used the concept of **framed literals** to keep track of literals that have been used as a resolvent in a previous step. These literals are saved rather than just deleted as in

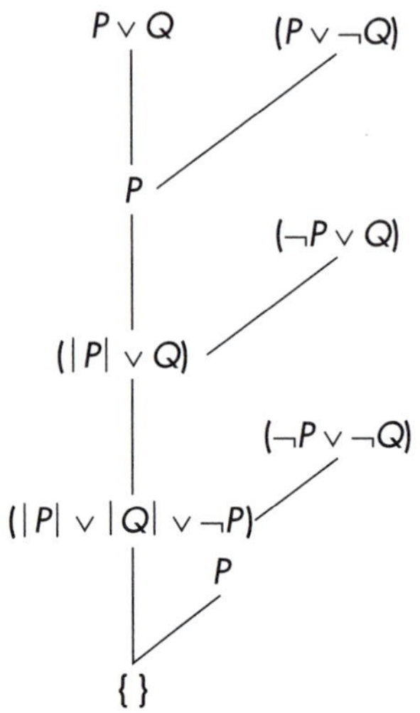

FIGURE 9.3

An example
of ordered linear
resolution from
Chang and Lee
(1973)

$$
\begin{array}{ll}
P \vee Q & (P \vee \neg Q) \\
\quad | & \\
\quad P & \\
\quad | & (\neg P \vee Q) \\
(|P| \vee Q) & \\
\quad | & (\neg P \vee \neg Q) \\
(|P| \vee |Q| \vee \neg P) & \\
\quad | & P \\
\quad \{\} &
\end{array}
$$

normal resolution, as knowing what literals have already been used can speed up the resolution process. In Figure 9.3, framed literals are represented as literals within vertical bars. For example, |P| represents the framed literal P, which was used in a previous resolution step as a resolvent. Chang and Lee call this method of framing literals and using ordered clauses and a linear strategy **ordered linear deduction,** or OL deduction.

The design of the prover is to use a new class, ResNode, to represent the search space nodes. ResNode is a subclass of the search class Node. To create a search space, we create a ResGraph class that is a subclass of the class DepthGraph and use a depth-first method of search. Two new classes are created to represent clauses in propositional logic (class Clause) and literals that form clauses (class Literal). It is up to the Clause class to maintain the order of literals in the clause, to mark literals as framed, and to perform the resolution operation.

9.6 A C++ THEOREM PROVER

The C++ code in this section implements an ordered linear resolution theorem prover. This program is based on the search library and the logic classes already introduced. It works on propositional logic statements that have already been translated into clauses of literals "or"ed together. For example, the clause $P \vee \neg Q \vee R$ is represented by [p, ~q, r].

The ResNode and ResGraph classes set up a structure for performing the OL resolution. They are based on the search library classes.

```
//file: resnode.h
#include <stdio.h>
#include "clause.h"
#include "ctable.h"
#include "literal.h"
#include "graph.h"

class ResGraph;

/*
 * Class ResNode represents the nodes in the search
 * graph. It contains the resolvent and the side
 * clause used with the resolvent to create the
 * next resolvent. If the node is the root node,
 * the resolvent will be the top clause and the
 * side clause will be empty. If the node is a
 * goal clause, the resolvent will be the empty
 * clause: [].
 */
class ResNode : public Node
{
  friend ResGraph;
  public:
      ResNode(Clause *, Clause *);
      ~ResNode();

      int operator==(const Node &) const;
      void display() const;
      IntrList<Node> *expand(int);
  private:
      Clause *resolvent,
          *side;
};

/*
 * Class ResGraph implements the search algorithm.
 * In this case the depth-first algorithm is
 * chosen. ResGraph also contains the table
 * consisting of the axioms (the theory) to be used
 * in the resolution proof.
 */
```

```
class ResGraph : public DepthGraph
{
  friend ResNode;
  public:
      ResGraph(ResNode *, ClauseTable &);
      void settable(ClauseTable &);
      int is_goal(const Node *);
  private:
      static ClauseTable *table;
};
```

The following file implements the theorem prover: It shows how the graph is expanded and searches for an empty clause.

```
//file: resnode.cpp
 #include "resnode.h"

ClauseTable *ResGraph::table;

ResNode::ResNode(Clause *resolv, Clause *sid)
{
  resolvent = resolv;
  side = sid;
}

ResNode::~ResNode()
{
  delete(resolvent);
}

/*
 * Since the resolution procedure centers on
 * resolvents, it is sufficient to check if the
 * resolvents are equal when comparing two ResNode
 * objects. The idea is that if B is the resolvent
 * of A and C and also of D and E, B has been
 * generated twice by seperate procedures, i.e., by
 * separate search paths. But only the resolvent is
 * of interest, and since B is really the same
 * resolvent, the ResNode objects that contain B
 * are effectively the same also.
 */
int ResNode::operator==(const Node &other) const
{
  const ResNode &resother = (ResNode &)other;
  return(*resolvent == *(resother.resolvent));
```

```
}

void ResNode::display() const
{
  if (side)
  {
      side->display();
      putchar('\n');
  }
  resolvent->display();
  putchar('\t');
}


/*
 * Expanding() a ResNode means finding side clauses
 * in the DB that can be used with the current
 * clause to produce resolvent clauses. For each
 * side clause and new resolvent that is found, a
 * successor ResNode object is created.
 */
IntrList<Node> *ResNode::expand(int)
{
  Clause
      *newclause;
  ResNode
      *tmp;
  IntrList<Node>
      *ret = new IntrList<Node>;

  int max = ResGraph::table->getsize();
  for (int i = 0; i < max; i++)
  {
      /*
       * Try to resolve the current clause with the
       * next clause in the DB. If you succeed,
       * check if the resolvent clause is a
       * tautology. If so, ignore it. If not, add
       * the clause to the successor list.
       * Tautologies are skipped because a
       * tautology is always true and does not add
       * any new information to the resolution
       * process.
       */
      newclause = resolvent->resolve
                  (*ResGraph::table->getclause(i));
if (newclause)
```

```
            {
              if (!newclause->is_tautology())
              {
                tmp = new ResNode(newclause,
                          ResGraph::table->getclause(i));
                ret->addtotail(tmp);
              }
              else
                  delete(newclause);
            }
        }
    return(ret);
}


ResGraph::ResGraph(ResNode *start, ClauseTable &ct)
          :DepthGraph(0, start)
{
    table = &ct;
}

void ResGraph::settable(ClauseTable &ct)
{
    table = &ct;
}

/*
 * If the resolvent is the empty clause, [], the
 * node is a goal node.
 */
int ResGraph::is_goal(const Node *n)
{
    ResNode *node = (ResNode *)n;
    return(node->resolvent->is_empty());
}
```

Much of the work in implementing ordered linear resolution is in the implementation of clauses. In the following file, the clauses must keep the literals in order, keep track of framed literals, and most important, perform the resolution operation.

```
//file: clause.h
#ifndef _Clause_H_
#define _Clause_H_

#include <stdio.h>
#include "literal.h"
```

```
#include "list.h"

/*
 * Class clause represents clauses as used in
 * resolution. A Clause object is created by
 * Clause("[p, q]"). Member function resolve() can
 * be called to resolve a clause with another
 * clause. If successful, this function will return
 * the resolvent of these two clauses. The reduce-
 * order operation as defined by Chang and Lee for
 * OL-resolution is implemented by private member
 * function reduce_order().
 */
class Clause
{
  public:
    Clause();
    Clause(const char *);
    Clause *clone() const;
      Clause &operator=(const Clause &other);
      Clause &operator=(const char *);
      int operator==(const Clause &) const;
    Clause *resolve(Clause &);
    int is_empty() const;
    void display() const;
      int is_tautology();
  private:
    oid merge_except(int, Clause &);
    void frame_last();
    void delete_framed();
    void reduce_order();
      void parse_string(const char *);

    IntrList<Literal> terms;
};

#endif
```

The following file implements the clauses for the theorem prover.

```
//file: clause.cpp
#include <stdarg.h>
#include "clause.h"

Clause::Clause()
```

```
{
}

Clause::Clause(const char *string)
{
  parse_string(string);
}

int Clause::operator==(const Clause &other) const
{
  return(terms == other.terms);
}

Clause *Clause::clone() const
{
  return(new Clause(*this));
}

Clause &Clause::operator=(const Clause &other)
{
  if (this != &other)
      terms = other.terms;
  return(*this);
}

Clause &Clause::operator=(const char *string)
{
  terms.clear(DoDel);
  parse_string(string);
  return(*this);
}

void Clause::display() const
{
  ROIntrListIterator<Literal> iter(terms);
  const Literal *lit;
  putchar('[');
  if ((lit = iter.getfirst()))
    lit->display();
  while ((lit = iter.getnext()))
  {
    printf(", ");
    lit->display();
  }
  putchar(']');
}
```

```
/*
 * Is_tautology() determines if the clause is a
 * tautology.
 */
int Clause::is_tautology()
{
  IntrListIterator<Literal> iter(terms);
  Literal *plit;

  /*
   * To check if a clause is a tautology, the
   * clause must be checked for a pair of literals
   * that are complementary to each other (one
   * positive, the other negative or the other way
   * around). Framed literals are not taken into
   * account.
   */
  for (plit = iter.getfirst(); plit; plit =
                                iter.getnext())
  {
    /* Skip framed literals. */
    if (!plit->is_framed())
    {
    /*
     * Get the next literal of the clause and
     * determine if its negation is also part of
     * the clause. If so, the clause is a tautology.
     */
    Literal lit = *plit;
    lit.negate();
    if (terms.lookup(&lit))
    return(1);
    }
  }
  return(0);
}

int Clause::is_empty() const
{
  return(terms.is_empty());
}

/*
 * Merge_except() merges the current clause with
 * another clause, except for the specified literal
 * of the other clause (this is usually one the
```

```
 *  literals resolved upon, namely the literal in
 *  the other clause that is the negation of the
 *  last literal of the current clause).
 */
void Clause::merge_except(int pos, Clause &other)
{
  IntrListIterator<Literal> iter(other.terms);
  Literal *lit;
  int i;

  for (i = 0, lit = iter.getfirst(); lit; lit =
                    iter.getnext())
  {
    if (pos != i++)
      /*
       * Add (a copy of) the literal to the current
       * clause, but do no create any duplicates.
       */
      if (!terms.lookup(lit))
          terms.addtotail(lit->clone());
  }
}


/*
 * Frame_last() frames the last literal of the
 * clause. Note that this must be done only if the
 * literal does not occur yet as a framed literal
 * in the clause. If it does, the last literal is
 * removed because a framed literal not followed by
 * any unframed literal must be removed.
 */
void Clause::frame_last()
{
  Literal lit = *terms.gettail();
  lit.make_framed();

  if (!terms.lookup(&lit))
      terms.gettail()->make_framed();
  else
      terms.remove_tail(DoDel);
}

/*
 * Delete_framed() removes from the clause every
 * framed literal that is not followed by an
```

```
 * unframed literal. By definition, these must be
 * the last literals of the clause.
 */
void Clause::delete_framed()
{
  Literal *lit;
  while ((lit = terms.gettail()) &&
                               lit->is_framed())
    terms.remove_tail(DoDel);
}


/*
 * Reduce_order() implements the reduce-order
 * operation. Note that we keep reducing the clause
 * as long as possible: if the result of a
 * reduced-order clause is reduceable itself, it is
 * reduced again. It is not really clear from Chang
 * and Lee's description if this should be done,
 * but this seems like a reasonable thing to do and
 * does not cause any problems as far as we know.
 */
void Clause::reduce_order()
{
  for (;;)
  {
      if (terms.is_empty())
          break;

      /*
       * Check if the negation of the last literal
       * of the clause appears as a framed literal
       * in the clause. If so, reduce the clause
       * (turn it into a reduced-order clause) by
       * removing the last literal. Next, remove
       * every framed literal not followed by any
       * unframed literal.
       */
    Literal lit = *terms.gettail();
    lit.negate();
    lit.make_framed();

    if (terms.lookup(&lit))
        terms.remove_tail(DoDel);
    else
        break;
```

```
        /* Delete framed literals not followed by any
         * unframed literal. */
      delete_framed();
  }
}


/*
 * Resolve() resolves the two clauses according to
 * the OL-resolution scheme. If this procedure
 * succeeds, the resulting resolvent is returned;
 * otherwise NULL is returned.
 */
Clause* Clause::resolve(Clause &other)
{
  Clause *result = NULL;
  int pos;

  /*
   * Determine the negation of the last literal of
   * the clause: get a copy of this literal and
   * negate it.
   */
  Literal neglast = *terms.gettail();
  neglast.negate();

  /*
   * Determine if the negated literal appears in
   * the other clause. If so, the clauses can be
   * resolved.
   */
  if ((pos = other.terms.find(&neglast)) >= 0)
  {
      /*
       * Create the resolvent. Get a copy of the
       * current clause. Frame the last literal.
       * Merge with the other clause, exempting the
       * negated literal found in the other clause.
       * Delete every framed literal not followed
       * by an unframed literal. Apply the reduce-
       * order operation.
       */
    result = clone();
    result->frame_last();
    result->merge_except(pos, other);
```

```
        result->delete_framed();
        result->reduce_order();
    }
    return(result);
}


/*
 * Parse_string() parses the supplied string. This
 * routine is used to create Clause objects. No
 * error checking is performed.
 */
void Clause::parse_string(const char *string)
{
    char *p, *end, *buf;

    if (!(buf = strdup(string)))
    {
        puts("Clause::Clause() out of memory");
        exit(0);
    }
    p = buf + 1;
    while (*p)
    {
        Boolean neg;
        Literal *lit;

        neg = false;
        while (*p == ' ')
            p++;
        if (*p == '~')
        {
            neg = true;
            p++;
        }
        if (end = strchr(p, ','))
        {
            *end = '\0';
            end++;
        }
        else
        {
            end = strchr(p, ']');
            *end = '\0';
        }
        lit = new Literal(neg, p);
```

```
        if (!terms.lookup(lit))
            terms.addtotail(lit);
        else
            delete lit;
        p = end;
    }
    delete(buf);
}
```

Literals are also defined with a special class. However, the C++ code is not included here. (Please refer to the C++ files provided with the text. The last code segment in this chapter is a main program to run the theorem prover.)

```
//file: run.cpp
#include "resnode.h"

int main()
{
    char
        *clauses[] = { "[p, q, r]",
        "[p, q, ~r]",
        "[p, ~q, r]",
        "[p, ~q, ~r]",
        "[~p, q, r]",
        "[~p, q, ~r]",
        "[~p, ~q, r]",
        "[~p, ~q, ~r]",
        NULL,
            };
    ClauseTable
        table(clauses);
    Clause
        topclause = clauses[0];
    ResGraph
        prover(new ResNode(topclause.clone(), NULL),
                                            table);

    if (prover.generate())
        prover.display();
    else
        puts("no solution found");
    putchar('\n');

    return(1);
}
```

9.7 OTHER SYSTEMS

Many other types of systems that aid in the development of theorems and proofs of theorems have been developed. In this section, we briefly introduce a few of them.

9.7.1 Boyer-Moore Theorem Prover

The Boyer-Moore Theorem Prover (BMTP) marked an important milestone in theorem prover research (Boyer and Moore, 1979; Barr and Feigenbaum, 1981). The primary application of the BMTP has been to prove facts and properties of programs, particularly LISP programs. The BMTP is very good at automating proofs by induction, a method that works well on purely recursive programs.

The BMTP is based on recursive function theory in which theorems can be stated and automatically proved. It works by continuously rewriting the current formula to be proved, and it uses heuristics to help decide how to rewrite the given formula. However, it does not perform backtracking. The representation used is very similar to that used by LISP, a circumstance that makes it relatively easy to prove facts about LISP programs. It has been used to prove the correctness of many algorithms, such as a string-searching algorithm and a simple compiler.

9.7.2 Theorem Discovery Programs

An important emerging class of programs are those that are able to discover theorems from a small set of relevant axioms. These programs focus on finding interesting theorems rather than on proving theorems. One such system is known as the Automated Mathematician (AM) and was written by Doug Lenat (1990; Rich, 1991). This system is able to conjecture many interesting statements that can then be fed into a theorem prover to be checked.

9.7.3 Interactive Theorem Checkers

Other systems that have been developed have more modest goals, but they work in much the same way as theorem provers do. Because systems such as the BMTP could not prove complex statements without some guidance as to necessary lemmas, a natural reaction is to develop a system to aid in proving more complex theorems. EKL (see Ketonen and Weening, 1984) is such a system. Its main goal is to facilitate the checking of mathematical proofs. EKL interacts with its user through finite-order predicate logic with typed lambda-calculus. Users enter proposed axioms, lemmas, and theorems in predicate logic and request the system to attempt to prove the lemmas and theorems by using the axioms given and any previously proven theorems. Because the system works interactively, users can examine where the proofs failed and can propose alternative lemmas or introduce new axioms.

Other such interactive systems are FOL (see Weyhrauch, 1980, in Nilsson, 1981).

9.7.4 Other FOPL Proof Methods

Other successful theorem proving mechanisms are different from means-ends, resolution, or tableau methods. A **Hilbert system** (sometimes called a Frege System) uses a forward-reasoning strategy that attempts to prove a statement by starting with the known facts and applying inference rules until the theorem is reached.

Natural deduction constitutes another family of proof mechanisms in which the aim is to formalize the kind of reasoning that people do in informal arguments. Bledsoe's natural deduction system uses strategies and heuristics to decompose a theorem into parts that are easier to prove (Bledsoe, 1977).

Sequent calculus merges natural deduction and the tableau method. The **Davis-Putnam procedure** is a quick procedure for propositional logic. All of these alternative methods are concisely presented by Fitting (1990), who also included proofs of soundness and completeness for these mechanisms.

9.8 SUMMARY

This chapter describes methods used for theorem provers and expands on the resolution proof procedure. Means-ends analysis, which is contained within the General Problem Solver system, works to reduce differences. Resolution is a powerful method for theorem proving that is based on a single inference rule. Tableau theorem provers are an efficient way to represent a large number of inference rules and a sound method on which to base provers. The basic resolution proof procedure can be augmented by the use of search strategies that allow it to be more easily implemented. An object-oriented, propositional logic, resolution theorem prover based on the ordered, linear resolution strategy is presented.

In summary, there are many proof methods that can be used to effectively prove statements in logic, only some of which are presented in this chapter. Proving statements based on a set of underlying facts will continue to be required of many AI applications in order to determine whether new facts are consistent with, provable by, or logically inferred by the accumulated knowledge.

9.9 REFERENCES

Theorem provers have long been a central theme in artificial intelligence and much longer for mathematicians. Martin Gardner (1958) describes several interesting logic machines and diagramming techniques that have been developed by logicians in the last several hundred years.

Formal specifications for systems are based on the ideas of logic and theorem proving. They are primarily used for specifying systems that must be provably correct, such as secure operating system kernels or communications protocols. Refer to Diller (1994) for a specification of Z, a popular language for formal system specification.

AI-based theorem provers and resolution are a central topic of Genesereth and Nilsson (1987) and Shinghal (1992). Chang and Lee (1973) and Fitting (1990) describe many types of automated theorem proving in great detail and provide excellent references on resolution and tableau theorem proving. See Fitting (1990) or Manna and Waldinger (1989) for more information on tableau theorem proving. See also Wos et al. (1985) and Nilsson (1980) for more theorem proving methods.

See Chang and Lee (1973), pp. 135–145, for complete information on the OL deduction algorithm.

9.10 EXERCISES

Warm-up Exercises

9.1. Create a tableau proof for $P \downarrow (Q \vee R)$.

9.2. Create a tableau proof for $\forall X.(P(X) \vee Q(X)) \rightarrow \exists X.(P(X) \vee \forall X(Q(X)))$.

9.3. Use linear resolution strategy to show that the following set of clauses is unsatisfiable:

$$P \vee Q$$
$$Q \vee R$$
$$R \vee W$$
$$\neg R \vee \neg P$$
$$\neg W \vee \neg Q$$
$$\neg Q \vee \neg R$$

9.4. Apply all the clause deletion strategies mentioned in this chapter with resolution to the following set of clauses:

$$\neg P \vee \neg Q \vee R$$

$$\neg P \vee S$$

$$\neg Q \vee S$$

$$P$$

$$Q$$

$$\neg R$$

Homework Exercises

9.5. Show that using only the unit strategy for choosing clauses in resolution is not complete. That is, show that there are some sets of unsatisfiable clauses for which unit resolution cannot produce a contradiction.

9.6. You showed (in Exercise 9.5) that using the unit strategy is not complete. If you use instead the unit strategy combined with the ordered resolution strategy, does this make it impossible to prove some things that are provable by unit resolution alone? If so, give an example; otherwise, give a proof that they behave the same.

9.7. Show that the ordered resolution strategy is not refutation complete.

9.8. Show that using both the ordered resolution strategy with the set of support resolution strategy is not complete by finding a counterexample.

9.9. Show that the tautology elimination clause deletion strategy has no effect on the satisfiability or unsatisfiability of a set of clauses.

9.10. Show that the subsumption elimination clause deletion strategy has no effect on the satisfiability or unsatisfiability of a set of clauses.

9.11. Apply resolution to the following set of clauses first without any deletion of clauses and list all possible resolutions (there should be 28 of them). Then apply all the deletion strategies mentioned in the text and again apply all possible resolutions.

$$P \vee Q$$

$$\neg P \vee R$$

$$\neg Q \vee R$$

9.12. Use hyperresolution to prove Exercise 9.11.

9.13. The strategies for resolution given in the text are not the only ones available, only some of the most common. Think of another resolution strategy for picking clauses to resolve. Is your strategy refutation complete? Give an informal justification of its completeness or a counterexample.

Programming Exercises

9.14. Modify the C++ ordered linear resolution theorem prover to use the unit-preference strategy. You may use whatever secondary resolution strategy that you wish. Your program should also apply the pure literal deletion strategy discussed in Section 9.3.1. Your program should output the list of clauses produced by the input file (which you should write a prompt for). The last line of the input file is the negation of the statement to be proved. Your program should also output each new clause produced by resolution and indicate the two clauses that were resolved together.

9.15. Modify the ordered linear resolution theorem prover given in Section 9.6 to include the other inference rules given in Chapter 4.

9.16. Write a program similar to the one you wrote for Exercise 9.14, except this time implement hyperresolution, by which as many as three clauses can be resolved with the nucleus.

9.17. Write a C++ program that implements, for propositional calculus, a reasoning mechanism based on the concept of network diagrams, as presented in Chapter 3 of Gardner (1958).

Projects

9.18. Write a tableau-based theorem prover in C++, using the search library and the tableau rules given in Section 9.4.

9.19. Write an interface to the C++ Prolog-like theorem prover that will take as input, FOPL statements and convert them to clausal form, using the procedure from Section 6.2.1.

9.20. Write an interface to the C++ ordered linear theorem prover to offer an interactive interface that allows clauses be input at the keyboard until "go" is entered. The program should allow input to be read from files and allow resetting of the prover to erase all previous clauses input.

9.21. Further investigate means-ends theorem provers and write one, using C++.

9.22. Investigate the formal specification Z and augment the resolution theorem prover given here to read a subset of Z specifications. Your program should be able to read the specification for an "Internal Telephone Directory" from Chapter 4 of Diller

(1994) and be able to prove statements about the functions the directory might perform.

9.23. Write a linear resolution theorem prover using class BackTrack of the C++ search library for propositional logic.

9.24. Extend the propositional logic theorem prover (from Exercise 9.23 or from Section 9.6) to handle FOPL.

10

PLANNING

10.1 THE PLANNING PROBLEM

Developing a plan is defined as finding a sequence of actions to accomplish a specified goal. One way to think of this problem is to consider a robot with a finite set of possible actions that it can perform. The problem for the robot is to assemble these actions into a sequence that will enable it to achieve its goals; and the problem of finding such a sequence of actions can be viewed as a search problem. That is, we can search through all possible sequences of actions for the sequences that lead to the goal. When viewed in this way, we can apply all the search techniques that we studied in Chapter 5.

The problem of planning is not simple, however. One complication is known as the frame problem, which was mentioned in Section 7.2.1. The frame problem arises because actions have the potential to change the state of the world. Therefore, the planner needs to specify exactly what does and what does not change. Take, for example, a robot that can change the color of objects next to it by using a spray can of paint. When the robot paints a nearby object, we need to state not only that the color of the object has changed but also that the color of other objects has *not* changed. One of the items we must specify is that the color of the robot does not change (unless we have a messy robot that also paints itself when it paints the object). Axioms that specify what does not change as the result of an action are called **frame axioms**.

A second problem that complicates the search for the appropriate sequence of actions is the dependence of portions of the

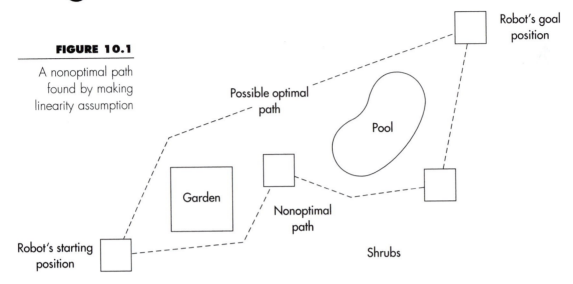

FIGURE 10.1

A nonoptimal path
found by making
linearity assumption

plan on one another. For example, consider the processing of batch computer jobs. If one programmer submits a job to format a filesystem and 10 minutes later submits another job to read data from the same filesystem, then the programmer has violated the **linearity assumption** of the batch job processor, namely, that jobs do not depend on one another and therefore can be done in any order. The batch job processor makes this assumption in order to more efficiently complete all jobs in its queue. However, in the filesystem jobs submitted by our misguided programmer, the second job must be executed before the first job or the expected plata will no longer be there.

A robot path-planning problem also shows how the linearity assumption can affect the solution. The problem is for the robot to find the shortest path from a starting position to a goal position, meanwhile avoiding objects along the path. If we assume that finding a path can be split into the separate tasks of finding paths around each object between the robot's position and the goal, then we are making a linearity assumption about the problem. And if we do make such an assumption, then we probably will not find an optimal path. Suppose we find the shortest path around the first object and the shortest path around the second object, and so on (Figure 10.1). We cannot simply string all these actions together and have the shortest path from the start to the goal. The optimal paths around the objects must have matching starting and ending positions as well as constituting an optimal path overall. This matching complicates the process, because the paths around objects may require nonmatching starting and ending points to be optimal for each object. Then those positions must be adjusted to try to optimize the entire path.

Planning introduces the need to generalize and save previously constructed plans. Suppose a robot is able to develop a plan to put out a fire in the computer room. Then it is desirable for the robot to be able to generalize that plan so that it can put out a fire in the lounge without having to regenerate an entire plan. If a second fire occurs in the computer room, the robot should be able to reexecute the same plan and put out the fire as soon as possible.

10.2 EXAMPLE OF PLANNING

Suppose we wanted to design a robot that would go to the moon to find gold there. The robot's job is to develop and execute a plan to find gold once it has been delivered to the moon. The robot can perform the following actions:

Move(P)	This action moves the robot to position *P* on the moon
Gather(G)	Gather gold that is lying on the ground in the robot's immediate visual field
Identify(R)	Identify rock types
BlowUp(R)	Blow up a rock into small pieces

We can represent the robot's actions more precisely in FOPL by using axioms of the form *Action* → (*Results* ← *Conditions*). *Action* refers to the action that we are trying to define; *Results* defines the consequences of applying the action; and *Conditions* defines what must be true to apply the action. Converting our actions above to this form gives

$$\forall P. Move(P) \rightarrow (Position(robot, P) \leftarrow Can\_move(robot))$$
$$\forall G. Gather(G) \rightarrow (Has(robot, G) \leftarrow See(robot, G))$$
$$\forall R(Type.Identify(R) \rightarrow (Identity(R, Type) \leftarrow (See(robot, R) \wedge Rock(R)))$$
$$\forall R(Pieces.Blowup(R) \rightarrow ((\neg Rock(R) \wedge Rock(Pieces)) \leftarrow (Rock(R)$$
$$\wedge Has(robot, explosives)))$$

The preceding axioms only define what does change; they do not define what does not change as a result of our actions. That is, we have not yet defined any frame axioms. We need to define how each action affects each of our predicates. For example, we need to define how the *Move* action affects all predicates that we use (*Position, Can_move, Has, See, Identity,* and *Rock*). Even for this small example, we would need to have at least 24 frame axioms to define what does not change. Some of these for *Move* are:

$$\forall P \forall X \forall Y. Move(P) \rightarrow (Has(X,Y) \leftarrow Has(X,Y))$$
$$\forall P \forall X \forall Y. Move(P) \rightarrow (See(X,Y) \leftarrow See(X,Y))$$
$$\forall P \forall X \forall Y. Move(P) \rightarrow (Rock(X) \leftarrow Rock(X))$$

For these axioms to work, we must define all frame axioms and also modify the *Move* axioms so that we update what is in the field of view of the robot. In addition, we should modify the *Blowup* action so that the robot's position changes before the rock blows up, to prevent the robot from blowing itself up!

10.3 STANFORD RESEARCH INSTITUTE PROBLEM SOLVER (STRIPS)[1]

STRIPS (Fikes and Nilsson, 1971) is one of the earliest robot problem-solving systems and has inspired many other planning systems. STRIPS was successful in addressing the frame problem by using a notation other than FOPL for describing what does and does not change with each action. STRIPS uses **add lists** to describe what is true as a result of applying an action and **delete lists** to describe what is no longer true as a result of an action. And to specify the necessary conditions for applying an action, they used a list of **preconditions**. These three lists completely describe each operator. For example, Table 10.1 shows how we can rewrite the actions given for the robot to find gold on the moon in this form. When writing our actions in STRIPS form, we no longer need explicit frame axioms because they are implicitly contained in the add and delete lists. Any predicate not contained in the add list or delete list of an operator is assumed to not be affected by application of the operator. However, we must be careful when constructing these actions because we can no longer use FOPL to ensure that we have considered all cases (i.e., we may miss an item in a delete list).

STRIPS uses the following steps to develop a plan:

1. Select a subgoal and try to prove it by using a theorem proven. If it is provable, go to step 4; otherwise, go to step 2.
2. Choose an action whose add list specifies clauses that allow the incomplete proof of step 1 to be continued. This action is chosen by using a mean-ends analysis technique to minimize the difference between the goal and the incomplete proof of it.

---

[1] Although called a problem solver at the time, such systems are now called planners. Stanford Research Institute has since been renamed SRI International.

Operator	Predicate type[a]	Predicate
Blowup(R)	P	*Rock(R)* ∧ *Has(robot,explosives)* ∧ *Position(R,P)* ∧ *Position(robot,P)*
	A	*None*
		Rock(Pieces)
	D	*Rock(R)*
		Has(robot,explosives)
Gather(G)	P	*See(robot,G)* ∧ *Identity(G,gold)*
	A	*Has(robot,G)*
	D	*See(robot,G)*
Identify(R)	P	*See(robot,R)* ∧ *Rock(R)* ∧ *Position(R,P)* ∧ *Position(robot,P)*
	A	*Identity(R,Type)*
	D	None
Move(P)	P	*Can_move(robot)* ∧ *Position(robot,X)*
	A	*Position(robot,P)*
	D	*Position(robot,X)*

[a] P, preconditions; A, addition list, D, delete list.

3. The precondition of the chosen action forms a new subgoal. Go to step 1 and try to prove the new subgoal.
4. If the subgoal is the goal, quit. Otherwise, apply the action (change the current state) that just had its preconditions established and go to step 1.

TABLE 10.1

Preconditions, addition lists, and delete lists defining the gold-collecting robot operators

The output of **STRIPS** is a list of actions that will achieve the original goal. This method of forming subgoals and then pushing them on a stack (i.e., Step 3) is sometimes called **goal stack planning**.

A useful construction for analyzing and saving plans is known as a **triangle table**. Figure 10.2 shows a triangle table that describes a robot's plan for finding gold on the moon. The actions are listed to the right of the table. The preconditions for each action are contained within the blocks to the left of the action. The add and delete lists are given below each action. The add and delete lists are listed to the left of the future actions that will require them. In addition, items in add and delete lists that are not used by future actions are not listed in the triangle table. If a column has conflicting entries, then there are conflicting postconditions (add and delete lists) and preconditions. Checking the plan by looking for consistent entries in each column gives us a method of checking whether the actions are independent of one another in this plan and may be reordered.

1	Can_move(robot) Position(robot,X)	Move(P)			
2	See(robot,G) Position(G,P) Rock(G)	Position(robot,P)	Identify(G)		
3	Has(robot,explosives) Position(G,P) Rock(G)	Position(robot,P)		Blowup(G)	
4	See(robot,G)		Identity(G,gold)	Rock(G-pieces) See(G-pieces)	Gather(G-pieces)
5					Has(robot,G-pieces)
	1	2	3	4	5

FIGURE 10.2

Triangle table for the gold-hunting robot

A triangle table can be viewed as a **macro** action and stored so that it can be reused. This particular table (Figure 10.2) might be stored as a "get-gold" macro action with its own preconditions list, add list, and delete list. This trangular table is constructed by finding a plan using the STRIPS algorithm.

Figure 10.3 shows a **kernel** for the *Blowup* action in this plan. Every condition in the kernel must be true before we can apply the *Blowup* operator in this scenario (as given in Figure 10.2). This gives us the ability to jump forward in the plan or to apply the plan with unknown starting conditions. In this example, it may so happen that the robot has landed next to a rock that is known to contain gold. If that is the case, then the robot should immediately blow it up and extract the gold rather than moving and attempting to identify another. Using the notion of a kernel may allow us to recover when the plan has been interrupted by unforeseen circumstances. For instance, if the robot has lost all of its explosives, it may still be able to perform its job by finding some gold nuggets lying on the ground.

10.4 OTHER PLANNING TECHNIQUES

We have discussed one planning technique in this rich area of AI research. Many other approaches are used, some of which are listed below.

10.4.1 Nonlinear Planning with Constraint Posting

Nonlinear plans are built, not from start to finish, but by simultaneously building different parts of the plan. Nonlinear planning is

	1	2	3
3	Has(robot,explosives) Position(G,P) Rock(G)	Position(robot,P)	
4	See(robot,G)		Identity(G,gold)
5			

FIGURE 10.3

Kernel for the *Blowup* action

used primarily because many problem domains require it, especially in those situations for which the linearity assumption is not met. As Figure 10.1 illustrated, when the linearity assumption is made, we may end up with a long path. However, if we view the same problem in a nonlinear fashion, we can find an optimal path. If we first choose all the intermediate positions for the robot, we can choose them so that they will produce an optimal path. Next, we can fill in the detail of how to get from each intermediate position to the next.

The idea of **constraint posting** is to incrementally add constraints to a plan being built. Find constraints can help in identifying the subset of possible plans. This refinement to nonlinear planning has been used in MOLGEN (Stefik, 1981a) and TWEAK (Chapman, 1987). These constraints can be hypothesized operators that may be useful, partial orderings between operators, bindings of variables, or any other constraint that helps refine the plan.

10.4.2 Hierarchical Planning

In **hierarchical planning,** an abstract level of planning is done first and the details of the plan are filled in later. These multiple levels of planning can be developed into a hierarchy of **abstraction spaces**. For example, we could view the task of a gold-hunting robot on the moon in a hierarchical, top-down fashion. First, we develop an overall plan: Get the robot to the moon, find the gold, and bring the robot and the gold back to earth. Then we can fill in the details by developing specific plans for each. The most famous system that used a hierarchical approach to planning was the ABSTRIPS system, described in Sacerdoti (1974), which built on the STRIPS system.

10.4.3 Reactive Systems

Reactive systems do not form plans per se. Instead, they react to the situation at hand, and the reaction does not involve the formation of a sequence of actions or plan. This idea is not particularly new. Simple reactive systems have been around for some time. Process control devices such as thermostats, pressure control values, and other regulators all are reactive devices; that is, in a given state, they either perform an action or not.

Reactive systems can be quite complex and can include many different states and actions. Their responsiveness makes them useful for situations where speed of action is essential and where unpredictable events may occur. For example, in a robot-controlled automobile, we may need a reactive system to cause the robot to stop the automobile when an object is detected in front of the automobile. For example, if a child runs in front of the automobile, then the robot must decide to stop quickly.

Most reactive systems maintain only a list of situation-action rules and are not capable of developing higher level plans. If the rules are complex enough (the action may in fact be a stored plan of actions), then the system is capable of exhibiting complex behavior. Once more traditional planners have stored many plans and begin to refer only to those stored plans, then it is possible to replace the planning system with a reactive system. See Mitchell (1990) for some recent work in this translation process.

10.4.4 Metaplanning

Metaplanning is a technique for reasoning, not only about the problem domain, but also about the planning process itself. This technique allows the planner to use different approaches, depending on the problem at hand. The planner may also be able to learn which techniques are best for each type of problem and to apply them appropriately (Stefik, 1981b).

10.4.5 Case-Based Planning

It is possible to reuse old plans indirectly to generate new plans. That is, we can use the structure of an old plan, change it on the basis of the problem we are trying to solve, and create a new plan (Hammond, 1986). Case-based reasoning is a technique used in some systems to handle commonsense concepts.

10.5 AN OBJECT-ORIENTED PLANNER

The planner developed in this section uses the same sort of STRIPS approach described in Section 10.3. It uses much of the previous work done in C++, such as the search library and logic classes. The planner is tested using examples from a "blocks world"—a simple

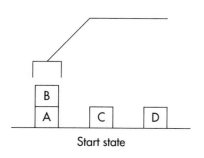
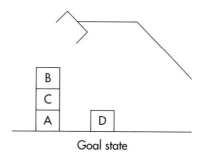

Start state   Goal state

FIGURE 10.4

Sample start state and goal state in a blocks world

world where blocks can be moved around to accomplish goals. This world has operators of "stack," "unstack," "pickup," and "putdown." These operators are completely defined using preconditions, add lists, and delete lists when we discuss the C++ code that implements them (see Frule.pp in Section 10.6). An example blocks world is given in Figure 10.4. In this world, we have a robotic gripper arm that is able to pick up the blocks and move them around. The predicates that apply to this world are as follows:

Predicate Name	Description
Clear(*block*)	The *block* has nothing on top of it and is not in the gripper.
Holding(*block*)	The *block* is in the gripper.
Arm(empty)	The gripper arm is empty.
On(*block1, block2*)	*block1* is sitting on top of *block2*
Ontable(*block*)	*block* is sitting directly on the table.

10.5.1 The Design

Some major classes are used in our STRIPS-like planner:

```
class StripsObject public Node
class Strips : public Depth Tree
class BasFact
class Fact : public BasFact, public Complex
class FactList : public BasFact, public PtrList<Fact>
class Action : public BasFact
class Frule
```

The first two classes in the program are defined by the statements *class StripsObject : public Node* and *class Strips : public DepthTree*. These are the basic problem-solving classes. Strips implements the search technique, and StripsObject represents the objects in the search tree. Class StripsObject is little more than a placeholder, it contains the configuration of the world (a description of the blocks world), the goal stack, and the action that was last applied to the world. These actions together make up the solution path: the plan.

The goal stack consists of different types of objects: simple goals, compound goals, and actions. For each of these, a different class is defined: Fact, FactList and Action, respectively. Classes Fact and FactList are also used in the state description of the world. Because these objects are different types but must all be stored on the same goal stack, we need a heterogeneous container that can handle several object types. This container is a list class that stores pointers to objects of *BasFact*. Fact objects are predicates; for instance *on(a, b)*. Class Fact is derived from one of the logic classes, class Complex. The objects of class Fact are simple goals.

The statement class *FactList : public BasFact, public PtrList<Fact>* defines the class containing complex goals. In other words, a FactList object is a collection of facts, for instance *on(a, b) & on(b, c)*.

Actions are objects belonging to the class defined by the statement *class Action : public BasFact*. An Action object represents the action that must be applied to the world, for instance *pickup(a)*. The information contained in an Action object is stored in two separate objects: a Complex object, which represents the "name" of the action (e.g., *pickup(a)*) and a pointer to an object of class Frule.

Class Frule represents the STRIPS F-rules. It contains the name of the rule, the precondition list, the add list, and the del (delete) list. Each of these lists is an object of type FactList. Frule objects are used in combination with objects of type Action: every Action object contains a pointer to an Frule object so that it knows which actions must be performed when it is applied to the world.

10.5.2 The Algorithm

Most of the work is done by process_strips(), defined in BasFact, and in the classes derived from it. This function takes a StripsObject and generates all its successors. The original idea was to have the generation of successors take place in expand(), where it logically should be. Here was the original method: Take the first object from the stack and pass to it the current configuration of the world; the object determines whether it itself is true in the world; if not, the object returns a list of "things" that either have not been satisfied yet (goals of a compound goal) or that will make the object true (substitutions or actions). If the object does not return anything, it is true and can be popped off the stack. When it comes off the stack, one or more new StripsObjects (the successors) are created, and the "things" that were returned by the stack object are applied to these successors.

This original method turned out to be impractical, because each stack object has its own notion of what these "things" should be, meaning there was no easy and uniform way to process and apply them to the new StripsObjects. Because the stack objects do know what must be done and how this can be done, the logical thing to do was to incorporate this procedure in the stack objects themselves instead of in the StripsObject class. As a consequence, the generation of successor nodes does not, strictly speaking, take place in the StripsObject class, where it normally would be done, but in the Fact, FactList, and Action classes, by means of process_strips(). Each of these classes has its own implementation of this function; each checks whether the object (i.e., an object of class Fact, FactList, or Action) is true in the world and, if not, determines how it can be made true. Each class uses this information to generate new StripsObjects, that is, the successors.

For more details on the implementation of the STRIPS-planner, see the comments accompanying the source code in the next section.

10.6 A C++ PLANNER

It is important to note that this planner uses the logic classes built in earlier chapters and the list class to produce the planner. The first step is writing the header file for our STRIPS-like planner.

```
//file: strips.h
#ifndef _STRIPS_H_
#define _STRIPS_H_

#include <list.h>
#include <logic.h>
#include <nodes.h>
#include <tree.h>

/*
 * StackItemType is used to differentiate stack
 * objects. This is useful when comparing stack
 * objects;  because the stack contains objects of
 * different types, the StackItemType tells us if
 * these objects can be comparedl.
 */
enum StackItemType { T_Fact, T_FactList, T_Action };
```

```
/* Forward declaration of class StripsObject */
   class StripsObject;

/*
 * BasFact is the base class for every class that
 * can be put on the stack. Three classes are
 * derived from this class: Fact, FactList and
 * Action. Since stack objects are stored on a
 * heterogeneous list a type object is used to
 * differentiate objects of one type from another.
 * The type of an object is determined by getstack-
 * type(). Member function process_strips()
 * generates the successors of an object of class
 * StripsObject, so this is where the real work is
 * done.
 */
class BasFact
{
  public:
    virtual ~BasFact();
    virtual int operator==(const BasFact &) const = 0;
    virtual StackItemType getstacktype() const = 0;
    virtual BasFact *basdup() const = 0;
    BasFact *clone() const;
    virtual void display() const = 0;
    virtual void process_strips(StripsObject *,
                          IntrList<Node> *) = 0;
    virtual void apply_subst(Substitution &) = 0;
};
/*
 * Class Fact represents a predicate: either a fact
 * in the world or a goal on the stack. For examples:
 * on(a, b) or on(a, X1).
 */
class Fact : public BasFact, public Complex
{
  public:
    Fact(const char *str);
    int operator==(const BasFact &) const;
    StackItemType getstacktype() const;
    BasFact *basdup() const;
    Fact *clone() const;
    void display() const;
    void process_strips(StripsObject *,
                          IntrList<Node> *);
```

```
      void apply_subst(Substitution &s);
  private:
    static StackItemType TypeId;
};


/*
 * Class FactList represents a conjunction of
 * precidates: either a collection of facts in the
 * world, i.e., a state description, or a compound
 * goal on the stack. For example: on(a, b) and
 * on(b, c).
 */
class FactList : public BasFact, public PtrList<Fact>
{
  public:
    FactList(int do_manage = 1);
    FactList &operator=(const FactList &);
    FactList &operator=(const char *);
    int operator==(const BasFact &) const;
    StackItemType getstacktype() const;
    FactList(const char *);
    BasFact *basdup() const;
    FactList *clone() const;
    void display() const;
    void process_strips(StripsObject *,
                        IntrList<Node> *);
    void apply_subst(Substitution &);
  private:
    void process(const char *);

    static StackItemType TypeId;
};

class Frule;
/*
 * Class Action represents an action that changes
 * one state desription into another. For example:
 * pickup(a). The changes introduced by the Action
 * object are represented by an object of class
 * F-rule.
 */
class Action : public BasFact
{
  public:
    Action(Complex &, Frule *);
```

```
      int operator==(const BasFact &other) const;
      StackItemType getstacktype() const;
      void display() const;
      void process_strips(StripsObject *,
                          IntrList<Node> *);
      void apply_subst(Substitution &s);
      BasFact *basdup() const;
      Action *clone() const;
      FactList* get_addlist() const;
      FactList* get_prelist() const;
      FactList* get_dellist() const;
   private:
      FactList *get_list(const FactList &) const;
      static StackItemType TypeId;

      Complex action;
      Frule *rule;
};


/*
 * Class F-rule represents the so called F-rules of
 * STRIPS. It consists of three components: a pre
 * condition formula, an add formula and a delete
 * list. The precondition formula consists of facts
 * that must be true in the world before the F-rule
 * can be applied. The add formula contains facts
 * that are added to the world and the delete list
 * facts that are removed from the world when the
 * F-rule is applied to the world.
 */
class Frule
{
    public:
        friend Action;
      Frule(char *, char *, char *, char *);
      void display() const;
        Action *create_action(Fact &);
    private:
      Complex name;
      FactList pre,
          del,
          add;
};


/*
```

```
 * Array of F-rule objects.
 */
#define MAXFRULE  4
extern Frule frulearr[MAXFRULE];

/*
 * Class StripsObject represents nodes in the search
 * tree. StripsObject contains the description of
 * the world, the goal stack, and the action object
 * that has last been applied. The solution path is
 * composed of these action objects.
 */
class StripsObject : public Node
{
    public:
       StripsObject();
       StripsObject(const char *, const char *);
       int operator==(const Node &) const;
         void display() const;
         IntrList<Node> *expand(int);
       StripsObject *dup() const;

       FactList world;
       PtrList<BasFact> stack;
         Complex action;
};

/*
 * Class Strips represents the search method that
 * is applied to the STRIPS problem. In this case,
 * depth-first search is selected.
 */
class Strips : public DepthTree
{
    public:
    Strips();
    Strips(StripsObject *);
    int is_goal(const Node *);
};

#endif
```

The following C++ program implements the C++ planner.

```
//file: strips.cpp
```

```
#include "strips.h"

StripsObject::StripsObject()
{
}

StripsObject::StripsObject(const char *wrld, const
char *stck)
{
  FactList *fl = new FactList(stck);

  world = wrld;
  stack.addtohead(fl);
}

int StripsObject::operator==(const Node &other)
                                               const
{
  if (!(world == ((StripsObject &)other).world))
      return(0);
  if (!(stack == ((StripsObject &)other).stack))
      return(0);
  return(action == ((StripsObject &)other).action);
}

void StripsObject::display() const
{
  if (action.notempty())
  {
      action.display();
      putchar('\n');
  }
}

/*
 * Dup() copies the complete StripsObject except
 * for the action.
 */
StripsObject *StripsObject::dup() const
{
  StripsObject *ret = new StripsObject;
  ret->world = world;
  ret->stack = stack;
  return(ret);
}
```

```
/*
 * Expand() generates the successors of the
 * StripsObject. In truth, the real work is done in
 * process_strips() defined in class BasFact and
 * the classes derived from it. Expand() takes the
 * first item from the stack and calls
 * process_strips() on it to process "itself".
 */
IntrList<Node> *StripsObject::expand(int)
{
  BasFact *object;
  IntrList<Node> *succs = new IntrList<Node>;

  /*
   * Get the first item of the stack. If the stack
   * is empty we're through.
   */
     object = stack.gethead();

  if (!object)
  {
    /*
     * Create a successor. The stack of this
     * successor will be empty, which will serve as
     * the stop condition.
     */
    StripsObject *kid = new StripsObject;
    succs->addtohead(kid);
  }

  /*
   * Use the item that was popped from the stack
   * to process the current StripsObject. This will
   * update the StripsObject and generate its
   * successors.
   */
  object->process_strips(this, succs);

  /*
   * Once we've expanded the object, the stack and
   * world are no longer needed (this would be
   * different if we were doing a graph search
   * instead of a tree search), so we call clear()
   * to free the memory used by them.
   */
```

```
    stack.clear(DoDel);
    world.clear(DoDel);
    return(succs);
}

Strips::Strips()
  : DepthTree(0)
{
}

Strips::Strips(StripsObject *start)
  : DepthTree(0, start)
{
}

int Strips::is_goal(const Node *g)
{
   const StripsObject *s = (StripsObject *)g;

   /*
    * The node is a goal node if the goal stack of
    * the node is empty.
    */
    return(s->stack.is_empty());
}
```

The remainder of the code can be found in the file *planner.cc* (not given here), which is the implementation of the other functions described in the file *strips.h*. The following file implements the Frule class for a block-stacking problem.

```
//file: frule.cpp
#include "strips.h"

/*
 * Note that the prelist and the dellist of each
 * F-rule are exactly the same, meaning we could
 * remove either of them. But for completeness's
 * sake, we keep both of them.
 */
Frule frulearr[MAXFRULE] = {
                Frule("stack(X, Y)",
                    "clear(Y) & holding(X)",
                    "clear(Y) & holding(X)",
                    "arm(empty) & on(X, Y) &
                                        clear(X)"),
```

```
      Frule("unstack(X, Y)",
        "on(X, Y) & clear(X) & arm(empty)",
        "on(X, Y) & clear(X) & arm(empty)",
        "holding(X) & clear(Y)"),

      Frule("pickup(X)",
        "ontable(X) & clear(X)
                    & arm(empty)",
        "ontable(X) & clear(X)
                    & arm(empty)",
        "holding(X)"),

      Frule("putdown(X)",
        "holding(X)",
        "holding(X)",
        "ontable(X) & arm(empty)
                    & clear(X)")
};
```

The following file includes test cases for the **STRIPS** planner. Cas 6 corresponds to the problem in Figure 10.4.

```cpp
//file: run.cpp
#include "strips.h"

int main()
{
  StripsObject *s1 = new StripsObject(
    "clear(a) & clear(b) & clear(c) & ontable(a)
              & ontable(b) & ontable(c)
              & arm(empty)",
    "on(a, b) & on(c, a)");

  StripsObject *s2 = new StripsObject(
    "clear(b) & clear(c) & ontable(a) & ontable(b)
              & on(c, a) & arm(empty)",
    "on(a, b) & on(b, c)");

  StripsObject *s3 = new StripsObject(
    "clear(a) & clear(b) & clear(c) & ontable(a)
              & ontable(b) & ontable(c)
              & arm(empty)",
  "holding(a) & on(b, c)");

  StripsObject *s4 = new StripsObject(
    "clear(c) & clear(b) & ontable(a) & ontable(b)
```

```
                    & arm(empty) & on(c, a)",
    "ontable(c) & on(b, c) & on(a, b)");

StripsObject *s5 = new StripsObject(
    "clear(c) & ontable(a) & on(b, a) & on(c, b)
            & arm(empty)",
    "on(a, b) & on(b, c)");

StripsObject *s6 = new StripsObject(
    "on(b, a) & ontable(a) & ontable(c)
            & ontable(d) & clear(b) & clear(c)
            & clear(d) & arm(empty)",
    "on(b, c) & on(c, a) & ontable(a) & ontable(d)");

Strips planner;

puts("** Plan for problem 1: **");
planner.set_startnode(s1);
if (planner.generate())
  planner.display();

printf("\n** Plan for problem 2: **\n");
planner.set_startnode(s2);
if (planner.generate())
  planner.display();

printf("\n** Plan for problem 3: **\n");
planner.set_startnode(s3);
if (planner.generate())
  planner.display();

printf("\n** Plan for problem 4: **\n");
planner.set_startnode(s4);
if (planner.generate())
  planner.display();

printf("\n** Plan for problem 5: **\n");
planner.set_startnode(s5);
if (planner.generate())
  planner.display();

printf("\n** Plan for problem 6: **\n");
planner.set_startnode(s6);
if (planner.generate())
  planner.display();
```

```
    return(1);
}
```

10.7 SUMMARY

There are many approaches and techniques that can be used for planning, and the general problem quickly becomes difficult. For example, consider the problem of planning the construction of a single-family home. To build a really effective solution to this problem, we need to be able to handle potential problems that can occur, make judgments about what the potential trade-offs are, and be able to determine the best alternative path on the basis of some criteria. In general, planning problems can utilize many of the same techniques we have seen from other areas of AI, such as heuristic search, knowledge representation, theorem proving, and common-sense reasoning. In this chapter we discuss planning in the context of simple planning, using a STRIPS-like approach.

10.8 REFERENCES

For a set of important papers in the area of planning, refer to *Readings in Planning* by J. Allen (1990). For more on STRIPS and ABSTRIPS, refer to Nilsson (1980), Cohen (1982), Volume 3, and Fikes and Nilsson (1971).

10.9 EXERCISES

Warm-up Exercises

10.1. Define the monkey and bananas problem given in Section 5.1.2 as a planning problem with operators, add lists, delete lists, and preconditions.

10.2. Write a triangle table to solve the monkey and bananas problem.

10.3. Consider planning a wedding. What does the plan need to generate? What knowledge is needed?

10.4. Consider planning a large convention in a particular city. List the factors that must be considered to plan the convention, the data that must be available, and the general method that could be taken to get a workable plan for the convention.

10.5. What could cause plans to fail in a wedding plan, such as one

302

that would be generated by your answer to Exercise 10.3?

10.6. What could cause plans to fail in a convention plan, such as one that would be generated by your answer to Exercise 10.4?

10.7. Describe criteria for determining whether a workable plan is "good" or "bad" in the context of the wedding planner. That is, if you had many plans that would produce a wedding, how could you tell which is the best?

Homework Exercises

10.8. Write (in **STRIPS** form) a planner for a wedding with the following constraints:

- Plan small (<100 people), medium (<300 and >100), and large (>300) weddings.

- Weddings consist of a reception, a ceremony, a honeymoon, a rehearsal dinner, picture-taking, and a wedding shower.

- You have input data about the availability of reception halls (number of people and dates), the number of people expected at the reception, and the date and time desired for the wedding.

- You should produce a reasonable ordering of events to occur and when they need to occur.

10.9. Consider the task defined by the following diagrams. The initial state is described by

(IN robot rooma)
(IN box1 roomb)
(OPEN door1)
(IN door1 rooma)
(IN door1 roomb)
(CONNECTS door1 rooma roomb)

The goal is described by

(NEXTTO robot box1)
(CLOSED door1)

The robot has three operators, described by:

GOTO X_obj	Puts the robot next to the X_obj and not next to anything else; Represent this by putting (NEXT TO robot *) in the delete list. It is applicable if the robot and X_obj are in the same room.

GOTHRU X_door	Puts the robot in the room that the door connects to. That is, it moves the robot from its current room to the connecting room. Initially, the robot must be next to the open X_door.
CLOSE X_door	Closes the open X_door :The robot must be next to the X_door.

Describe the three operators by giving their preconditions, delete list, and add list. Describe a plan for achieving the goal and draw a diagram giving the symbolic descriptions (use the predicates above) of the sequence of states that would be achieved if the plan were executed. (Exercise adapted from Bundy et al., 1978.)

10.10. Write the rest of the frame axioms necessary for the robot that is searching for gold on the moon. Also modify the definitions of the actions so that the robot does not blow itself up and keeps track of the objects in its field of vision.

10.11. The C++ planner presented here will get caught in an infinite loop on some problem specifications and goal states. Find one such problem and associated goal state that will cause this problem.

10.12. In Exercise 10.11, you specified one such problem that could occur with the C++ planner presented here. Characterize all such problems and goals that could cause the planner to get caught in a loop.

10.13. 10- Consider the problem of trying to develop a plan when there are many, many options at each step for actions to take. Specifically, it is not realistic to try to use the planning techniques presented here for planning a chess game, move by move. However, how might you use these sorts of planning techniques to choose a higher level plan or strategy?

Programming Exercises

10.14. Implement the wedding planner by using the STRIPS-like C++ framework provided. Make up at least 10 reception hall vendors, church names, etc., and run the problem for a wedding of 350 people on June 1.

10.15. Implement a planner by using the framework given in Exercise 10.9. Use the framework to implement a STRIPS planner that will be able to plan its way out of an arbitrarily complex maze specified in the form given in Exercise 10.9.

10.16. Expand the STRIPS-like C++ planner to produce triangle tables.

10.17. As noted in Exercise 10.11, the C++ planner presented in Section 10.6 loops on some problems. Devise a scheme so that the planner will not loop on these problems. Explain how this scheme might alter the functioning of the planner and modify the program to use your scheme.

Projects

10.18. Create a planner to plan airline trips on the basis of available flight data. Your planner should take into account layover time, number of connections, avoidance of bad airports and airlines, and a particular individual's preferences for these criteria.

10.19. Create a versatile birthday party planner. The planner should take into account the person's age (a party for a 7-year-old will be very different from a 70-year-old's party), the number of people expected, the type of entertainment that might be applicable (e.g., a clown for a 7-year-old-or a band for a person more than 15), and the types of food that be appropriate.

10.20. Create the wedding planner by using data from the phone book in your local area to determine the available reception halls, capacity, food available, and so on. Make up data about availability and add data about other wedding-related tasks such as floral arrangements, invitations, and photographer.

NATURAL LANGUAGE PROCESSING

Language is a part of

our organism and

no less complicated

than it.

LUDWIG WITTGENSTEIN, 1915

11.1 ISSUES IN NATURAL LANGUAGE

A machine that interacts with humans in a natural way must be able to interpret and produce natural language. Most people in the world can not write computer programs or even type effectively, so they are prohibited from using the power of the computer in their daily lives, except in highly specialized applications. In response to this obvious deficiency, much work has been done to produce machines that both understand and produce natural language.

In this chapter we will focus on the understanding of natural language. The production of natural language appears on the surface to be a simpler problem. But, in fact, it includes many of the same difficulties that understanding language does. To generate speech that makes sense to humans requires an understanding of the situation at hand as well as a deep understanding of how language is used in those situation.

A view of the steps required to understand spoken language is given in Figure 11.1. The initial steps are similar to those that a compiler performs in translating a program to machine code. First, we must determine what words have been spoken. This is the **lexical analysis** step, and it requires some understanding of what words are and the various ways they can be used, so that the appropriate words can be recognized (i.e., recognizing "their" rather than "there"). Lower level analysis must also occur so that a stream of sound waves can be translated into words and other elementary

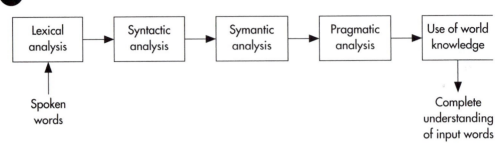

FIGURE 11.1

Steps in understanding language

segments of meaning (called tokens). This process includes splitting the sound waves into phonemes (elements of sound, like "th") and into morphemes (elements of meaning, like "-ing"). Take, for example, the phrase "great ships." "Great ships" sounds very much like "gray chips." To distinguish one from the other requires careful lexical analysis.

The next phase shown in Figure 11.1 is **syntactic analysis**. In this phase, the stream of tokens is analyzed to determine whether or not it is part of the language in question. If it is a legal sentence, then a **parse tree** that indicates the structure of the sentence is produced. In other words, the parse tree divides the sentence into subject, verb, object phrase, and so on. We will discuss this phase in Section 11.2. Consider the problem of trying to determine whether the phrase "Oh no—Bilbo!" is a legal English sentence. This phrase is not a sentence, but we still might need to parse it to determine what was said, particularly if Bilbo also has a gun!

The third phase shown in Figure 11.1 is **semantic analysis**. The purpose of this phase is to convert the parse tree to a representation of language that details the meaning of the sentence, such as conceptual graphs. This phase will also be discussed in this chapter. Consider, for example, a sentence such as "Professors that give hard exams to students make them sweat." We need to determine the meaning of different parts of the sentence: the students doing the sweating (not the professors)? What does it mean to sweat? Do students have to do work to complete exams (they aren't just given as gifts)?

The last two phases, **pragmatic analysis** and **world knowledge**, integrate the semantic knowledge of the sentence into the context of the discourse and of the world, respectively. Both of these phases are still being actively studied and will not be covered in this chapter. Consider a statement like "Hang on just a minute." On the basis of the pragmatic analysis, we would find that this statement is a figure of speech that is either asking us to wait or questioning what was said. In other words, we would realize that the statement is not asking us to grasp some object for one minute of time.

Consider a statement like "To be or not to be: that is the question." The speaker of this statement assumes that the listener knows that Shakespeare wrote this phrase and that it carries with it Shakespeare's context. So, to fully understand what is being said, the listener needs to have knowledge of the world and common human experiences and background. Many jokes depend on pragmatic analysis and world knowledge.

11.2 FORMAL LANGUAGES

Formal language theory is at the heart of the design of computer languages. It is also a prerequisite for much of the work that has been done in the syntactic analysis of natural language. For a complete discussion of the theory of languages, see Hopcroft and Ullman, 1979.

A language is defined by using a **grammar** that consists of the following four parts:

- A set of **terminals**, denoted as Σ. The terminal symbols of the language are the basic building blocks of a language. For example, we might designate the letters of the alphabet as terminal symbols (as well as whatever delimiters are necessary) of a language that uses words. A special terminal that is often included in the set is e, which represents the empty string.

- A set of **nonterminals**, denoted as N. Nonterminals represent higher level constructs of the grammar, such as a sentence or a word. These constructs are used as intermediate quantities in the generation of an outcome consisting only of terminal symbols. For example, the nonterminal word generates a string of letters (terminal symbols).

- A set of **productions**, denoted as P. The productions are the rules defining how we generate legal sentences in the grammar. For example, we may have a production such as *<Sentence>* → *<Noun_Phrase> <Verb_Phrase>*. This rule says that a sentence (a nonterminal) is made up of a noun phrase (another nonterminal) followed by a verb phrase (a third kind of nonterminal). Another production might be *<verb>* → *sit | eat | swim*, which means that the verb nonterminal can be either "its," "eat," or "swim."

- A **start symbol**, denoted as S. The start symbol defines the structural unit (or building block) of the language. For example, in English the start symbol might represent an English sentence; in a programming language the start symbol might represent a program.

Symbol	Meaning in EBNF
<a>	*a* is a nonterminal
<a> → *<b>*	Nonterminal *a* can be replaced by terminal *b*
<a> | *<b>*	Either *a* or *b* can be used
[*a*]	*a* can optionally be used
[*abc*]*	*abc* can be replaced zero or more times
[*abc*]⁺	*abc* can be replaced one or more times

TABLE 11.1

Symbols for EBNF
grammar productions

A grammar is formally defined as an ordered list of these components:

$$G = \{\Sigma, N, P, S\}$$

11.2.1 Extended Backus-Naur Form

A notation commonly used for writing the productions of grammars is Backus-Naur Form (BNF). We will use an extended version of BNF, called **Extended Backus-Naur Form** (EBNF). The symbols used in constructing EBNF grammar production rules are given in Table 11.1.

Let's use EBNF to define numbers that have integral exponents:

number> → [+ \| –] { *<decnum>* \| [*<decnum>*] × 10$^{<integer>}$ }

<decnum> → { *<unsigned_int>* \| [*<unsigned_int>*].*<unsigned_int>* }

<integer> → [+ \| –] *<unsigned_int>*

<unsigned_int> → *<digit>*⁺

<digit> → >{1 \| 2 \| 3 \| 4 \| 5 \| 6 \| 7 \| 8 \| 9 \| 0}

Chomsky hierarchy. Noam Chomsky developed a mathematical description of four different classes of languages, which are now know as Chomsky types zero through three. He was attempting to develop a mathematical theory of natural languages. The four types are

- Chomsky type 0: recursively enumerable languages
- Chomsky type 1: context-sensitive languages
- Chomsky type 2: context-free languages
- Chomsky type 3: regular languages

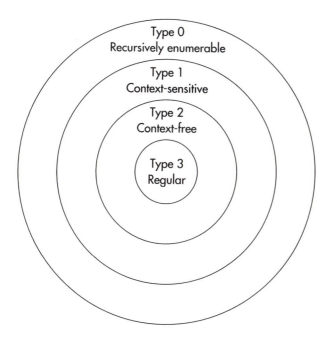

FIGURE 11.2

Language containment in the Chomsky hierarchy

Each of these classes included the ones below it (Figure 11.2). For example, the set of recursively enumerable languages includes context-sensitive, context-free, and regular languages.

Regular languages. A regular language is the simplest type of formal languages and is recognizable by a finite-state machine. In EBNF, the grammars for these languages can be written in what is called **regular** form; that is, these rules are nonrecursive and can be written with no more than one nonterminal on each side of the production. For example, $<A> \to b$ and $<A1> \to <A2>b$ are rules with regular form. If all rules have the form of the preceding examples, then the grammar is termed **left-linear**. If they have the form $<A> \to b<A2>$ or $<A> \to b$, then the grammar is termed **right-linear**. The following productions constitute a right-linear, regular grammar:

$$<S> \to a <A>$$
$$<A> \to b <B>$$
$$<B> \to c <A>$$
$$<B> \to d$$

where $<S>$ is the start symbol. This grammar describes sentences consisting of *ab*, followed by zero or more occurrences of *cb*, followed by a single *d*.

Regular grammars and languages are simple. In fact, they are so simple that they cannot describe some useful language constructs. Take, for example, a language that consists of all sets of balanced parentheses. In reading a sequence of parentheses, we may nest to an arbitrary depth before finding a matching parenthesis. To be able to match all the remaining parentheses, we need to have enough states to keep track of them. Because we can have an arbitrary depth of nesting, we may need an arbitrary number of states in our finite-state machine. However, we cannot have an arbitrary number of states in our finite-state machine and therefore cannot recognize these nested parentheses.[1] Therefore, we need to study more powerful formalisms for grammars.

Context-free languages. Context-free grammar rules have the form

$$<A> \rightarrow \alpha$$

where α is a sequence of zero or more terminals and nonterminals. A simple context-free grammar is

$$<S> \rightarrow (<S>)$$
$$<S> \rightarrow x$$

This grammar produces the languages of all matched parentheses around a single x. And this grammar can describe the language noted above, the one that could not be described by using a regular grammar.

Context-sensitive languages. Content-sensitive grammar rules have the form

$$\alpha \rightarrow \beta$$

where the length of α is less than or equal to the length of β in terms of the number of terminals and nonterminals that they contain. These rules can be written in the normal form $\alpha_1<A>\alpha_2 \rightarrow \alpha_1\beta\alpha_2$. This normal form suggests the name "context-sensitive." The nonterminal $<A>$ is taken in a context—that of being between α_1 and α_2—and it is only in this context that this rule applies.

Recursively enumerable languages. A language is recursively enumerable if it can be expressed by arbitrary production rules with any sequence of terminals and nonterminal on each side of the production.

---

[1] The fact that regular grammars (and finite-state machines) are not able to count and to retain that count for later use is often paraphrased. For example, regular grammar cannot create matched sets of parentheses, as that would require counting the number of unmatched parentheses.

We call such languages recursively enumerable because we can write a program that produces all sentences in the language in some order; that is, the program enumerates them. However, for any particular input sentence, our program may never be able to determine whether or not that sentence is in the language. If all we can do is enumerate all sentences in the language, we may never reach the input sentence in our lifetime. And because our program may not reach the input sentence, we are unable to state whether or not the sentence is in the language. Consequently, languages this general are not yet useful because of the pragmatic constraints on our ability to parse them.

11.2.2 Parse Trees

Given the following grammar, we can proceed to structure that tells us which grammatical rules were used to produce any legal sentence in the language defined by the grammar. The structure we still use is a parse tree (Figure 11.3).

$<S> \rightarrow <NP> <VP>$

$<NP> \rightarrow <N>$

$<NP> \rightarrow <Art> <N>$

$<VP> \rightarrow <V>$

$<VP> \rightarrow <V> <NP>$

$<Art> \rightarrow$ a

$<Art> \rightarrow$ the

$<N> \rightarrow$ wombat

$<N> \rightarrow$ hobbit

$<N> \rightarrow$ crumpet

$<V> \rightarrow$ eats

$<V> \rightarrow$ sleeps

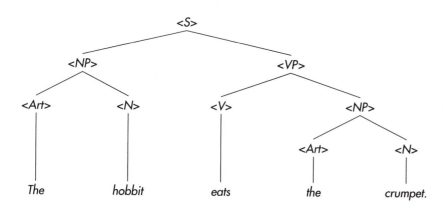

FIGURE 11.3

A simple parse tree

At the bottom of the parse tree are the individual tokens or words that make up the sentence. At the very top of the tree is the start symbol, in this case, *<S>*. Each branching of the tree indicates the application of a rule. For example, at the top of the tree we have two branches emanating from the *<S>* node. They are labeled *<NP>* and *<VP>*. This particular branching indicates that we applied the rule *<S>* → *<NP>* *<VP>* to derive this sentence.

A **left-most derivation** is found if we always expand the left-most node first whenever possible (similar to a depth-first search). A **right-most derivation** is found if we always expand the right-most node first.

11.2.3 Other Issues

A grammar is called **ambiguous** if there exists more than one parse tree for some sentence in the grammar. For example, if the left-most derivation is different from the right-most derivation for any sentence, then the language is ambiguous.

Language parsers usually take either a **top-down** or **bottom-up** approach. A top-down parser begins with the start symbol and applies rules until it gets down to the token level. It then checks its choices by determing whether the token or word matches the type designated for it. Many top-down parsers take into account a number of tokens (called the number of **look-ahead** symbols) in order to make better decisions on which rules to apply. This is particularly helpful if there are many rules that apply at one time but only one can be chosen. Bottom-up parsers work by examining the words or tokens first. Most computer language compilers work in a bottom-up fashion.

11.3 DEFINITE CLAUSE GRAMMARS

The rules for definite clause grammars (DCG) are usually written directly in Prolog, as most Prologs support DCGs. We use a similar type of context-free rule structure in the C++ parser in Section 11.6. They perform a top-down, left-most derivation parsing of the input sentence. Consider the following rule:

$$sentence(Number, sentence(NP, VP)) \rightarrow$$
$$noun\_phrase(Number, NP),$$
$$verb\_phrase(Number, VP).$$

This rule says that a sentence is made up of a verb phrase and a noun phrase. It also ensures that the number of the verb phrase matches the number of the noun phrase; that is, if the verb phrase is plural, then the noun phrase must be plural also. This DCG rule is automatically translated into the following Prolog rule:

>*sentence(Number,sentence(NP,VP), List, Rest)*
>*noun_phrase(Number, NP, List, Rest0),*
>*verb_phrase(Number, VP, Rest0, Rest).*

Consequently, a query to parse a particular sentence must have the form *sentence(Number, Parse_Tree, [the, hobbit, eats, the, crumpet],* []). The sentence to parse must be in difference list format for the parsing to work correctly. That is, List and Rest represent the sentence together. The actual sentence passed is the difference of the two. Normally, one places the entire sentence in the List argument and Rest contains the empty list, so that the program can check to see if the sentence can be parsed with the given grammar.

11.4 TRANSITION NETWORKS

Transition networks (TNs) are used for parsing simple languages and are based on the notion of a finite-state machine. The transition between states depends on the next symbol (word or token) that is read from the input stream, and it is labeled by the object that must be parsed before it proceeds to the next node. A special symbol (ε) is used to represent those situations in which no input needs to be parsed before proceeding to the next node.

Augmented transition networks (ATNs) expand on the transition network principle by allowing some context-sensitive language constructs and also by allowing attached procedures to check the context-sensitive properties of the language. The network allows us to check for agreement between verb and subject. ATNs also use framelike structures for nonterminal and terminals in the grammar, with slots for context-sensitive characteristics, like number.

The transition network in Figure 11.4 is based on the following context-free grammar:

>*<S> → <NP> <VP> | <Aux><NP><VP> | <NP> <Aux> <VP>*
>*<VP> → <Verb><NP>*<PP>**
>*<NP> → <Adj>*<Noun> | <det><Adj>*<Noun>*
>*<PP> → <Prep> <NP>*

The rules for *<VP>* (verb phrase) are embedded within the TN for sentences. The meanings of the abbreviations used in these rules are listed in Table 11.2.

Abbreviation	Meaning	Example
Aux	auxiliary verb	has
Adj	adjective	fuzzy
NP	noun phrase	the kitten
VP	verb phrase	eat the hotdog
PP	prepositional phrase	for the dog
Det	determinism	the
Prep	preposition	of

TABLE 11.2

Abbreviations used in rules for the transition network in Figure 11.4

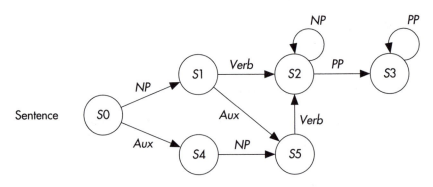

FIGURE 11.4

Very simple TN for English

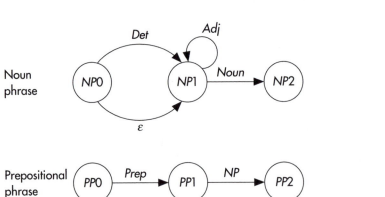

11.5 CATEGORIES OF NATURAL LANGUAGE WORK

There are many areas of work in natural language where **AI** plays a major role. Some of the most active areas of current research are

- *Discourse.* Researchers are developing programs that program produce meaningful conversations between the program and the user. Tutoring systems or programs acting as expert consultants are two systems that use discourse.

- *Explanation generation.* Anytime a program must try to explain its results to the user of the program, it requires this capability.

- *Dictionaries.* Programs of this type create and maintain dictionaries of words that can be used by other programs.

- *Natural language understanding.* Researchers in this area continue to refine ways to extract meaning from natural language. They also are concerned with disambiguating sentence meaning and describing techniques for making inferences from natural language segments.

- *Machine translation.* The goal of this research area is to produce programs that can automatically translate one language into another.

11.6 C++ NATURAL LANGUAGE PARSER

We can use C++ and the search library presented in Section 5.8 to parse a context-free grammar. The following header file for a sample parser for a simple grammar defines class interfaces. Note that the AND/OR search definitions are used because they are a natural fit for DCG-like rules. AND nodes in the tree represent where two parts of the rule must be in order. For example, *<S>* → *<NP>*, *<VP>* would be represented as an AND node in the search tree. OR nodes represent the alternative parsings for a nonterminal. For example, the rule *<VP>* → *<V>* | *<V><NP>* would be represented with an OR node.

```
//file: parser.h
#ifndef _parser_H_
#define _parser_H_

#include <stdio.h>
#include <stdarg.h>
#include "tree.h"
#include "list.h"
#include "xstring.h"

/*
 * Item defines symbolic names for the syntactic
 * categories used for the CF-PSG rules and the
```

```
 * words in the lexicon. Note that if the parser is
 * extended with rules that contain new syntactic
 * categories, Item must be updated accordingly.
 */
enum Item
{
  S,
  VP,
  IV,
  TV,
  TV2,
  NP,
  NP1,
  N,
  DET,
  CN,
};


#define END -1

/*
 * Class Rules represents CF-PSG rules, i.e., rules
 * like 'S -> NP VP' and 'NP -> DET N'. The
 * arguments passed to the constructor of Rule are
 * of type Item. The first Item represents the LHS
 * (left-hand side) of the rule and the rest the
 * RHS (right-hand side) of the rule. A variable
 * argument list is used so that the size of the
 * rule is not limited. The last argument passed
 * must be END. Class Rule contains two data
 * fields: the head (LHS) of the rule and the body
 * (RHS) of the rule.
 */
class Rule
{
  public:
      Rule(Item, ...);
      void display() const;
      const List<Item> *match(Item) const;
  private:
      Item head;
      List<Item> body;
};


/*
```

```
 * Class Word defines words that will be stored in
 * the lexicon used by the parser. Class Word
 * contains two data fields: the word itself (a
 * string) and the syntactic category of this word.
 */
class Word
{
  public:
      Word(Item, const char *);
      void display() const;
      int match(Item, const char *) const;
  private:
      Item head;
      String word;
};

extern Rule rules[];
extern int MaxRule;
extern Word lexicon[];
extern int MaxWord;

/*  Element
 *
 * Class Element is a representation of the nodes
 * generated during the search, and it serves as an
 * abstraction of the syntactic categories. Note
 * that expand() is implemented instead of
 * do_operator() because there is not a fixed
 * number of operators for this problem (every LHS
 * of a CF-PSG may be rewritten to a RHS containing
 * a variable number of syntactic categories). The
 * Item element represents the syntactic category
 * of the word that was parsed by this Element
 * object. The solution path is made up of these
 * elements.
 */
class Element : public OrNode
{
  public:
    Element(Item);
    Item get_item() const;

    int operator==(const Node &) const;
    void display() const;
    IntrList<Node> *expand(int);
```

```
    private:
      Item
      item;
};

/*
 * Parse represents the search algorithm. Because a
 * depth-first search of an AND/OR tree must be
 * performed, Parse is derived AODepthTree. Class
 * Parse contains the sentence to be parsed (an \
 * array of char *) and an index to this sentence
 * indicates which word will be parsed next. The
 * number of words in the sentence is determined by
 * 'size'.
 */
class Parse : public AODepthTree
{
  public:
    Parse(char **, int, Element *);
    int is_terminal(const AONode *);
  private:
    char
      **sentence;
    int
      index,
        size;
};

#endif
```

The following code implements a context-free parser based on the class definitions given in *parser.h*.

```
//file: parser.cpp
#include "parser.h"

/*
 * Table defines string values for the syntactic
 * categories defined in Item.
 */
char
  *table[] = {"s", "vp", "iv", "tv", "tv2", "np",
            "np1", "n", "det", "cn"};

Rule::Rule(Item item1, ...)
```

```
{
  Item p;
  va_list args;

  va_start(args, item1);
  head = item1;

  while ((p = va_arg(args, Item)) != END)
       body.addtotail(p);

  va_end(args);
}

void Rule::display() const
{
  ROListIterator<Item> iter(body);
  int i;
  Item n;

  printf("%s -> ", table[head]);

  n = iter.getfirst();
  printf("%s ", table[n]);
  for (i = 1; i < body.getcount(); i++)
  {
    n = iter.getnext();
      printf("%s ", table[n]);
  }
  putchar('\n');
}

/*
 * Match() checks whether the specified item matches
 * the head (LHS) of the rule and if true returns
 * the body (RHS) of the rule.
 */
const List<Item> *Rule::match(Item item) const
{
  return(item == head ? &body : NULL);
}

Word::Word(Item item, const char *wrd)
{
  head = item;
  word = wrd;
}
```

```
void Word::display() const
{
  cout << table[head] << ":" << word << "\n";
}

int Word::match(Item item, const char *wrd) const
{
  return(head == item && word == wrd);
}

Parse::Parse(char **sntnc, int length, Element
             *start) : AODepthTree(0, start)
{
  sentence = sntnc;
  index = 0;
  size = length;
}

Element::Element(Item it)
{
  item = it;
}

void Element::display() const
{
  printf("%s\n", table[item]);
}

/*
 * The equality operator is not used anywhere in
 * the program, but it must be implemented because
 * it is defined pure virtual in OrNode.
 */
int Element::operator==(const Node &other) const
{
  return(item == ((Element &)other).item);
}

Item Element::get_item() const
{
  return(item);
}

/*
 * To expand a node, every rule in the rules DB is
```

```
 * checked to see if its LHS is of the same
 * syntactic category as the node. If a match is
 * found, then an AND node is created, and for
 * each of the syntactic categories of the RHS of
 * the rule a new node is created that is added as
 * a successor to the AND node. Keep in mind that
 * the terminology of AND and OR nodes used here
 * differs from normal usage.
 */
IntrList<Node> *Element::expand(int )
{
  IntrList<Node> *ret = new IntrList<Node>;
  int i;

  for (i = 0; i < MaxRule; i++)
  {
      const List<Item> *rhs;
      AndNode *andnode;

    if ((rhs = rules[i].match(item)))
    {
      Item lhs_element;
        ROListIterator<Item> iter(*rhs);
        int d;

        andnode = new AndNode();
        lhs_element = iter.getfirst();
      andnode->addsucc(new Element(lhs_element));
      for (d = 1; d < rhs->getcount(); d++)
        {
           lhs_element = iter.getnext();
          andnode->addsucc(new Element(lhs_element));
        }

        ret->addtotail(andnode);
    }
  }
  return(ret);
}

/*
 * A node is terminal if the syntactic category of
 * the item to be parsed is terminal (in a
 * linguistic sense) itself and if it matches the
 * word (pointed to by the index) that the item
```

```
 * represents in the sentence. First, the syntactic
 * category of the item is searched in the lexicon.
 * If it can't be found there, the item does not
 * represent a terminal syntactic category. Next,
 * the word belonging to this syntactic category
 * according to the lexicon is compared with the
 * word in the input string. If both conditions
 * are satisfied, the item is considered parsed and
 * hence terminal.
 */
int Parse::is_terminal(const AONode *node)
{
  int
    i;

  if (index >= size)
      return(0);

  for (i = 0; i < MaxWord; i++)
      if (lexicon[i].match(((Element *)node)->
                      get_item(), sentence[index]))
      {
        index++;
        return(1);
      }

  return(0);
}
```

The following files define a sample grammar and a use of that grammar from a program.

```
//file: data.cpp
#include "parser.h"

/*
 * Rules[] contains the CF-PSG rules that are used
 * by the parser to rewrite a LHS category to new
 * categories. The size of the array is indicated
 * by MaxRule.
 */
Rule
  rules[] = {
             Rule(S, NP, VP, END),
            Rule(NP, NP1, END),
```

```
                Rule(NP, DET, N, END),
                Rule(VP, IV, END),
                Rule(VP, TV, NP, END),
                Rule(VP, TV2, CN, S, END),
            };

int MaxRule = 6;

/*
 * Lexicon[] contains the words that the parses
 * recognizes. The size of the array is indicatd by
 * MaxWord.
 */
Word
  lexicon[] = {
                Word(TV, "kills"),
              Word(TV2, "thinks"),
              Word(IV, "sleeps"),
              Word(NP1, "john"),
              Word(N, "man"),
              Word(DET, "the"),
              Word(CN, "that"),
            };

int MaxWord = 7;



=======================================================


//file: run.cpp
#include "parser.h"

int main(int argc, char *argv[])
{
  if (argc == 1)
  {
    printf("Usage: %s <string>\n", argv[0]);
    exit(0);
  }
  Parse
    sentence(++argv, argc -1, new Element(S));
  if (sentence.generate())
    sentence.display();
}
```

11.7 SUMMARY

This chapter presents some of the basics of natural language parsing techniques. Clearly, as more understanding of language is needed, more advanced techniques should be used to understand the semantics of natural language. We present a simple grammar parsing algorithm that directly uses the search library algorithms presented in Chapter 5. Many of the issues faced in parsing natural languages are representative of the difficult problems that AI faces in general. Problems such as disambiguating a sentence to understand which of the possible meanings is most likely, using commonsense knowledge, and integrating world knowledge into problem solving are all general problems that AI faces.

11.8 REFERENCES

Excellent general references for natural language parsing and understanding are Grishman (1986) and Allen (1995). Boden (1977), Winograd and Flores (1986), and Minsky (1986) provide easily readable texts that detail some of the difficulties in natural language understanding. Refer to Winograd (1983) for details on many methods for parsing natural language, such as transformational grammars, ATNs, and feature and function grammars. See the January 1996 Communications of the ACM for several articles on the current state of natural language processing. For more on DCGs in Prolog, see Pereira (1980), Bratko (1990), and Sterling (1991).

11.9 EXERCISES

Warm-up Exercises

11.1. Produce a parse tree for the following English sentences:

That is true in a pig's eye.

Follow the yellow brick road to the castle.

Cats may bite, but they also purr.

A penny saved is a penny earned.

Some of these sentences have several possible parse trees. For those sentences, diagram two parse trees and explain what information could be used to pick the proper parsing for the given situation. You will have to expand the grammar given in Section 11.2.2 to parse these sentences. When you use a rule not given in Section 11.2.2, state it in a separate list.

11.2. Consider the sentence "Put the red apple on the white book on the table with the black top."

   a. Show all the syntactically valid parsings of this sentence. Assume any reasonable grammar that you like.

   b. What semantic information and knowledge about the world could be used to help select the appropriate parsing and meaning of this command? Could some parsings be discarded as nonsensical without any further information (that is, making some reasonable assumptions)? If so, which ones?

11.3. In the following paragraph, determine to what object each of the pronouns refers?

   Otis went to AI class. The instructor attempted to explain ATN parsers. He decided that he was confusing them with state diagrams. To better occupy his time, he left it and went to study them in the library.

   The referents of some pronouns may not be clear. Identify the possible choices and what information is needed to clarify the connection between the pronoun and its inferent.

11.4. Consider a phrase like "It isn't soup yet!" To fully understand this phrase, one needs to understand much more than just these four words and to what "it" refers. Explain the knowledge that a reader would have to know in order to understand this phase.

Homework Exercises

11.5. Write context-free grammars describing the syntax of each of the following:

   a. All strings of length one or more over the set of terminals: {*blank,a,b,c*}.

   b. Sequences of lowercase letters or digits, starting with a letter.

11.6. Design a TN to parse the language described in Exercise 11.5(a).

11.7. Design a TN to parse the language described in Exerccise 11.5(b).

11.8. Write a TN to recognize verb phrases involving auxiliary verbs. The grammar should specifically handle the following types of verb phrases in a sentence:

should have eaten

will eat

would eat

could have eaten

ate

eat

had been eating

11.9. Consider the problem of specifying a natural-language-like interface to an intelligent tutoring system (ITS) that teaches the user how write a C++ program. The intent of the ITS is to act as a tutor for students who are just beginning to learn C++.

a. Write a grammar to define a language for interacting with the ITS.

b. Show a parsing, using your grammar from (a) for both of the following sentences:

- What are the parameters of *cout*?
- Tell me how to overload an operator.

11.10. Identify each of the following grammars by its most restrictive Chomsky type. Also, give a concise English description of the language produced by each grammar.

a. $<S> \rightarrow <A><C>a<B>$

$<C>a \rightarrow aa<C>$

$<C><B> \rightarrow <D><B>$

$<C><B> \rightarrow <E>$

$a<D> \rightarrow <D>a$

$<A><D> \rightarrow <A><C>$

$a<E> \rightarrow <E>a$

$<A><E> \rightarrow \varepsilon$

b. $a<S>b \rightarrow <S>$

$<S> \rightarrow a<S>b$

$<S> \rightarrow b$

c. $<S> \rightarrow 0<A>$

$<A> \rightarrow 0<A><B>$

$$<A> \rightarrow 1$$
$$<A> \rightarrow 1$$

11.11. The European Economic Community has decided to pay each farmer a subsidy of one English pound per leg for every animal on his farm. A farmer must send in his claim for a subsidy in a form similar to the following examples (derived from a problem in Bundy, 1978):

Six chickens and four cows and seventy-seven pigs.

One hundred and twenty-seven hens and one horse.

  a. Write a suitable context-free grammar for these returns. (Assume that the only animals that exist are mentioned in the above examples and also that any particular farmer can have no more than 999 of a particular animal.)

  b. Is your grammar ambiguous?

Programming Exercises

11.12. Extend the context-free grammar given in Section 11.6 to handle composite sentences with connectives *if, then, and, or, neither, nor,* and *but.* That is, your program should be able to handle the following sentences (as well as the original set) and produce an interpretation:

Bill paints and Raju sings.

If Amy sings, then every teacher listens.

Arjun listens but Raju talks.

Mark neither likes Al nor likes pizza.

Mary paints or Mary sings.

A teacher teaches or a teacher paints.

All singers sing and Raju sings.

Note that you will have to extend the grammar to include the other verbs and nouns listed in the examples. Prompt for the name of a file from which to read a set of sentences that are written in English, like the examples.

11.13. Use the context-free parser in Section 11.6 as a front end to the resolution theorem prover given in Chapter 9. Your program should read statements written as English sentences from a file and should consider the last sentence to be the goal.

12

Oᴛʜᴇʀ ʀᴇᴀsᴏɴɪɴɢ TECHNIQUES

"I am endeavoring,

Ma'am," Spock said

with dignity, "to

construct a mneu-

monic circuit out of

stone knives and

12.1 REASONING TECHNIQUES

bearskins."

In earlier chapters we discussed many techniques for reasoning
such as first-order predicate logic and the knowledge-manipulating
rules of expert systems. In this chapter, we discuss other reasoning
techniques including case-based reasoning, nonmonotonic reasoning, and reasoning about special topics such as time, knowledge,
and belief. Many other reasoning techniques, such as model-based
reasoning, constraint-based reasoning, and qualitative reasoning,
are also widely used, but they are not included here.

12.2 CASE-BASED REASONING

Case-based reasoning (CBR) starts with a library of stored scenarios, or **cases,** that it uses to analyze new situations. One of the first
examples of this type of system was Hammond's CHEF program,
which could create new recipes based on existing recipes. When a
new recipe was proposed to the system, it would look for similar
recipes and then modify one old recipe to meet the conditions of the
requested new recipe. The challenges in case-based reasoning are
devising a storage method that allows cases to be reusable and a
matching routine that will match a new situation to an existing
case.

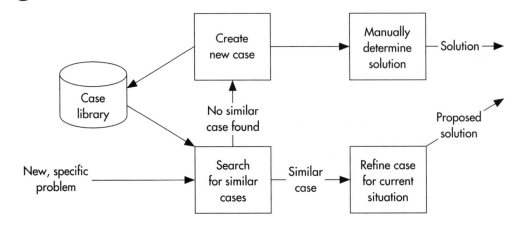

FIGURE 12.1

Architecture of
case-based reasoning
system

Corporations use CBR systems at their help desks, which are staffed by groups of people who respond to customer-reported problems. Corporate computer centers usually have help desks that employees can call to report a problem. Software companies have problem report lines for customers to call when they need advice.

Figure 12.1 shows a case-based reasoning system that includes a **case library,** which is the set of all cases that are known to the CBR system. The case library can be thought of as a specific kind of knowledge base that only contains cases. When a new problem is presented to the system, it checks the case library for a similar case. If a similar case is found, then the system will attempt to modify the case (if necessary) to produce a potential solution to the new problem. If there is no case that matches, then it will create a new entry in the case library. If there are multiple cases that apply to the new problem, then the system picks one to try first.

Example 1. *Using CBR with a rule-based system.* An interesting way to combine a rule-based system and a CBR system was described by Golding and Rosenbloom (1991). The combined system would check to see whether the problem to be solved was similar to a known exception to the rules (as in the case library). If it was similar, it would use the exception to guide the solution to the problem. The application they tackled was pronouncing surnames. They found that cases are good at identifying specific exceptions, whereas rules were good at identifying broad trends. The procedure combining the two approaches provided better solutions than either method alone could, because exceptions could be specified at any point in the path to a solution:

```
Until the input problem is solved do:
{
```

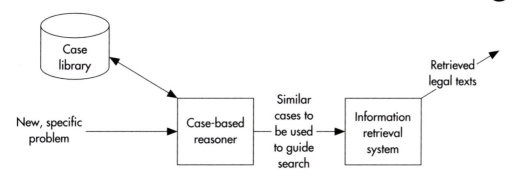

Use the rules to select an operator to apply
toward the solution
    Search for cases that would contradict this
choice of operator
    If a contradicting case is found **then**
        apply the operator suggested by the case
    else
        apply the operator the rules suggested
}

FIGURE 12.2

Integrating CBR with
an information
retrieval system

Example 2. *Using CBR with an information retrieval system.*
Rissland and Daniels (1995) devised an innovative approach to for-
mulating queries to a large set of documents by using a CBR system. One application involved accessing a subset of tax laws; another was accessing bankruptcy law. Direct translation of the huge
number of laws to a case library was not feasible because of the limitations of the CBR indexing methods, to say nothing of the extensive effort required to convert laws to cases. So, the approach was
to have a smaller case library that is used to formulate queries to
the large set of law documents, which are accessed through an
existing information retrieval system (Figure 12.2). In other words,
the intent of the system was to have a case library just large enough
to allow it to formulate queries that enable the case.law document
system to find more relevant cases.

12.3 NONMONOTONIC REASONING

In the systems discussed so far, addition of new information to a
knowledge base has not necessitated the removal of any existing
information. In other words, when new information is added to a
knowledge base, the size of the knowledge base grows (in terms of
statements). Reasoning systems of this type, in which the knowledge

base never shrinks, are called monotonic reasoning systems. These systems simply verify that the new information is consistent with the current knowledge base. However, some techniques may require us to retract existing information from the knowledge base when new statements are added. In this type of reasoning, we reevaluate prior assumptions on the basis of the current knowledge base. In other words, if a new statement violates some of the prior assumptions, we are forced to retract one or more of the offending assumptions. Because the overall size of the knowledge base does not necessarily grow when new statements are added, this type of reasoning is termed **nonmonotonic** reasoning.

12.3.1 Closed World Assumption

The closed world assumption (CWA) provides a relatively simple base for nonmonotonic reasoning. The **closed world assumption** declares that if a fact is not explicitly stated or if its negation is not provably true, then it is assumed to be false. For example, suppose that we are given the following set of predicates as our entire knowledge base:

Pig(arnold)

Dog(lassie)

Cat(garfield)

$\forall X.(Pig(X) \rightarrow Likes(X,mud))$

Here we are stating that Arnold is a pig, Lassie is a dog, Garfield is a cat, and every pig likes mud. So the complete known universe of objects (of any type) is *{arnold, lassie, garfield, mud}*. Using the CWA,[1] we attempt to prove every known predicate for every known object. Our known predicates make up the set *{Pig, Dog, Cat, Likes}*. We can prove only that *Likes(arnold, mud)*. No other combination of object and predicate is provable beyond those stated in the set. Therefore, to prove any other combination of the given objects and predicates, we must add more statements to our knowledge base.

The following list of statements is known as a CWA extension:

1. *Likes(arnold, mud)*

2. ¬*Pig(lassie)*

3. ¬*Pig(garfield)*

4. ¬*Dog(arnold)*

---

[1] Here, we are using an additional assumption called the **domain-closure assumption,** which declares that no other objects are in the domain other than those that are named.

5. $\neg Dog(garfield)$

6. $\neg Cat(arnold)$

7. $\neg Cat(lassie)$

8. $\neg Pig(mud)$

9. $\neg Dog(mud)$

10. $\neg Cat(mud)$

11. $\neg Likes(lassie, mud)$

12. $\neg Likes(garfield, mud)$

13. $\neg Likes(arnold, arnold)$

14. $\neg Likes(arnold, lassie)$

15. $\neg Likes(arnold, garfield)$

16. $\neg Likes(lassie, lassie)$

17. $\neg Likes(lassie, garfield)$

18. $\neg Likes(lassie, arnold)$

19. $\neg Likes(garfield, garfield)$

20. $\neg Likes(garfield, lassie)$

21. $\neg Likes(garfield, arnold)$

22. $\neg Likes(mud, mud)$

23. $\neg Likes(mud, lassie)$

24. $\neg Likes(mud, arnold)$

25. $\neg Likes(mud, garfield)$

Even for our initial very small knowledge base, the CWA extension rapidly becomes very large. In reality, the complete CWA extension is rarely calculated. Instead, we normally assume that only a fact that is not able to be proved is false. So, we would not know that $\neg Likes(mud, lassie)$[2] is assumed to be true until we tried to prove that $Likes(mud, lassie)$.

12.3.2 Predicate Completion

In Section 12.3.1 we listed the CWA extension of a set of facts. However, instead of listing each instantiated clause to indicate the CWA extension, we can formulate rules that give the same information. This enables us to concisely describes what is assumable and to completely define what each predicate means. This allows theorem provers to have an efficient representation of what can be assumed

---

[2] Actually, this is a nonsense expression that would translate to "mud does not like lassie." However, the full CWA extension adds predicates for all constant terms, even constants like "mud."

and what can not. Starting with the same set of predicates used in Section 12.3.1, we can declare that Lassie is the only dog, Garfield the only cat, and Arnold the only pig. We can do this by adding the following **predicate completions** (a predicate completion of a given predicate logically states every case that satisfies the predicate and excludes every case that does not satisfy the predicate):

$$\forall X.(Dog(X) \equiv equal(X, lassie))$$
$$\forall X.(Cat(X) \equiv equal(X, garfield))$$
$$\forall X.(Pig(X) \equiv equal(X, arnold))$$

These three rules eliminate the need for the explicit CWA extension statements 2 through 10 in Section 12.3.1.

The predicate completion for the *Likes* predicate is

$$\forall Y \forall X.(Likes(X, Y) \equiv (equal(X, arnold) \wedge equal(Y, mud)))$$

This single predicate completion allows us to easily prove the CWA extension statements 11 through 25 in Section 12.3.1.

12.3.3 Default Logic

There is another form of reasoning that allows default values to be selected if certain conditions are met. For example, suppose that we know that

$$Politician(charlie)$$

Given that Charlie is a politician, we might want to assume (unless told otherwise) that

$$Wants(charlie, donations)$$
$$\exists X.(Promised(charlie, X) \rightarrow \neg Kept(charlie, X))$$
$$Gives\_speeches(charlie)$$

In fact, we would like to have a general rule that applies to all politicians, so that we can use these assumptions for any known politician. We can specify these rules as

$$\frac{\alpha}{\dfrac{\beta}{\beta}}$$

where we know α to be true, and, if β is consistent with the current knowledge base, then we can assume β. So, putting one of our politician rules in this form, we get

$$\frac{\begin{array}{c} politician(X) \\ \exists Y.(Promised(X,Y) \rightarrow \neg Kept(X,Y)) \end{array}}{\exists Y.(Promised(X,Y) \rightarrow \neg Kept(X,Y))}$$

When the set of default logic rules is large, it is possible to have conflicting rules that apply to a particular individual. For example, suppose we also had a rule that said an engineer does not give speeches and we then tried to add Marge, who is both a politician and a mechanical engineer. Further suppose we have a rule that says all politicians give speeches. We would then have to decide whether to assume that Marge gives speeches or not, on the basis of two, conflicting default logic rules. In this case, we could probably resolve the issue by saying that a politician is extremely likely to give speeches, whereas the inability of an engineer to give speeches is less certain. Resolving such conflicts automatically is difficult, especially when there is a large number of possibly conflicting assumptions that can be made.

12.3.4 Truth Maintenance Systems

To use nonmonotonic logic, we must maintain the set of interrelated facts and reflect the effects of new information on previous inferences and assumptions. A **truth maintenance system** (TMS) performs this function by keeping track of the interrelated assumptions and making the necessary changes in the knowledge base.

In a nonmonotonic reasoning system, any new statement added to the knowledge base may negate previously made assumptions. Furthermore, there may be many theorems that have already been proved on the basis of the now-negated assumptions. So, when a new statement comes into the system, all associated theorems and assumptions must be checked to see whether they are still valid. Whenever a sentence is deleted from a knowledge base, the effect is the same: The assumptions that were made on the basis of that sentence, as well as the theorems based on the sentence and any ensuing assumptions must be checked to see whether they still are provable with the remaining set of axioms.

12.4 KNOWLEDGE AND BELIEF: USING MODAL LOGIC

Modal logic augments first-order predicate logic with **modal operators** that augment logic sentences to represent properties of the sentence. For example, the sentence could be true only at given times (temporal logics), known to be true by an agent (knowledge modals), or believed by an agent (belief modals).

By using what are known as modal operators, we can extend FOPL to represent the knowledge and beliefs of entities. **Modal operators** operate on an FOPL logic sentence to produce the sentence's value under the given mode or situation. In this section, we will only discuss the use of modal operators in the context of the belief and knowledge of a particular agent (see Genesereth and Nilsson, 1987).

Let's define our modal operators as follows:

$$K_\alpha(\phi) \equiv K(\alpha,\phi) \equiv \text{Agent } \alpha \text{ knows statement } \phi$$
$$B_\alpha(\phi) \equiv B(\alpha,\phi) \equiv \text{Agent } \alpha \text{ believes statement } \phi$$

For these operators to behave as we expect knowledge and belief to behave, we must define additional axioms. Note that ϕ and φ must be **closed** statements; that is, they must not contain any unquantified variables.

- **Distribution axiom**

  $(K_\alpha(\phi) \wedge K_\alpha(\phi \rightarrow \varphi)) \rightarrow K_\alpha(\varphi)$

  This axiom allows α to use modus ponens on its knowledge. Another way of writing this axiom is

  $K_\alpha(\phi \rightarrow \varphi) \rightarrow (K_\alpha(\phi) \rightarrow K_\alpha(\varphi))$

  Writing the axiom in this way produces a distribution property of the knowledge modal operator K.

- **Knowledge axiom**

  $K_\alpha(\phi) \rightarrow \phi$

  If an agent knows a statement, then it must be true. This axiom disallows α from knowing false statements.

- **Positive introspection axiom**

  $K_\alpha(\phi) \rightarrow K_\alpha(K_\alpha(\phi))$

  This axiom states that, if α knows a fact, then α knows that it knows the fact.

- **Negative introspection axiom**

  $\neg K_\alpha(\phi) \rightarrow K_\alpha(\neg K_\alpha(\phi))$

  Sometimes we include this axiom, which implies that α is not completely ignorant of knowledge. The axiom states that, if α does not know a fact, then α knows that it do not know the fact.

Axioms to define the belief modal operator, *B,* are less rigorous than those used to define knowledge, because the belief of a statement should require less proof than that needed to know the statement. Other axioms can be included for belief, and the notion of belief is much less well defined than that of knowledge. The axioms for belief follows.

- **Not-a-fool axiom**

$\neg B_\alpha(False)$

This axiom disallows someone from believing a falsehood.

- **Positive introspection axiom for belief**

$B_\alpha(\phi) \rightarrow B_\alpha(B_\alpha(\phi))$

We can define knowledge in terms of belief by the following axiom:

$K_\alpha(\phi) \equiv B_\alpha(\phi) \wedge \phi$

This axiom simply says that knowledge can be defined as belief in a fact. For α to have any knowledge of ϕ's existence, α must at least believe the fact of ϕ's existence (see Figure 12.3).

To order to prove a statement about an agent's beliefs, we need to ensure that we work entirely within what the agent believes. For example, if $B_{Otis}(Cow(elsie))$ and $B_{Otis}(\forall X.(Cow(X) \rightarrow Eats(X,grass)))$, then we can conclude $B_{Otis}(Eats(elsie,grass))$. Even this simple example assumes that Otis believes (or knows) the rule for Modus Ponens (i.e., $B_{Otis}((P \wedge (P \rightarrow Q)) \rightarrow Q)$) and the rule for Universal Instantiation (Section 4.4). If we are careful to always work within the agent's belief system, then we can apply normal resolution to prove facts.

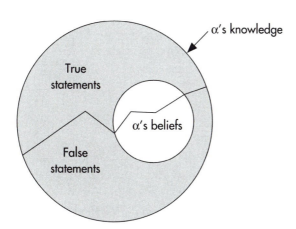

338

The modal operator method is not the only method for representing beliefs and knowledge, but it does show how FOPL can be extended to deal with higher level concepts.

12.5 SUMMARY

Logic can be used to reason in more complex situations, such as those dealing with case-based reasoning and nonmonotonic reasoning. Case-based reasoning is a method that has been highly successful in applications that use preexisting cases to solve new problems. It has also been successfully used as an adjunct to other reasoning methods and systems, such as rule-based systems. Nonmonotonic reasoning and its associated assumptions keep reasoning systems computationally feasible by allowing us to make reasonable assumptions without including every fact (and its negation) in the knowledge base. We also discussed the use of modal operators (in the form of knowledge and belief modal operators) that can be used to reason about knowledge and to give agents a way to reason about their knowledge and other agents' knowledge and beliefs.

12.6 REFERENCES

For information about CBR, refer to Janet Kolodner's "Judging Which Is the Best Case for a Case-Based Reasoner," in *Proceedings of the Case-Based Workshop* (1989) and Hammond's "CHEF: A model of case-based planning" (1986). For nonmonotonic reasoning, see Genesereth and Nilsson (1987) and Ramsay (1988). Another important method for nonmonotonic reasoning is known as circumscription. The details of the method appeared in a paper by McCarthy in Webber and Nilsson (1981). Saul Kripke's work on modal logics can be found in *Semantic Considerations on Modal Logic* (Oxford University Press, 1971).

12.7 EXERCISES

Warm-up Exercises

12.1. Nonmonotonic logic can save tremendous amounts of computation and make many more problems tractable. Give an simple example where the CWA can make an invalid assumption.

12.2. Consider the definition of a case-based reasoner for U.S. legal decisions. How should it handle a case such as the O. J. Simpson case? The Menendez brothers' case?

12.3. Consider a CBR system that helps someone select an interesting movie (a movie advisor) to rent from a vast selection of possible movies. The user of the system specifies characteristics of a movie he or she wishes to see (say, "drama," "less than two hours long," and "has won major academy awards"), and the CBR system looks for a movie that matches these characteristics. Specify the information that is needed in a case.

12.4. For the movie rental advisor in Exercise 12.3, specify how three sample characteristics could be deemed similar enough to allow a movie to be chosen.

12.5. For the movie rental advisor in Exercise 12.3, how would you handle the fact that the user would not like to rent a movie they have already seen?

12.6. Consider a knowledge base consisting of the following facts and rules. Give the CWA extention of this set of predicates.

$Dog(rufus)$

$Cat(fluffy)$

$Turtle(pokey)$

$\forall X.(Dog(X) \rightarrow Eats(X, meat))$

$\forall X.(Cat(X) \rightarrow Eats(X, milk))$

12.7. Apply predicate completion to the set of predicates in Exercise 12.6.

12.8. Write a rule in default logic form for specifying that cats usually drink milk.

12.9. Write a rule in default logic form for specifying that a fuzzy, purring cat probably will not bite.

12.10. Translate the following statement (which uses the Belief system) into English.

$B_{Marius}(B_{Otis}(\forall X.(Cat(X) \rightarrow Fuzzy(X))) \wedge \exists X.(Cat(X) \rightarrow Fuzzy(X)))) \wedge Fuzzy(fluffy)$

Homework Exercises

12.11. As described in Chapter 8, R++ has the ability to add rules to the definition of an object. Could R++ be used to support the CWA? If so, sketch out how objects could implement rules that use the CWA. If not, describe why R++ does not have the power to support CWA with its object-based rules.

12.12. Develop an object representation for the movie rental advisor cases (Exercises 12.3, 12.4, and 12.5).

12.13. Apply predicate completion to the following set of predicates:

$$\forall X \forall Y \forall Z.(P(X,Y) \wedge P(Y,Z) \rightarrow P(X,Z))$$

$$\forall X \forall Y.(P(X,Y) \wedge P(Y,X) \rightarrow X = Y)$$

$$\forall X \forall Y.(P(a,Y) \rightarrow P(X,b))$$

12.14. Prove that if one knows ϕ, then one cannot also know $\neg\phi$ or more formally:

$$K_\alpha(\phi) \rightarrow \neg K_\alpha(\neg\phi)$$

Programming Exercises

12.15. Revise the C++ production system in Section 8.6 to implement a simple CBR-like approach. Create cases that require four propositions to be true. Implement a mechanism that will return a case as matching if three of the propositions match the incoming problem to be solved.

12.16. Modify the C++ theorem prover in Section 9.6 to implement the CWA when a new axiom is added by using a statement like *assert*.

Projects

12.17. Develop a case-based reasoner in C++ that will help people buy homes. The program will take as input the specifications of a home that people wish to buy. The case library consists of a set of homes for sale. Develop an object representation for the cases. In determining the criteria for is a similar case, be sure to consider cases where the house is likely to meet the requirements of the buyer such as being within a mile or two of their specified region, having more bathrooms than specified, being close to their specified maximum or minimum price.

12.18. Modify the C++ theorem prover in Section 9.6 to use CWA and to allow deletion of axioms (by using a *retract* mechanism). Also, when an axiom is deleted, any theorems that have been proved by using that axiom or that have been added by CWA need to be retracted. Theorems or axioms that were proved by the deleted axiom but which can be proved in an alternative way with the remaining axioms should be retained.

EMERGING APPLICATION AREAS OF ARTIFICIAL INTELLIGENCE

"Robbie was a non-vocal robot. He couldn't speak. He was made and sold in 1996. Those were the days before extreme specializa-tion, so he was sold as a nursemaid—"

"As what?"

"As a nursemaid—"

ISAAC ASIMOV, 1950

13.1 ACTIVE AREAS OF AI WORK

This chapter explores three important and rapidly evolving areas of applied artificial intelligence:

- Very large knowledge bases (VLKB)
- Intelligent agents and agent-oriented programming
- Knowledge discovery in databases (KDD)

All three of these fields are relatively new (even though some research has been going on for a long time) and have only recently become fields of widespread interest in the AI community.

13.2 VERY LARGE KNOWLEDGE BASES

There is a move toward very large knowledge bases because of two converging trends: (1) The maturity of knowledge representation schemes and the move toward solving larger problems, and (2) the need for knowledge bases to include information from existing, large database systems. These two trends are forcing us to develop techniques that enable programs to handle large collections of knowledge. A related trend involves the development of database systems to support more knowledge-base-like features. We expect that knowledge bases will contain tens or hundreds of millions of rules or frames in the future (Lenat, 1990). Thus it is important that algorithms that use such knowledge bases be efficient.

The most ambitious project to develop a large knowledge base is the *Cyc* project. A second large knowledge-based system is PARKA, which uses a frame-based knowledge representation scheme and parallel algorithms (Evett, Hendler, and Andersen, 1993).

13.2.1 *Cyc* Project

The *Cyc* project (Lenat, 1990; Guha and Lenat, 1990) is a 10-year undertaking to produce a knowledge base that contains common-sense knowledge. The project is led by Doug Lenat and R. Guha at Cycorp, Inc., and has been in progress for about eight years.[1] It exemplifies the problems that occur in representing knowledge on a large scale and offers solutions to some of those problems.

The name *Cyc* is meant to imply the inverse of "encyclopedia"; *Cyc* will contain the information that is *not* contained in an encyclopedia, namely, commonsense knowledge. The intent is to provide *Cyc* with the commonsense knowledge that is needed to understand other information and make inferences in the real world. The hope is that *Cyc* can eventually understand natural language and other domains where commonsense knowledge is crucial. Two of its fundamental assumptions are that this sort of initial, commonsense knowledge base must be carefully built by hand and that there is no simple way to represent the totality of commonsense knowledge.

13.2.2 Structure of *Cyc* Knowledge Base

An interesting problem that the *Cyc* project encountered was the need to express its knowledge at two levels. One level is essentially first-order predicate logic (FOPL) and is called EL-CycL (the epistemological level *Cyc* language). The other level is called the heuristic level *Cyc* language (HL-CycL). HL-CycL expresses exactly the same information as the EL-CycL but is intended to represent that knowledge so that it can be used efficiently. The user interacts with *Cyc* at the EL-CycL level and, if needed, the Tell/Ask interface communicates with the heuristic level (Figure 13.1).

EL-CycL extends FOPL to include constructs to represent equality and allow some default values. An example (from Guha and Lenat, 1990) is the statement $fans(Stallone,x) \land \neg ab_n(x) \supset$

---

[1] The project was begun at the Microelectronics and Computer Technology Corporation.

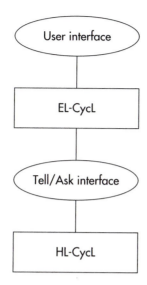

FIGURE 13.1

Cyc's knowledge is duplicated at heuristic and FOPL levels

moviesSeen(*x,Rocky*), where ⊃ means →. This statement means that if *x* is a fan of Sylvester Stallone and he is not abnormal, then he will have seen the movie *Rocky*. The phrase $\neg ab_n(x)$ represents a nonmonotonic construct (see Chapter 12). Once expressed in EL-CycL, the statement would also be translated to the heurisitic level (HL-CycL) so that it could be used efficiently with other knowledge.

Cyc also uses the concept of **microtheories.** This concept allows a set of knowledge statements to be grouped together. It also allows abstractions to be formed at different levels of granularity and conflicting theories to be represented.

13.2.3 *Cyc* Ontology

A key component of *Cyc*'s knowledge structure is the representation of its **ontology**—its classifications for objects. It is a hierarchy of superset and subset relationships, much like an object-oriented class hierarchy. A very small subset (*Cyc* has over 5000 defined classifications) of the hierarchy of classifications (which *Cyc* calls **collections**) is shown in Figure 13.2. The Thing collection refers to what was called the universal type in Chapter 7.

13.2.4 *Cyc* Applications

Cyc is currently being tested in many research collaborations with Cycorp. Current projects involve using the *Cyc* knowledge base to extract information from databases and to disambiguate word senses, resolve references, and interpret the meaning of ellipses. It is

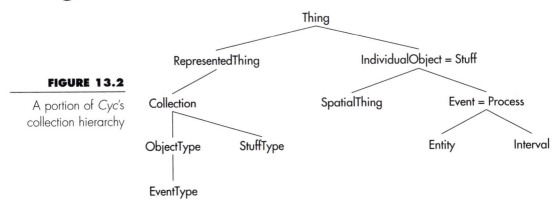

FIGURE 13.2

A portion of *Cyc's*
collection hierarchy

hoped these latter projects will aid in understanding natural language.

13.3 INTELLIGENT AGENTS

In an exam for a course in numerical analysis, one of the authors was required to show all derivations in writing. While the author was cranking out the problem by hand, he also programmed his calculator to solve the problem numerically so that he would have an approximate solution. The calculator took over half an hour to find a solution to the problem, and luckily it was precisely the same as the one the author found by hand. The author's calculator and the simple program that it used might be called an agent working on behalf of the author. While it was not particularly intelligent, it did perform a useful function for its owner, essentially independently. So, we could say that an **intelligent agent** is an entity to which we can assign a consistent mental state. Take, for example, the problem of finding useful references in the library. Suppose we had to find information about poisonous frogs. We could send a hired assistant to the library with that information in hand. Once the assistant got to the library, it would be very helpful if he could use some intelligence in the search. If he found information about *rañas* and recognized that *raña* means "frog" in Spanish, then he might bring back more useful information.

13.3.1 Defining Agents Formally

Goodwin (1993) formally defines properties of agents and describes a framework for formally describing agents in the Z specification language (Spivey, 1989). Goodwin's agent system interacts with its environment as shown in Figure 13.3.

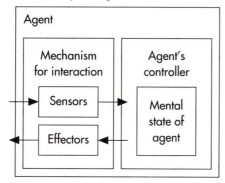

FIGURE 13.3

A definition of an agent-oriented system

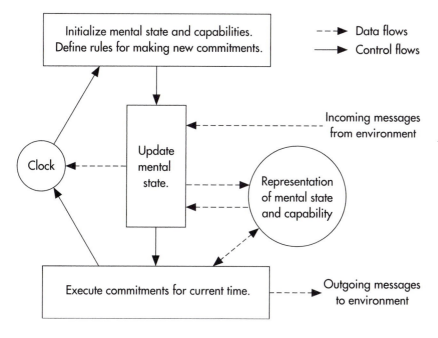

FIGURE 13.4

A data and control flow diagram of Shoham's agent interpreter

Goodwin's definition of an agent-oriented system is very similar to that of robotic systems. However, in an agent-oriented system, we explicitly require a mental state of the agent to be maintained. Each intelligent agent has **sensors** to measure the environment and **effectors** to produce changes in or interact with the outside environment. Russell and Norvig (1995) define three types of agents: a **reflex agent,** which responds to what it senses from its environment; a **goal-based agent,** which will act to achieve its goals; and a **utility-**

based agent, which acts to maximize its own internal metrics, or "happiness." The operational environment is the environment with which the agent interacts. For example, for an intelligent information-gathering agent that looks for relevant information on the World-Wide Web (WWW), the environment is both the Web itself and the interaction with the person who started the agent. This type of agent has sensors that are capable of reading information on the Web and can traverse the Web's links. Its effectors are its methods of sharing its information with the person who started the agent.

The mental state of the agent is maintained through an "agent interpreter" (Figure 13.4). For example, an intelligent agent might function by passing through a cycle that includes a fulfillment of goals and commitments to its environment and an update of its mental state, which is based on changes in the environment or in its goals and commitments, or both.

13.3.2 Information Retrieval Agents

A very popular form of intelligent agents is an **information retrieval agent,** which is an intelligent agent whose main function is to find and gather relevant information. As mentioned earlier, the advent of the World-Wide Web has made such agents useful.

Information retrieval agents must go through a multistep process to find relevant information (Knoblock and Arens, 1994). So, it is worthwhile for the agents to develop a plan that is based on the information they have and includes the following steps:

1. Selecting the information sources to investigate.
2. Mapping the queries into the information source's language. This step involves reformulating the query into a language and terminology that the source will recognize and understand.
3. Generating a query plan for implementing the queries. This step involves determining the order in which queries need to be performed (some queries may depend on information to be gathered from other sources) and in which any other processing needs to be performed before, between, or after the queries.

An information retrieval agent may have difficulty determining what information is stored in a given information source (such as a Web site), because various information sources are likely to have very different formats and very different ways of expressing their contents. To cope with this problem, efforts have been made to standardize the information content of information sources by developing languages such as the site description languages SL_0 and SL_1 (Levy, Sagiv, and Srivastava, 1994).

13.4 AGENT-ORIENTED PROGRAMMING

Agent-oriented programming (AOP) is a type of programming that uses "agents" as a basic unit, rather than objects, as in OOP. The intent of agent-oriented programming is to provide an environment in which programming agents and building agents can interact with one another. Such an infrastructure greatly simplifies the creation of intelligent agents and makes it possible to study the properties of agents and their interactions.

According to Shoham (1993), an agent-oriented programming system has three primary components:

1. *Formal language for specifying an agent.* This component is used to describe the internal, mental state of an agent. It should be able to define the beliefs of an agent and its commitments and goals.

2. *Programming language for instructing and defining the agent.* This component allows agents to be created and commanded.

3. *An "agentifier."* This component converts existing devices into intelligent, programmable agents.

Shoham (1993) has created a programming language called AGENT-0 that defines and instructs agents and can be used within the AOP paradigm. AGENT-0 is a relatively simple programming language that works for the agent model given in Figure 13.4. Such an agent has commitments and beliefs that help in guiding its actions. AGENT-0 only supports commitments that the agent can directly execute. It does not allow agents to commit to complex conditions or statements that require planning. Beliefs are expressed as a sequence of facts that are considered to be true by the agent. A program is partially defined in Backus-Naur Form (from Shoham, 1993):

```
<program>    ::= timegrain := <time>
   CAPABILITIES := (<action> <mentalcondition>)*
   INITIAL BELIEFS := <fact>*
   COMMITMENT RULES := <commitrule>
```

Thus, an agent is expressed in terms of its capabilities, what it can commit to, and its initial set of beliefs. With AGENT-0, the programmer can also add time qualifiers to facts and actions so that the agent can deal with the relative timing of events and actions.

Shoham views AOP as a specialization of OOP; in other words, AOP uses specific versions of OOP's more general concepts. In particular, OOP has the object as its basic unit, whereas AOP has the agent as its basic unit. Agents have an internal state and behavior, just as objects do. However, objects are not constrained with regard to the type of state and behavior, whereas agents must exhibit beliefs, commitments, capabilities, and goals. Agents and objects both use message-passing to communicate with one another and can instruct other agents (or objects) to execute an internal method. But agents have specific types of messages to communicate with other agents, whereas OOP does not have any constraints on the types of messages. In both systems, there is a form of inheritance, with classes (or groups) of agents sharing (or inheriting) properties with (or from) other agents. Because agent-oriented programming is a specialization of OOP, it can be performed in an OOP system or language.

13.5 KNOWLEDGE DISCOVERY IN DATABASES

Knowledge Discovery in Databases (KDD) is a very active field of interdisciplinary research.[1] It depends on database and artificial intelligence techniques, including machine learning, search, and knowledge representation. Data mining, which has also been called (with some slight difference in meaning and approach) data archaeology and data dredging, is a key step in KDD. **Data mining** is the set of methods for extracting heretofore unrecognized patterns in data. AI techniques can be applied to data mining as well as other steps of KDD.

According to Fayyad, Piatetsky-Shapiro, and Smyth (1995), "knowledge discovery in databases is the nontrivial process of identifying valid, novel, potentially useful, and ultimately understandable patterns in data." This definition has several key words in it that need to be explained:

- *nontrivial* implies that an AI search is required to find something useful in the data. In other words, the process is not just a simple calculation or a straightforward summary of the data.
- *pattern* is a description of a subset of the data that is shorter than the complete listing of the subset of data. More formally, Fayyad, Piatetsky-Shapiro, and Smyth (1995) define it as an expression in a formal language that describes a subset of the data.

---

[1] The field has had workshops at the national conference of the American Association of Artificial Intelligence since 1989. It just had its first international conference, KDD and Data Mining, in 1995 in Montréal, Québec.

- *validity of patterns* is a measure of the certainty of the patterns found in the data.

- *novel* means that patterns should be new to the system (and preferably to everyone).

- *potentially useful* means that the patterns found in the data can be measured by a utility function.

- *data* is the set of all facts in the database.

- *ultimately understandable* means understandable by humans as a real pattern in the data.

The need for KDD and data mining has never been greater. Vast stores of data containing vast amounts of knowledge exist in very large databases (VLDB), but it is difficult to find and extract that knowledge. As database technology becomes better able to handle larger and larger VLDBs, it becomes even more important to have automated methods to analyze and extract interesting patterns from that data. The trend toward establishing **data warehouses** for storing an entire enterprise's data and then analyzing the data to improve the enterprise is increasing the need for KDD. The popularity of analysis support methods and tools, such as those supporting on-line analytical processing (OLAP), illustrate the need to extract knowledge from these VLDBs.

The high-level process for KDD involves five key steps (Figure 13.5), of which data mining is only one:

- *Data selection.* The process of selecting a subset of the data to be analyzed. If the database is very large, then this step can be critical to selecting a subset that may produce interesting patterns and is not so large that it is impractical to analyze.

- *Preprocessing.* The intent of this step is to clean up noisy data by removing outliers, by providing missing information, and by identifying known trends.

- *Transformation.* The process of transforming values into a format that will normalize them to a common scheme. This step is useful if the data come from different databases (and therefore have different data models and semantics) or if the data can be put into another form that helps the data mining process.

- *Data mining.* The process of choosing the type of data mining to do (e.g., data clustering, trend analysis, model fitting, goal testing), picking appropriate methods, and then extracting patterns in data.

- *Interpretation and evaluation.* The data mining step might produce many patterns. The key is to select patterns that are

FIGURE 13.5

KDD process from the database to extracted knowledge

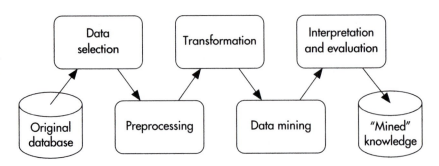

interesting and useful and to retain those and discard the rest. Those interesting patterns then need to be integrated with previously selected patterns to determine whether changes have occurred or whether inconsistent knowledge has been found.

Example 1. *The Recon System.* Recon is a system that develops rule-based models from the contents of relational databases and other input files (Refer to E. Simoudis, R. Kerber, and B. Livezey, 1994). It integrates many independently developed tools such as neural networks, deductive databases, and data visualization tools. The Recon user uses this set of tools to help guide Recon to develop a rule-based model. The Recon system has been used in applications including manufacturing, investment, banking, fraud detection, and market data analysis. For example, it has been used to analyze historical data for 8000 stocks and produce a rule-based model for future performance of investments. This stock model was then used to develop specific stock portfolios.

Example 2. *The SKICAT system.* The SKICAT (Sky Image Cataloging and Analysis Tool) system has no initial database (Figure 13.6; U. Fayyad, N. Weir, and S. Djorgovski, 1993). It is able to turn the incoming data into knowledge at a sufficient surety that the raw data need not be stored or further analyzed. It functions as a classifier of celestial objects that are extracted from digitized photographs taken by telescopes. This task is extremely tedious and error prone when done by hand. Its basic classifier was trained by a learning algorithm based on objects that were previously classified by astronomers. Storage of 3000 high-resolution photographic plates would require about 1 Terabyte of space. But SKICAT has avoided this storage problem by extracting the knowledge.

Even though this system was relatively small in scope, it was extremely successful in identifying objects that were too faint to be identified by human experts. As such, it has improved the reliability and speed of the image-cataloging process.

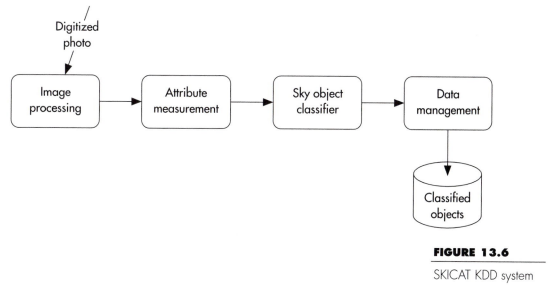

Digitized photo

| Image processing | → | Attribute measurement | → | Sky object classifier | → | Data management |

Classified objects

FIGURE 13.6

SKICAT KDD system

13.6 SUMMARY

Three areas of applied artificial intelligence are the focus of this chapter. Large knowledge bases will continue to become more effective and more efficient, and their functionality will likely merge with traditional database systems to create truly integrated data and knowledge-based systems. Agent-oriented programming and intelligent agents are needed to filter and assimilate the huge amounts of information that are being generated at an ever-increasing rate. Knowledge discovery in databases is related to both VLKB and the need to process and extract relevant facts from large amounts of information. While these three areas appear on the surface to be only marginally related, they are all being spurred by the same explosion of information.

13.7 REFERENCES

The *Cyc* project is well documented by Lenat (1990) and Guha and Lenat (1990). Good sources of information about intelligent agents are Woolridge (1995), Shoham (1993), Goodwin (1993), Russell and Norvig (1995), and the papers collected in the *Proceedings of the Twelfth National Conference on Artificial Intelligence* (Seattle, WA: AAAI, 1994). KDD is best documented by the *Proceedings* of the First International Conference on KDD and Data Mining Proceedings, held in Montréal, Québec, in 1995 (AAAI Press). Other sources are the KDD workshop proceedings from 1989 to 1994 from

AAAI Press. An object-oriented library in C++ has been developed for machine learning; the library is called MLC++. Refer to Kohavi (1995) for information on the MLC++ programming environment and Kohavi (1994) for information on the MLC++ library C++ classes. The library is available for research and education via *ftp* from Stanford University.

13.8 EXERCISES

Warm-up Exercises

13.1. Suppose we wanted an intelligent agent to act as an assistant for KDD. This intelligent agent would be sent off to perform the KDD process and to extract interesting patterns in databases. Is it useful to incorporate intelligent agents with KDD? Why or why not?

13.2. Current data mining techniques have difficulty handling very large sets of data. It appears that the running time cannot be larger than $O(n^{1.5})$, where n is the number of records of data for the data mining algorithm. Consequently, the data-selection step is critical, so that algorithms with higher running time can still be used. Do you think it is likely that data mining techniques will ever be able to effectively process databases with billions of records without any data-selection step? Why or why not?

13.3. Identify an application (in addition to those mentioned in the chapter) for *cyc*, once it is successfully completed.

13.4. Consider an intelligent agent to help find interesting television programming for you to watch. This agent will have access to the programming schedule for all available channels on your system (say, about 1000 channels are available) and to brief descriptions of the programs scheduled to air. What effectors and sensors are needed by this agent? What are the goals of the agent?

13.5. The previous problem proposes a television-watching agent. One danger of such an agent is that it will suggest only programs that you have liked before or very similar programs that you have watched before, and not show you anything truly interesting or new to you. Describe an approach that would minimize this danger and help the agent find new types of interesting programs for you to watch.

13.6. Cast the definition of an expert system in terms of an intelligent agent.

Homework Exercises

13.7. For the television-watching, intelligent agent (Exercises 13.4 and 13.5), define the information needed by the agent, its required internal state, its effectors and sensors, and the goals of the agent. Describe how this agent might be implemented, using AI techniques and existing information systems.

13.8. Consider the definition of softbots (software robots) as "intelligent agents that are given a set of tasks to perform." An example of a softbot is Rodney, a softbot designed to do UNIX system operations and administration (Etzioni, Lesh, and Segal, 1994). It might perform tasks such as monitoring system security, doing backups, monitoring file system usage, and compressing files. Modify the definition of an intelligent agent to make it a complete softbot definition. Is your softbot definition significantly different from the definition of an intelligent agent?

13.9. *Cyc*'s goal of building a very large set of commonsense knowledge is extremely ambitious. Some people have said that if this project fails, then the entire field of symbolic AI will have also failed and should be abandoned for other approaches. What is your opinion? Why?

Programming Exercises

13.10. Develop an electronic mail agent that will prioritize mail messages on the basis of a set of rules. It should include rules like

- If a message is a response to another message, then order the messages by arrival time, with the earliest message always being the original message.
- Read messages from your manager (and her manager, etc.) first.
- If a message contains a particular set of keywords or phrases, read them first.
- If a message is from an important individual, read it first.

Note that the rules given are not sufficient and that another rule establishing a precedence order for the application of these four rules must be written

13.11. Develop a simple data mining tool. Pick a simple, normalized relational database that contains six tables. Your tool should be able to take that set of relational tables (which make up a database), merge them into one large, denormalized table, and then be able to search for simple relationships between the columns of data as specified by general rules (see a data base text, such as Ullman, 1988, for more functional dependence). For example, it should be able to check for simple relationships between columns (where column variables are *A*, *B*, *C*, etc.):

- If values in *A* are a function of values in *B*, then flag pattern *FD(B,A)* *to* indicate that there is a possible functional dependency between *A* and *B*.
- If values in *A* are always smaller than values in *B*, then flag pattern *LT(A,B)* to indicate that there may be an ordering relationship.
- Define a greater-than (*GT*) relationship.

Projects

13.12. Extend your data mining tool from Exercise 13.10 to create a tool that will take an initial, nonnormalized relation (containing data) and search for possible functional dependencies. The tool should use column names to determine likely candidates that might require normalization and then test its hypotheses on the actual data. Once the functional dependencies have been tested (although they still may not be valid), the tool should create output relations that are likely to be in Boyce-Codd Normal Form (BCNF). See Ullman (1988) for a description of BCNF.

13.13. Create an intelligent agent to monitor a transmission control protocol/internet protocol-based network. It should monitor traffic, looking for abnormal patterns. When it finds an abnormal pattern in traffic, it should report it via electronic mail. The agent should first monitor traffic (say, for a week) to determine the normal patterns (you can use statistical methods, such as control charting to determine what is normal) and then begin to look for variances from those patterns.

13.14. Create an intelligent agent similar to Rodney, except your agent will only look in users' directories for files that are security risks. For example, if it finds a file *setuid*-ed to root, it will flag that file as a security risk. Other examples are *.profile* files that are writable by others. Investigate possible security problem indicators in the UNIX system and develop rules to guide the intelligent agent. Use a book such as Fielder and Hunter (1986) to determine the needed rules. Pfleeger (1989) and Amoroso (1994) are good general security references.

ARTIFICIAL INTELLIGENCE PAST AND FUTURE

Experience has shown that science frequently develops most fruitfully once we learn to examine the things that seem the simplest, instead of those that seem the most mysterious.

MARVIN MINSKY, 1990

14.1 BRIEF HISTORY OF COMPUTING AND AI

The quest for intelligent machines has been a passion for humans for many hundreds of years. With seventeenth-century devices such as Blaise Pascal's calculating machine (called the *Pascaline*) and Gottfried Wilhelm Leibniz's more complicated machine also came dreams of building intelligent devices. In the early 1800s, Charles Babbage (along with Lady Ada Lovelace) developed more advanced mechanical computing devices, called the *difference engine* and the *analytical engine*. They incorporated into these devices many of the fundamental ideas of computing, including program instructions, subroutines, and the basics of computer architecture. However, the fruition of those ideas was not realized until the development of programmable computers in the 1940s. Nevertheless, with each advance, the hopes for truly intelligent machines increased.

Beliefs about the potential intelligence of computers was encouraged by the naming and use of several early computers. For example, the 1940s ENIAC (Electronic Numerical Integrator and Computer) was often referred to as the "super brain." The 1950s UNIVAC (Universal Automatic Computer) correctly predicted a U.S. presidential election on national broadcast television. After the final voting results were in, this prediction was viewed as remarkable because of the closeness of the election. For many years, the UNIVAC typified computers in the public's mind.

In the 1950s, workers finally were able to seriously explore the possibility of using electronic computers to imitate, if not duplicate, human intelligence. In a 1958 paper, Simon and Newell (1958) predicted that by 1968 a computer would be the world chess champion. This statement typifies the optimism of the time. Only in 1996 was a computer able to beat the world champion in a game of chess: IBM's *Deep Blue* program beat Gary Kasparov in one game of a six-game match (and tied some other games).

The first conference on artificial intelligence was held in 1956, and many of the pioneers of AI were active participants. John McCarthy (now at Stanford University) organized the conference, and early researchers in the field, such as Marvin Minsky, Alan Newell, Herb Simon, and Art Samuel, attended. The conference produced the term *artificial intelligence* to describe the emerging field. McCarthy is generally given credit for having suggested and promoted use of the new name; later (in 1959), he also produced the popular AI language LISP (list processing language).

AI continued to grow in popularity and success in the 1960s with the further development of other important new programs. Daniel Bobrow produced a program called *Student* that could solve algebra problems from English text problems and rivaled the performance of average high school students in that task. Thomas Evans generated a program that could solve analogy problems, as mentioned in the exercises of Chapter 7. Also, expert systems were born with the development of Ed Feigenbaum's *DENDRAL* system. *DENDRAL* could process mass spectrograph data produced by a complex molecule and determine the probable identity of the molecule. A spectrograph allows identification of the component atoms of the molecule but does not immediately show how the atoms are arranged. Analysis is required to determine possible molecular structures.

An interesting program called *ELIZA* was developed by Joseph Weizenbaum in 1966. The program (which can be found in many forms for most programming languages) simulates a psychological therapist. The program works by responding to simple patterns it finds in the "patient's" questions and statements. The program was able to successfully persuade some people that the program was actually performing useful psychotherapy. Although Weizenbaum never claimed that the program was intelligent, *ELIZA* continued to be hailed (by others) as exemplary of the possibilities of AI or to be used as a target of criticism against AI.

Terry Winograd's 1970 doctoral thesis also received rave reviews. His program was called *SHRDLU,* and it was used to instruct the computer to move blocks around in a simulated "blocks world." The program used planning and natural language to allow users to specify goals that would be satisfied in the blocks world. For example, a

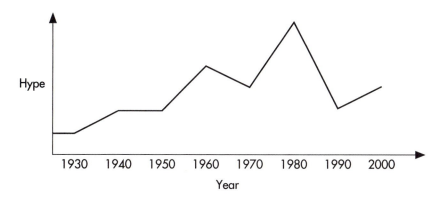

Hype

Year

FIGURE 14.1

Trends in popular
hype for AI

user could specify "move the red block on top of the yellow rectangular solid." *SHRDLU* would then attempt to perform the task.

As indicated in Figure 14.1, the amount of hype about the potential of AI stayed relatively constant until it surged upward after the 1956 conference. Another big spike in the amount of hype and expectations occurred in the 1980s when hope developed that expert systems would solve many of the world's hard problems. However, disappointment soon followed, when it became clear that expert systems were more aptly used on more limited set of applications; and the hype dropped off dramatically until the mid-1990s, when the need to process vast amounts of information has caused the press to popularize the use of AI again.

The work in AI has more recently been characterized by Raymond Kurzweil (1990), who described three primary ages of AI:

- *Age of Recursion* (50s to 70s). This age was characterized by programs that used a small set of ideas and could perform many intelligent tasks, such as recursion and heuristic search. Much of the work done during this time still forms the foundation for problem-solving techniques used in AI algorithms.

- *Age of Knowledge* (late 60s to 80s). This age was characterized by the realization that the ability to represent and manipulate knowledge was critical to the solution of many problems. Semantic networks and many knowledge representation techniques were created during this time.

- *Age of Application*[1] (80s to present). This age has been characterized (so far) by the successful application and expansion of AI techniques into many areas. Applications such as vision,

---

[1] Kurzweil did not give this age a name, but he did go on to describe many of the successful uses and research efforts for AI at the time.

pattern recognition, machine learning, agent-oriented programming, virtual reality, and expert systems are widespread at this time.

AI has also developed two camps of research, often characterized as *neats* and *scruffies*. The *neats* tend to develop theory that is useful in understanding and characterizing intelligent behavior. The *scruffies* tend to develop systems that may or may not have a solid theoretical basis but do appear to work on the problem at hand. Communication and joint work between the two camps enables each to effectively build off the other's work. If a *neat* develops a new theoretical concept, then a *scruffy* uses that technique to develop or enhance a solution to his problem. If on the other hand, a *scruffy* develops a successful program or approach, then *neats* make gains when they extract the theoretical implications from the results.

14.2 FUTURE CONSIDERATIONS FOR AI

Artificial intelligence continues to evolve rapidly and will undoubtedly see many successes in its future. While it is not clear where these successes will be, it is clear that there is sufficient momentum in many areas of research to propel some of them to their goals.

14.2.1 Future Possibilities of AI

AI has many unattained goals. Indeed, many of these goals have existed from the outset of modern AI, but are only now becoming reachable because of the power of machines and improving techniques. AI goals that are close[2] to being realized are

- Automatic translation of documents and speech from one natural language to another
- Ability to converse in natural language with a computer
- Intelligent vehicles that can avoid accidents, perform route planning, and negotiate congested roadways
- Development of large and usable knowledge bases, such as automated access to documents in the Library of Congress
- A world champion chess machine

There are other goals of AI that are still beyond the reach of current technology:

---

[2] Perhaps these goals are realizable in the next five to ten years.

- Intelligent servants and assistants to perform a wide variety of household or office tasks
- Programs that can learn on their own by using printed material
- Creative programs that can apply their creativity to a wide range of problems
- Programs that can be given a vague goal; put into a new, complex situation; and then understand and achieve the goal

14.2.2 Future of Object-Oriented AI

Object-oriented artificial intelligence (OOAI) will continue to be developed and pursued on many fronts. OOAI is an implementation environment for artificial intelligence techniques that use the OO design and programming paradigm. As work continues on the development of AI theory, those developments will often be deployed by using OOAI, because the object-oriented paradigm continues to be the predominate programming paradigm. The increasing popularity of object-oriented database management systems and the emerging field of OO-related patterns (see Coplien and Schmidt,1995) will also encourage development and use of AI techniques that use the same paradigm.

14.2.3 Ethical Considerations of AI

Artificial intelligence, much like any field of computer science or engineering, produces new technologies that may have unexpected consequences and implications. However, AI has a few unique considerations, because its developers are trying to produce intelligent agents, whose use raises many ethical issues.

For example, consider the development of an intelligent mutual funds sales agent that sells mutual funds over the phone. The sales agent program sounds like a real person and can answer practically any question about mutual funds as well as engage in "small talk" with the customer. It turns out that this program is able to fool about 99% of the customers that it talks to and is able to effectively sell mutual funds. Using the program has led to the following situations: (1) Customers don't know that they are being sold the funds by an automated agent. When they find out, they are usually outraged. (2) The mutual fund company finds that the program is able to sell almost as many funds as its best sales agent and always outperforms the average sales agents. As a result, the company is considering replacing all live agents with automated ones. (3) The company is considering "enhancing" the effectiveness of the agent by tying the agent into demographics and marketing data that is specific to a customer. Then the agent could call when the customer is likely to be home and could use the information to chitchat and to play on the known (or likely) fears of the customer. One might mitigate the bad use of this particular program by having the agent notify customers during the call that it is not a real person, or by having the human agents concentrate on those customers who don't like to talk to the automated agent (once they find out), or by not using any sensitive data (such as playing on fears) in the demographics data—or all of the above.

Other AI uses could be viewed as criminal behavior by many. Suppose programmers developed intelligent programs that were used to

- Create a gambling robot (which looks human) that could count cards and enhance the odds sufficiently to win more than it loses
- Develop destructive agents that could actively seek to destroy something (like a jail cell, or a disk drive, or the contents of computer memory, or a checking account balance)
- Create a robot that could falsify signatures or documents, or could appear like someone or something else

Although most uses of AI will not have such clearly negative ethical implications, a few will open up the opportunity for unethical behavior. Consider an intelligent program that peruses publicly available records for a life insurance company. Given an applicant, it will look for any information it can find that might be relevant to life span. It might compile lists of the customer's magazine subscriptions, credit balances, and past addresses, and then use that information to determine what rate to charge. Whether this action is unethical is less clear because it would be possible for a human to compile the same lists, given sufficient time. It also would probably be legal for a human to do this research. However, if it becomes easy for the insurance company to find out that you subscribe to *Cholesterol Weekly* and to *Pipe-Smokers' Journal*, then you may feel that your privacy has been invaded.

As these ethical problems become more common, we hope and expect that researchers will institute review boards for the purpose of coming to consensus on proper and ethical use of particular technologies. Review boards have already proved effective in other areas of advanced technology, such as medicine and molecular biology.

14.3 REFERENCES

Much of the history of AI and details on important applications can be found in *The Handbook of Artificial Intelligence*, Volumes 1–4, by

A. Barr and E. A. Feigenbaum (1982, 1989). Kurzweil's 1990 book contains photographs, interviews, and articles by and about many of the influential people of AI. It also contains descriptions of many AI applications and interesting facts on the history of computing and computers. Kurzweil includes a detailed chronology of many of the important events in AI and computing.

14.4 EXERCISES

Warm-up Exercises

14.1. Consider the ethical problems in developing an AI agent that could infiltrate your customers' computer systems to find out whether they are using your software or not. Further consider the ethical problems in actually using the software to gather that information.

14.2. In Exercise 14.1, you considered the ethical problems in developing a spying agent and using it. Are the ethical problems any different (or worse) if, after you use the agent, you act on the information by sending threatening notes to those customers who are using the software but not paying for it?

14.3. AI is concerned with trying to develop intelligent software. Suppose that a unit of code (software) is only moderately intelligent (say, it has the intelligence of a wharf rat) but has developed an instinct for survival. The unit would evade attempts to be captured or killed and keep moving over the network to other machines to evade capture. The software is not harmful in any way. What are the ethical considerations in eliminating this unit of software by capturing and erasing it?

14.4. Reconsider Exercise 14.3, except this time think of the intelligent "rat" as a "dirty rat." That is, it is harmful in some way.

14.5. Consider the development of an AI program that will perform all the work you do for your employer. You are able to set the program loose and not even show up at your office. Your employer is happy with the work done. You continue to collect paychecks, and even get another job. Are there any ethical problems with this scenario? If so, what are they?

14.6. Reconsider Exercise 14.5. Suppose the employee decides to "reuse" the program with multiple employers and claims to be doing "work" for them all, but is really using the program to do all the work. Are there ethical problems with this scenario? If so, what are they?

14.7. Consider the development of a tax-evasion program. The program is able to move your assets and income so that they cannot be tracked by the tax authorities. This practice could be viewed as taking advantage of a loophole in the tax laws, because you are able to hide your assets by legal means. What are the ethical considerations?

14.8. Reconsider Exercise 14.7. This time, you don't use the program yourself. You just sell it to as many people as you can, for $2,000 a copy. What are the ethical considerations?

14.9. Consider that an AI researcher creates a robot that can learn new behaviors. The robot is sent out into society. The robot joins forces with a group of bank robbers and learns from them. Shortly thereafter, the robot has learned plenty from his friends and sets off on his own. The robot robs a bank, shoots a guard, and then heads for the hills. Should the AI researcher be responsible? What if the authorities ask the researcher to shut off the robot, but the researcher refuses?

Homework Exercises

14.10. Investigate the history of logic diagrams and identify techniques that could be used in a modern theorem proving system. Start with the book by Gardner (1958); also refer to Sowa (1995).

14.11. Review books that predict a dire future for civilization, such as *1984* by George Orwell (1949), *Brave New World* by Aldous Huxley (1932), and *Future Shock* by Alvin Toffler (1970). Have any of these books accurately predicated the adverse role of technology? How might AI in the future make some of these predications materialize?

14.12. How could the use of reusable objects adversely affect civilization? What happens when a heavily used object (let's say, one central to all operating systems in use) has a latent error?

14.13. Find reports from the 1956 AI conference. Investigate the claims made for AI at that time, as well as the hopes and goals for AI. Report on the accuracy of the claims and how many of the hopes and goals have actually been achieved (by any method) today.

14.14. Suppose that a program is written that *is* clearly more intelligent than humans. To what purpose should we put such a program? What should be done if the program refuses to perform that purpose?

APPENDIX:
C++ TOPICS TUTORIAL

This appendix is extracted, by permission of the authors, from material in an on-line C++ guide called *C++ Annotations*, Version 3.4.13, written by Frank B. Brokken and Karel Kubat of the State University of Gröningen in the Netherlands. A current version of this material (and their other online material) can be obtained via *ftp* from

ftp.icce.rug.nl/pub/http

or via the World Wide Web at

http://www.icce.rug.nl/docs/cplusplus/cplusplus.html

We have duplicated here, for convenience, introductions to several key topics in C++, which students not familiar with C++ (but know C) can use in addition to the material in the text.

A.1 CLASSES

The use of classes is further explained in this section. Two special member functions, the constructor, and the destructor, are introduced.

In steps, we will construct a class `Person`, which could be used in a database application to store a name, an address and a phone number.

The definition of a `Person` thus far is as follows:

```
class Person
{
  public:                    // interface functions
    void setname (char const *n);
    void setaddress (char const *a);
    void setphone (char const *p);
```

```
        char const *getname (void);
        char const *getaddress (void);
        char const *getphone (void);

    private:                            // data fields
        char *name;                     // name of person
        char *address;                  // address field
        char *phone;                    // telephone number
};
```

The data fields in this class are `name`, `address` and `phone`. The fields are `char*`s, which point to allocated memory. The data are `private`, which means that they can only be accessed by the functions of the class `Person`.

The data are manipulated by interface functions that take care of all communication with code outside the class; they either set the data fields to a given value (e.g., `setname()`), or they inspect the data (e.g., `getname()`).

A.1.1 Constructor and destructor

A class in C++ may contain two special functions that are involved in its internal workings. These functions are the constructor and the destructor.

The constructor

By definition, the constructor function has the same name as the corresponding class. The constructor has no return value specification, not even `void`. For example, for the class `Person` the constructor is `Person::Person()`. The C++ run-time system makes sure that the constructor of a class, if defined, is called when an object of the class is created. Of course, it is possible to define a class that has no constructor at all; in that case the run-time system either calls no function or it calls a dummy constructor (which performs no actions) when a corresponding object is created. Naturally, the actual generated code depends on the compiler. (A compiler-supplied constructor in a class that contains composed objects will "automatically" call the member initializers and therefore does perform some actions.)

If an object is a local nonstatic variable in a function, the constructor is called when the function is executed. If an object is a global or a static variable, the constructor is called when the program starts—even before `main()` is executed. This is illustrated in the following listing:

```
#include <stdio.h>
// a class Test with a constructor function
class Test
{
  public:     // 'public' function:
    Test ();                   // the constructor
};

Test::Test ()              // here is the
{                          // definition
  puts ("constructor of class Test called");
}

// and here is the test program:
Test
  g;                       // global object
void func ()
{
  Test                     // local object
    l;                     // in function func()

  puts ("here's function func()");
}

int main ()
{
  Test                             // local object
    x;                             // in function main()
  puts ("main() function");
  func ();
  return (0);
}
```

The listing shows how a class `Test` consisting of only one function—the constructor—is defined. The constructor performs only one action: printing a message. The program contains three objects of the class `Test`: one global object, one local object in `main()`, and one local object in `func()`.

Concerning the definition of a constructor, it is important to note the following:

- The constructor has the same name as its class.
- The constructor may not be defined with a return value. This is true for the declaration of the constructor in the class definition, as in

```
class Test
{
  public:
    /* no return value here */ Test ();
};
```

and also holds true for the definition of the constructor function, as in

```
/* no return value here */ Test::Test ()
{
}
```

The constructor function in the example above has no arguments; it is therefore also called the **default constructor**. This is, however, no requirement per se. Later we shall see that it is possible to define constructors with arguments.

The constructor of the three objects of the class `Test` in the above listing are called in the following order:

- The constructor is first called for the global object g.
- Next the function `main()` is started. The object x is created as a local variable of this function, and hence the constructor is called again. After this we expect to see the text `main() function`.
- Finally the function `func()` is activated from `main()`. In this function the local object l is created, and hence the constructor is called. After this, the message `here's  function func()` appears.

As expected, the program yields the following output (the text in parentheses is for illustrative purposes):

```
constructor of class Test called (global object g)
constructor of class Test called (object x in main())
main() function
constructor of class Test called object l in func())
here's function func()
```

The destructor

The second special function is the destructor. This function is the opposite of the constructor in the sense that it is invoked when an object ceases to exist. For objects that are local nonstatic variables, the destructor is called when the function in which the object is defined is about to return; for static or global variables the destructor is called before the program terminates. Even when a program is interrupted using an `exit()` call, the destructors are called for objects which exist at that time.

When defining a destructor for a given class, the following rules apply:

- The destructor function has the same name as the class, but it is prefixed by a tilde.
- The destructor has neither arguments nor a return value.

A destructor for the class `Test` from the previous section could be declared as follows:

```
class Test
{
  public:
    Test ();          // constructor
    ~Test ();         // destructor
};
```

A first application

One of the applications of constructors and destructors is the management of memory allocation. This is demonstrated using the class `Person`.

As illustrated at the beginning of this section, the class `Person` contains three `private` pointers, all `char*`s. These data members are manipulated by the interface functions. According to the internal workings of the class, when a name, address, or phone number of a `Person` is defined, memory is allocated to store these data. An obvious setup is described below:

- The constructor of the class makes sure that the data members are initially 0-pointers.
- The destructor releases all allocated memory.
- The defining of a name, address or phone number (by means of the `set...()` functions) consists of two steps. First, previously allocated memory is released. Next, the string which is supplied as an argument to the `set...()` function is duplicated in memory.

    - Inspecting a data member using one of the `get...()` functions simply returns the corresponding pointer: either a

0-pointer, indicating that the data is not defined, or a pointer to allocated memory holding the data.

The `set...()` functions are illustrated below. Strings are duplicated in this example by an imaginary function `xstrdup()`, which would duplicate a string or terminate the program when the memory pool is exhausted.

```
// interface functions set...()
void Person::setname (char const *n)
{
  free (name);
  name = xstrdup (n);
}


void Person::setaddress (char const *n)
{
  free (address);
  address = xstrdup (n);
}


void Person::setphone (char const *n)
{
  free (phone);
  phone = xstrdup (n);
}
```

Note that the statements `free(...)` in this list are executed unconditionally. This never leads to incorrect actions: when a name, address, or phone number is defined, the corresponding pointers address previously allocated memory that should be freed. When the data are not (yet) defined, then the corresponding pointer is a 0-pointer and `free(0)` performs no action. Furthermore, it should be noted that this code example uses the standard C function `free()`, which should be familiar to most C programmers. The `delete` statement, which has more C++ "flavor," will be discussed later.

The interface functions `get...()` are listed below:

```
  // interface functions get...()
char const *Person::getname ()
{
  return (name);
}


char const *Person::getaddress ()
```

```
{
  return (address);
}

char const *Person::getphone ()
{
  return (phone);
}
```

Finally, following are the destructor, constructor, and class definition:

```
// class definition
class Person
{
  public:
    Person ();              // constructor
    ~Person ();             // destructor

    // functions to set fields
    void setname (char const *n);
    void setaddress (char const *a);
    void setphone (char const *p);

    // functions to inspect fields
    char const *getname (void);
    char const *getaddress (void);
    char const *getphone (void);

  private:
    char *name;             // name of person
    char *address;          // address field
    char *phone;            // telephone number
};

// constructor
Person::Person ()
{
  name = address = phone = 0;
}

// destructor
Person::~Person ()
{
  free (name);
  free (address);
```

```
free (phone);
}
```

To demonstrate the use of the class `Person`, a code example follows below. An object is initialized and passed to a function `printperson()`, which prints the contained data. Note the usage of the reference operator & in the argument list of the function `printperson()`. This way only a reference to a Person object is passed instead of a whole object. That `printperson()` does not modify its argument is evident from the fact that the argument is declared `const`. Also note that the example does not show where the destructor is called; this action occurs implicitly when the function `main()` terminates and hence when its local variable p ceases to exist.

It should also be noted that the function `printperson()` could be defined as a `public` member function of the class `Person`.

```
void printperson (Person const &p)
{
  printf ("Name                    : %s\n"
      "Address : %s\n"
      "Phone   : %s\n",
    p.getname (), p.getaddress (), p.getphone ());
}

int main ()
{
  Person
    p;

  p.setname ("Linus Torvalds");
  p.setaddress ("E-mail: Torvalds@cs.helsinki.fi");
  p.setphone (" - not sure - ");

  printperson (p);
  return (0);
}
```

The preceding code fragment can only serve as an example, because most C++ compilers will actually fail to parse the code. The reason for this is that the function `printperson()` receives a `const` argument but calls functions for this argument which might or might not modify it (these are the functions `getname()`, `getaddress()`, and `getphone()`). Given this setup, the "const-ness" of the argument to `printperson()` cannot be guaranteed—hence, the compiler will not produce working code. The solution would of course be to tell the compiler that `getname()`, `getaddress()`, and `getphone()` will not modify the object at hand, but we postpone this modification to Section A.1.2.

When `printperson()` receives a fully defined `Person` object (containing a name, address, and phone number), the data are correctly printed. However, when a `Person` object is only partially filled, (with only a name, for example) `printperson()` passes 0-pointers to `printf()`. This anesthetic feature can be remedied with a little more code:

```
void printperson (Person const &p)
{
  if (p.getname ())
    printf ("Name    : %s\n", p.getname ());
  if (p.getaddress ())
    printf ("Address : %s\n", p.getaddress ());
  if (p.getphone ())
    printf ("Phone   : %s\n", p.getphone ());
}
```

Constructors with arguments

In the preceding definition of the class `Person`, the constructor and destructor have no arguments. C++ allows the constructor to be defined with an argument list that is supplied when an object is created.

For the class `Person`, a constructor that expects three strings—the name, address, and phone number—may be handy:

```
Person::Person (char const *n, char const *a, char
const *p)
{
  name = xstrdup (n);
  address = xstrdup (a);
  phone = xstrdup (p);
}
```

The constructor must be included in the class definition. For example, a declaration in a header file would then look as follows:

```
class Person
{
  public:
    Person::Person (char const *n,
      char const *a, char const *p);
};
```

Since C++ allows function overloading, such a declaration of a constructor can coexist with a constructor without arguments. The class `Person` would thus have two constructors.

The use of a constructor with arguments is illustrated in the following code fragment. The object a is initialized at its definition.

```
int main ()
{
  Person
    a ("Karel", "Rietveldlaan 37", "426044"),
    b;
}
```

The order of construction

The possibility of defining arguments with constructors offers us the chance to monitor at which exact moment in a program's execution an object is created or destroyed. This is shown in the following listing, using a class `Test`:

```
class Test
{
  public:
    // constructors:
    Test ();                   // argument-free
    Test (char const *name);   // with a name argument
    // destructor:
    ~Test ();

  private:
    // data:
    char *n;                   // name field
};

Test::Test ()
{
  n = strdup ("without name");
  printf ("Test object without name created\n");
}

Test::Test (char const *name)
{
  n = strdup (name);
  printf ("Test object %s created\n", n);
}
```

```
Test::~Test ()
{
  printf ("Test object %s destroyed\n", n);
  free (n);
}
```

By defining objects of the class `Test` with specific names, the construction and destruction of these objects can be monitored.

```
Test
  globaltest ("global");

void func ()
{
  Test
    functest ("func");
}

int main ()
{
  Test
    maintest ("main");

  func ();
  return (0);
}
```

This test program leads to the following expected output:

```
Test object global created
Test object main created
Test object func created
Test object func destroyed
Test object main destroyed
Test object global destroyed
```

A.1.2 Const **member functions and** const **objects**

The keyword `const` is often seen in the declarations of member functions following the argument list. This keyword is used to indicate that a member function does not alter the data fields of its object but only inspects them. Using the example of the class `Person`, the `get...()`, functions could be declared `const`:

```
class Person
{
  public:
     .

     .
     // functions to inspect fields
     char const *getname (void) const;
     char const *getaddress (void) const;
     char const *getphone (void) const;

  private:           .          .
};
```

As is illustrated in this fragment, the keyword const occurs *following* the argument list of functions. Whatever appears *before* the keyword const cannot be altered and does not alter data.

The same specification must be repeated in the definition of member functions:

```
char const *Person::getname () const
{
   return (name);
}
```

A member function, which is declared and defined as const, cannot alter any data fields of its class. In other words, a statement like

```
name = 0;
```

in the above const function getname() would lead to a compilation error.

The purpose of const functions lies in the fact that C++ allows const objects to be created. For such objects, only the functions that do not modify it (such as the const member functions) may be called. The only exceptions to the rule are the constructor and destructor; these are called "automatically." This feature is comparable to the definition of a variable int const max = 10. Such a variable may be initialized at its definition. Analogously, the constructor can initialize its object at the definition, but subsequent assignments may not take place.

The following example shows how a const object of the class Person can be defined. At the definition of an object the data fields are initialized (this is an action of the constructor):

```
Person
  const me ("Karel", "karel@icce.rug.nl", "426044");
```

Following this definition, it would be illegal to try to redefine the name, address, or phone number for the object me; a statement such as

```
me.setname ("Lerak");
```

would not be accepted by the compiler.

Generally it is a good habit to declare member functions that do not modify their object as const. This allows the definition of const objects.

A.1.3 The operators new **and** delete

The C++ language defines two operators that are specific for the allocation and deallocation of memory. These operators are new and delete.

A pointer variable to an int is used to point to memory that is allocated by new. This memory is later released by the operator delete. The most basic example of the usage of these operators is given below:

```
int
  *ip;

ip = new int;
. .
delete ip;
```

Note that new and delete are operators and therefore do not require parentheses, unlike functions such as malloc() and free().

Allocating and deallocating arrays

When the operator new is used to allocate an array, the size of the variable is placed between square brackets following the type:

```
int
  *intarr;

intarr = new int [20];  // allocates 20 ints
```

The syntactical rule for the operator new is that this operator must be followed by a type, optionally followed by a number in square brackets. The type and number specification lead to an expression that is used by the compiler to deduce the size; in C an expression like `sizeof(int[20])` might be used.

An array is deallocated by using the operator `delete`:

```
delete [] intarr;
```

In this statement, the array operators `[]` indicate that an array is being deallocated. The rule of thumb is that whenever `new` is followed by `[]`, `delete` should be followed by it as well.

new and delete and object pointers

The operators `new` and `delete` are also used when an object of a given class is allocated. The advantage of the operators over functions such as `malloc()` and `free()` lies in the fact that `new` and `delete` call the corresponding constructor or destructor. This is illustrated in the following example:

```
Person
    *pp;                    // pointer to Person object

pp = new Person;            // now constructed
.
. delete pp;                // now destroyed
```

The allocation of a new `Person` object, pointed to by `pp`, is a two-step process. First, the memory for the object itself is allocated. Second, the constructor is called which initializes the object. In the above example the constructor is the argument-free version; it is however also possible to choose an explicit constructor:

```
pp = new Person ("Frank", "Oostumerweg 17",
                                "05903-2223");     .
.
delete pp;
```

Like the construction of an object, the destruction is also a two-step process. First the destructor of the class is called to deallocate the memory the object uses. Then the memory used by the object itself is freed.

Dynamically allocated arrays of objects can also be manipulated with `new` and `delete`. In this case, the size of the array is given between the `[]` when the array is created:

```
Person
  *personarray;

personarray = new Person [10];
```

The compiler will generate code to call the default constructor for each object which is created. To release such an array, the array operators `[]` must be used with the `delete` operator:

```
delete [] personarray;
```

The presence of the `[]` ensures that the destructor is called for by each object in the array. Note that `delete personarray` would only release the memory of the array itself.

The function `set_new_handler()`

The C++ run-time system makes sure that when memory allocation fails, an error function is activated. By default this function returns the value 0 to the caller of `new`, so the pointer that is assigned by `new` is set to zero. The error function can be redefined, but it must comply with a few prerequisites, which are, unfortunately, compiler-dependent. For the Microsoft C/C++ compiler version 7, the prerequisites are

- The function is supplied one argument, a `size_t` value which indicates how many bytes should have been allocated (the type `size_t` is usually identical to `unsigned`).
- The function must return an `int`, which is the value passed by `new` to the assigned pointer.

The Gnu C/C++ compiler `gcc`, which is present on many Unix platforms, requires that the error handler

- has no argument (a `void` argument list).
- returns no value (`void` return type).

For example, the redefined error function might print a message and terminate the program. The error function is included in the allocation system by the function `set_new_handler()`, defined in the header file `new.h`. On some compilers, notably the Microsoft C/C++ 7 compiler, the installing function is called `_set_new_handler()` (note the leading underscore).

The implementation of an error function is illustrated below. This implementation applies to the Microsoft C/C++ requirements:

```
#include <new.h>
#include <stdlib.h>
#include <stdio.h>

int out_of_memory (size_t sz)
{
  printf
("Memory exhausted, can't allocate %u bytes\n", sz);
  exit (1);

  return (0);          // return an int to satisfy the
                       // declaration
}

int main ()
{
  int
    *ip;
  long
    total_allocated = 0L;

// install error function
set_new_handler (out_of_memory);

// eat up all memory
puts ("Ok, allocating..");
while (1)
{
    ip = new int [100];
    total_allocated += 100L;
    printf ("Now got a total of %ld bytes\n",
    total_allocated);
}

return (0);
}
```

The advantage of an allocation error function lies in the fact that, once installed, new can be used without wondering whether the allocation succeeded or not; on failure the error function is automatically invoked and the program exits. It is good practice to install a new handler in each C++ program, even when the actual code of the program does not allocate memory. Memory allocation can also fail in not directly visible code, such as when streams are used or when strings are duplicated by low-level functions.

Often, even standard C functions that allocate memory, such as strdup(), malloc(), realloc(), etc., trigger the new handler when memory allocation fails. This means that once a new handler is installed, such functions can be used in a C++ program without testing for errors. However, compilers exist where the C functions do not trigger the new handler.

A.1.4 The keyword `inline`

Let us take another look at the implementation of the function `Person::getname()`:

```
char const *Person::getname () const
{
  return (name);
}
```

This function is used to retrieve the name field of an object of the class `Person`. In a code fragment, like

```
Person
  frank ("Frank", "Oostumerweg 23", "2223");

puts (frank.getname ());
```

the following actions take place:

- The function `Person::getname()` is called.
- This function returns the value of the pointer `name` of the object `frank`.
- This value, which is a pointer to a string, is passed to `puts()`.
- The function `puts()` finally is called and prints a string.

The first part of these actions leads to time loss, since an extra function call is necessary to retrieve the value of the `name` field. Sometimes a faster process, in which the `name` field becomes immediately available, may be desirable, thus avoiding the call to `getname()`. This can be realized with `inline` functions, which can be defined in two ways.

`Inline` functions within class definitions

Using the first method to implement `inline` functions, the code of a function is defined *in a class definition itself*. For the class `Person`, this would lead to the following implementation of `getname()`:

```
class Person
{
  public:
    .

    .
    char const *getname (void) const
      {return (name);}
    .
};
```

Note that the code of the function `getname()` now literally occurs in the definition of the class `Person`. The keyword `const` occurs after the function declaration and before the code block.

The effect can be clearly illustrated. When `getname()` is called in a program statement, the compiler generates the code of the function instead of a call. This construction is called an inline function because the compiler "inserts" the actual code of the function.

`Inline` functions outside class definitions

The second way to implement inline functions leaves a class definition intact, but mentions the keyword `inline` in the function definition. The class and function definitions then are

```
class Person
{
public:
  .

  .
  char const *getname (void) const;
  .
private:
  .

  .
};

inline char const *Person::getname () const
{
  return (name);
}
```

Again the compiler will insert the code of the function `getname()` instead of generating a call.

When to use `inline` functions

When should `inline` functions be used and when not? There are a number of simple rules of thumb:

- In general, `inline` functions should *not* be used.
- Defining `inline` functions can be considered if a fully developed and tested program runs too slowly and shows "bottlenecks" in certain functions. A profiler, which runs a program and determines where most of the time is spent, is necessary for such optimization.
- `inline` functions can be used when member functions consist of one very simple statement (such as the return statement in the function `Person::getname()`).
- It is useful to implement an `inline` function only when the time spent during a function call is long compared to the code in the function. An example where an `inline` function has no effect at all is the following:

```
void Person::printname () const
{
  puts (name);
}
```

This function, which is presumed to be a member of the class `Person` for the sake of the argument, contains only one statement, but it is a statement that takes relatively a long time to execute. In general, functions which perform input and output spend lots of time. The effect of the conversion of this function `printname()` to `inline` would therefore lead to unmeasurable time gain.

`inline` functions have one disadvantage: the actual code is inserted by the compiler and must therefore be known compile-time. Therefore an `inline` function can never be located in a run-time library. Practically, this means that an `inline` function is placed near the definition of a class, usually in the same header file. The result is a header file that shows not only the *declaration* of a class but also part of its *implementation*.

A.1.5 Objects in objects: Composition

Objects are often used as data fields in class definitions. This is referred to as **composition**. For example, the class `Person` could hold information about the name, address, and phone number, but additionally a class `Date` could be used to include information about the birth date:

```
class Person
{
  public:
    // constructor and destructor
    Person ();
    Person (char const *nm, char const *adr,
        char const *ph);
    ~Person ();

    // interface functions
    void setname (char const *n);
    void setaddress (char const *a);
    void setphone (char const *p);
    void setbirthday (int yr, int mnth, int d);

    char const *getname () const;
    char const *getaddress () const;
    char const *getphone () const;
    int getbirthyear () const;
    int getbirthmonth () const;
    int getbirthday () const;

  private:
    // data fields
    char *name, *address, *phone;
    Date birthday;
};
```

The class `Date` could consist of three `int` data fields to store year, month, and day. These data fields would be set and inspected using interface functions `setyear()`, `getyear()`, etc.

The interface functions of the class `Person` would then use `Date`'s interface functions to manipulate the birth date. The function `getbirthyear()` is an example of the class `Person`:

```
int Person::getbirthyear () const
{
  return (birthday.getyear ());
}
```

Composition is not extraordinary or C++ specific; in C it is quite common to include `structs` or `unions` in other compound types.

Composition and `const` objects: Member initializers

Composition of objects has an important consequence for the constructor functions of the "composed" (embedded) object. Unless explicitly instructed otherwise, the compiler generates code to call the default constructors of all composed classes in the constructor of the composing class. Often it is desirable to initialize a composed object from the constructor of the composing class. This is illustrated for the composed class `Date` in a `Person`. In this fragment it assumed that a constructor for a `Person` should be defined expecting six arguments: the name, address, and phone number in addition to the year, month, and day of the birth date. It is further assumed that the composed class `Date` has a constructor with three `int` arguments for the year, month, and day:

```
Person::Person     (char const *nm, char const *adr,
                    char const *ph,
                    int d, int m, int y)
   : birthday      (d, m, y)
{
  name = strdup (nm);
  address = strdup (adr);
  phone = strdup (ph);
}
```

Note that following the argument list of the constructor `Person::Person()`, the constructor of the data field `Date` is specifically called, supplied with three arguments. This constructor is explicitly called for the composed object `birthday`. This occurs even *before* the code block of `Person::Person()` is executed. This means that when a `Person` object is constructed and when six arguments are supplied to the constructor, the `birthday` field of the object is initialized even before `Person`'s own data fields are set to their values. The constructor of the composed data member is also referred to as **member initializer**.

When several composed data members of a class exist, all member initializers can be called by using a "constructor list": this list consists of the constructors of all composed objects, separated by commas.

When member initializers are *not* used, the compiler automatically supplies a call to the default constructor (i.e., the constructor without arguments). In this case a default constructor *must* be defined in the composed class.

Not using member initializers can also lead to inefficient code. Consider the following code fragment where the `birthday` field is not initialized by the `Date` constructor, but instead the `setday()`, `setmonth()`, and `setyear()` functions are called:

```
Person::Person (char const *nm, char const *adr,
```

```
            char const *ph,
            int d, int m, int y)
{
  name = strdup (nm);
  address = strdup (adr);
  phone = strdup (ph);

  birthday.setday (d);
  birthday.setmonth (m);
  birthday.setyear (y);
}
```

This code is inefficient because the default constructor of `birthday` is called (this action is implicit), and subsequently, the desired date is set explicitly by member functions of the class `Date`.

This method is not only inefficient but may even not work when the composed object is declared as `const`. A data field like `birthday` is a good candidate for being `const`, since a person's birthday is not likely to change. This means that when the definition of a `Person` is changed so that the data member `birthday` is declared as `const`, the implementation of the constructor `Person::Person()` with six arguments *must* use member initializers. The call to `birthday.set...()` would be illegal, since this is no `const` function. The rule of thumb is the following: when composition of objects is used, the member initializer method is preferred to explicit initialization of the composed object. This not only leads to more efficient code but also allows the composed object to be declared as `const`.

A.1.6 Friend functions and friend classes

As we have seen in the previous sections, `private` data or function members are normally only accessible by the code which is part of the corresponding class. However, situations may arise in which it is desirable to allow the explicit access to `private` members of one class to one or more other classless functions or member functions of classes. Consider the following code example (all functions are `inline` for purposes of brevity):

```
class A              // class A: just stores an
{                    // int value via the constructor
  public:            // and can retrieve it via
    A (int v)        // getval
      { value = v; }
    int getval ()
```

```
                 { return (value); }

   private:
     int value;
};

void decrement (A &a)   // function decrement: tries
{          // to alter A's private data
   a.value-;
}

class B                  // class B: tries to touch
{          // A's private parts
   public:
     void touch (A &a)
       { a.value++; }
};
```

This code will not compile, since the function decrement() and the function touch() of the class B attempt to access a private data member of A.

We can explicitly allow decrement() to access A's data, and we can explicitly allow the class B to access these data. To accomplish this, the offending classless function decrement() and the class B are declared to be friends of A:

```
class A
{
   public:
     friend class B;            // B's my friend, I
                                              trust him

// decrement() is also a good pal
friend void decrement (A
     &what);
     .         .
};
```

Concerning friendship between classes, the following should be noted:

- Friendship is not mutual by default. This means that even though B is declared as a friend of A, A is not given the right to access B's private members.
- Friendship, when applied to program design, is an escape mechanism which creates exceptions to the rule of data hid-

ing. Using friend classes should therefore be minimized to those cases where it is absolutely essential.

A.2 CLASSES AND MEMORY ALLOCATION

In contrast to the set of functions that handle memory allocation in C (`malloc()` etc.), the operators `new` and `delete` are specifically meant to be used with the features that C++ offers. Following are important differences between `malloc()` and `new`:

- The function `malloc()` doesn't "know" what the allocated memory will be used for. For example, when memory for `int`s is allocated, the programmer must supply the correct expression using a multiplication by `sizeof(int)`. In contrast, `new` requires the use of a type; the `sizeof` expression is implicitly handled by the compiler.
- The only way to initialize memory allocated by `malloc()` is to use `calloc()`, which allocates memory and resets it to a given value. In contrast, `new` can call the constructor of an allocated object where initial actions are defined. This constructor may be supplied with arguments.

The comparison between `free()` and `delete` is analogous; `delete` makes sure that when an object is deallocated, a corresponding destructor is called.

The calling of constructors and destructors when objects are created or destroyed, has a number of consequences which shall be discussed in this section. Many problems in program development in C are caused by incorrect memory allocation or memory leaks: memory is not allocated, not freed, not initialized; boundaries are overwritten; etc. C++ does not "magically" solve these problems, but it does provide a number of handy tools. In this section the following topics are discussed:

- assignment operator and operator overloading
- `this` pointer
- copy constructor

A.2.1 Classes with pointer data members

In this section we shall again use the class `Person` as an example:

```
class Person
```

```
{
  public:
    // constructors and destructor
    Person ();
    Person (char const *n, char const *a,
            char const *p);
    ~Person ();

    // interface functions
    void setname (char const *n);
    void setaddress (char const *a);
    void setphone (char const *p);

    char const *getname (void) const;
    char const *getaddress (void) const;
    char const *getphone (void) const;

  private:
    // data fields
    char *name;
    char *address;
    char *phone;
};
```

In this class the destructor is necessary to prevent that memory, once allocated for the fields `name`, `address`, and `phone`, from becoming unreachable when an object ceases to exist. In the following example a `Person` object is created, after which the data fields are printed. After this, the `main()` function stops, which leads to the deallocation of memory. The destructor of the class is also shown for illustration purposes.

Note that in this example an object of the class `Person` is also created and destroyed with a pointer variable using the operators `new` and `delete`.

```
Person::~Person ()
{
  delete name;
  delete address;
  delete phone;
}

void main ()
{
  Person
```

```
    kk ("Karel", "Rietveldlaan",
      "050-426044"),
    *bill = new Person ("Bill Clinton",
        "White House",
        "09-1-202-142-3045")

  printf("%s, %s, %s\n",
    kk.getname (), kk.getaddress (),
                                    kk.getphone ());
  printf("%s, %s, %s\n",
    bill->getname (), bill->getaddress (), bill->
                                    getphone ());

  delete bill;
}
```

The memory occupied by the object kk is released automatically when main() terminates. The C++ compiler makes sure that the destructor is called. However, the object pointed to by bill is handled differently. The variable bill is a pointer, and a pointer variable is, even in C++, in itself no Person. Therefore, before main() terminates, the memory occupied by the object pointed to by bill must be explicitly released; hence the statement delete bill. The operator delete will make sure that the destructor is called, thereby releasing the three strings of the object.

A.2.2 The assignment operator

Variables that are structs or classes can be directly assigned in C++ in the same way that structs can be assigned in C. The default action of such an assignment is a byte-by-byte copying from one compound type to the other.

Let us now consider the consequences of this default action in a program statement:

```
void printperson (Person const &p)
{
  Person
    tmp;

  tmp = p;
  printf ("Name:    %s\n"
      "Address:    %s\n"
      "Phone:      %s\n",
    tmp.getname (), tmp.getaddress (), tmp.getphone
());
}
```

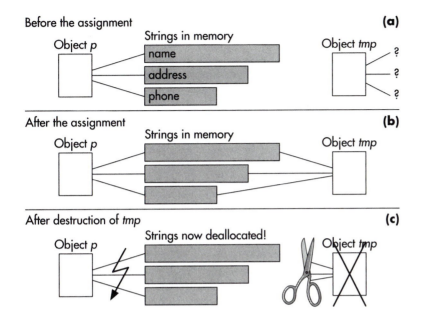

Before the assignment **(a)**

Object p   Strings in memory   Object *tmp*

name

address

phone

After the assignment **(b)**

Object p   Strings in memory   Object *tmp*

FIGURE A.1

After destruction of *tmp* **(c)**

Object p   Strings now deallocated!   Object *tmp*

We shall follow the execution of this function step by step.

- The function printperson() expects a reference to a Person as its parameter p. So far, nothing extraordinary is happening.
- The function defines a local object tmp. This means that the default constructor of Person is called, which—if defined properly—resets the pointer fields name, address and phone of the tmp object to zero.
- Next, the object referenced by p is copied to tmp. By default, this means that sizeof(Person) bytes from p are copied to tmp. Now a potentially dangerous situation has arisen. The actual values in p are **pointers**, pointing to allocated memory. Following the assignment this memory is addressed by two objects, p *and* tmp.
- The potentially dangerous situation develops into an acutely dangerous situation when the function printperson() terminates: the object tmp is destroyed. The destructor of the class Person releases the memory pointed to by the fields name, address, and phone. Unfortunately, this memory is also in use by p! The incorrect assignment is illustrated in Figure A.1.

FIGURE A.2

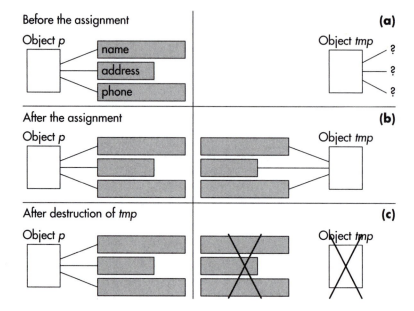

Before the assignment   (a)

After the assignment   (b)

After destruction of *tmp*   (c)

After the execution of `printperson()`, the object that was referenced by p may still contain valid pointers to strings, but they are pointers which address deallocated memory. This action is undoubtedly not a desired effect of a function like the above. The deallocated memory will likely become occupied during subsequent allocations, thereby causing the previously held strings to become lost.

In general, it can be concluded that *every class that contains a constructor and a destructor and also contains pointer fields to address allocated memory is a potential candidate for trouble.* There is, of course, a possibility to intervene, discussed in the next section.

Overloading the assignment operator

Obviously, the right way to assign one `Person` object to another, is *not* to copy the contents of the object byte by byte. A better way is to make an equivalent object, one with its own allocated memory but that contains the same strings.

The "right" way to duplicate a `Person` object is illustrated in Figure A.2. There are several ways to achieve this effect. One solution consists of the definition of a special function to handle assignments of objects of the class `Person`. The purpose of this function would be to create a copy of an object, one with its own `name`, `address`, and `phone` strings. Such a member function might be

```
void Person::assign (Person const &other)
{
  // delete our own previously used memory
  delete name;
  delete address;
  delete phone;

  // now copy the other's data
  name = strdup (other.name);
  address = strdup (other.address);
  phone = strdup (other.phone);
}
```

Using this tool we could rewrite the offending function func():

```
void printperson (Person const &p)
{
  Person
    tmp;

  // make tmp a copy of p, but with its own
  // allocated strings
  tmp.assign (p);

  printf ("Name:    %s\n"
      "Address:   %s\n"
      "Phone:     %s\n",
    tmp.getname (), tmp.getaddress (),
                              tmp.getphone ());

  // now it doesn't matter that tmp gets destroyed
}
```

In itself this solution is valid, although it is purely symptomatic. This solution requires the programmer to use a specific member function instead of the operator =; the problem, however, remains if this rule is not strictly adhered to. Our experience shows that *errare humanum est*; therefore, a solution that doesn't enforce exceptions is preferable.

The problem of the assignment operator is solved by using operator overloading, the syntactic possibility of C++ to redefine the actions of an operator in a given context. Overloading the assignment operator is probably the most common form of operator overloading. However, a word of warning is appropriate: the fact that C++ allows operator overloading does not mean that this feature should be used at all times. A few rules should be observed:

- Operator overloading should be used in situations where an operator has a defined action that is not desired due to its negative side effects. A typical example is the above assignment operator in the context of the class `Person`.

- Operator overloading can be used in situations where the usage of the operator is common and when no ambiguity in the meaning of the operator is introduced by redefining it. An example may be the redefinition of the operator + for a class which represents a complex number. The meaning of a + between two complex numbers is quite clear and unambiguous.

- In all other cases it is preferable to define a member function, instead of redefining an operator.

Using these rules, operator overloading is minimized which helps keep source files readable. An operator simply does what it is designed to do. Therefore, in our vision, the operators << and >> in the context of streams are misleading; the stream operations do not have anything in common with the bitwise shift operations.

The function `operator=()`

To achieve operator overloading in a context of a class, the class is simply expanded with a `public` function which states the operator. A corresponding function is then defined.

For example, to overload the addition operator + a function `operator+()` would be defined. The function name consists of the keyword `operator` and the operator itself.

In our case we define a new function `operator=()` to redefine the actions of the assignment operator. A possible extension to the class `Person` could therefore be:

```
// new declaration of the class
class Person
{
  public:
      .
      .
      void operator= (Person const &other);
      .
      .
  private:
      .
      .
};
```

```
// definition of the function
void Person::operator= (Person const &other)
{
  // deallocate old data
  delete name;
  delete address;
  delete phone;

  // make duplicates of other's data
  name = strdup (other.name);
  address = strdup (other.address);
  phone = strdup (other.phone);
}
```

The function `operator=()`, presented earlier, is the first version of the overloaded assignment. We shall present better and less bug-prone versions later.

The actions of this member function are similar to those of the previously proposed function `assign()`, but the name makes sure that this function is also activated when the assignment operator = is used. In fact there are two ways to call this function:

```
Person
  pers ("Frank", "Oostumerweg 23", "2223"),
  copy;

// first possibility
copy = pers;

// second possibility
copy.operator= (pers);
```

It is obvious that the second possibility, in which `operator=()` is explicitly stated, is not used often. However, the code fragment illustrates the similarity of the two methods of calling the function.

A.2.3 The `this` pointer

As we have seen, a member function of a given class is always called in the context of some object of the class; there is always an implicit "substrate" for the function to act on. C++ defines a keyword, `this`, to address this substrate (`this` is not available in the `static` member functions, to be discussed later). The `this` keyword is a pointer variable, which always contains the address of the object in question. The `this` pointer is implicitly declared in each member function (whether `public` or `private`); therefore, it is as if each member function of the class `Person` would contain the following declaration:

```
extern Person *this;
```

A member function like `setname()`, which sets a name field of a `Person` to a given string, could therefore be implemented with or without the `this` pointer:

```
// alternative 1: implicit use of this
void Person::setname (char const *n)
{
  delete name;
  name = strdup (n);
}

// alternative 2: explicit use of this
void Person::setname (char const *n)
{
  delete this->name;
  this->name = strdup (n);
}
```

Explicit use of the this pointer is not very frequent. However, there are a number of situations where the this pointer is needed.

Preventing self-destruction with `this`

As we have seen, the `operator =` can be redefined for the class `Person` in such a way that two objects of the class can be assigned, leading to two copies of the same object. As long as the two variables are different, the previously presented version of the function `operator=()` will function properly; the memory of the assigned object is released, after which it is allocated again to hold new strings. However, when an object is assigned to itself (called auto-assignment), a problem occurs: the allocated strings of the assigned are first released, but this also leads to the releasing of the strings of the right-hand side variable:

```
void fubar (Person const &p)
{
  p = p;                      // auto-assignment!
}
```

In this example, it is perfectly clear that something unnecessary, possibly even wrong, is happening. Auto-assignment can also occur in more hidden forms:

```
Person
   one,
   two,
   *pp;

pp = &one;
.

.

*pp = two;
.

.

one = *pp;
```

The problem of the auto-assignment can be solved by using the `this` pointer. In the overloaded assignment operator function we simply test whether the address of the right-hand side object is the same as the address of the current object. If so, no action needs to be taken. The definition of the function `operator=()` then becomes

```
void Person::operator= (Person const &other)
{
  // only take action if address of current object
  // (this) is NOT equal to address of other
  // object (&other):

  if (this != &other)
  {
      delete name;
      delete address;
      delete phone;

      name = strdup (other.name);
      address = strdup (other.address);
      phone = strdup (other.phone);
  }
}
```

This is the second version of the overloaded assignment function. A better version remains to be discussed.

Note the use of the address operator in the statement

```
if (this != &other)
```

The variable `this` is a pointer to the "current" object, while `other` is a reference, which is an "alias" to an actual `Person` object.

The address of the other object is therefore &other, while the address of the current object is this.

Associativity of operators and this

The syntax of C++ states that the associativity of the assignment operator is to the right-hand side, as in

```
a = b = c;
```

The expression b = c is evaluated first, and the result is assigned to a.

The implementation of the overloaded assignment operator so far does not permit such constructions, as an assignment using the member function returns nothing (void). We can therefore conclude that the previous implementation does circumvent an allocation problem, but is not quite syntactically correct.

The syntactical problem can be illustrated as follows. When we rewrite the expression a = b = c to the form that explicitly mentions member functions, we get

```
a.operator= (b.operator= (c));
```

This is syntactically incorrect, since the subexpression b.operator=(c) yields void, and the class Person contains no member functions with the prototype operator=(void).

This problem can also be remedied by using the this pointer. The overloaded assignment function expects as its argument a reference to a Person object; in the same way it can return a reference to such an object. This reference can then be used as an argument for a nested assignment.

It is customary to let the overloaded assignment return a reference to the current object (i.e., *this) as a const reference. The (final) version of the overloaded assignment operator for the class Person thus becomes:

```
// declaration in the class
class Person
{
  public:
    .
    .
    Person const &operator= (Person const &other)
    .
    .
```

```
};
// definition of the function
Person const &Person::operator= (Person const &other)
{
  // only take action when no auto-assignment occurs
  if (this != &other)
  {
    // deallocate own data
    delete address;
    delete name;
    delete phone;

    // duplicate other's data
    address = strdup (other.address);
    name = strdup (other.name);
    phone = strdup (other.phone);
  }

  // return current object, compiler will make sure
  // that a const reference is returned
  return (*this);
}
```

A.2.4 The copy constructor: Initialization vs. assignment

In the following sections we shall look closer at another use of the
operator =. We shall use a class String as an example. This class is
meant to handle allocated strings and is defined as follows:

```
class String
{
  public:
    // constructor, destructors
    String ();
    String (char const *s);
    ~String ();

    // overloaded assignment
    String const &operator= (String const &other);

    // interface functions
    void set (char const *data);
    char const *get (void);

  private:
```

```
// one data field: ptr to allocated string
char *str;
};
```

Concerning this definition we remark the following:

- The class contains a pointer `char  *str` to address allocated memory. For this reason, the class has a constructor and destructor. A typical action of the constructor would be to set the `str` pointer to 0. A typical action of the destructor would be to release the allocated memory.

- For the same reason the class has an overloaded assignment operator. The code of this function would look like this:

```
String const &String::operator= (String const
&other)
{
  if (this != &other)
  {
    delete str;
    str = strdup (other.str);
  }
  return (*this);
}
```

- The class has, besides a default constructor, a constructor which expects one string argument. Typically this argument would be used to set the string to a given value, as in

```
String
  a ("Hello World!\n");
```

- The only interface functions are to set the string part of the object and to retrieve it.

  Consider the following code fragment. The statement references are discussed below the example.

```
String
  a ("Hello World\n"),    // see (1)
  b,                       // see (2)
  c = a;                   // see (3)

int main ()
{
```

```
    b = c;                    // see (4)
    return (0);
}
```

- Statement 1 shows an initialization. The object a is initialized with a string "Hello World". This construction of the object a therefore uses the constructor that expects one string argument. It should be noted here that this form is identical to

```
String
  a = "Hello World\n";
```

  Even though this code fragment uses the operator =, this is no *assignment*. Rather it is an *initialization* and hence construction.

- In statement 2 a second String object is created. Again a constructor is called, but since no special arguments are present, this is the default constructor.

- In statement 3 a new object c is created. Again a constructor is called. The new object is also initialized with (the data of) object a. This form of initialization has not been discussed yet. Since we can rewrite this statement in the form

```
String
  c (a);
```

  this initialization suggests that a constructor is called, with a (reference to a) String object as argument. Such constructors, called **copy constructors,** are quite common in C++.

- In statement 4 one object is assigned to another. Because no object is *created* in this statement, this is just an assignment, using the overloaded assignment operator.

The simple rule that applies here is that *whenever an object is created, a constructor is needed*. The form of the constructor is still the following:

- The constructor has no return value.
- The constructor is defined in a function with the same name as the corresponding class.
- The argument list of the constructor can be deduced from the code; the argument is either present between parentheses or following a =.

We conclude therefore that, given code statement 3, the class String must be rewritten to define a **copy constructor**:

```
// class definition
class String
{
  public:
    .
    .
    String (String const &other);
    .
    .
};

// constructor definition
String::String (String const &other)
{
  str = strdup (other.str);
}
```

The actions of the copy constructor are similar to those of the overloaded assignment operator function: an object is *duplicated,* so that it contains its own allocated data. The copy constructor function is, however, simpler in the following respect:

- A copy constructor doesn't need to deallocate previously allocated memory. Since the object in question has just been created, it cannot already have its own allocated data.
- A copy constructor never needs to check whether autoduplication occurs. No variable can be initialized with itself.

The copy constructor has other important tasks, all of which are related to the fact that the copy constructor is always called when an object is created and initialized with another object, even when this new object is a hidden or temporary variable.

- When a function takes an object as argument, instead of a pointer or a reference, C++ calls the copy constructor to pass a copy of an object as the argument. This argument, which usually is passed via the stack, is therefore a new object, created and initialized with the data of the passed argument. This is illustrated in the following code fragment:

```
void func (String s) // no pointer, no reference
```

```
{                          // but the String itself
  puts (s.get ());
}

int main ()
{
  String
    hi ("hello world");

  func (hi);
  return (0);
}
```

In this code fragment, hi itself is not passed as an argument, but instead a temporary (stack) variable is created using the copy constructor. This temporary variable is known within func() as s. Note that by defining func() with a reference argument, extra stack use and a call to the copy constructor would have been avoided.

The copy constructor is also implicitly called when a function returns an object. This situation occurs when, for example, a function returns keyboard input in a String format:

```
String getline ()
{
  char
    buf [100];          // buffer for keyboard input

  gets (buf);           // read buffer

  String
    ret = buf;          // convert to String

  return (ret);         // and return it
}
```

A hidden String object is here initialized with the return value ret (using the copy constructor) and is returned by the function. The local variable ret itself ceases to exist when getline() terminates.

To demonstrate that copy constructors are not called in all situations, consider the following rewritten function getline():

```
String getline ()
{
  char
    buf [100];                  // buffer for kbd input
```

```
    gets (buf);                  // read buffer
    return (buf);                // and return it
}
```

This code fragment is quite valid, even though the return value char* doesn't match the prototype String. In this situation, C++ will try to convert the char* to a String; this is indeed possible, given a constructor that expects a char* argument. This means that the copy constructor is *not* used in this version of getline(). Instead, the constructor expecting a char* argument is used.

Similarities between the copy constructor and operator=()

The similarities between the copy constructor and the overloaded assignment operator are reinvestigated in this section. We present here two primitive functions that often occur in "our" code and that we think are quite useful.

- The duplication of (private) data occurs in the copy constructor and in the overloaded assignment function.
- The deallocation of used memory occurs in the overloaded assignment function and in the destructor.

Duplication and deallocation can be coded in two primitive functions, say copy() and destroy(), which are used in the overloaded assignment operator, the copy constructor, and the destructor. When we apply this method to the class Person, we can rewrite the code. First, the class definition is expanded with two private functions copy() and destroy(). The purpose of these functions is to *unconditionally* copy the data of another object or to deallocate the memory of the current object. Hence, these functions implement "primitive" functionality:

```
// class definition, only relevant functions are
                                              shown here
class Person
{
  public:
    // constructors, destructor
    Person (Person const &other);
    ~Person ();

    // overloaded assignment
    Person const &operator= (Person const &other);
    .
```

```
  private:
    // data fields
    char *name, *address, *phone;

    // the two primitives
    void copy (Person const &other);
    void destroy (void);
};
```

Next, we present the implementation of the functions copy() and destroy():

```
// copy(): unconditionally copy other object's data
void Person::copy (Person const &other)
{
  name = strdup (other.name);
  address = strdup (other.address);
  phone = strdup (other.phone);
}

// destroy(): unconditionally deallocate data
void Person::destroy ()
{
  delete name;
  delete address;
  delete phone;
}
```

Finally, the three public functions in which other object's memory is copied or in which memory is deallocated are rewritten:

```
// copy constructor
Person::Person (Person const &other)
{
  // unconditionally copy other's data
  copy (other);
}

// destructor
Person::~Person ()
{
  // unconditionally deallocate
  destroy ();
}
```

```
// overloaded assignment
Person const &Person::operator= (Person const
&other)
{
  // only take action if no auto-assignment
  if (this != &other)
  {
    destroy ();
    copy (other);
  }

  // return (reference to) current object for
  // chain-assignments
  return (*this);
}
```

A.2.5 More operator overloading

The following sections present more examples of operator overloading.

Overloading operator []

As one more example of operator overloading, we present here a class that is meant to represent an array of ints. Indexing the array elements occurs with the standard array operator [], but additionally the class checks for boundary overflow. An example of the use of the class follows.

```
int main ()
{
  Intarray
    x (20);                       // 20 ints

  for (register int i = 0; i < 20; i++)
    x [i] = i * 2;                // assign the elements

  for (i = 0; i <= 20; i++)
    printf ("At index %d: value %d\n",
        i, x [i]);

  return (0);
}
```

This example shows how an array is created to hold 20 ints. The elements of the array can be assigned or retrieved. This example should produce a run-time error, which is generated by the class `Intarray`; the last `for` loop causes a boundary overflow, since `x[20]` is addressed while legal indexes are range from 0 to 19. The definition of the class follows:

```
class Intarray
{
   public:
     // constructors, destructor etc.
     Intarray (int sz = 1);    // default size: 1 int
     Intarray (Intarray const &other);
     ~Intarray ();
     Intarray const &operator= (Intarray const
&other);

     // the interface
     int &operator[] (int index);

   private:
     // data
     int *data, size;
};
```

Concerning this class definition, note:

- The class has a constructor with a default `int` argument, specifying the array size. This function serves also as the default constructor, since the compiler will substitute 1 for the argument when none is given.

- The class uses an internal pointer to address allocated memory. Hence, the necessary tools are provided: a copy constructor, an overloaded assignment function, and a destructor.

- The interface is defined as a function that returns a reference to an `int`. This allows an expression like `x[10]` to be used on the left-hand side *and* on the right-hand side of an assignment. We can therefore use the same function to retrieve and to set data of the class.

The member functions of the class follow.

```
// constructor
Intarray::Intarray (int sz)
{
  // check for legal size specification
```

```
  if (sz < 1)
  {
    printf
("Intarray: size of array must be >= 1, not %d!\n",
                                                sz);
    exit (1);
  }

  // remember size, create array
  size = sz;
  data = new int [sz];
}

// copy constructor
Intarray::Intarray (Intarray const &other)
{
  // set size
  size = other.size;

  // create array
  data = new int [size];

  // copy other's values
  for (register int i = 0; i < size; i++)
    data [i] = other.data [i];
}

// overloaded assignment
Intarray const &Intarray::operator= (Intarray const
                                                &other)
{
  // take action only when no auto-assignment
  if (this != &other)
  {
    // set size
    size = other.size;
    // remove previous memory, create new array
    delete [] data;
    data = new int [size];
    // copy other's data
    for (register int i = 0; i < size; i++)
      data [i] = other.data [i];
  }
  return (*this);
}
```

```
// here is the interface function
int &Intarray::operator[] (int index)
{
  // check for array boundary over/underflow
  if (index < 0 || index >= size)
  {
    printf
      ("Intarray: boundary overflow or underflow, "
       "index=%d, should range from 0 to %d\n",
       index, size - 1);
    exit (1);
  }

  // emit the reference
  return (data [index]);
}
```

Cin, cout, cerr operators

A class can be adapted for use with the C++ streams `cout` and `cerr` and the operator `<<`. Adaptation of a class for use with `cin` and its operator `>>` occurs in a similar way and is not illustrated here.

The implementation of an overloaded operator `<<` in the context of `cout` or `cerr` involves the base class of `cout` or `cerr`, which is `ostream`. This class is declared in the header file `iostream.h` and defines only overloaded operator functions for "basic" types, such as, `int`, `char*`, etc. The purpose of this section is to show how an operator function can be defined that processes a new class, say `Person`, so that constructions such as the following one become possible:

```
Person
  kr ("Kernighan and Ritchie", "unknown",
"unknown");

cout << "Name, address and phone number of Person
                                          kr:\n"
     << kr
     << '\n';
```

The statement `cout << kr` involves the operator `<<` and its two operands, an `ostream&` and a `Person&`. The proposed action is defined in a classless operator function `operator<<()` expecting two arguments:

```
// declaration in, say, person.h
```

```
extern ostream &operator<< (ostream &, Person const &);

// definition in some source file
ostream &operator<< (ostream &stream, Person const
                                                &pers)
{
  return (stream << "Name:     " << pers.getname ()
           << "Address: " << pers.getaddress ()
           << "Phone:    " << pers.getphone ()
       );
}
```

Concerning this function, note the following:

- The function must return a (reference to) ostream object to enable "chaining" of the operator.
- The two operands of the operator << are stated as the two arguments of the overloading function.
- The class ostream provides the member function opfx(), which flushes any other ostream streams tied with the current stream. The function opfx() returns 0 when an error has been encountered.

An improved form of the function would therefore be

```
ostream &operator<< (ostream &stream, Person const
&pers)
{
  if (! stream.opfx ())
    return (stream);
  .
  .
}
```

A.2.6 Conclusion

Two important extensions to classes have been discussed in this section—the overloaded assignment operator and the copy constructor. As we have seen, classes with pointer data that address allocated memory are potential sources of semantic errors. The two introduced extensions are the only measures against unintentional loss of allocated data.

The conclusion therefore is that as soon as a class is defined where pointer data are used, an overloaded assignment function and a copy constructor should be implemented.

A.3 INHERITANCE

When programming in C, it is common to take a **top-down** approach to problem solutions. Functions and actions of the program are defined in terms of sub-functions, which again are defined in sub-sub-functions, and so on. This yields a hierarchy of code: `main()` at the top, followed by a level of functions that are called from `main()`, etc.

In C++ the dependencies between code and data can also be defined in terms of classes that are related to other classes. This looks like composition, where objects of a class contain objects of another class as their data. But the relation described here is of a different kind: a class can be *defined* by means of an older, preexisting, class, leading to a situation in which a new class has all the functionality of the older class and additionally introduces its own specific functionality. Instead of composition, where a given class *contains* another class, we mean here derivation, where a given class *is* another class.

Another term for derivation is **inheritance;** here the new class inherits the functionality of an existing class, while the existing class does not appear as a data member in the definition of the new class. When speaking of inheritance, the existing class is called the **base class**, while the new class is called the **derived class**.

Derivation of classes is often used when the methodology of C++ program development is fully exploited. In this section we first address the syntactical possibilities that C++ offers for deriving classes from other classes. Then we address the peculiar extension to C that is thus offered by C++.

As we have seen in the object-oriented approach to problem solving (Chapter 2), classes are identified during the problem analysis, after which objects of the defined classes can be declared to represent entities of the problem at hand. The classes are placed in a hierarchy, where the top-level class contains the least functionality. Each derivation, and hence descent, in the hierarchy adds functionality in the class definition.

In this section we use a simple vehicle classification system to build a hierarchy of classes. The first class is `Vehicle`, which implements as its functionality the possibility to set or retrieve the weight of a vehicle. The next level in the object hierarchy are land, water, and air vehicles. The initial object hierarchy is illustrated in Figure A.3.

A.3.1 Related types

The relationship between the proposed classes representing different kinds of vehicles is now further illustrated. The figure shows the

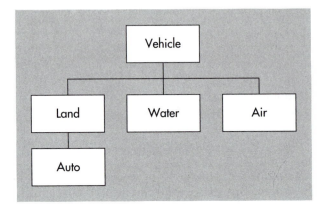

FIGURE A.3

object hierarchy in vertical direction: an `Auto` is a special case of a `Land` vehicle, which in turn is a special case of a `Vehicle`. The class `Vehicle` is thus the "greatest common denominator" in the classification system. For the sake of example, we implement in this class the functionality to store and retrieve the weight of a vehicle:

```
class Vehicle
{
  public:
    // constructors
    Vehicle ();
    Vehicle (int wt);

    // interface
    int getweight () const;
    void setweight (int wt);

  private:
    // data
    int weight;
}
```

Using this class, the weight of a vehicle can be defined as soon as the corresponding object is created. At a later stage the weight can be redefined or retrieved.

To represent vehicles that travel over land, a new class `Land` can be defined with the functionality of a `Vehicle`, but in addition to its own specific information. For the sake of example, we assume that we are interested in the speed of land vehicles *and* in their weight. The relationship between `Vehicles` and `Lands` could of course be represented with composition, but that would be awkward—composition would suggest that a `Land` vehicle *contains* a vehicle, while the relationship should be that the `Land` vehicle *is* a special case of a vehicle.

A relationship in terms of composition would also introduce needless code. Consider the following code fragment, which shows a class `Land` using composition (only the `setweight()` functionality is shown):

```cpp
class Land
{
  public:
    void setweight (int wt);
  private:
    Vehicle v;     // composed Vehicle
};

void Land::setweight (int wt)
{
  v.setweight (wt);
}
```

Using composition, the `setweight()` function of the class `Land` would serve only to pass its argument to `Vehicle::setweight()`. Thus, as far as weight handling is concerned, `Land::setweight()` would introduce no extra functionality, just extra code. Clearly this code duplication is redundant: a `Land` should *be* a `Vehicle`, not *contain* one.

The relationship is better achieved with inheritance. `Land` is *derived* from `Vehicle`; therefore `Vehicle` is the base class of the derivation.

```cpp
class Land: public Vehicle
{
  public:
    // constructors
    Land ();
    Land (int wt, int sp);

    // interface
    void setspeed (int sp);
    int getspeed () const;

  private:
    // data
    int speed;
};
```

By postfixing the class name `Land` in its definition by `public Vehicle`, the derivation is defined. The class `Land` now contains all the functionality of its base class `Vehicle` plus its own specific information. The extra functionality consists here of a constructor with two arguments and interface functions to access the `speed` data member. (The derivation in this example mentions the keyword `public`. C++ also implements `private` derivation, which is not often used and which we will therefore leave to the reader to uncover.)

To illustrate the use of the derived class `Land`, consider the following example:

```
Land
  veh (1200, 145);

int  main ()
{
  printf ("Vehicle weighs %d\n"
      "Speed is %d\n",
    veh.getweight (), veh.getspeed ());
  return (0);
}
```

This example shows two features of derivation. First, `getweight()` is no direct member of a `Land`; nevertheless it is used in `veh.getweight()`. This member function is an implicit part of the class, inherited from its "parent" vehicle.

Second, although the derived class `Land` now contains the functionality of `Vehicle`, the `private` fields of `Vehicle` remain private in the sense that they can be accessed only by member functions of `Vehicle` itself. This means that the member functions of `Land` *must* use the interface functions (`getweight()`, `setweight()`) to address the `weight` field, just as with any other code outside the `Vehicle` class. This restriction is necessary so that the aspect of data hiding remains ensured. The class `Vehicle` could, for example, be recoded and recompiled, after which the program could be relinked. The class `Land` itself could remain unchanged.

In this example we assume that the class `Auto`, which represents automobiles, should be able to represent the weight, speed, and name of a car. This class is therefore derived from `Land`:

```
class Auto: public Land
{
  public:
    // constructors
    Auto ();
```

```
    Auto (int wt, int sp, char const *nm);

    // copy constructor
    Auto (Auto const &other);

    // assignment
    Auto const &operator= (Auto const &other);

    // destructor
    ~Auto ();

    // interface
    char const *getname () const;
    void setname (char const *nm);

  private:
    // data
    char const *name;
};
```

In this class definition, `Auto` is derived from `Land`, which in turn is derived from `Vehicle`. We speak here of **nested derivation**—`Land` is `Auto`'s direct base class, while `Vehicle` is the indirect base class.

Note the presence of a destructor, a copy constructor, and overloaded assignment function in the class `Auto`. Since this class uses a pointer to address allocated memory, these tools are needed.

A.3.2 The constructor of a derived class

As mentioned previously, a derived class inherits the functionality of its base class. In this section, the effects of the inheritance on the constructor of a derived class are explored.

As can be seen from the definition of the class `Land`, a constructor exists to set both the `weight` and the `speed` of an object. The poor man's implementation of this constructor could be:

```
Land::Land (int wt, int sp)
{
  setweight (wt);
  setspeed (sp);
}
```

This implementation has a disadvantage. The C++ compiler will generate code to call the default constructor of a base class from each constructor in the derived class unless explicitly instructed otherwise. This can be compared to the situation that arises in composed objects. The result in the above implementation is therefore that (a) the default constructor of a `Vehicle` is called, which probably initializes the weight of the vehicle, and that (b) subsequently the weight is redefined by calling `setweight()`.

Of course, the better solution is to directly call the constructor of `Vehicle` that expects an `int` argument. The syntax to achieve this places the constructor to be called (supplied with an argument) following the argument list of the constructor of the derived class:

```
Land::Land (int wt, int sp)
  : Vehicle (wt)
{
  setspeed (sp);
}
```

A.3.3 Redefining member functions

The actions of all functions that are defined in a base class (and that are therefore also available in derived classes) can be redefined. This feature is illustrated in this section.

Let's assume that the vehicle classification system should be able to represent trucks, which consist of two parts, the front part with an engine and a trailer. Both the front part and the trailer have their own weight, but the `getweight()` function should return the combined weights. The definition of a `Truck` therefore starts with the class definition, derived from `Auto`, but expanded to hold one more `int` field to represent additional weight information. Here we choose to represent the weight of the front part of the truck in the `Auto` class and to store the weight of the trailer as the additional field:

```
class Truck: public Auto
{
  public:
    // constructors
    Truck ();
    Truck (int engine_wt, int sp, char const *nm,
        int trailer_wt);

    // interface: to set two weight fields
    void setweight (int engine_wt, int trailer_wt);
    // and to return combined weight
    int getweight () const;

  private:
    // data
```

```
      int trailer_weight;
};

// example of constructor
Truck::Truck (int engine_wt, int sp, char const
*nm,
      int trailer_wt)
  : Auto (engine_wt, sp, nm)
{
  trailer_weight = trailer_wt;
}
```

Note that the class `Truck` now contains two functions that are already present in the base class:

- The function `setweight()` is already defined in `Vehicle`. The redefinition in `Truck` poses no problem—this functionality is simply redefined to perform actions specific to a `Truck` object. The definition of a new version of `setweight()` in the class `Truck` will hide the version of `Vehicle`: for a `Truck` only a `setweight()` function with two `int` arguments can be used.
- The function `getweight()` is also already defined in `Vehicle`, with the same argument list as in `Truck`. In this case, the class `Truck` *redefines* this member function.

The following code fragment presents the redefined function `getweight()`:

```
int Truck::getweight () const
{
  return
    (        // sum of:
      Auto::getweight () +      // engine part plus
      trailer_weight            // the trailer
    );
}
```

Note that in this function the call `Auto::getweight()` explicitly selects the `getweight()` function of the class `Auto`. An implementation like

```
return (getweight () + trailer_weight);
```

would not be correct, as this statement would lead to infinite recursion and hence to an error in the program execution.

A.3.4 Multiple inheritance

In the previously described derivations, a class was always derived from *one* base class. C++ also implements **multiple derivation**, in which a class is derived from several base classes, thus inheriting the functionality of more than one "parent" at the same time.

For example, let's assume that a class Engine exists with the functionality to store information about an engine such as the serial number, the power, the type of fuel, etc.

```
class Engine
{
  public:
    // constructors and such
    Engine ();
    Engine (char const *serial_nr, int power,
        char const *fuel_type);

    // tools needed because we have pointers in
    // the class
    Engine (Engine const &other);
    Engine const &operator= (Engine const &other);
    ~Engine ();

    // interface to get/set stuff
    void setserial (char const *serial_nr);
    char const *getserial () const;
    void setpower (int power);
    int getpower () const;
    void setfueltype (char const *type);
    char const *getfueltype () const;

  private:
    // data
    char const *serial_number, fuel_type;
    int power;
};
```

To represent an Auto with all information about the engine, a class MotorCar can be derived from Auto *and* from Engine. By using multiple derivation, the functionality of an Auto *and* of an Engine are swept into a MotorCar:

```
class MotorCar: public Auto, public Engine
{
  public:
```

```
    // constructors
    MotorCar ();
    MotorCar (int wt,  int sp,  char const *nm,
            char const *ser,  int pow,  char const
                                                *fuel);
};

MotorCar::MotorCar (int wt,  int sp,  char const *nm,
           char const *ser,  int pow,  char const *fuel)
    : Engine (ser,  pow,  fuel),  Auto (wt,  sp,  nm)
{
}
```

A few remarks concerning this derivation:

- The keyword public is present both before the class name Auto and before the class name Engine, because the default derivation in C++ is private. Therefore the keyword public must be repeated before each base class specification.
- The multiply derived class MotorCar introduces no "extra" functionality of its own but only combines two preexisting types into one aggregate type. Thus, C++ offers the possibility to simply sweep multiple simple types into a more complex type. This feature of C++ is very often used. Usually it pays to develop "simple" classes each with its strict, well-defined functionality. More functionality can always be achieved by combining several small classes.
- The constructor that expects six arguments contains no code of its own. Its only purpose is to activate the constructors of the base classes. Similarly, the class definition contains no data or interface functions—here it is sufficient that all interface is inherited from the base classes.

Also note the syntax of the constructor: following the argument list, the two base class constructors are called, each supplied with the correct arguments. It is also noteworthy that the *order* in which the constructors are called is defined by the *derivation*, and *not* by the statement in the constructor of the class MotorCar.

- First, the constructor of Auto is called, since MotorCar is derived from Auto.
- Then, the constructor of Engine is called.
- Last, any actions of the constructor of MotorCar itself are executed (in this example, there are none).

The multiple derivation in this example may feel a bit awkward because the derivation implies that MotorCar *is* an Auto and at the same time *is* an Engine. A relationship "a MotorCar *has* an Engine" would be expressed as composition by including an Engine object in the data of a MotorCar. However, consider the unnecessary code duplication in the interface functions for an Engine where composition is used (here we assume that a composed object engine of the class Engine exists in a MotorCar):

```
void MotorCar::setpower (int pow)
{
  engine.setpower (pow);
}

int MotorCar::getpower () const
{
  return (engine.getpower ());
}

// etceteras, repeated for set/getserial(),
// and set/getfueltype()
```

Such simple interface functions are better avoided by using derivation. Alternatively, when insisting on the *has* relationship and hence on composition, the interface functions could be avoided using inline functions.

A.3.5 Conversions between base classes and derived classes

When using inheritance in the definition of classes, it can be said that an object of a derived class is simultaneously an object of the base class. This has important consequences, which are discussed in this section.

Conversions in object assignments

We define two objects, one of a base class and one of a derived class:

```
Vehicle
  v (900);        // vehicle with weight 900 kg
Auto
  a (1200, 130, "Ford");
    // automobile with weight 1200 kg,
    // max speed 130 km/h, make Ford
```

Object a is now initialized with its specific values. However, an `Auto` is at the same time a `Vehicle`, making the assignment from a derived object to a base object possible:

```
v = a;
```

In this assignment the object v now receives the value 1200 as its `weight` field. A `Vehicle` has neither a `speed` field nor a `name` field, so these data are therefore not assigned.

However, the conversion from a base object to a derived object poses problems. What data should a statement like

```
a = v;
```

substitute for the fields `speed` and `name`, which are missing in the right-hand side `Vehicle`? Such an assignment would not be accepted by the compiler.

Therefore, the following general rule applies: when assigning related objects, an assignment where some data are dropped is legal (an assignment where data would have to be left blank is not legal). This rule is a syntactic one and also applies when the classes in question have their overloaded assignment functions.

The conversion of an object of a base class to an object of a derived class can of course be explicitly defined, if necessary. For example, to achieve the correct working of a statement

```
a = v;
```

the class `Auto` would need an assignment function accepting a `Vehicle` as its argument. It would then be the programmer's responsibility to decide what to do with the missing data:

```
Auto const &Auto::operator= (Vehicle const &veh)
{
  setweight (veh.getweight ());
  .
  . code to handle other fields should
  . be supplied here
  .
}
```

Conversions in pointer assignments

We define the following objects and one pointer variable:

```
Land
  l (1200, 130);
Auto
  a (500, 75, "Daf");
Truck
  t (2600, 120, "Mercedes", 6000);
Vehicle
  *vp;
```

Subsequently we can assign vp to the addresses of the three objects of the derived classes:

```
vp = &l;
vp = &a;
vp = &t;
```

Each of these assignments is perfectly legal. However, an implicit conversion of the type of the derived class to a `Vehicle` is made because vp is defined as a pointer to a `Vehicle`. Hence, when using vp, only the member functions that manipulate the weight can be called; this is the only functionality of a `Vehicle` and therefore the only functionality that can be accessed by using a pointer to a `Vehicle`.

The restriction in functionality has further importance for the class `Truck`. The statement `vp = &t`, vp points to a `Truck`; nevertheless, `vp->getweight()` will return 2600, and 8600 (the combined weight of the cabin and the trailer, 2600 + 6000) would be returned by `t.getweight()`.

When a function is called using a pointer to an object, the *type of the pointer*, not the object itself, determines which member function is available and executed. In other words, C++ always implicitly converts the object that is pointed to the type of the pointer.

Of course, an explicit type cast is a way around the implicit conversion:

```
Truck
  truck;
Vehicle
  *vp;

vp = &truck;      // vp now points to a truck object
  .
  .
  .
Truck
```

```
   *trp;

trp = (Truck *) vp;
printf ("Make: %s\n", trp->getname ());
```

The second to last statement of this code fragment specifically casts a Vehicle* variable to a Truck* in order to assign the value to the pointer trp. This code will only work if vp indeed points to a Truck and a function getname() is available; otherwise, unexpected behavior of the program may result.

A.3.6 Storing base class pointers

Because pointers to a base class can be used to address derived classes, they can be useful in developing general-purpose classes that can process objects of the derived types. A typical example of such processing is the storage of objects, be it in an array, a list, a tree or another appropriate storage method. Classes that are designed to store objects of other classes are therefore often called **container classes**. The stored objects are then *contained* in the container class.

As an example, we present the class VStorage, which is used to store pointers to Vehicles. The actual pointers may be addresses of Vehicles themselves but may also refer to derived types, such as Autos.

The definition of the class follows:

```
class VSTorage
{
  public:
    // constructors, destructor
    VStorage ();
    VSTorage (VStorage const &other);
    ~VStorage ();

    // overloaded assignment
    VStorage const &operator= (VStorage const
&other);

    // interface:
    // add Vehicle* to storage
    void add (Vehicle *vp);
    // retrieve first Vehicle*
    Vehicle *getfirst (void) const;
    // retrieve next Vehicle*
    Vehicle *getnext (void) const;
```

```
private:
   // data
   Vehicle **storage;
   int nstored, current;
};
```

Concerning this class definition, note the following:

- The class contains three interface functions: one to add a Vehicle* to the storage, one to retrieve the first Vehicle* from the storage, and one to retrieve next pointers until no more are in the storage. The class could therefore be used in the following manner:

```
Land
   l (200, 20);     // weight 200, speed 20
Auto
   a (1200, 130, "Ford");      // weight 1200,
                               // speed 130,
                               // make Ford
VStorage
   garage;          // the storage

garage.add (&l);   // add to storage
garage.add (&a);
     .
Vehicle
   *anyp;
int
   total_wt = 0;

for (anyp = garage.getfirst (); anyp; anyp =
                               garage.getnext())
   total_wt += anyp->getweight ();

printf ("Total weight: %d\n", total_wt);
```

This example demonstrates how derived types (one Auto and one Land) are implicitly converted to their base type (a Vehicle) so that they can be stored in a VStorage. Base-type objects are then retrieved from the storage; the function getweight(), defined in the base type, being greatest common denominator can be used to compute the combined weight.

- The class `VStorage` contains all the tools to ensure that two `VStorage` objects can be assigned to one another, etc. These tools are the overloaded assignment function and the copy constructor.

- The actual internal workings of the class become apparent once the `private` section is seen. The class `VStorage` maintains an array of pointers to `Vehicles` and needs two `ints` to store the number of objects and which object is "current," to be returned by `getnext()`.

The class `VStorage` will not be further explained because similar examples appear in the next sections. It is important to note that by providing class derivation and base/derived conversions, C++ is a powerful tool. These features of C++ allow the processing of all derived types by one generic class.

Class `VStorage` could even be used to store all types that may be derived from a `Vehicle` in the future. It seems a bit paradoxical that the class should be able to use code that isn't even there yet, but there is no real paradox: `VStorage` uses a certain protocol, defined by the `Vehicle` and obligatory for all derived classes.

The class `VStorage` has one disadvantage: when we add a `Truck` object to a storage, then a code fragment like

```
Vehicle
  *any;
VStorage
  garage;
.  .
any = garage.getnext ();
printf ("%d\n", any->getweight ());
```

will *not* print the combined weight of the front part and the trailer. Only the weight stored in the `Vehicle` portion of the truck will be returned via the function `any->getweight()`.

There is, of course, a remedy to this slight disadvantage, discussed in the next section.

A.4 POLYMORPHISM, LATE BINDING, AND VIRTUALITY

As we saw in Section A.3, C++ provides the tools to derive classes from one base type, to use base class pointers to address derived objects, and subsequently to process derived objects in a generic class.

Concerning the allowed operations on all objects in such a generic class, we have seen that the base class must define the actions to be performed on all derived objects. In the example of the `Vehicle`, this was the functionality to store and retrieve the weight of a vehicle.

When using a base class pointer to address an object of a derived class, the pointer type normally determines which actual function will be called. This means that the code example from Section A.3.6, which uses the storage class `VStorage`, will incorrectly compute the combined weight when a `Truck` object is in the storage—only one weight field, of the front part of the truck, is taken into consideration. The reason for this is obvious: a `Vehicle *vp` calls the function `Vehicle::getweight()` and not `Truck::getweight()`, even when that pointer actually points to a `Truck`.

However, the opposite is also possible. C++ makes it possible that a `Vehicle *vp` calls a function `Truck::getweight()` when the pointer actually points to a `Truck`. The term for this feature of C++ is **polymorphism**: the pointer `vp` assumes several forms when pointing to several objects. In other words, `vp` might behave like a `Truck*` when pointing to a `Truck`, or like an `Auto*` when pointing to an `Auto`.

A second term for this feature is **late binding**. This name refers to the fact that the decision concerning function to call (one of the base class or one of the derived classes) cannot be made at compile-time. The correct function is selected at run-time.

A.4.1 Virtual functions

The default behavior of the activation of a member function by a pointer is that the *type* of the pointer determines the function. For example, a `Vehicle*` will activate `Vehicle`'s member functions, even when pointing to an object of a derived class. This is referred to as **early** or **static binding,** because the type of function is known at compile-time. The **late** or **dynamic binding** is achieved in C++ with **virtual functions**.

A function becomes virtual when its declaration starts with the keyword `virtual`. Once a function is declared `virtual` in a base class, its definition remains `virtual` in all derived classes, even when the keyword `virtual` is not repeated in the definition of the derived classes.

As far as the vehicle classification system is concerned, the two member functions `getweight()` and `setweight()` may be declared as `virtual`. The following class definitions illustrate the classes `Vehicle`, the overall base class of the classification system, and `Truck`, which has `Vehicle` as an indirect base class. The functions `getweight()` of the two classes are also shown:

```cpp
class Vehicle
{
  public:
    // constructors
    Vehicle ();
    Vehicle (int wt);

    // interface.. now virtuals!
    virtual int getweight () const;
    virtual void setweight (int wt);

  private:
    // data
    int weight;
}

// Vehicle's own getweight() function:
int Vehicle::getweight () const
{
  return (weight);
}

class Land: public Vehicle
{
  .
  .
}

class Auto: public Land
{
  .
  .
}

class Truck: public Auto
{
  public:
    // constructors
    Truck ();
    Truck (int engine_wt, int sp, char const *nm,
           int trailer_wt);

    // interface: to set two weight fields
    void setweight (int engine_wt, int trailer_wt);
    // and to return combined weight
```

```
    int getweight () const;

  private:
    // data
    int trailer_weight;
};

// Truck's own getweight() function
int Truck::getweight () const
{
  return (Auto::getweight () + trailer_wt);
}
```

Note that the keyword `virtual` appears only in the definition of the base class `Vehicle`; it need not be repeated in the derived classes (though a repetition would not be an error).

The effect of the late binding is illustrated in the next fragment:

```
Vehicle
  v (1200);          // vehicle with weight 1200
Truck
  t (6000, 115,      // truck with cabin weight 6000,
                     // speed 115,
     "Scania",       // make Scania, trailer weight
                     // 15000
     15000);

Vehicle
  *vp;     // generic vehicle pointer

int main ()
{
  // see below (1)
  vp = &v;
  printf ("%d\n", vp->getweight ());

  // see below (2)
  vp = &t;
  printf ("%d\n", vp->getweight ());

  // see below (3)
  printf ("%d\n", vp->getspeed ());

  return (0);
}
```

Since the function getweight() is defined as virtual, late binding is used here; in the statements below the (1) mark, Vehicle's function getweight() is called. In contrast, the statements under (2) use Truck's function getweight().

Statement (3), however, will still lead to a syntax error. A function getspeed() is not a member of Vehicle and hence cannot be called using a Vehicle*.

The rule is that when using a pointer to a class, *only the functions that are members of that class can be called*. These functions can be virtual, but this only affects the type of binding (early vs. late).

Polymorphism in program development

When functions are defined as virtual in a base class (and hence in all derived classes), and when these functions are called using a pointer to the base class, the pointer can assume more forms; it is polymorph. In this section we illustrate the effect of polymorphism on the manner in which programs in C++ can be developed.

A vehicle classification system in C might be implemented with Vehicle being a union of structs and having an enumeration field to determine which actual type of vehicle is represented. A function getweight() would typically first determine what type of vehicle is represented and then inspect the relevant fields:

```
typedef enum          /* type of the vehicle */
{
  is_vehicle,
  is_land,
  is_auto,
  is_truck,
} Vtype;

typedef struct        /* generic vehicle type */
{
  int weight;
} Vehicle;

typedef struct        /* land vehicle: adds speed */
{
  Vehicle v;
  int speed;
} Land;

typedef struct        /* auto: Land vehicle + name */
{
```

```
    Land l;
    char *name;
} Auto;
/* truck: Auto + trailer */
typedef struct
{
    Auto a;
    int trailer_wt;
} Truck;
/* all sorts of vehicles in 1 union */
typedef union
{
    Vehicle v;
    Land l;
    Auto a;
    Truck t;
} AnyVehicle;
/* the data for a all vehicles */
typedef struct
{
    Vtype type;
    AnyVehicle thing;
} Object;
/* how to get weight of a vehicle */
int getweight (Object *o)
{
    switch (o->type)
    {
      case is_vehicle:
        return (o->thing.v.weight);
      case is_land:
        return (o->thing.l.v.weight);
      case is_auto:
        return (o->thing.a.l.v.weight);
      case is_truck:
        return (o->thing.t.a.l.v.weight +
            o->thing.t.trailer_wt);
    }
}
```

A disadvantage of this approach is that the implementation cannot be easily changed. If we wanted to define a type Airplane, which would add the functionality to store the number of passengers, then we would have to reedit and recompile the code.

In contrast, C++ offers the possibility of polymorphism. The advantage is that "old" code remains usable. In C++ the implementation of an extra class `Airplane` would mean one extra class, possibly with its own (virtual) functions `getweight()` and `setweight()`. A function like

```
void printweight (Vehicle const *any)
{
  printf ("Weight: %d\n", any->getweight ());
}
```

would still work; the function wouldn't even need to be recompiled, since late binding is in effect.

How polymorphism is implemented

Understanding the implementation is not necessary for using this feature of C++, though it does explain why there is a cost of polymorphism in terms of memory usage. The fundamental idea of polymorphism is that the C++ compiler does not know which function to call at compile-time; the correct function can be selected only at run-time. That means that the address of the function must be stored somewhere, to be looked up prior to the actual call. This "somewhere" must be accessible from the object in question. For example, when a `Vehicle *vp` points to a `Truck` object, then `vp->getweight()` calls a member function of `Truck`; the address of this function is determined from the actual object to which `vp` points.

The most common implementation is the following. An object that contains virtual functions holds as its first data member a hidden field pointing to an array of pointers that hold the addresses of the virtual functions. It must be noted that this implementation is compiler-dependent and is by no means dictated by the C++ ANSI definition.

The table of the addresses of virtual functions is shared by all objects of the class. It even may be the case that two classes share the same table. The overhead in terms of memory consumption is therefore

- One extra pointer field per object, which points to:
- One table of pointers per (derived) class to address the virtual functions.

Therefore, a statement like `vp->getweight()` first inspects the hidden data member of the object pointed to by `vp`. In the case of the vehicle classification system, this data member points to a

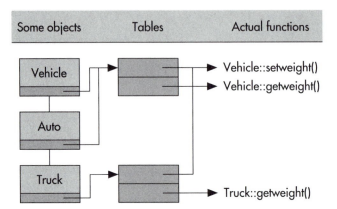

FIGURE A.4

table of two addresses: one pointer for the function `getweight()` and one pointer for the function `setweight()`. The actual function called is determined from this table.

The organization of the objects concerning virtual functions is further illustrated in Figure A.4. All objects that use virtual functions must have one (hidden) data member to address a table of function pointers. The objects of the classes `Vehicle` and `Auto` both address the same table. The class `Truck`, however, introduces its own version of `getweight()`. Therefore, this class needs its own table of function pointers.

A.4.2 Pure virtual functions

Until now, the base class `Vehicle` contained its own concrete implementations of the virtual functions `getweight()` and `setweight()`. In C++, however, it is also possible only to *mention* virtual functions in a base class and not define them. The functions are concretely implemented in a derived class. This approach defines a **protocol**, which has to be followed in the derived classes.

The special feature of only *declaring* functions in a base class and not *defining* them is that derived classes must take care of the actual definition: the C++ compiler will not allow the definition of an object of a class that doesn't concretely define the function in question. Thus, the base class enforces a protocol by declaring a function by its name, return value, and arguments; however, the derived classes must take care of the actual implementation. The base class itself is therefore only a *model* to be used for the derivation of other classes. Such base classes are also called **abstract classes**.

The functions that are only declared but not defined in the base class are called **pure virtual functions**. A function is made pure virtual by preceding its declaration with the keyword `virtual` and by postfixing it with = 0. An example of a pure virtual function occurs in the following listing, where the definition of a class `Sortable` requires that all subsequent classes have a function `compare()`:

```
class Sortable
{
  public:
    virtual int compare (Sortable const &other)
const = 0;
};
```

The function `compare()` must return an `int` and receives a reference to a second `Sortable` object. Its action might be to compare the current object with the `other` one. The function is not allowed to alter the other object, as `other` is declared `const`. Furthermore, the function is not allowed to alter the current object, as the function itself is declared `const`.

The base class can be used as a model for derived classes. As an example, consider the following class `Person`, capable of comparing two `Person` objects by the alphabetical order of their names and addresses:

```
class Person: public Sortable
{
  public:
    // constructors, destructors, and stuff
    Person ();
    Person (char const *nm, char const *add, char
                                      const *ph);
    Person (Person const &other);
    Person const &operator= (Person const &other);

    // interface
    char const *getname () const;
    char const *getaddress () const;
    char const *getphone () const;
    void setname (char const *nm);
    void setaddress (char const *add);
    void setphone (char const *ph);

    // requirements enforced by Sortable
    int compare (Sortable const &other) const;

  private:
    // data members
```

```
        char *name, *address, *phone;
};

int Person::compare (Sortable const &o)
{
  Person
    const &other = (Person const &)o;
  register int
    cmp;

  // first try: if names unequal, we're done
  if ( (cmp = strcmp (name, other.name)) )
    return (cmp);
  // second try: compare by addresses
  return (strcmp (address, other.address));
}
```

Note that in the implementation of `Person::compare()`, the argument of the function is not a reference to a `Person` but a reference to a `Sortable`. Remember that C++ allows function overloading: a function `compare(Person const &other)` would be an entirely different function from the one required by the protocol of `Sortable`. Therefore, in the implementation of the function, we cast the `Sortable&` argument to a `Person&` argument.

A.4.3 Comparing only `Persons`

Sometimes it may be useful to know in the concrete implementation of a pure virtual function what the `other` object is. For example, the function `Person::compare()` should make the comparison *only* if the other `object` is a `Person` too: imagine what the statement

```
strcmp (name, other.name)
```

would do if the `other` object was not a `Person` and hence did not have a `char *name` data member.

We therefore offer an improved version of the protocol of the class `Sortable`. This class is expanded to require that each derived class implements a function `int getsignature()`:

```
class Sortable
{
   .
   .    virtual int getsignature () const = 0;
   .    .
```

```
};
```

The concrete function `Person::compare()` can now compare names and addresses if the signatures of the current and other object match:

```
int Person::compare (Sortable const &o)
{
  register int
    cmp;

  // first, check signatures
  if ( (cmp = getsignature () - o.getsignature ()) )
    return (cmp);

  Person
    const &other = (Person const &)o;

  // next: if names unequal, we're done
  if ( (cmp = strcmp (name, other.name)) )
    return (cmp);
  // last try: compare by addresses
  return (strcmp (address, other.address));
}
```

The crux of the matter is the function `getsignature()`. This function should return a unique `int` value for its particular class. An elegant implementation is the following:

```
class Person: public Sortable
{
  . .
  // getsignature() now required too
  int getsignature () const;
}

int Person::getsignature () const
{
  static int    // Person's own tag, I'm quite sure
    tag;        // that no other class can access it

  return ( (int) &tag );   // hence, &tag is unique
                           // for Person
}
```

A.4.4 Virtual destructors

When the operator `delete` releases memory which is occupied by a dynamically allocated object, a corresponding destructor is called to ensure that internally used memory of the object can also be released. Now consider the following code fragment, in which the two classes from the previous sections are used:

```
Sortable
  *sp;
Person
  *pp = new Person ("Frank", "frank@icce.rug.nl",
                                        "633688");

sp = pp;                   // sp now points to a Person
  .
  .
delete sp;                 // object destroyed
```

In this example, an object of a derived class (`Person`) is destroyed using a base class pointer (`Sortable*`). For a "standard" class definition, the destructor of `Sortable` is called instead of the destructor of `Person`.

C++, however, allows virtual destructors. By preceding the declaration of a destructor with the keyword `virtual`, we can ensure that the right destructor is activated even when called via a base class pointer. The definition of the class Sortable would therefore become

```
class Sortable
{
  public:
    virtual ~Sortable ();
    virtual int compare (Sortable const &other)
const = 0;
    .
    .
};
```

Should the virtual destructor of the base class be a *pure* virtual function or not? In general, the answer to this question would be no, because for a class such as `Sortable`, the definition should not *force* derived classes to define a destructor. In contrast, `compare()` is a pure virtual function; in this case, the base class defines a protocol that must be adhered to.

By defining the destructor of the base class as `virtual`, though not purely so, the base class offers the possibility of redefinition of the destructor in any derived classes. The base class doesn't enforce the choice.

The conclusion, therefore, is that the base class must define a destructor function, which is used in the case that derived classes do *not* define their own destructors. Such a destructor could be an empty function:

```
Sortable::~Sortable ()
{
}
```

A.4.5 Virtuality in multiple inheritance

As was previously mentioned, it is possible to derive a class from several base classes at once. Such a derived class inherits the properties of all its base classes. Of course, the base classes themselves may be derived from classes that are higher in the hierarchy.

A slight difficulty in multiple inheritance may arise when more than one "path" leads from the derived class to the base class. This is illustrated in the following code fragment, in which a class Derived is doubly derived from a class Base.

```
class Base
{
  public:
    void setfield (int val)
      { field = val; }
    int getfield () const
      { return (field); }
  private:
    int field;
};

class Derived: public Base, public Base
{
};
```

Due to the double derivation, the functionality of Base now occurs twice in Derived. This leads to ambiguity: When the function setfield() is called for a Derived object, *which* function should that be, since there are two? In such a duplicate derivation, many C++ compilers will fail to generate code and correctly identify the error.

The above code clearly duplicates its base class in the derivation. Such a duplication can be easily avoided here. But duplication of a

FIGURE A.5

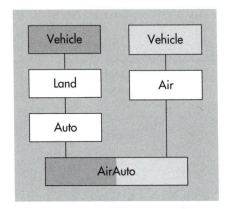

FIGURE A.6

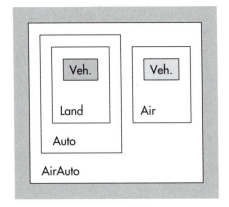

base class can also occur via nested inheritance, where an object is derived from, say, an `Auto` and from an `Air`. Such a class would be needed to represent a flying car (such as the one James Bond drives in *The Man with the Golden Gun*). An `AirAuto` would ultimately contain two `Vehicles`, and hence two `weight` fields, two `setweight()` functions, and two `getweight()` functions.

Ambiguity in multiple inheritance

Let's investigate why an `AirAuto` introduces ambiguity when derived from `Auto` and `Air`.

- An `AirAuto` is an `Auto`, hence a `Land`, and hence a `Vehicle`.
- However, an `AirAuto` is also an `Air`, and hence a `Vehicle`.

This duplication of `Vehicle` data is further illustrated in Figure A.5. The internal organization of an `AirAuto` is shown in Figure A.6.

The C++ compiler will detect the ambiguity in an `AirAuto` object and will therefore fail to produce code for a statement like

```
AirAuto
  cool;

printf ("%d\n", cool.getweight());
```

The question of which member function `getweight()` should be called cannot be resolved by the compiler. The programmer has two possibilities to resolve the ambiguity explicitly.

- First, the function call where the ambiguity occurs can be modified. This is done with the scope resolution operator:

  ```
  // let's hope that the weight is kept in the Auto
  // part of the object.
  printf ("%d\n", cool.Auto::getweight ());
  ```

  Note that the scope operator and the class name occur before the name of the member function itself.

- Second, a dedicated function `getweight()` could be created for the class `AirAuto`:

  ```
  int AirAuto::getweight () const
  {
    return (Auto::getweight ());
  }
  ```

The second possibility is preferable, since it relieves the programmer who uses the class `AirAuto` of special precautions.

Besides these explicit solutions, there is a more elegant one, discussed in the next section.

Virtual base classes

As is illustrated in the figure, more than one object of the type `Vehicle` is present in one `AirAuto`. The result is not only an ambiguity in the functions that access the `weight` data but also the presence of two `weight` fields. This is somewhat redundant, since we can assume that an `AirAuto` has just one weight.

We can achieve that only one `Vehicle` be contained in an `AirAuto`. This is done by ensuring that the base class that is multiply present in a derived class is defined as a **virtual base class**. When a base class `B` is a virtual base class of a derived class `D`, then

FIGURE A.7

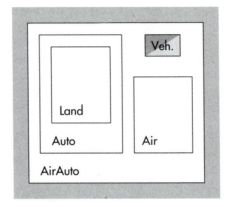

B may be present in D. The compiler will leave out the inclusion of the members of B when these are already present in D.

For the class AirAuto, this means that the derivation of Land and Air is changed:

```
class Land: virtual public Vehicle
{
    .   .
};

class Air: virtual public Vehicle
{
    .   .
};
```

The virtual derivation ensures that via the Land route, a Vehicle is only added to a class when not yet present. The same holds true for the Air route. This means that we can no longer say by which route a Vehicle becomes a part of an AirAuto; we can say only that there is one Vehicle object embedded.

The internal organization of an AirAuto after virtual derivation is shown in Figure A.7.

Concerning virtual derivation we make the following remarks:

- Virtual derivation is, in contrast to virtual functions, a pure compile-time issue: whether or not a derivation is virtual defines how the compiler builds a class definition from other classes.
- In the example, it would suffice to define either Land or Air with virtual derivation. That would also have the effect that

one definition of a `Vehicle` in an `AirAuto` would be dropped. Defining both `Land` and `Air` as virtually derived is, however, by no means erroneous.

- The fact that the `Vehicle` in an `AirAuto` is no longer "embedded" in `Auto` or `Air` has a consequence for the chain of construction. The constructor of an `AirAuto` will directly call the constructor of a `Vehicle`; this constructor will not be called from the constructors of `Auto` or `Air`.

Consequently, the ambiguity in the calling of member functions of a base class is avoided using virtual derivation. Duplication of data members is also avoided.

When virtual derivation is not appropriate

In contrast to the previous definition of a class such as `AirAuto`, situations may arise where the double presence of the members of a base class is appropriate. To illustrate this, consider the definition of a `Truck`:

```
class Truck: public Auto
{
  public:
    // constructors
    Truck ();
    Truck (int engine_wt, int sp, char const *nm,
        int trailer_wt);

    // interface: to set two weight fields
    void setweight (int engine_wt, int trailer_wt);
    // and to return combined weight
    int getweight () const;

  private:
    // data
    int trailer_weight;
};

// example of constructor
Truck::Truck (int engine_wt, int sp, char const *nm,
        int trailer_wt)
  : Auto (engine_wt, sp, nm)
{
  trailer_weight = trailer_wt;
}
```

```
// example of interface function
int Truck::getweight () const
{
  return
    (                                  // sum of:
      Auto::getweight () +             // engine part plus
      trailer_wt                       // the trailer
    );
}
```

This definition shows how a Truck object is constructed to hold two weight fields—one via its derivation from Auto and one via its own int trailer_weight data member. Of course, such a definition is valid, but it could be rewritten. We could let a Truck be derived from an Auto *and* from a Vehicle, thereby explicitly requesting the double presence of a Vehicle—one for the weight of the engine and cab, and one for the weight of the trailer.

A small item of interest here is that a derivation like

```
class Truck: public Auto, public Vehicle
```

is not accepted by the C++ compiler because a Vehicle is already part of an Auto and is therefore not needed. An intermediate class resolves the problem; we derive a class TrailerVeh from Vehicle, and Truck from Auto and TrailerVeh. All ambiguities concerning the member functions are then resolved in the class Truck:

```
class TrailerVeh: public Vehicle
{
  public:
    TrailerVeh (int wt);
};

TrailerVeh::TrailerVeh (int wt)
  : Vehicle (wt)
{
}

class Truck: public Auto, public TrailerVeh
{
  public:
    // constructors
    Truck ();
    Truck (int engine_wt, int sp, char const *nm,
           int trailer_wt);
```

```
        // interface: to set two weight fields
        void setweight (int engine_wt, int trailer_wt);
        // and to return combined weight
        int getweight () const;
};

// example of constructor
Truck::Truck (int engine_wt, int sp, char const *nm,
         int trailer_wt)
   : Auto (engine_wt, sp, nm), TrailerVeh
(trailer_wt)
{
}

// example of interface function
int Truck::getweight () const
{
   return
      (        // sum of:
         Auto::getweight () +       // engine part plus
         TrailerVeh::getweight ()   // the trailer
      );
}
```

A.5 TEMPLATES

Most modern C++ compilers support a "super-macro-mechanism" which allows programmers to define generic functions or classes, based on a hypothetical argument or other entity. The generic functions or classes become concrete code once their definitions are used with real entities. The generic definitions of functions or classes are called **templates**.

A.5.1 Template functions

The definition of a template function is very similar to the definition of a concrete function, except for the fact that the arguments to the function are named in a symbolic way. This is best illustrated with an example:

```
template <class T>
void swap (T &a, T &b)
{
```

```
    T
      tmp = a;

    a = b;
    b = tmp;
}
```

In this example, a template function `swap()` is defined, which acts on any type as long as variables (or objects) of that type can be assigned to each other and can be initialized by one another. The generic type used in the function `swap()` is called here T, as given in the first line of the code fragment.

The code of the function performs the following tasks:

- First, a variable of type T is created (this is `tmp`) and initialized with the argument `a`.
- Second, the variables referred to by `a` and `b` are swapped, using `tmp` as an intermediate.

The actual references `a` and `b` could refer to `int`s, `double`s, or any other type. Note that the definition of a template function is similar to a `#define` in the sense that the template function is not code yet; it only becomes code once it is used.

As an example of the use of this template function, consider the following code fragment (we use the class `Person` as illustration):

```
int main ()
{
  int
    a = 3,
    b = 16;
  double
    d = 3.14,
    e = 2.17;
  Person
    k ("Karel", "Rietveldlaan 37", "426044"),
    f ("Frank", "Oostumerweg 17",  "2223");

  swap (a, b);
  printf ("a = %d, b = %d\n", a, b);

  swap (d, e);
  printf ("d = %lf, e = %lf\n", d, e);

  swap (k, f);
```

```
  printf ("k's name = %s, f's name = %s\n",
      k.getname (), f.getname ());

  return (0);
}
```

Once the C++ compiler encounters the use of the template function `swap()`, concrete code is generated. This means that three
functions are created—one to handle `ints`, one to handle `doubles`,
and one to handle `Persons`. The compiler generates mangled
names to distinguish between these functions; for example, internally the functions may be named `swap_int_int()`, `swap_dou-`
`ble_double()`, and `swap_Person_Person()`. It should furthermore be noted that, as far as the class Person is concerned, the definition of `swap()` requires a copy constructor and an overloaded
assignment operator.

The fact that the compiler only generates concrete code once a
template function is used has an important consequence. The definition of a template function can never be collected in a run-time
library; it must be present in, say, a header file.

A.5.2 Template classes

The "super-macro-mechanism" offered by templates can be used to
define generic classes, which are intended to handle any type of
entity. Typically, template classes are container classes and represent arrays, lists, stacks, or trees.

A template class: `Array`

As an example, we present here a template class `Array`, which can
be used to store arrays of any elements:

```
#include <stdio.h>
#include <stdlib.h>

template<class T>
class Array
{
  public:
    // constructors, destructors and such
    virtual ~Array (void)
      { delete [] data; }
    Array (int sz = 10)
      { init (sz); }
    Array (Array<T> const &other);
```

```
      Array const &operator= (Array<T> const &other);

      // interface
      int size (void) const;
      T &operator[] (int index);

    private:
      // data
      int n;
      T *data;
      // initializer
      void init (int sz);
};

template <class T>
void Array<T>::init (int sz)
{
  if (sz < 1)
  {
    fprintf (stderr,
         "Array: cannot create array of size < 1\n"
             "requested: %d\n", sz);
    exit (1);
  }
  n = sz;
  data = new T [n];
}

template <class T>
Array<T>::Array (Array<T> const &other)
{
  n = other.n;
  data = new T [n];
  for (register int i = 0; i < n; i++)
    data [i] = other.data [i];
}

template <class T>
Array<T> const &Array<T>::operator= (Array<T> const
                                            &other)
{
  if (this != &other)
  {
    delete [] data;
    n = other.n;
    data = new T [n];
```

```
    for (register int i = 0; i < n; i++)
      data [i] = other.data [i];
  }
  return (*this);
}


template <class T>
int Array<T>::size (void) const
{
  return (n);
}


template <class T>
T &Array<T>::operator[] (int index)
{
  if (index < 0 || index >= n)
  {
    fprintf (stderr,
  "Array: index out of bounds, must be between" " 0
                                           and %d\n"
        " requested was: %d\n",
        n - 1, index);
    exit (1);
  }
  return (data [index]);
}
```

Concerning this definition it is important to note the following:

- The definition of the class starts with

  ```
  template <class T>
  ```

- This is similar to the definition of a template function—this line holds the symbolic name T, referring to the type which will be handled by the class.
- In the class definition, all functions that have an Array as their argument (such as the copy constructor) refer to this argument as an Array<T>.
- In the function definitions, the class name is referred to as Array<T> because, similar to name mangling in template functions, the compiler will modify the class name Array to a new name when the class is concretely used. The symbolic name T will then become a part of the new class name.

Concerning the statements in the template, note the following:

- The template class `Array` uses two data members: a pointer to an allocated array (`data`) and the size of the array (`n`).
- The class contains a copy constructor, (virtual) destructor, and overloaded assignment function, since it addresses allocated memory.
- Note the statement `delete [] data` in the destructor and overloaded assignment. This statement makes sure that, when `data` points to an array of objects, the destructor for the objects is called prior to the deallocation of the array itself.
- The statement `data[i] = other.data[i]` in the overloaded assignment copies the data from another `Array`. This statement may actually copy memory byte by byte or activate an overloaded assignment operator when the stored data is, say, a `Person`.

When dealing with the template class `Array` and, in general, all template classes, it is important to note that the template itself must be known to the compiler at compile-time. This usually means that the code of the template class is appended to the class definition, say in a header file `array.h`.

Using the `Array` class

The template class `Array` is used as illustrated in the following example:

```
#include <stdio.h>
#include "array.h"

#define PI 3.1415

int main ()
{
  Array <int>
    intarr;

  for (register int i = 0; i < intarr.size (); i++)
    intarr [i] = i << 2;

  Array <double>
    doublearr;
```

```
  for (i = 0; i < doublearr.size (); i++)
    doublearr [i] = PI * (i + 1);

  for (i = 0; i < intarr.size (); i++)
    printf ("intarr [%d]    : %d\n"
        "doublearr [%d]: %g\n",
        i, intarr [i],
        i, doublearr [i]);

  return (0);
}
```

Note that the actual type of the array must be supplied when defining an object of the template class.

The class can, of course, be used with any type (or class) as long as arrays of the type can be allocated and entities of the type can be assigned. For a class such as Person, this means that a default constructor and overloaded assignment function are needed. An illustration follows:

```
int main ()
{
  Array <Person>
    staff (2);          // array of two persons

  Person
    one,
    two;

  .                     // code assigning names and
  .                     // addresses and phone numbers
  .                     // isn't shown

  staff [0] = one;
  staff [1] = two;

  printf ("%s\n%s\n",
    staff [0].getname (), staff [1].getname ());

  return (0);
}
```

Since the above array staff consists of Persons, the Person's interface functions, such as getname(), can be called for elements in the array.

Evaluation of template classes

In this section we have seen two approaches to the construction of container classes:

- The `Storable/Storage` approach defines a "storable" prototype with a pure virtual function `duplicate()`. During the storage, in the class `Storage`, this function is called to duplicate an object. This approach imposes the need for a duplicating function for each object derived from `Storable` so that it may be placed in a `Storage`.
- The template approach, using the template class `Array`, poses no such restrictions when it is used. Following a definition of an `Array` object, to hold, say, `Persons`, as in

```
Array <Person>
  staff;
```

the array can be used without modifying or adapting the class `Person`.

This comparison suggests that templates are a much better approach to container classes. There is, however, one disadvantage—whenever a template class with a given type (`Person` or `Vehicle` or whatever) is used, the compiler must construct a **new "real" class**, each with its own mangled name (say `ArrayPerson`, `ArrayVehicle`). A function such as `init()`, which is defined in the template class `Array`, then occurs twice in a program, once as `ArrayPerson::init()` and once as `ArrayVehicle::init()`. Of course, this holds true not only for `init()` but for all member functions of a template class.

In contrast, the `Storable/Storage` approach requires only two new functions, one duplicator for a `Person` and one for a `Vehicle`. The code of the container class itself occurs only once in a program.

We can therefore conclude the following:

- When a program uses only one container class, the template approach is preferable—it is easier to use and requires no special precautions or conversions as far as the contained class is concerned.
- When a program uses several instances of a container class, the `Storable/Storage` approach is preferable—it prevents needless code duplication, though it does require special adaptations of the contained class.

BIBLIOGRAPHY

Abramson, H., and Rogers, M. H. (1989). *Meta-Programming in Logic Programming*, MIT Press, Cambridge, MA.

Adeli, H. (1990). *Knowledge Engineering Applications*, Volume 2, McGraw-Hill, New York, NY.

Aho, A. V., Sethi, R., and Ullman, J. D. (1986). *Compilers: Principles, Techniques and Tools*, Addison-Wesley, Reading, MA.

Albert, P. (1988). "KOOL: Merging Object Frames and Rules," in DeMongeot, J., Herve, T., Rialle, V., and Roche, C., Eds., *Artificial Intelligence and Cognitive Sciences*, Manchester University Press, Manchester, England, pp. 15–21.

Allen, J. (1987). *Natural Language Understanding*, Benjamin/Cummings, Menlo Park, CA.

Allen, J., Hendler, J., and Tate, A., Eds. (1990). *Readings in Planning*, Morgan Kaufmann, San Mateo, CA.

American Association for Artificial Intelligence (1988). *Proceedings of the Seventh National Conference on Artificial Intelligence*, Saint Paul, MN.

American Association for Artificial Intelligence (1990). *Proceedings of the Eighth National Conference on Artificial Intelligence*, Boston, MA.

American Association for Artificial Intelligence (1991). *Proceedings of the Ninth National Conference on Artificial Intelligence*, Anaheim, CA.

American Association for Artificial Intelligence (1992). *Proceedings of the Tenth National Conference on Artificial Intelligence*, San Jose, CA.

American Association for Artificial Intelligence (1993). *Proceedings of the Eleventh National Conference on Artificial Intelligence*, Washington, D.C.

American Association for Artificial Intelligence (1993). *Proceedings of the Fifth Innovative Applications of Artificial Intelligence*, Washington, D.C.

American Association for Artificial Intelligence (1994). *Proceedings of the Twelfth National Conference on Artificial Intelligence*, Seattle, WA.

American Association for Artificial Intelligence (1994). *Proceedings of the Sixth Innovative Applications of Artificial Intelligence*, Seattle, WA.

American Association for Artificial Intelligence (1995). *Proceedings of the Seventh Innovative Applications of Artificial Intelligence*, Montréal, Québec.

American Association for Artificial Intelligence (1995). *Proceedings of the International Joint Conference on Artificial Intelligence*, Montréal, Québec.

Amorosso, E. (1994). *Fundamentals of Computer Security Technology*, Prentice-Hall, Englewood Cliffs, NJ.

Anthony, T. (1985). "The Metals Analyst: An Expert System for Identifying Metals and Alloys," GE corporate R&D Report #85CRC181, General Electric Corporation, Schenectady, NY.

Appelt, D. E. (1985). *Planning English Sentences*, Cambridge University Press, Cambridge, England.

Apt, K. R., and Pedreschi, D. (1990). *Studies in Pure Prolog: Termination*, Centrum voor Wiskunde en Informatica, Report CS-R9048, Stichting Mathematisch Centrum, Amsterdam, The Netherlands.

Aravind, J., Webber, B., and Sag, I. (1981). *Elements of Discourse Understanding*, Cambridge University Press, Cambridge, England.

Arikawa, A., Goto, S., Ohsuga, S., and Yokomori, T., Eds. (1990). *Algorithmic Learning Theory*, Springer-Verlag, Berlin, Germany.

Arnold, A. (1972). *The World Book of Children's Games*, Fawcett, Greenwich, CN.

Asimov, I. (1950). *I, Robot,* Fawcett, Greenwich, CN.

Aslett, M. J. (1991). *A Knowledge Based Approach to Software Development—ESPRIT Project ASPIS,* North-Holland, Amsterdam, The Netherlands.

Asperti, A., and Longo, G. (1991). *Categories, Types, and Structures: An Introduction to Category Theory for the Working Computer Scientist,* MIT Press, Cambridge, MA.

Association for Computing Machinery (1977). *Proceedings of the Symposium on Artificial Intelligence and Programming Languages,* New York, NY.

Association for Computing Machinery (1986). *Object-Oriented Programming—Systems, Languages and Applications Conference Proceedings,* New York, NY.

Association for Computing Machinery (1987). *Object-Oriented Programming—Systems, Languages and Applications Conference Proceedings,* New York, NY.

Association for Computing Machinery (1988). *Object-Oriented Programming—Systems, Languages and Applications Conference Proceedings,* New York, NY.

Association for Computing Machinery (1989). *Object-Oriented Programming—Systems, Languages and Applications Conference Proceedings,* New York, NY.

Association for Computing Machinery (1990). *Object-Oriented Programming—Systems, Languages and Applications Conference Proceedings,* New York, NY.

Association for Computing Machinery (1991). *Object-Oriented Programming—Systems, Languages and Applications Conference Proceedings,* New York, NY.

Association for Computing Machinery (1992). *Object-Oriented Programming—Systems, Languages and Applications Conference Proceedings,* New York, NY.

Association for Computing Machinery (1993). *Object-Oriented Programming—Systems, Languages and Applications Conference Proceedings,* New York, NY.

Association for Computing Machinery (1994). *Object-Oriented Programming—Systems, Languages and Applications Conference Proceedings,* New York, NY.

Association for Computing Machinery (1995). *Object-Oriented Programming—Systems, Languages and Applications Conference Proceedings,* New York, NY.

Association for Computing Machinery (1996). *Object-Oriented Programming—Systems, Languages and Applications Conference Proceedings,* New York, NY.

AT&T (1992). *Object-Oriented Technology,* AT&T Best Current Practices, Berkeley Heights, NJ.

AT&T (1995). *R++ User Manual,* Middletown, NJ.

Baase, S. (1988). *Computer Algorithms: Introduction to Design and Analysis,* Second Edition, Addison-Wesley, Reading, MA.

Barkakati, N. (1991). *Object-Oriented Programming in C++,* SAMS, Carmel, IN.

Barnier, W., and Chan, J. B. (1989). *Discrete Mathematics with Applications,* West Publishing, Saint Paul, MN.

Barr, A., and Feigenbaum, E. A. (1981). *The Handbook of Artificial Intelligence,* Volumes 1-3, Addison-Wesley, Reading, MA.

Barr, A., and Feigenbaum, E. A. (1989). *The Handbook of Artificial Intelligence,* Volume 4, Addison-Wesley, Reading, MA.

Besnard, P. (1989). *An Introduction to Default Logic,* Springer-Verlag, Berlin, Germany.

Bischoff, M. B., Shortliffe, E. H., Scott, A. C., Carlson, R. W., and Jacobs, C. D. (1983). "Integration of a Computer-based Consultant into the Clinical Setting," in *Proceedings of the Seventh Annual Symposium on Computer Applications in Medical Care,* pp. 149–152.

Bledsoe, W. W. (1971). "Splitting and Reduction Heuristics in Automatic Theorem Proving," *Artificial Intelligence,* **2**(1):55–77.

Bledsoe, W. W. (1977). "Non-Resolution Theorem Proving," *Artificial Intelligence,* **9**(1): 1–35. Also in Webber, B. L., and Nilsson, N. J. (1981), *Readings in Artificial Intelligence,* Morgan Kaufmann, Los Altos, CA, pp. 91–108.

Blish, J. (1968). *Star Trek 2,* Bantam, Toronto, Ontario.

Boden, M. (1977). *Artificial Intelligence and Natural Man,* Basic Books, New York, NY.

Booch, G. (1991). *Object-Oriented Design, with Applications*, Benjamin/Cummings, Redwood City, CA.

Booch, G. (1994). *Object-Oriented Analysis and Design, with Applications*, Second Edition, Benjamin/Cummings, Redwood City, CA.

Booch, G. (1996). *Object Solutions: Managing the Object-Oriented Project*, Addison-Wesley, Menlo Park, CA.

Bowen, K. A. (1991). *Prolog and Expert Systems*, McGraw-Hill, New York, NY.

Boyer, R. S., and Moore, J. S. (1979). *A Computational Logic*, Academic Press, New York, NY.

Brachman, R. J., and Levesque, H. J. (1985). *Readings in Knowledge Representation*, Morgan Kaufmann, Los Altos, CA.

Bratko, I. (1990). *PROLOG: Programming for Artificial Intelligence*, Second Edition, Addison-Wesley, Workingham, England.

Brazdil, P. B., and Konolige, K., Eds. (1990). *Machine Learning, Meta-Reasoning and Logics*, Kluwer Academic, Boston, MA.

Brewka, G. (1991). *Nonmonotonic Reasoning: Logical Foundations of Commonsense*, Cambridge University Press, Cambridge, England.

Bronson, G., and Menconi, S. (1988). *A First Book of C: Fundamentals of C Programming*, West Publishing, Saint Paul, MN.

Brownston, L., Farrell, R., Kant, E., and Martin, N. (1985). *Programming Expert Systems in OPS5: An Introduction to Rule-Based Programming*, Addison-Wesley, Reading, MA.

Bryant, N. (1988). *Managing Expert Systems*, John Wiley and Sons, New York, NY.

Bundy, A., and others (1978). *Artificial Intelligence: An Introductory Course*, North-Holland, Amsterdam, The Netherlands.

Burris, S., and Sankappanavar, H. P. (1981). *A Course in Universal Algebra*, Springer-Verlag, New York, NY.

Bynum, S., Noble, R., and Todd, C. (1995). "The GE Compliance Checker: A Generic Tool for Assessing

Mortgage Loan Resale Requirements," in *Proceedings of the Seventh Innovative Applications of Artificial Intelligence Conference*, American Association for Artificial Intelligence, Menlo Park, CA, pp. 29–40.

Carberry, S. (1990). *Plan Recognition in Natural Language Dialogue*, MIT Press, Cambridge, MA.

Carroll, L. (1897). *Symbolic Logic, Part I: Elementary*, MacMillan. Republished (1958) by Dover, New York, NY.

Chang, C.-L., and Lee, R. C.-T. (1973). *Symbolic Logic and Mechanical Theorem Proving*, Academic Press, New York, NY.

Chapman, D. (1987). "Planning for Conjunctive Goals," *Artificial Intelligence*, **32**(3):333–377.

Charniak, E., and McDermott, D. (1985). *Introduction to Artificial Intelligence*, Addison-Wesley, Reading, MA.

Charniak, E., Riesbeck, C. K., and Meehan, J. R. (1987). *Artificial Intelligence Programming*, Second Edition, Lawrence Erlbaum Associates, Hillsdale, NJ.

Chomsky, N. (1957). *Syntactic Structures*, Mouton, The Hague, The Netherlands.

Clocksin, W. F., and Mellish, C. S. (1987). *Programming in Prolog*, Third Edition, Springer-Verlag, Berlin, Germany.

Coad, P., and Nicola, J. (1993). *Object-Oriented Programming*, Yourdon Press, Englewood Cliffs, NJ.

Coad, P., and Yourdon, E. (1991). *Object-Oriented Analysis*, Yourdon Press, Englewood Cliffs, NJ.

Coad, P., and Yourdon, E. (1991). *Object-Oriented Design*, Yourdon Press, Englewood Cliffs, NJ.

Cohen, D. N. (1981). *Knowledge-based Theorem Proving and Learning*, UMI Research Press, Ann Arbor, MI.

Colmerauer, A., Kanaui, H., Roussel, P., and Pasero, R. (1973). *Un système de communication homme-machine en français*, Groupe de Recherche en Intelligence Artificielle, Université d'Aix-Marseille.

Coplien, J. (1991). *Advanced C++ Programming Styles and Idioms*, Addison-Wesley, Reading, MA.

Coplien, J., and Schmidt, D. C., Eds. (1995). *Pattern Languages of Program Design*, Addison-Wesley, Reading, MA.

Cormen, T. H., Leiserson, C. E., and Rivest, R. L. (1990). *Introduction to Algorithms*, McGraw-Hill, New York, NY.

Curry, H. B. (1950). *A Theory of Formal Deducibility*, Notre Dame University Press, Notre Dame, IN.

Czejdo, B., Eick, C. F., and Taylor, M. (1993). "Integrating Sets, Rules, and Data in an Object-oriented Environment," *IEEE Expert*, February 1993, pp. 59–66.

Davis, E. (1990). *Representations of Commonsense Knowledge*, Morgan Kaufmann, San Mateo, CA.

Dean, T., Allen, J., and Aloimonos, Y. (1995). *Artificial Intelligence: Theory and Practice*, Benjamin/Cummings, Redwood City, CA.

De Mántaras, R. L. (1990). *Approximate Reasoning Models*, Ellis Horwood, Chichester, England.

DeMongeot, J., Herve, T., Rialle, V., and Roche, C., Eds. (1988). *Artificial Intelligence and Cognitive Sciences*, Manchester University Press, Manchester, England.

Devanbu, P., Brachman, R. J., Selfridge, P. G., and Ballard, B. W. (1991). "LaSSIE—A Knowledge-based Software Information System," *Communications of the ACM*, **34**(5; May, 1991):34–49.

Diller, Antoni (1994). *Z—An Introduction to Formal Methods*, John Wiley and Sons, Chichester, England.

Dodd, A. (1990). *An Advanced Logic Programming Language*, Volume 2: *Prolog-2 Encyclopaedia*, Intellect (republished by Ablex), Oxford, England.

Dodd, A. (1990). *An Advanced Logic Programming Language*, Volume 1: *Prolog-2 User Guide*, Intellect (republished by Ablex), Oxford, England.

Duffy, D. A. (1991). *Principles of Automated Theorem Proving*, John Wiley and Sons, Chichester, England.

Ege, R. K. (1992). *Programming in an Object-Oriented Environment*, Academic Press, San Diego, CA.

Ellis, M. A., and Stroustrup, B. (1990). *The Annotated C++ Reference Manual*, Addison-Wesley, Reading, MA.

Embley, D. W., Kurtz, B. D., and Woodfield, S. N. (1992). *Object-Oriented Systems Analysis: A Model-Driven Approach*, Prentice Hall, Englewood Cliffs, NJ.

Ercoli, P., and Lewis, R. (1988). *Artificial Intelligence Tools in Education: Proceedings for the IFIP TC3 Working Conference on Artificial Intelligence Tools in Education*, Frascati, Italy, 26–28 May 1987, North-Holland, Amsterdam, The Netherlands.

Etzioni, O., Lesh, N., and Segal, R. (1994). "Building Softbots for UNIX (Preliminary Report)," in *Software Agents: Papers from the 1994 Spring Symposium*, Technical Report SS-94-03, American Association for Artificial Intelligence, Menlo Park, CA, pp. 9–16.

Evans, T. G. (1968). "A Heuristic Program to Solve Geometric Analogy Problems," in Minsky, M., Ed., *Semantic Information Processing*, MIT Press, Cambridge, MA, pp. 271–353.

Evett, M. P., Hendler, J. A., and Andersen, W. A. (1993). "Massively Parallel Support for Computationally Effective Recognition Queries," in *Proceedings of the Eleventh National Conference on Artificial Intelligence*, American Association for Artificial Intelligence, Menlo Park, CA, pp. 297-302.

Eysenck, H. J. (1982). *A Model for Intelligence*, Springer-Verlag, Berlin, Germany.

Fayyad, U. M., and Simoudis, E. (1995). *Knowledge Discovery in Databases*, Tutorial MA1 of the Fourteenth International Joint Conference on Artificial Intelligence, American Association for Artificial Intelligence, Menlo Park, CA.

Fayyad, U. M., Piatetsky-Shapiro, G., and Smyth, P. J. (1995). "From Knowledge Discovery to Data Mining: An Overview," in Fayyad, U. M., Piatetsky-Shapiro, G., Smyth, P. J., and Uthurusamy, R., Eds., *Advances in Knowledge Discovery and Data Mining*, AAAI Press, Menlo Park, CA.

Fayyad, U. M., Piatetsky-Shapiro, G., Smyth, P. J., and Uthurusamy, R., Eds. (1995). *Advances in Knowledge Discovery and Data Mining*, AAAI Press, Menlo Park, CA.

Fayyad, U. M., Weir, N., and Djorgovski, S. G. (1993). "Automated Analysis of a Large-Scale Sky Survey: The SKICAT System," in Piatetsky-Shapiro, G., Ed., *Proceedings of the AAAI-93 Workshop on KDD*, AAAI Press, Menlo Park, CA.

Feigenbaum, E. A. (1977). "The Art of Artificial Intelligence: Themes and Case Studies of Knowledge Engineering," in *Proceedings of the International Joint Conference on Artificial Intelligence*, Volume 2, MIT Press, Cambridge, MA, p. 2.

Feigenbaum, E. A., and Feldman, J., Eds. (1963). *Computers and Thought*, McGraw-Hill, New York, NY.

Fielder, D., and Hunter, B. H. (1986). *UNIX System Administration*, Hayden, Indianapolis, IN.

Fikes, R. E., and Nilsson, N. J. (1971). "STRIPS: A New Approach to the Application of Theorem Proving to Problem Solving," *Artificial Intelligence*, 2(3–4):189–208.

Fikes, R. E., Hart, P. E., and Nilsson, N. J. (1972). "Learning and Executing Generalized Robot Plans," *Artificial Intelligence* 3(4):251–288. Also in Webber, B. L., and Nilsson, N. J. (1981), *Readings in Artificial Intelligence*, Morgan Kaufmann, Los Altos, CA, pp. 231–249.

Fitting, M. (1990). *First-Order Logic and Automated Theorem Proving*, Springer-Verlag, New York, NY.

Ford, N. (1989). *Prolog Programming*, John Wiley and Sons, Chichester, England.

Forgy, C. L.(1994). *RAL/C and RAL/C++: Rule-Based Extensions to C and C++*, Production Systems Technologies, Pittsburgh, PA.

Forgy, C., and Hrishenko, S. (1991). *Rule-extended Algorithmic Language: User's Guide*, Productions Systems Technologies, Pittsburgh, PA.

Forgy, C., and Hrishenko, S. (1991). *Rule-extended Algorithmic Language: Language Guide*, Productions Systems Technologies, Pittsburgh, PA.

Formica, A., Missikoff, M., and Vazzana, S. (1991). "An Object-oriented Data Model for Artificial Intelligence Applications," *Lecture Notes in Computer Science*, Springer Verlag, New York, pp. 26–41.

Frege, G. (1884). *Foundations of Arithmetic: A Logico-mathematical Enquiry into the Concept of Number*, Austin, J. L., Trans. Published by Harper, New York, NY, 1960.

Frey, R. L. (1956). *According to Hoyle: Rules of Games*, Fawcett, Greenwich, CN.

Fu, K. S. (1968). *Sequential Methods in Pattern Recognition and Machine Learning*, Academic Press, New York, NY.

Fu, K. S., Ed. (1971). "*Pattern Recognition and Machine Learning*," Proceedings of the Japan-U.S. Seminar on the Learning Process in Control Systems, Plenum Press, New York, NY.

Gaines, B. R., and Boose J. H., Eds. (1990). *Machine Learning and Uncertain Reasoning*, Volume 3, *Knowledge-Based Systems*, Academic Press, London, England.

Gal, A., Lapalme, G., Saint-Dizier, P., and Somers, H. (1991). *Prolog for Natural Language Processing*, John Wiley and Sons, Chichester, England.

Gardner, Martin (1958). *Logic Machines and Diagrams*, McGraw-Hill, New York, NY.

Genesereth, M. R., and Fikes, R. E. (1992). "Knowledge Interchange Format, Version 3.0, Reference Manual," June 1992 version, Stanford Logic Group Report-Logic-92-1, Computer Science Department, Stanford University.

Genesereth, M. R., and Nilsson, N. J. (1987). *Logical Foundations of Artificial Intelligence*, Morgan Kaufmann, Los Altos, CA.

Gerlernter, H. (1963). "Realization of a Geometry Theorem-proving Machine," in Feigenbaum, E. A., and Feldman, J., Eds. (1963), *Computers and Thought*, McGraw-Hill, New York, NY, pp. 134–152.

Ginsburg, M. L. (1985). "Counterfactuals," Computer Science Department Report STAN-CS-84-1029, Stanford University, Stanford, CA.

Ginsburg, M. L. (1993). *Essentials of Artificial Intelligence*, Morgan Kaufmann, San Mateo, CA.

Goldberg, D. E. (1989). *Genetic Algorithms in Search, Optimization, and Machine Learning*, Addison-Wesley, Reading, MA.

Golding, A. R., and Rosenbloom, P. S. (1991). "Improving Rule-Based Systems Through Case-Based Reasoning," in *Proceedings of the Ninth National Conference on Artificial Intelligence*, American Association for Artificial Intelligence, Menlo Park, CA, pp. 22–27.

Goodwin, R. (1993). "Formalizing Properties of Agents," School of Computer Science, Carnegie Mellon University, CMU-CS-93-159, May, Pittsburgh, PA.

Gorlen, K. E., Orlow, S. M., and Plexico, P. S. (1990). *Data Abstraction and Object-Oriented Programming in C++*, John Wiley and Sons, Chichester, England.

Graham, Ian, and Jones, Peter L. (1988). *Expert Systems: Knowledge, Uncertainty and Decision*, Chapman and Hall, London, England.

Grishman, R. (1986). *Computational Linguistics: An Introduction*, Cambridge University Press, Cambridge, England.

Guha, R. V., and Lenat, D. B. (1990). "Cyc: A Midterm Report," *AI Magazine*, **11**(3):32–59.

Hammond, K. (1986). "Chef—A Model of Case-based Planning," in *Proceedings of the National Conference on Artificial Intelligence*, AAAI Press, Menlo Park, CA.

Hammond, K., (1989). *Case-Based Planning: Viewing Planning as a Memory Task*, Academic Press, New York, NY.

Harris, M. D. (1985). *Introduction to Natural Language Processing*, Reston, Reston, VA.

Hayes-Roth, F., Waterman, D. A., and Lenat, D. B. (1983). *Building Expert Systems*, Addison-Wesley, Reading, MA.

Henrion, M., Schacter, R., Kanal, L., and Lemmer, J., Eds. (1990). *Uncertainty in Artificial Intelligence 5*, North-Holland, Amsterdam, The Netherlands.

Higa, K., Morrison, M., Morrison, J., and Sheng, O. R. L. (1992). "Object-Oriented Methodology for Knowledge Base/Database Coupling," *Communications of the ACM*, **35**(6):99–113.

Hofstadter, D. R. (1979). *Gödel, Escher, Bach: An Eternal Golden Braid*, Vintage, New York, NY.

Hofstadter, D. R. (1985). *Metamagical Themas: Questing for the Essence of Mind and Pattern*, Bantam, Toronto, Ontario.

Hofstadter, D. R., and Dennett, D. C. (1981). *The Mind's I: Fantasies and Reflections on Self and Soul*, Bantam, Chicago, IL.

Hölldobler, S., Ed. (1989). *Foundations of Equational Logic Programming*, Springer-Verlag, Berlin, Germany.

Holtzmann, P., and Fischer, R. (1993). "GCESS: A Symptom-driven Diagnostic Shell and Related Applications," in *Proceedings of the Fifth Innovative Applications of Artificial Intelligence Conference*, American Association for Artificial Intelligence, Menlo Park, CA, pp. 61–74.

Holtzner, S., and the Peter Norton Computing Group (1990). *C++ Programming: The Accessible Guide to Professional Programming*, Brady, New York, NY.

Hopcroft, J. E., and Ullman, J. D. (1979). *Introduction to Automata Theory, Languages and Computation*, Addison-Wesley, Reading, MA.

Hornstein, N. (1984). *Logic as Grammar: An Approach to Meaning in Natural Language*, MIT Press, Cambridge, MA.

Horstmann, C. S. (1991). *Mastering C++: An Introduction to C++ and Object-Oriented Programming for C and Pascal Programmers*, John Wiley and Sons, New York, NY.

Hu, D. (1989). *C/C++ for Expert Systems*, Management Information Source, Portland, OR.

Hu, D. (1990). *Object-Oriented Environment in C+: A User-Friendly Interface*, Management Information Source, Portland, OR.

Huet, G., and Plotkin, G., Eds. (1991). *Logical Frameworks*, Cambridge University Press, Cambridge, England.

Huxley, A. (1932). *Brave New World*, Harper & Row, New York, NY.

IEEE Computer Society (1984). *IEEE 1984 Workshop on Principles of Knowledge-Based Systems*, Proceedings, December 3–4, Denver, CO. IEEE Computer Society Press, Silver Spring, MD.

Ince, D. (1991). *Object-Oriented Software Engineering with C++*, McGraw-Hill, London, England.

Jackson, P., Reichgelt, H., and van Harmelen, F., Eds. (1989). *Logic-Based Knowledge Representation*, MIT Press, Cambridge, MA.

Jakobson, G., Weissman, M., Goyal, S. (1995). "IMPACT: Development and Deployment Experience of Network Event Correlation Applications," in *Proceedings of the Seventh Innovative Applications of Artificial Intelligence Conference*, American Association for Artificial Intelligence, Menlo Park, CA, pp. 70–76.

Kernighan, B. W, and Ritchie, D. M. (1978). *The C Programming Language*, Prentice-Hall, Englewood Cliffs, NJ.

Ketonen, J., and Weening, J. S. (1984). "EKL—An Interactive Proof Checker User's Reference Manual," Computer Science Department Report STAN-CS-84-1006, Stanford University, Stanford, CA.

Kim, S. H. (1991). *Knowledge Systems Through Prolog*, Oxford University Press, New York, NY.

Knoblock, C. A., and Arens, Y. (1994). "An Architecture for Information Retrieval Agents," in *Software Agents, Papers from the 1994 Spring Symposium*, Technical Report SS-94-03, American Association for Artificial Intelligence, Menlo Park, CA, pp. 49–56.

Knuth, D. E. (1973). *The Art of Computer Programming*, Volume 1: *Fundamental Algorithms*, Second Edition, Addison-Wesley, Reading, MA.

Knuth, D. E. (1973). *The Art of Computer Programming*, Volume 3: *Sorting and Searching*, Addison-Wesley, Reading, MA.

Kohavi, R., and Sommerfield, D. (1995). "MLC++, Machine Learning Library in C++, MLC++ Utilities 1.1," unpublished report available from mlc@cs.stanford.edu.

Kohavi, R., John, G., Long, R., Manley, D., and Pfleger, K. (1994). "MLC++: A Machine Learning Library in C++," in *Tools with Artificial Intelligence*, IEEE Computer Society Press, Piscataway, NJ, pp. 740–743. Also available by anonymous ftp from starry.stanford.edu:pub/ronnyk/mlc/toolsmlc.ps.

Kolodner, J. (1989). "Judging Which is the Best Case for a Case-Based Reasoner," in *Proceedings of the Case-Based Workshop*, American Association for Artificial Intelligence, Menlo Park, CA.

Konigsberger, H. K., and de Bruyn, F. W. G. M. (1990). *Prolog from the Beginning*, McGraw-Hill, London, England.

Kowalski, R. A. (1974). *Predicate Logic as a Programming Language*, International Federation for Information Processing, Geneva, Switzerland, pp. 569–574.

Kreutzer, W., and McKenzie, B. (1991). *Programming for Artificial Intelligence: Methods, Tools and Applications*, Addison-Wesley, Sydney, Australia.

Kripke, S. A. (1963). "Semantic Considerations on Modal Logic," *Acta Philosophica Fennica*, **16**:83–94.

Kulkarni, D., and Simon, H. A. (1987). *The Processes of Scientific Discovery: The Strategy of Experimentation*, Technical Report AIP-5, Carnegie-Mellon University, Pittsburgh, PA.

Kurzweil, R. (1990). *The Age of Intelligent Machines*, MIT Press, Cambridge, MA.

Ladd, S. (1990). *C++ Techniques and Applications*, M & T Books, Redwood City, CA.

Lee, J. K., and others (1995). "DAS: Intelligent Scheduling Systems for Shipbuilding," in *Proceedings of the Seventh Innovative Applications of Artificial Intelligence Conference*, American Association for Artificial Intelligence, Menlo Park, CA, pp. 90–106.

Lenat, D. B. (1990). *Building Large Knowledge-Based Systems: Representation and Inference in the Cyc Project*, Addison-Wesley, Reading, MA.

Lenzerini, M., Nardi, D., and Simi, M., Eds. (1991). *Inheritance Hierarchies in Knowledge Representation and Programming Languages*, John Wiley and Sons, Chichester, England.

Levy, A. Y., Sagiv, Y., and Srivastava, D. (1994). "Towards Efficient Information Gathering Agents," in *Software Agents, Papers from the 1994 Spring Symposium*, Technical Report SS-94-03, American Association for Artificial Intelligence, Menlo Park, CA, pp. 64–70.

Lifschitz, V., Ed. (1990). *Formalizing Common Sense: Papers by John McCarthy*, Ablex, Norwood, NJ.

Lifschitz, V., Ed. (1991). *Artificial Intelligence and Mathematical Theory of Computation: Papers in Honor of John McCarthy*, Academic Press, Boston.

Lippman, S. B. (1989). *C++ Primer*, Addison-Wesley, Reading, MA.

Lloyd, J. W. (1984). *Foundations of Logic Programming*, Springer-Verlag, Berlin, Germany.

Lucas, P. J. (1992). *The C++ Programmer's Handbook*, Prentice Hall, Englewood Cliffs, NJ.

Luger, G. F., and Stubblefield, W. A. (1989). *Artificial Intelligence and the Design of Expert Systems*, Benjamin/Cummings, Redwood City, CA.

Luger, G. F., and Stubblefield, W. A. (1993). *Artificial Intelligence: Structures and Strategies for Complex Problem Solving*, Second Edition, Benjamin/Cummings, Redwood City, CA.

Lukaszewicz, W (1990). *Non-Monotonic Reasoning, Formalization of Commonsense Reasoning*, Ellis Horwood, Chichester, England.

Luker, P. A, and Birtwistle, G., Eds. (1987). *Simulation and AI: Proceedings of the Conference on AI and Simulation*, San Diego, CA, January 14–16, Simulation Councils, Inc., San Diego, CA.

Madachy, J. S. (1979). *Madachy's Mathematical Recreations*, Dover, New York, NY.

Manna, Z. (1974). *Mathematical Theory of Computation*, McGraw-Hill, New York, NY.

Manna, Z. (1980). *Lectures on the Logic of Computer Programming*, Society for Industrial and Applied Mathematics, Philadelphia, PA.

Manna, Z., and Pnueli, A. (1992). *The Temporal Logic of Reactive and Concurrent Systems: Specification*, Springer-Verlag, New York, NY.

Manna, Z., and Waldinger, R. (1985). *The Logical Basis for Computer Programming*, Volume 1: *Deductive Reasoning*, Addison-Wesley, Reading, MA.

Manna, Z., and Waldinger, R. (1989). *The Logical Basis for Computer Programming*, Volume 2: *Deductive Systems*, Addison-Wesley, Reading, MA.

McGregor, J. D., and Sykes, D. A. (1992). *Object-Oriented Software Development: Engineering Software for Reuse*, Van Nostrand Reinhold, New York, NY.

McKeown, K. (1985). *Text Generation*, Cambridge University Press, Cambridge, England.

Meyer, B. (1991). *Object-Oriented Software Construction*, Prentice Hall, New York, NY.

Miller, P., Blumenfucht, S., and Black, H.(1984). "An Expert System Which Critiques Patient Workup: Modeling Conflicting Expertise," in *Computers and Biomedical Research*, Volume 17, pp. 554–569.

Minsky, M. Ed. (1968). *Semantic Information Processing*, MIT Press, Cambridge, MA.

Minsky, M. (1986). *The Society of Mind*, Simon and Schuster, New York, NY.

Mitchell, T. M. (1990). "Becoming Increasingly Reactive," in American Association for Artificial Intelligence, *Proceedings of the Eighth National Conference on Artificial Intelligence*, Boston, MA, pp. 1051–1058.

Nagel, E., Suppes, P., and Tarski, A. (1962). *Logic, Methodology and Philosophy of Science: Proceedings of the 1960 International Congress for Logic, Methodology and Philosophy of Science*, Stanford University, Stanford, CA.

Nelson, M. M., and Illingworth, W. T. (1991). *A Practical Guide to Neural Nets*, Addison-Wesley, Reading, MA.

Newell, A. (1956). "The Logic Theory Machine," *IRE Transactions on Information Theory*, **2**:61–79.

Newell, A., and Simon, H. A. (1963a). "Computers in Psychology," in R. D. Luce, R. R. Bush, and E. Galanter, Eds., *Handbook of Mathematical Psychology*, Volume 1, John Wiley and Sons, New York, NY, pp. 361–428.

Newell, A., and Simon, H. A. (1963b). "GPS: A Program that Simulates Human Thought," in Feigenbaum, E. A., and Feldman, J., Eds. (1963), *Computers and Thought*, McGraw-Hill, New York, NY, pp. 279–293.

Newell, A., and Simon, H. A. (1972). *Human Problem Solving*, Prentice-Hall, Englewood Cliffs, NJ.

Nilsson, N. J. (1980). *Principles of Artificial Intelligence*, Tioga, Palo Alto, CA.

Nilsson, N. J. (1984). "Probabilistic Logic," Technical Note 321, SRI International, Menlo Park, CA.

Nilsson, N. J. (1985). *Triangle Tables: A Proposal for a Robot Programming Language*, Technical Note 347, SRI International, Menlo Park, CA.

Nilsson, N., J. (1965). *The Mathematical Foundations of Learning Machines*, Morgan Kaufmann, San Mateo, CA, republished in 1990.

Nilsson, U., and Maluszynski, J. (1990). *Logic, Programming and Prolog*, John Wiley and Sons, Chichester, England.

Odeh, M. H., and Padget, J. A. (1993). "Object-Oriented Execution of OPS5 Production Systems," in *Object-Oriented Programming—Systems, Languages and Applications Conference Proceedings*, Association for Computing Machinery, New York, NY, pp. 178–190.

O'Keefe, R. A. (1990). *The Craft of Prolog*, MIT Press, Cambridge, MA.

Pang, G. K. H., and MacFarlane, A. G. J. (1987). "An Expert Systems Approach to Computer-Aided Design of Multivariable Systems," *Lecture Notes in Control and Information Sciences*, Number 89, Springer-Verlag, Berlin, Germany.

Partridge, D. A. (1986). *Artificial Intelligence: Applications in the Future of Software Engineering*, Ellis Horwood, Chichester, England.

Pearl, J. (1983). *Search and Heuristics*, North-Holland, Amsterdam, The Netherlands.

Pearl, J. (1984). *Heuristics: Intelligent Search Strategies for Computer Problem Solving*, Addison-Wesley, Reading, MA.

Pearl, J., (1988). *Probabilistic Reasoning in Intelligent Systems: Networks of Plausible Inference*, Morgan Kaufmann, San Mateo, CA.

Pereira, F. C. N., and Shieber, S. M. (1987). *Prolog and Natural-Language Analysis*, Center for the Study of Language and Information, Stanford University, Stanford, CA.

Pereira, F. C. N., and Warren, D. H. D. (1980). "Definite Clause Grammars for Language Analysis—A Survey of the Formalism and a Comparison with Augmented Transition Networks," *Artificial Intelligence*, **13**(3):231–278.

Pfleeger, C. P. (1989). *Security in Computing*, Prentice Hall, Englewood Cliffs, NJ.

Pollock, J. L. (1989). *How to Build a Person: A Prolegomenon*, MIT Press, Cambridge, MA.

Polya, G. (1945). *How to Solve It: A New Aspect of Mathematical Method*, Second Edition, Princeton University Press, Princeton, NJ.

Prata, S. (1991). *C++ Primer Plus*, Waite Group Press, Mill Valley, CA.

Pratt, V. (1985). *Logical Algorithms*, unpublished draft textbook, Stanford, CA.

Ramsay, A. (1988). *Formal Methods in Artificial Intelligence*, Cambridge University Press, Cambridge, England.

Raymond, D., and Wood, D. (1994). "The Grail Papers, Version 2.0," Department of Computer Science, Waterloo University, Waterloo, Canada.

Resnick, L., Borgida, A., Brachman, R., McGuinness, D., Patel-Schneider, Peter, and Zalondek, K. (1991). "CLASSIC Description and Reference Manual for the COMMON LISP Implementation, Version 1.2," AT&T Internal Memorandum, July 31, 1991.

Rich, E. (1983). *Artificial Intelligence*, McGraw-Hill, New York, NY.

Rich, E., and Knight, K. (1991). *Artificial Intelligence*, Second Edition, McGraw-Hill, New York, NY.

Rissland, E. L., and Daniels, J. J. (1995). "Using CBR to Drive IR," in *Proceedings of the International Joint Conference on Artificial Intelligence*, American Association for Artificial Intelligence, Menlo Park, CA, pp. 400–407.

Robey, B. L., Fink, P. K., Venkatesan, S., and Redfield, C. L. (1993). "The DRAIR Advisor: A Knowledge-Based System for Materiel Deficiency Analysis," in *Proceedings of the Fifth Innovative Applications of Artificial Intelligence Conference*, American Association for Artificial Intelligence, Menlo Park, CA, pp. 169–182.

Roche, C. (1988). "Object in Expert Systems," in DeMongeot, J., Herve, T., Rialle, V., and Roche, C., Eds. (1988), *Artificial Intelligence and Cognitive Sciences*, Manchester University Press, Manchester, England, pp. 3-14.

Ross, P. (1989). *Advanced Prolog: Techniques and Examples*, Addison-Wesley, Reading, MA.

Roussel, P. (1975). *PROLOG: Manuel de référence et d'utilization*, Groupe d'Intelligence Artificielle, Université d'Aix-Marseille, Marseille, France.

Rowe, N. C. (1988). *Artificial Intelligence Through Prolog*, Prentice Hall, Englewood Cliffs, NJ.

Rumbaugh, J., Blaha, M., Premerlani, W., Eddy, F., and Lorensen, W. (1991). *Object-oriented Modeling and Design*, Prentice Hall, Englewood Cliffs, NJ.

Russell, S., and Norvig, P. 1995. *Artificial Intelligence: A Modern Approach*, Prentice Hall, Englewood Cliffs, NJ.

Sacerdoti, E. D. (1974). "Planning in a Hierarchy of Abstraction Spaces," *Artificial Intelligence*, **5(2)**:115–135.

Sacerdoti, E. D. (1975). "The Nonlinear Nature of Plans," in *Proceedings of the Fourth International Conference on Artificial Intelligence (IJCAI-75)*, Tbilisi, Georgia, pp. 206–214.

Sag, I. A. (1986). *Grammatical Hierarchy and Linear Precedence*, Center for the Study of Language and Information Report CSLI-86-60, Stanford University, Stanford, CA.

Sager, N. (1981). *Natural Language Information Processing*, Addison-Wesley, Reading, MA.

Sakamura, K. Ed. (1990). *TRON Project 1990: Open-Architecture Computer Systems*, Springer-Verlag, Tokyo, Japan.

Sangal, R. (1991). *Programming Paradigms in LISP*, McGraw-Hill, New York, NY.

Schalkoff, R. J. (1990). *Artificial Intelligence: An Engineering Approach*, McGraw-Hill, New York, NY.

Schank, R. C., and Abelson, R. P. (1977). *Scripts, Plans, Goals, and Understanding*, Laurence Erlbaum Associates, Hillsdale, NJ.

Schank, R. C., and Colby, K. (1973). *Computer Models of Thought and Language*, W. H. Freeman, San Francisco, CA.

Schank, R. C., and Riesbeck, C. K. (1981). *Inside Computer Understanding*, Lawrence Erlbaum Associates, Hillsdale, NJ.

Schildt, H. (1987). *Artificial Intelligence Using C*, Osborne McGraw-Hill, Berkeley, CA.

Schneider, F. (1988). "An Implementation of Frames in SmallTalk," in DeMongeot, J., Herve, T., Rialle, V., and Roche, C., Eds., *Artificial Intelligence and Cognitive Sciences*, Manchester University Press, Manchester, England, pp. 139–146.

Schöning, U. (1989). *Logic for Computer Scientists*, Birkhäuser, Boston, MA.

Sedgewick, R. (1988). *Algorithms*, Second Edition, Addison-Wesley, Reading, MA.

Sedgewick, R. (1990). *Algorithms in C*, Addison-Wesley, Reading, MA.

Self, J. Ed. (1988). *Artificial Intelligence and Human Learning: Intelligent Computer-Aided Instruction*, Chapman and Hall, London, England.

Senator, T. E., and others (1995). "The FinCEN Artificial Intelligence System: Identifying Potential Money Laundering from Reports of Large Cash Transactions," in *Proceedings of the Seventh Innovative Applications of Artificial Intelligence Conference*, American Association for Artificial Intelligence, Menlo Park, CA, pp. 156–170.

Sethi, R. (1989). *Programming Languages: Concepts and Constructs*, Addison-Wesley, Reading, MA.

Shafer, G., and Pearl, J., Eds. (1990). *Readings in Uncertain Reasoning*, Morgan Kaufmann, San Mateo, CA.

Shanahan, M., and Southwick, R. (1989). *Search, Inference and Dependencies in Artificial Intelligence*, Ellis Horwood, Chichester, England.

Shapiro, E. (1987). *The Encyclopedia of Artificial Intelligence*, John Wiley and Sons, New York, NY.

Shavlik, J. W., and Dietterich, T. G., Eds. (1990). *Readings in Machine Learning*, Morgan Kaufmann, San Mateo, CA.

Shinghal, R. (1992). *Formal Concepts in Artificial Intelligence,* Chapman and Hall, London.

Shlaer, S., and Mellor, S. J. (1988). *Object-Oriented Systems Analysis: Modeling the World in Data,* Yourdon Press, Englewood Cliffs, NJ.

Shoham, Y. (1993). "Agent-Oriented Programming," *Artificial Intelligence,* **37**(2):51–92.

Shufelt, J. A., and Berliner, H. J. (1993). "Generating Knight's Tours Without Backtracking from Errors," Carnegie Mellon University, Computer Science technical report, CMU-CS-93-161.

Silverman, B., Hwang, V., and Post, S., Eds. (1990). *The Fifth Annual AI Systems in Government Conference,* Proceedings, May 6-11, Washington, D.C. IEEE Computer Society Press, Los Alamitos, CA.

Simoudis, E., Kerber, R., and Livezey, B. (1994). "Recon: A Framework for Database Mining," in *Intelligent Hybrid Systems,* by Kumaran (ed.), Addison-Wesley, London, England.

Simon, H. A., and Newell, A. (1958). "Heuristic Problem Solving: The Next Advance in Operations Research," *Operations Research,* **6**:1–10.

Smart, G., and Langeland-Knudsen, J. (1986). *The CRI Directory of Expert Systems,* Learned Information, Copenhagen, Denmark.

Smith, D. N. (1991). *Concepts of Object-Oriented Programming,* McGraw-Hill, New York, NY.

Snyers, D., and Thayse, A. (1987). *From Logic Design to Logic Programming: Theorem Proving Techniques and P-Functions,* Springer-Verlag, Berlin, Germany.

Solow, D. (1990). *How to Read and Do Proofs: An Introduction to Mathematical Thought Processes,* John Wiley and Sons, New York, NY.

Sowa, J. F. (1984). *Conceptual Structures: Information Processing in Mind and Machine,* Addison-Wesley, Reading, MA.

Sowa, J. F. (1995). *Knowledge Representation,* draft to be published by PWS Publishing Company, Boston, MA.

Spivey, J. M. (1989). *The Z Notation: A Reference Manual,* Prentice Hall, Englewood Cliffs, NJ.

Spivey, J. M. (1992). *The Z Notation: A Reference Manual,* Second Edition, Prentice Hall, New York, NY.

Steele, G. L., Jr. (1984). *Common Lisp: The Language,* Digital Press, Pittsburgh, PA.

Stefik, M. (1981a). "Planning with Constraints (MOLGEN: Part 1)," *Artificial Intelligence,* **16**(2):111–139.

Stefik, M. (1981b). "Planning and Meta-planning (MOLGEN: Part 2)," *Artificial Intelligence,* **16**(2):141–169.

Sterling, L., Ed. (1990). *The Practice of Prolog,* MIT Press, Cambridge, MA.

Sterling, L., and Shapiro, E. (1986). *The Art of Prolog: Advanced Programming Techniques,* MIT Press, Cambridge, MA.

Stroustrup, B. (1986). *The C++ Programming Language,* Addison-Wesley, Reading, MA.

Stroustrup, B. (1991). *The C++ Programming Language,* Second Edition, Addison-Wesley, Reading, MA.

Tarski, A. (1956). *Logic, Semantics, Metamathematics: Papers from 1923 to 1938,* Clarendon Press, Oxford, England.

Tello, E. R. (1989). *Object-Oriented Programming for Artificial Intelligence: A Guide to Tools and System Design,* Addison-Wesley, Reading, MA.

Tennant, H. (1981). *Natural Language Processing,* Petrocelli, New York, NY.

Thayse, A., Ed. (1988). *From Standard Logic to Logic Programming: Introducing a Logic-Based Approach to Artificial Intelligence,* John Wiley and Sons, Chichester, England.

Toffler, A. (1970). *Future Shock,* Bantam, Toronto, Ontario.

Tolkien, J. R. R. (1937). *The Hobbit,* Ballantine, New York, NY.

Tsang, C. P., Ed. (1990). *AI '90—Proceedings of the 4th Australian Joint Conference,* World Scientific, Singapore.

Turing, A. M. (1950). "Computing Machinery and Intelligence," *Mind*, Volume LIX, No. 236, pp. 433–460.

Turner, R. (1984). *Logics for Artificial Intelligence*, Ellis Horwood, Chichester, England.

Ullman, J. D. (1988). *Principles of Database and Knowledge-base Systems*, Volume 1, Computer Science Press, Rockville, MD.

Ullman, J. D. (1989). *Principles of Database and Knowledge-base Systems*, Volume 2: *The New Technologies*, Computer Science Press, Rockville, MD.

Ullman, J. D. (1992). *Foundations of Computer Science*, Computer Science Press, New York, NY.

Ullman, J. D. (1994). *Elements of ML Programming*, Prentice Hall, Englewood Cliffs, NJ.

USENIX Association (1989). *USENIX C++ Conference Proceedings*, Berkeley, CA.

USENIX Association (1990). *USENIX C++ Conference Proceedings*, Berkeley, CA.

Van Eijck, J. Ed. (1991). *Logics in AI: European Workshop JELIA '90*, Amsterdam, The Netherlands, September, 1990 Proceedings, Springer-Verlag, Berlin, Germany.

Van Heijenoort, J. (1967). *From Frege to Gödel: A Source Book in Mathematical Logic, 1879–1931*, Harvard University Press, Cambridge, MA.

Walker, A., McCord, M., Sowa, J. F., and Wilson, W. G. (1990). *Knowledge Systems and Prolog: Developing Expert, Database and Natural Language Systems*, Second Edition, Addison-Wesley, Reading, MA.

Walker, D. E., Ed. (1978). *Understanding Spoken Language*, Elsevier, North-Holland, New York, NY.

Webber, B. L., and Nilsson, N. J. (1981). *Readings in Artificial Intelligence*, Morgan Kaufmann, Los Altos, CA.

Weyhrauch, R. (1980), "Prolegomena to a Theory of Mechanized Formal Reasoning," *Artificial Intelligence*, **13**(1, 2):133–170. Also in Webber, B. L., and Nilsson, N. J. (1981), *Readings in Artificial Intelligence*, Morgan Kaufmann, Los Altos, CA, pp. 173–191.

White, M., and Goldsmith, J. (1990). *Standards and Review Manual for Certification in Knowledge Engineering: Handbook of Theory and Practice*, Systemsware Corporation, Rockville, MD.

Whitehead, A. N., and Russell, B. (1913). *Principia Mathematica*, Volumes 1–3, Cambridge University, Cambridge, England.

Wiener, R. S., and Pinson, L. J. (1988). *An Introduction to Object-Oriented Programming and C++*, Addison-Wesley, Reading, MA.

Wiener, R. S., and Pinson, L. J. (1990). *The C++ Workbook*, Addison-Wesley, Reading, MA.

Wilensky, R. (1984). *LISPcraft*, Norton, New York, NY.

Wilks, Y., Ed. (1989). *Theoretical Issues in Natural Language Processing*, Lawrence Erlbaum Associates, Hillsdale, NJ.

Winograd, T. (1983). *Language as a Cognitive Process*, Volume 1: *Syntax*, Addison-Wesley, Reading, MA.

Winograd, T., and Flores, F. (1986). *Understanding Computers and Cognition*, Ablex, Norwood, NJ.

Winston, P. H. (1984). *Artificial Intelligence*, Second Edition, Addison-Wesley, Reading, MA.

Wirth, N. (1988). *Programming in Modula-2*, Fourth Edition, Springer-Verlag, Berlin, Germany.

Witten, I. H. (1986). *Making Computers Talk*, Prentice Hall, Englewood Cliffs, NJ.

Wooldridge, M., and Jennings, N. R. (1995). "Intelligent Agents: Theory and Practice," submitted for publication to *Knowledge Engineering Review*.

Wos, L. (1988). *Automated Reasoning: 33 Basic Research Problems*, Prentice Hall, Englewood Cliffs, NJ.

Wos, L., Overbeek, R., Lusk, E., and Boyle, J. (1984). *Automated Reasoning: Introduction and Applications*, Prentice-Hall, Englewood Cliffs, NJ.

Zadeh, L. (1983). "Commonsense Knowledge Representation Based on Fuzzy Logic," *Computer*, **16**:61–65.

INDEX